THE GREAT DEFENDER

THE GREAT DEFENDER

A Biography of
Father John Flanagan DCL STL (Polegate)
by Sarah Morrison

JANUS PUBLISHING COMPANY
London, England

First published in Great Britain 1989 by Newmark Editions
Republished 1995
by Janus Publishing Company
Edinburgh House,
19 Nassau Street, London W1N 7RE

Copyright © Sarah Morrison 1995

British Library Cataloguing-in-Publication Data.
A catalogue record for this book is available from
the British Library.

ISBN 1 85756 197 X

All rights reserved. No part of this publication may be reproduced, stored in a retrieval system or transmitted in any form or by any means, electronic, mechanical, photocopying, recording or otherwise, without the prior permission of the publisher.

The right of Sarah Morrison to be identified as the author of this work has been asserted by her in accordance with the Copyright, Designs and Patents Act 1988.

Index Christine Headley

Cover Design Linda Wade

Printed and bound in England by
Antony Rowe Ltd, Chippenham, Wiltshire

*To the memory
of*
The Reverend Father John W Flanagan DCL, STL
St. George's Catholic Church, Polegate, Sussex, England.
That undaunted Defender of the Faith
in Britain during the period of doctrinal
and moral confusion which followed upon Vatican II.
To that beacon of pure light –
the touchstone of orthodoxy –
this book is gratefully and affectionately dedicated.

APPRECIATION

I am deeply indebted to the following for their invaluable help given to me:-

1. Major Sir Patrick Wall M.P.
   For his help and interest.
2. Miss Leta Kerin (Solicitor)
   For reviewing legally.
3. To my friends – Priests and laity – in giving me continuous encouragement and help during the period (eight months) of writing Father Flanagan's biography.

To all of them, my heartfelt thanks.
S.F. MORRISON

CONTENTS

Editorial		xi
Preface		xiii

PART ONE

I	The Seminary Life	1
II	Father Flanagan: A Learned Churchman	6
III	The Worship of Man Part One	24
IV	The Worship of Man Part Two	30
V	The Worship of Man Part Three	33
VI	Articles II-IV	39
VII	Who is Judas?	65
VIII	The Encyclical *Humanae Vitae* Still Under Attack	67
IX	Some Extracts from *Newsletter* Editorials	84
X	October Synod in Rome: Reports	91
XI	Can Christianity Survive the 20th Century?	95
XII	Further Extracts from the *Newsletter*	104
XIII	The International Catechetical Congress (Rome) and other reports	139
XIV	A Periscope on Teilhard de Chardin	145
XV	Theological Commission	152
XVI	An Account of Sudden Illness . . . and Articles	160
XVII	*Christian Order* and the Old Mass	189
XVIII	We ask . . . We beg our Bishops 10 important points	213
XIX	The Scandal of 'Holy Communion in the Hand'	232
XX	The Last Five Days in the Life of Father Flanagan	261
XXI	Tributes paid to Father Flanagan	266
XXII	The 'Good Shepherd' of Shepherd's Bush	275

PART TWO

XXIII	Suffering and Injustice	303
XXIV	Writers of Like Minds	313

Father Flanagan (front row) at the Vatican with the Clergy in the presence of (St.) Pope Pius XII

Father Flanagan with colleagues in Rome

THE GREAT DEFENDER

THE LORD IS RISEN INDEED
AND HATH APPEARED TO SIMON
(St. Luke Ch. 24:34)

EDITORIAL

IT IS VERY difficult as well as painful for those of us who were so closely involved with the work of Father John Flanagan to be able to assess, even remotely, the impact of his life on our times. This must be left to future Church historians.

There is no doubt, however, that the death of Father Flanagan has left a void which cannot be filled. Like the disciples who thought that the end had come with the death and burial of Christ after the crucifixion, so we too feel that all is lost, all is finished. In the words of the psalmist – *'HOMO SICUT FOENUM DIES EJUS TANQUAN FLOS AGRI SIC EFFLOREBIT'* 'Man's days are as the grass, as the flower of the field so shall he flourish'. But when the wind shall pass over, it shall be no more. He was taken from us at a time when, although he had suffered much from ill-health during his life, he appeared to have been given a new lease of life. He was writing pamphlets, dealing with correspondence and numerous other matters connected with the life of the Church, right up to the time of his death; and it was only a week or two prior to his death that he had posted off his final newsletter of the Catholic Priests' Association. This latter publication was always very much looked forward to by the priest and lay members of the Association. Why was this? Chiefly because Father Flanagan was not afraid to speak but on important issues as they arose in the day to day life of the Church. He was not only a mine of information as to what was happening but he was also a very effective exposer of error, whether it was to be found in high places or in low places. His scholarly mind would get to the root of these errors and being the clear thinker and writer that we was, it was not difficult for him to expose false conclusions drawn from false arguments, and in such a way that all could understand.

Father Flanagan had a rare flair for being 'on the spot'. For instance, when the vexed question of Communion in the hand arose and a pamphlet was produced by the National Liturgical Commission in support of the practice, he immediately brought out another pamphlet. 'The Case against Communion in the Hand' in which he corrected the errors and refuted the fallacious arguments of those who were trying to foist an unjustifiable option on unsuspecting Catholics, for he was not only a man of prayer but a priest ever guarding the Church's greatest treasure, the Blessed Sacrament. Had not Christ said WATCH as well as PRAY?

Perhaps the two things which he feared most would eventually destroy the Church if allowed to go unchecked were the Commissions which he felt were taking over the duties and responsibilities which pertained to bishops, and the blind eye which the hierarchy are turning towards ex-priests and the ex-religious who are allowed to roam the country speaking to groups here and there, and poisoning the minds of other priests and the religious, as well as the laity, with their theories which are against Catholic truth because they are against Catholic doctrine. Father Flanagan maintained that the hour had come when we must present out petitions at the feet of the Holy Father himself if the Church in this country is to be saved from the indifferentism to Catholic truth which has struck at its very roots.

Father Flanagan was attacked on all sides but he never flinched. He longed for one thing and one thing above all, namely, the unity of the Church under the supreme Pontiff. He loved the priests under his care with a great love. His love for his fellow priests was only second to his love of God which was boundless. 'ECCE SACERDOS MAGNUS QUI IN DIEBUS SUIS PLACUIT DEO'. Perhaps the greatest tribute we can pay him is for each and every one of us to support that loyal band of orthodox priests and pray for the Paraclete to come and strengthen us. May he send us one as full of zeal as Father Flanagan to lead us into the way of Truth.

PREFACE

TU ES SACERDOS IN AETERNUM
(Thou art a Priest forever)

'Keep them I pray thee, dearest Lord
Keep them, for they are thine
Thy priests, whose lives burn out
Before thy consecrated shrine.
Keep them, as spotless as the Host
That daily they caress
Their every thought, and word, and deed
Deign, dearest Lord, to bless'

The above prayer was chosen by Father John W. Flanagan for his Ordination card on the occasion of his Ordination to the sacred priesthood at the Cathedral, Newry, Co. Down, Ireland on 20 December 1936.

'TU ES SACERDOS IN AETERNUM' and how true to this supreme calling Father Flanagan remained, all through his priestly life, teaching and ministering for the greater honour and glory of God's Church upon earth.

He died defending it, as will be recorded by this biography.

Since Father Flanagan's death on the 27 March 1977, I have received many requests from Priests and laity to write his life. Having had the great privilege of knowing and helping him in so many different ways from 1953 to 1977, I felt it a duty in conscience to embark on this important work.

I will follow closely each phase. I will not exaggerate, nor will I delete, for here was a great priest – a great churchman, teacher and defender of orthodoxy, whose love of God was immense, but whose sufferings, both physical and mental were the ultimate of human endurance. One would have had to see, to believe. I saw. Physical for the very many illness he bore, both medical and surgical, but nothing could compare with the mental sufferings meted out by those from within the confines of the Church.

Today, five years following his death, I often wonder how certain members of the Hierarchy – and the – clergy feel, when celebrating a Requiem Mass and on uttering the following words of the Mass; 'The souls of the virtuous are in the hands of God, no torment will ever touch them' and again, when they read the Gospel of Matthew 5: 1-12 ie., 'Seeing the crowds, Jesus went up the hill. There He sat down and was joined by his disciples.

Then, He began to speak. This is what He taught them:-

'Blessed are the poor in spirit,
   for theirs is the Kingdom of Heaven. '
'Blessed are the meek,
   for they shall possess the earth. '
'Blessed are they that mourn,
   for they shall be comforted. '
'Blessed are they that hunger and thirst after justice,
   for they shall be filled. '
'Blessed are the merciful,
   for they shall obtain mercy. '
'Blessed are the clean of heart,
   for they shall see God. '
'Blessed are the peacemakers,
   for they shall be called the children of God. '
'Blessed are you, when people abuse you,
   and speak all kinds of calumny against you on my account.
Rejoice and be glad,
   for your reward will be great in Heaven. '

While the story of the life of Father John Flanagan unfolds, retain in memory, Christ's words in the eighth Beatitude. May his holy soul rest in peace with his God, whom he loved so much on earth and is now happy with in Heaven – forever, in the sight of the Beatific Vision.

I will now proceed to write this biography of a great priest, to the very best of my ability, neither adding or subtracting, but with continuous prayer to the Holy Spirit, and to the Holy Mother of God – seat of Divine Wisdom, that truth will prevail in every word I write.

To Commence, I will first record in full four tributes paid to Father Flanagan following his death. Many more will follow at the end of book, but these four will speak the life and times of this 'Man of God'.

Tribute No. 1

From Bishop Bernard D. Stewart
(Retd.) Sandhurst,   W. Australia Sacred Heart Cathedral,
                                        Bendigo, Victoria, 3550.

29 May 1981

Dear Miss Morrison,

    My acquaintance with Father Flanagan arose from the grave challenge to the Church after Vatican Council II. Dogmatic and moral teachings were under constant attack not only from traditional enemies, but far worse, from 'the enemies within the gate'.

    I was consoled when I first learned of the Priests Association and appreciated its official publication, which contained so much vigorous writing and informed defence of church teaching, notably from the pen of Father Flanagan. Father Flanagan was kind enough to notice and publish some of my own writings in the same field. I was most grateful for this help from such an able theologian and deeply regretted his being taken from the scene of combat, where men of his calibre and highly place, are conspicuous by their absence.

    It is my prayer that Holy Mother Church will come forth stronger, from today's turmoil, which the late Father Flanagan strove so valiantly to overcome.

With every blessing.

Yours sincerely in Christ,
Bernard D. Stewart.

TRIBUTE NO. 2
The following are the Bidding Prayers for Father Flanagan's Requiem Mass (1 April 1977) spoken by his very close friend. Father Hugh Byron, Wisbech, Cambridgeshire.

Let us pray:

O Lord we beg of Your mercy, that by the intercession of Your Immaculate Mother, the soul of John Flanagan,
Your good servant and priest may quickly enter into fellowship with Your saints and in their company enjoy peace without ending.
Through Christ our Lord.

Lord may we all have the courage like John Flanagan Your priest, to speak out boldly in defence of Your Church and her teachings, no matter what the price may be
Lord Hear Us.

Lord like Your servant, may our lives be characterised by complete integrity and absolute single-mindedness of purpose.
Lord, Hear Us.

O God, teach us the lesson Your son and priest John Flanagan had learnt so well namely to suffer misunderstanding, frequently to bear calumny, and permanently contempt and division, and to be able manfully to unite it all with the sufferings of Your Divine Son.
Lord Hear Us.

May the countless souls who privately wished him well in his efforts, but who felt unable publicly to support him, quickly come to a more noble frame of mind.
Lord Hear Us.

Let us commend ourselves and the soul of John Flanagan to the maternal care of Mary, the Mother of God
Hail Mary.

O Lord, in life You honoured John Flanagan with the sublime

dignity of being one of Your priests. Since it was his constant faith on earth, that his priesthood was eternal, may he even now, be enjoying that same priesthood in Heaven, and thus daily, be interceding for us.

Through Christ Our Lord

AMEN.

A summary of the Oration, given at the committal of Father Flanagan's mortal remains at St. Mary's Catholic Cemetery, Kensal Green, London, April 1977.

Father Hugh Byron said, there was no priest in these islands, who was really worthy to bury this extraordinary Priest, who was an outstanding 'Soldier of Jesus Christ'.

He had chiefly, come to his premature end through the ceaseless battles he fought to defend Christ's Church against both its enemies and friends, and to uphold the authority of Christ's Vicar on earth – the Pope.

His death now left the British Isles – certainly England – bereft of a champion to defend the Catholic cause.

Many thousands of the faithful laity in England must feel fatherless and leaderless. Those scores of Priests and religious who had come to Father Flanagan by night (like Nicodemus of old) must now be experiencing, even more chillingly, the dark night of the soul, in their respective dioceses and Religious Orders.

Yet God could raise up a successor if he wished, especially if there were even a few souls who deserved it.

(Remember how Sodom and Gomoraah could have been saved).

In my own parish – Father Byron went on to say – I have recently discovered a fourteen-year-old girl who spends a full hour on her knees before retiring each night. Perhaps there is a little boy or girl like her in every city in England.

If our dear church is not so spared, the fault will certainly not lie at John Flanagan's graveside.

May he, who lived his priestly life so nobly, generously, and tempestuously, now possess that rest he has very richly earned.

HIS CRUCIFIXION OVER – MAY HIS RESURRECTION QUICKLY DAWN.

Tribute No. 3

A tribute to Father John Flanagan (RIP) of Polegate
by Father George Walker PP.,
Chesham Bois,
Bucks

'He was a faithful and wise servant whom His Lord had placed over His family.'

The recent death of Father John Flanagan leaves a void in the minds and hearts of priests and laity in this country and abroad. The priests of the International Priests Association are now without their leader. They are bewildered, the laity are bewildered, not knowing what the future holds. Father John is laid to rest wearing the vestments of his calling, a priest forever according to the Order of *Melchizedek* of old.

A mighty multitude mourns for his passing, a good and holy priest, a father and a friend who loved everyone.

What services had he rendered to gain our love? The simple answer is, that he proved himself, by being a faithful and wise servant, discharging faithfully his pastoral duties. When his Master called him, He found him diligently defending God's Holy Church and we have the warrant Holy Writ declaring that blessed is that servant – Yes! Jesus Christ himself has pronounced him blessed – whom, when his Lord shall come, he shall find him so doing.

It is superfluous to speak of the works and the virtues of Father John Flanagan. His life is all before us.

He lived in the hearts and minds of his associates. Make no mistake about it, he was the living centre in the heart as of his brethren.

You all know so much of him and you so love his memory, that if I were to speak forever, you would not think that I had said enough; and no delineation of his priestly character would ever reach that most truthful estimate which you have all formed of his goodness and his holiness.

The holy office of the priesthood should not be assumed as of our own choice – that the doors of the Sanctuary should be opened only for those whom God has called, and preordained to this high ministry 'neither doth any man' says St. Paul, 'take the honour to himself, but he that is called by God, as Aaron was'. (Heb. V4). John Flanagan was called by God and fought with every fibre of his being, the cause of God and his Holy Church.

His deep abiding loyalty to God, to His Church and to the Holy Father, the Pope – cannot be questioned. He was a fearless champion for the things that are right. One thing he gave to his priest associates was courage. He made us realise the dignity of our calling. His great ambition was to enroll all priests loyal to the Church, in our association, that by force of numbers would defend the Papacy. As one of the founder-members of the International Priests' Association some years ago, I remember the high hopes he had of such an Association. His words were, 'We will fight without fear – modernism and humanism – by pen and by word of mouth – and love the brethren with an intense love. He seemed to foresee the troubles that now beset the Church.

The many changes that have taken place in the Church over the past few years have caused havoc in the minds of priests and laity. They are unable to put up an inward defence against the things that are sick and sad immediately around them – against the elements of destruction. There are so many things now within the Church that seem to be in a continual state of contradiction. This contradiction will never be solved, so long as both poles of this tension are recognised as having equal claims. One or other must give way. Two of our Bishops are primarily responsible. I remember Father Flanagan ringing me up and saying, 'By the way, so-and-so is mitre hunting.' How right he was. A few days later, I was able to ring him and say, 'you were right, you know, so-and-so, is now my Auxiliary Bishop.' Thank God, this is no longer so, for who in God's name would wish to be associated with the architects of the 'Windsor Statement.' They should be stopped in their tracks. Enough is enough. Father Flanagan would wish all his priest associates to stand up and shout. 'Enough, you have already gone too far.' But now, who have we got to tell us what to do? No Father Flanagan. No one ready to stand up – no one with the moral fibre of 'Flanagan'. Surely there is some one who will emerge?

In this transitional time in which we are living, the gulf is glaringly obvious, between traditional ecclesiastical thought and utterance, on one hand possibility of an understanding between the two, seems to become steadily more remote. Father John Flanagan foresaw all this, and was anxious for priest and people.

He made his standpoint crystal clear to everyone, for without a firm standpoint of one's own, one is helpless
when any change or upheaval, brought about by spiritual trends of the time, brings about a change in outlook.

We must always be conscious of where we stand, this gives us security, peace and freedom.

Father Flanagan warned us that the many disturbing things now happening in the Church, should serve as a pointer for our future. Unless all indications are deceptive other more vicious attacks are being prepared.

The social position of priests will come under serious attack. Priests must not neglect to watch carefully the findings of the 'Windsor Statement'. The position of the priests will be brought very low. This is why Father Flanagan thought that an Association might even the balance.

Unfortunately, there were priests who laughed at his ideas. There were Bishops who disapproved of Father Flanagan, and those who stood by him. Please God, that they will eventually realise, that these priests are loyal to Holy Mother Church, as they themselves should be.

The Church in England is looking for leadership and guidance. The situation must be rectified as soon as possible. Where will this leadership come from? How long are we going to have to wait? When will priests and laity know the minds of the Bishops? The Bishops have lost their credibility, and they are going to have to work hard to regain it. Who cares these days about a Bishop? I have heard it said, 'I wouldn't go to the other side of the street to meet one.' I would not go so far as this. To the priests of the Church it was said, 'KEEP THE DEPOSIT'. This we must do.

It was Father Flanagan's greatest desire, that all the members of the Association would show and give loyalty to their Bishops and realise fully, the heavy responsibility they have to carry. He ardently sought the blessing of the Bishops for the Association, and hoped that one day, they would recognise the value of the International Catholic Priests' who were ready to do everything possible for the defence of the Church.

God gave us Father Flanagan, a priest according to his own heart, and what is better, he gave us the grace to follow him to hear his voice.

It may only be on the 'LAST DAY' that we could sum up the

results of his constant, earnest and laborious ministry of the Word. For him, the fruits are all gathered in Heaven. The promise is, 'that they who instruct many into justice, shall shine like stars for all eternity.' (Dan. XII. 3).

TRIBUTE NO. 4

From: Daniel Allen Griffiths
of the Holy Shroud Information Centre
(Nottingham)

In all my life (and I am seventy three), I never had the privilege of meeting, still less working so closely with a Priest who was a Catholic Priest in every sense of the Word. His burning zeal for the TRUTH OF CATHOLICISM was something that burnt with an all devouring flame. Despite a severe heart attack some six years ago, (caused by a vicious attack in the so-called *Catholic Herald* on his veracity), Father John found, not only time to defend his beloved Catholic Church on every front and every occasion, but would give a talk on the Holy Shroud, whenever the invitation was received.

The mail was huge and he had to set up a scheme of preferentials each day, but for the Holy Shroud with its message of Divine Love and extra proof of the Resurrection, Father Flanagan of Polegate would always give priority.

Despite all the work that was involved in the International Catholic Priests Association, he was always anxious for all to hear and see the Holy Shroud talks.

He would phone me after a talk I had given and want to hear news of it. How many were there? Was it well received? Any questions? Father Flanagan found time to translate the voluminous report of the recent examination of the Holy Shroud in the tome *SINDONE*. He had not finished this work when the good Lord gave him the rest he so desperately needed.

He died, consoled the night before his rest, in knowing that he could do no more than get the bewildered, bemused, anxious and distraught Catholics of this land to write to the successor of St. Peter, and implore the Holy Father to aid them.

Lord,
Send us another Father Flanagan of Polegate.

Father Flanagan (fourth left front row) in his Ordination Group

PART ONE

I

THE SEMINARY LIFE
as told by his life long friend
Father ROBERT MOLLOY DCL.,DD., (CORK)

ON LEARNING OF the death of Father John Flanagan, I experienced a sense of deep personal loss, Our friendship covered over forty five years. I was his guest in Polegate many times. For me then his passing was not just another person gone to his reward, another Priest, whose death was lamented by many who knew him intimately. As a man, and as a priest, he was no ordinary person - extraordinary is the only word that tries to convey what I want to say.

After completing his second level education with honours at his home school in Portarlington (Co. Laois), Father Flanagan felt he had a call to the priesthood, more particularly to the missionary priesthood. In September 1930 he proceeded to the Junior Seminary of the Society of African Missions in Co. Mayo. There he would pursue an intensive course in ecclesiastical Latin; he had never taken that subject in his second level studies. After one year, his professors were satisfied that his grasp of the language would be more than equal to the demands that ecclesiastical studies ahead would make on him.

In September 1931 he moved to the Novitiate House of the Society in Galway. There we first met together with twenty-four other young men - with senior certificates - and from all corners of Ireland, all determined to be priests; or missionary priests, to serve God, wherever the Superiors would decide.

That number was a sign of the times. No wonder that in later years, Father John would show such respect for the past and its values. The words 'Modern Man' made him squirm.

Concurrently, with a two year course in spiritual formation we pursued our studies in Scholastic Philosophy. In the second year, he was chosen as 'speaker' for the house; his very many talents came to light and his leadership qualities were noted.

He was serious, resolute and yet companionable withal. He was seen to be a strong, manly man, with courage, integrity, forthrightness and a subdued sense of politeness, which had its own attraction.

He never set out to impress. Creating an 'image' would never be part of his technique.

1933 - 1937

In July 1933 he was accepted into the Society of African Missions. He was solidly set along the road to the priesthood in that Society. The four years that followed were passed in the Society's Theological College (Major Seminary) near Newry, Co. Down.

He led his class all the way. He identified with all student activities, was a keen footballer and a good debater, many times we joked with him about his 'weak subject' – plainchant.

The manliness that was his, simply went on maturing. More and more, we came to see, that he did not mind being unpopular, because of a stand he felt he should take on some issue. A strong sense of independence became more and more evident.

Reactions to this, there often were, as is understandable. It must have caused him discomfiture, if not suffering.

In those days, higher studies at University level was not an accepted pattern of formation in Missionary Institutes. 'The Charity of Christ presses us,' to use St Paul's words, compelled these Societies to meet the crying demand for pastoral priests in the Nigeria and Liberia of those days.

The urgency then, was, to build up an indigenous Church, even if it fell somewhat short of the ideal requirements.

Nigeria, now, has its own Cardinal and Hierarchy. Even among the laity, in the late thirties, tertiary education was the exception.

Father John, ordained a priest on 20 December 1936 in Newry Cathedral, Co. Down, with nineteen others, and with theology studies completed in 1937, was an obvious choice for further studies. Following the normal procedure, he would be notified of his assignment to one of the many Mission territories in West Africa, given over to the care of the Society of African Missions (Irish Province). But, to his great surprise, should I say shock? – he was appointed to Rome, to pursue higher studies in Canon Law – a branch of our ecclesiastical studies. Normally, this would be a three year course.

The choice of Father Flanagan surprised none of those who studied with him. Obviously, the area of law would provide the fullest challenge for his keen intellect.

1937 – 1939

He was enrolled as a Candidate for Canon Law Studies at the Lateran University in Rome and he read a distinguished course.

After two years he was conferred with a *Licentiate Summa Cum Laude* (Highest distinction possible at that point of his studies).

Well, I remember, seeing the official parchment, which carried these words. I can also say, that never in his later years, did that testimonial adorn the wall of his room. Legitimate and normal though this would have been, it was not the style of the man.

1939 – 1946

He returned to Ireland in July 1939 for a holiday, convinced that he would be returning to Rome in September to pursue his Doctorate, but, as things turned out, this would have to await another time. War was declared in September of that year. Much more thought had to be given to sending or not sending, students back for studies. As it turned out, Father Flanagan's superiors decided, that his skills were needed in our Newry House of Ecclesiastical Studies, especially in Canon Law. He would take up the chair of Canon Law studies there. Under his guidance, the subject took on an altogether new dimension for the students.

His insight was both practical and penetrating and open discussion became a feature of his course.

1947 – 1948

In 1947, he was asked to return to Rome and as expected defended his doctorate with distinction in June 1948.

Returning to Ireland 1948 he again took over the Chair of Canon Law in our seminary in Newry.

Naturally enough, his reputation quickly reached beyond our seminary. One Bishop, who had, as he said, always got a brilliant answer to knotty canonical problems, made this comment, 'He is the only Canonist I know, who will solve your problem over the phone, and quote the correct Canons word for word. '

But while all who consulted him or listened to him lecturing, recognised in him a keen Canonist; they came to appreciate him even more, as a man full of compassion. He was never too busy for a troubled heart. He had light and warmth for people whose problems were not canonical.

His heart was as big as his brain.

It is noteworthy, that in 1946, he was a delegate to the Irish Provincial assembly in Cork.

His health began to give cause for concern. Prudent care of his health was not one of his virtues, though he would not apply that to his demands on others.

In 1947, he was chosen as delegate to the Society's General Assembly, held at Rome.

Although the posts he filled and the voted-in delegations he got to – Society Chapters spoke highly of the regard with which he was held, during those years from 1930 – 1952.

1952

A number of reasons, notably his health, led to his incardination into the Diocese of Southwark. A highly placed ecclesiastic of that diocese, who had responsibility for 'clearing' Father's papers of recommendation for the diocese, said, when returning him the papers; 'Keep these, Father, they will prove of inestimable value for your canonisation', a touch of humour indeed, but a message conveyed, nevertheless.

The mention of canonisation prompts me to add a few words about another dimension of Father John. It is the spiritual dimension. Obviously, the various dimensions of a personality are not in watertight compartments.

Intellect, heart and activity, in combination, give us 'the man', and when these three are answering to God within, then they are shaping 'the man of God.'

The scriptures tell us, 'No man knoweth the things of a man, but the spirit of a man that is within him.'

Consequently, we only know what we are given or what we can see.

Father John was not the person to give such motivations from within, and so, we are left with what could be seen.

St. Augustine, it was, who said, 'Faith is to believe, what you do not see, the reward for this, is to see what you believe.'

I came to see in Father Flanagan, over the years – a man of faith – living the faith he knew – and sharing the faith with others.

Those of us who saw his Church in Polegate, could see his sense of God coming through. Nothing was too good for God's House.

Present at his Mass, one sensed a reverence. Despite indifferent health for long years, he was never far from his pastoral work or from his presbytery. He was 'at home' for all who needed him.

Those of us who saw him at Lourdes with his pilgrimage from Polegate, saw what the Mother of God meant to him.

He was their Spiritual Leader, and led them everywhere, though it cost him dearly, in weariness, due to declining health.

Those of us, who listened, while he spoke on the Shroud of Turin- saw his zeal to get such a message across – such evidence of the love of our Saviour, and the correlative call to return that love.

There is no need for me to spell out how earnestly he shared his faith. He pulled no punches, he feared no opposition, where truths of faith were being adulterated, as he saw it, where morals were being adapted to meet the needs of modern man and where conscience was becoming once again, a new name for private judgement.

He had nothing but scorn for the argument, 'But everybody is doing it'. He knew how St Thomas More answered that impassioned plea from his closest friends.

In matters of religion, Father John would warmly subscribe, I submit, to the trenchant words of Cardinal Manning, 'The will of the majority is not either reason or right.'

> These then, were his priorities:-
> To know the faith.
> To live the faith.
> To share the faith.

These were the warp and woof of the spirituality of the man and priest, friend and classmate, whom I knew as John Flanagan, and whom scores of thousands knew as Father Flanagan of Polegate.

II

FATHER FLANAGAN
A Learned Churchman

FATHER FLANAGAN WAS a simple and kind priest. He loved and practiced the simple things of life. Every hour available to him was given to the life for which God called and ordained him. His care for the spiritual and temporal welfare of his people was his constant concern.

On Father Flanagan's arrival as Assistant Priest to St. Osmund's Parish at Barnes, London SW13 in 1953, it was very obvious to me – a District Nursing Sister in the area – that his appointment to St. Osmund's would prove, *not only* what we had now among us, a very learned churchman, but a sick man.

This formed my very first impressions of Father Flanagan.

In my professional capacity, there were many occasions for my calling upon Father Flanagan's help, in dealing with my patients, when spiritual help was to mean much more than medical or nursing care. It was from this very angle, that Father Flanagan shone, like a beacon of light, in the darkness and despair of souls about to meet their Creator. No words of mine could ever describe fully, the joy, solace and love, Father Flanagan exuded to the sick and dying. I say this, in this biography, for I was there to witness it.

As I first met Father Flanagan, he had just alighted from a bus outside the church. He was returning from a London hospital, where he had undergone a series of tests, to discover what was, as yet, an undiagnosed condition. I remember clearly, the stark facial pallor, and thinking that there was deep seated trouble ahead for this priest. It turned out as such, which I will later disclose.

During the next five years at Barnes, Father Flanagan proved himself as the priest of the people. He was loved by all of the parishioners.

I will cover just two or three. It is as follows, while doing my daily rounds of the district, I noticed the erect figure of Father Flanagan walking down Castelnau (principal thoroughfare) towards Barnes Village, at a regular given time each morning. He always carried a small parcel under his arm. He did not possess a car, nor could he drive. His means of transport around the parish were either his familiar green bicycle, or by walking.

One morning I stopped my car and offered Father Flanagan a lift, but he politely thanked me, saying he preferred to walk.

Some time after this, I called to see a faithful parishioner who had undergone major surgery some months previously. When advising her about the facilities available to her from the County Health Department, especially help with meals and household chores, she wouldn't even hear of it saying that by doing so, her beloved 'help' without whom she could not live would disappear. Her beloved 'help' was no other than Father Flanagan, and I now relate her story as told to me.

Each morning at a certain time (if possible) Father Flanagan came to see her, bringing with him a small fresh loaf from the local bakery (parcel underarm!). He proceeded to the village supermarket, bought a 'Bird's Eye' complete dinner, took it to the flat, heated it in the oven and served it to his dear parishioner. Next, he went to the coal bunker, filled two buckets of coal, made up the fire and then took his leave until the next day. The story was beautiful, but typical of this priest, and the supreme joy he gave to one, who was, herself, the church's stalwart.

As providence so deigned, I was to be a future help to Father in his 'home-mission' work for the Church, but never did he tell me the story of the little parcel, nor did I say that I knew, even though we discussed the person concerned, then at her rest with God.

After doing midnight calls on my very ill patients, I have often seen Father Flanagan cycling back to the presbytery after keeping some hours vigil at the bedside of a dying parishioner, thus relieving the tired relatives of the constant strain.

Then there were the lapsed, where a priest could not enter, but I could, for as the nurse, I was needed. At one such home of what was a Church of England family (although no member practiced), I was called to give nursing care to the elderly mother, in her 80's. She was dying. On pulling out the bedstead, in order to work from the opposite side, there before my eyes was a large picture of Our Lady of Perpetual Succour *under the bed!*

On immediate contact with her daughter, I explained the importance of this holy picture of Our Blessed Lady. She is the Queen of Heaven and Earth, and I was sure that this same family would treat with great reverence a picture of the present Queen Mother of England. This picture of God's Heavenly Mother was much more important. How did it come to be under the bed? The answer was that the old mother was a baptised Catholic but lapsed early in her youth.

I took the picture to the bedside, held it up before her dying eyes and asked if I could send for a Priest. She nodded, 'Yes', so in a short space of time Father Flanagan arrived and all received him very graciously. The old lady died shortly after and received the full benefit of a Requiem Mass celebrated by Father Flanagan. There was a whole trail of non-Catholics present at the funeral, stemming from that one case of lapse.

In later years I was to hear Father Flanagan preach on the lapsed, and give the above case as an example of the tragedy of even one lapsed member.

Then there was the 'Miracle of the Rosary', which can only be attributed to the direct intervention of Our Blessed Lady.

It was the Vigil of the Feast of Our Lady of Lourdes, 10 February 1957. Requested by her General Practitioner, I called at an early hour to visit a patient suffering from terminal cancer. She had just been discharged from a London hospital and needed to receive further home-nursing care. She was a wonderful little Polish lady.

On entering the flat, I met her husband (a Canadian) who seemed a very disgruntled man full of complaints regarding no doctors' visit etc., etc.

I sensed friction somewhere, I entered the sickroom and I remember that face so well, flushed and anxious. She was only in her early 50's. In giving her nursing care, I found under her pillow a Rosary in bits and pieces! In her agony she scrambled for every bead. I immediately assured her that I also carried my Rosary. I being Irish, she being Polish, we shared the same love of Our Blessed Lady.

What joy this brought to the dying lady. When asked if she had received the Sacraments, she became completely frustrated and pointed to the next room and her husband. I felt the story was unfolding. I approached him and informed him that it was not a medical doctor that was required, but a Doctor of the Church. (Sometimes I felt that uniforms could work miracles too!) I would send for a priest immediately. He was quite docile.

Father Flanagan was soon to arrive in that room and never, never, will I forget the cries of joy from that dear Polish Lady as Father Flanagan and she were together. I was then called in to be present for the anointing.

Next day, Feast of Our Lady of Lourdes, Father Flanagan came with Holy communion. I brought Lourdes water. The husband kept out of sight during that period, and it was a very happy day for Father Flanagan, this little lady and myself.

She died shortly afterwards, and her last words to me were 'I'll wait for you', and I bet she will.

Her husband had prevented her from practising her Catholic faith for many years. She held tight to her Rosary all those years, hence the bits and pieces under her pillow which were priceless, and with which no jewel or diadem could compare.

By 1958, the Bishop Cowderoy of Southwark appointed Father Flanagan to found a new parish in the South East of England, to be known as the Parish of Hampden Park/Polegate, Sussex.

This parish consisted of the two extreme ends of the Mother Church of Our Lady of Ransom, Eastbourne, Sussex, being cut off to form this new cell. Polegate already had a little church, known as St. George's Church, accommodating approximately 100 people. It was in very poor condition and needed much work and cash to bring it up to standard – but the Father's priority had to start with the new Church at Hampden Park.

At that particular time the Catholic climate was poor in this area, for two thirds of Catholic laity were lapsed, and so the great burden of getting their Church and parish formed fell on the shoulders of those faithful few who worked so hard and remained so faithful to their own first parish priest. From that beginning to the end of his life, they were never to forget what he sacrificed for them. So, with only a derelict house, plus an orchard in a swamp at the back of the house to start with, the struggle was heavy and hard. **There was no money to begin with.** The old derelict house with the rain coming through the roof and down the walls and the window frames rotten with dry rot both outside and inside made a depressing entrance for any priest, and when this priest was already a sick man, left food for thought.

A priest friend of Father Flanagan's called to see him on his visit from the Mission field. He was shocked to see the conditions prevailing, saying, 'We have much better than this, on the missions.' Needless to say, it is often the case, that the Home Missions suffer most.

The house, as well as being derelict, was absolutely empty of any kind of household furniture and equipment necessary to start, not even a bed. So it was then that Providence guided that I would come and help. With my own personal belongings, the first presbytery took shape and I would now throw myself into what was for me the challenge of my life, helping this priest in every way possible.

Father Flanagan now installed in his presbytery, his first move was to get a Mass Centre organised from the house, pending the building of a new Church. Both the Father and myself got busy immediately, transforming a large downstairs room into what was to be known as 'The MASS ROOM.' This old dilapidated house, known as 106 Brodrick Road, Hampden Park, was about to become the predecessor of what was to follow, namely the beautiful church of St. Joachim, which I will later describe.

In just six weeks the Mass Room was ready for opening. It was the 15 August 1958 and that beautiful Feast of the Assumption of Our Blessed Lady into Heaven. There were just twenty-two people present at that first Mass. Soon the children began to arrive, all the doors were opened wide, and the children sat on the stairs. It was the mission beginning – this time the home mission, and its new parish.

The adjoining room, which was to be dining room/sitting room (when there was time available to sit!)/sacristy/confessional etc., etc., is a memory never to be defaced. Yet it all worked out well. Every one pulled their weight in helping. Those good, but few parishioners, to name but a few of them, included Janet and Stewart Thorpe, Patrick Neville, Ella and Colin Smitherman, Molly Wright, Cora Fox, Bill and Bert Lane, Nora O'Neill, Eileen Bell, Mrs Beeze and Mrs Martin. There were others who came in later, but the above are the people I first met when it all began. Some have now gone to their rest with God and must be sharing, with Father Flanagan's soul, their great reward from their eternal Father (RIP).

To continue with the founding of the new Parish cash had to be found from somewhere to start. No help whatsoever came from the diocese, and only once did Father Flanagan receive a small share from the Rosary Sunday Collection for poor parishes. Because of constant rain coming through the roof, the Father approached the Parish Priest (Eastbourne Canon Curtin,) for funds to repair it. An amount was given, which together with the Father's own personal capital of two hundred pounds, made the roof safe.

Here, I must relate, that for some unknown reason there seemed to be an atmosphere of antipathy towards Father Flanagan from Diocesan level. There was no mistaking, Father Flanagan carried the cross of Christ and like Christ, bore it manfully.

To gather funds for Church building Father Flanagan organised a football pool. He became its Promoter. We proceeded through the surrounding parishes, canvassing and collecting for new members, and in so doing, built up a substantial income to start the foundations of the church.

In exactly nine months, the foundation stone was laid – that date was 14 May 1959. Exactly **one year** later, 14 May 1960, our new church opened and the first Mass was celebrated by Father Flanagan.

One can imagine the joy immediately following the consecration of that first mass, to see the Sanctuary Lamp lit for the very first time! Father Flanagan had wished the church to be named 'Church of Our Lady of Perpetual Succour'. Bishop Cowderoy ruled this wish out and requested it to be called 'St Joachim's Church'. While very disappointed about this, Father Flanagan agreed, and so our new church St Joachim was born. This great love of our life, our new Church, was a true gift from God, for we now had the Divine Presence of Christ among us in His Tabernacle for the very first time.

I was determined that the three principal parts of the church would be free from all debt from the very moment of its inception, so with the great joy and love I donated, in memory of my deceased family, the foundation stone, the Tabernacle and requisites for high altar, the crucifix plus the beautiful statue, as it was then, of Our Lady of Lourdes. God's first home, His Tabernacle would be free from debt, and we would now work hard to gather in and pay the huge debts already upon us, and this we did, to complete by 1965. But, the story is only beginning! (Re. Our Beautiful Lady Chapel which will follow later).

To describe St Joachim's, it was built to form a cross. The reredos behind the High Altar was in grey slate stone, to represent the Hill of Calvary. There hung the crucifix.

The Baptistry, a beautiful circular or dome-like enclosure was placed at the entrance, and above this enclosure, seven little windows (or panes of glass) representing the Seven Sacraments.

The two arms to project from centre were, to the right, the Sacristy and to the left the Chapel of Our Blessed Lady.

The Sanctuary complete, we would make Our Lady's Chapel worthy of the honour and veneration God's Mother deserved, and we did just that.

My close friend, Winifred O'Doherty, from my native county of Donegal, Ireland, crossed over to Eastbourne to join me on a pilgrimage to Lourdes, for the success of our parish, its priest, and its lapsed. We also had another mission on hand, we would bring back to the Lady Chapel a statue of Our Lady of Lourdes. This statue was specially made by a stonemason in the Pyrenees, and because of the lapsed condition prevailing, a small piece of the rock from the Holy Grotto was embedded in the base. This statue in its packing case, was taken to the Grotto the evening before its departure from Lourdes to St Joachim's, via the Dieppe/Newhaven sea route.

Can you imagine my joy, as this treasured container arrived at 'Maryland' the new presbytery just purchased for the sum of £2,700.00 in 1959? Its name of 'Roselands' changed to 'Maryland' by Father Flanagan.

I remember the Father's joy also, as we both placed this statue on the altar of its new chapel. Friends from Dublin (now deceased) provided the four large brass candlesticks for the altar, and the beautiful altar-frontal (blue and white) donated by the Catenians.

We were now ready for the official opening. It would be Rosary Sunday 1960. The chapel was ablaze with candlelight, which reflected onto the blue white terrazzo floor beneath altar, and through the hexagonal blue blocks forming the entrance arch leading from central aisle.

Rosary and Benediction of the Most Blessed Sacrament, with Father Flanagan wearing his brand new cope, which, together with six sets of Mass Vestments, were made by my kind friends from the Dublin (Skerries) Branch of the Foreign Mission Society, of which I was previously a member when I lived and nursed in the North of Ireland. It was a marvellous feeling for us to have now, both the main body of the Church and the Lady Chapel fully furnished and completed. Stations of the cross were wooden, carved, and came from Oberammergau.

Father Flanagan's next plan was to have a Mission, which would cover both ends of his parish i.e. St Joachim's and St George's Church. Two Franciscian Priests, Father Anthony and Father Camillus, came to give this mission, which proved very fruitful, *Deo Gratias*.

With all this strain of work, and battling continuously against ill health, Father's life was a very unhappy one. The reason for this was that we had in the parish, a certain group of people who had plenty to say, but did nothing to help in this work and who were determined to have Father removed from the parish.

The consisted of those who were professionals in different spheres, and indeed, should have been leaders in helping their priest who was involved in the founding of this new parish from scratch. There were even members of the guild of the 'Blessed Sacrament' present!

Then, there were certain members of the clergy near at hand, associated with this particular group. There was marked hostility towards Father Flanagan from this combined group. Finally, a letter from the Vicar General to Father Flanagan, 'to get out as soon as possible'.

Prior to this final assault, Father Flanagan, in his condition, felt he could take no more, the parish would be divided and we would leave our beautiful new church and parish, and proceed to St George's, Polegate, once again to embark on making this a parish in its own right.

Needless to say this whole episode caused great suffering among our faithful parishioners, loyal to the Father. A special scroll, (with ninety-eight per cent of parishioners signing it) protesting against the manner in which

Father Flanagan had been treated and supporting him all the way, had been sent by Registered Post to Bishop Cowderoy, with not even the courtesy of a reply. The enemy was in our midst and we knew it.

There was no o justice then, as there is no justice today, both from within and without the confines of the Church.

We moved to the new presbytery called 'Villa Maria' by 20 September 1965, and plans for the complete renovation of St George's would begin, which would bring this church up to Vatican II standard. After only six weeks in residence, a very severe attack of illness struck again. This time I stressed that a change of doctor would be absolutely necessary. Father fully agreed, and so, Doctor Ashforth from Eastbourne took full charge of the Father's care. With immediate X-rays taken (for the first time!) and subsequent tests to follow, diagnosis proved that immediate surgery was necessary. The final result was shattering. At Esperance Nursing Home this operation was performed and disclosed the true cause, namely, total disintegration of the left kidney.

I will add here, that in the early 1960's, a psychiatrist had been called in during one of these attacks. Father Flanagan was fully aware of the trend of medical thought in his case, i.e. 'Neurosis'. How wrong can one be? Here was the answer, after long hard years of suffering, starting back in the late forties.

What a year of suffering for Father Flanagan! By the autumn of 1966, there was little hope for his life, for the second kidney gave cause for concern. The Father's general condition became toxic. He was told by his surgeon that he was 'skating on thin ice'. Father Flanagan wished to return to his presbytery, to be near his little church. By that same evening he had returned, reminding him of our continuous petitioning to our Lady of Lourdes, and prayer can move mountains. Pilgrimages to Lourdes commenced continuous Masses were offered, and the great miracle happened. The Father made a miraculous recovery, slow but sure. By 1968 he was once again ascending the altar of God, and thereafter to commence the greatest work of all, namely, to defend the Church and Magisterium in the dark days of turmoil following Vatican II.

I will now embark on this important part of his life for this biography, but before doing so, I will include here a letter from one of Father Flanagan's most faithful parishioners, who, like many of us, felt very hurt at the manner in which Father Flanagan was treated by his neighbouring brother clergy.

This following letter was written by Mrs Molly Smart.

'In 1965, a year after my husband's death (sudden) Father Flanagan worried about my distress, as he always was concerned about people, bereaved or ill, suggested I take on the job of Sacristan at St Georges. I accepted gladly and from then I worked closely and devotedly with the Father in this capacity, until he died so suddenly and so tragically one Sunday morning.

During all those years, and even during the Father's many and serious illnesses, I cannot recall he ever received help or visits from priests of the Eastbourne parishes. He told me there were many occasions in Esperance Nursing Home when visiting priests would pass his room without even calling to ask how he was. Apart from this, St George's Parish seemed to be 'out of bounds' for Eastbourne clergy, who did not support our fund – raising events or social gatherings. I can only assume that this was done deliberately to hurt Father Flanagan. Once when I talked to the Father about this, he shrugged his shoulders and said 'Don't worry, I am sure they will all come to my funeral.' They did, and as they crowded on to the sanctuary, I sadly remembered Father's prophetic words.

I will always remember this holy priest with gratitude and affection.

(Signed) Molly Smart.

I will now, as previously promised, relate the drastic happening to our beautiful Lady Chapel of St Joachim's Church.

To start, shortly after Father Flanagan moved to St George's, Polegate, and a new Priest, Father Scott had taken over the parish of St Joachim, Hampden Park, changes took place, either by his own wish, or that of his Bishop. (Cashman). The lovely statue of Our Lady of Lourdes was removed from her altar, and placed on the bare ground beside the altar. It caused great pain to all those concerned in putting it there. The statue remained in this position for some years.

There was a change of parish clergy, a new parish priest, but Our Lady's statue remained on the bare floor. A new parishioner made a small box-like stand upon which he placed the statue, thus rising it approximately one foot higher. Needless to say, this caused great sorrow and a delegation to the then parish priest, Father Bradley, suggested that Our Lady's Statue be replaced on her altar. Father Flanagan died before accomplishing this, but after the Father's funeral (March 1977) I approached this priest, and gave him the message about Father Flanagan's intentions. Father Bradley said he 'would see'. He did not see, but on his being moved to another parish in

1980, the new priest, Father Corcoran, finished the demolition job started by others.

Father Corcoran saw to it that Our Lady was stripped of her chapel, built a breeze-brick wall under the arch, (formerly described) and turned this lovely chapel of Our Lady into a Social Centre for the people!! All this, in spite of the fact that there was a site – and still is – available to build a hall at the back of the church.

A shelf on the wall of the sanctuary is the final resting place for this statue of Our Lady of Lourdes. I protested vigorously by letter. Result, no answer, 'Closed Shop'. The beautiful chapel which had been officially opened on Rosary Sunday in 1960, was well and truly removed from the Body of the church on Rosary Sunday 1980.

Would this dastardly act from 'those within the confines' bring tears? It did. Catholics of the area were not truly informed of the final ending to their Chapel, and when they were, it was too late to complain and protest.

Not content with depriving the Church of its Lady Chapel, this same priest has now removed the Altar Rails. One wonders what is to happen next to our churches at the hands of Bishops and priests.

The following, taken from a CPA *Newsletter*.

NO ALTAR RAILS

Where once I knelt awaiting
   The reception of my King
The Lord of Hosts, upon my tongue-
   Great joy, this act did bring.
My heart is sad, as I behold
   The 'Space', where now I stand
NO ALTAR RAIL – my 'TABLE'
   Removed – by a ruthless hand.

In memory of a loved one,
   This Altar Rail bestowed-
To beautify God's dwelling place,
   Where the fire of live once glowed.
Here's where the little children
   On their First Communion Day,
Received the 'Bread of Heaven'-
   In the old, time-honoured way.

The Bridegroom waits the happy bride,
   Beside the Altar Rail-
The dear departed, rest awhile-
   Ere they take 'the last long trail'-
How often have we witnessed
   The lone one – kneeling there,
As near to God as possible-
   In rapt and silent prayer!

The castle has its ramparts-
   Where watching soldiers keep
A keen look out for danger,
   While those within, do sleep.
Our Altar Rails – the ramparts-
   Guarding Our Lord and King,
Remove them, then – what danger,
   May this wanton action bring?

The vandals of past history,
   Destroyed – and sacked – at will,
Their **HATRED** of 'Things Sacred',
   Our hearts with sorrow fill.
Today, our hearts are breaking
   As we see the Godless way,
Our churches are denuded-
   By the vandals of **OUR** day!

Ecclesiastic vandals-
   The worst, of any kind,
THEY are the men responsible,
   For the deep distress of mind-
Of the meek- obedient- 'Faithful',
   Now rudely pushed aside,
No word of pity spoken,
   For the grief they cannot hide!

The 'wind of change' – blows chill
And we are caught in great distress.
Help us, dear Lord, to hold on tight-
And not succumb, to faithlessness.
With **YOU,** as our example,
Of **PERFECTION** – rudely slain-
Our eyes will ever turn to YOU-
And will not look in vain!

GERTRUDE GADEN
18 September 1976

The Formation of the Catholic Priests Association
February 20th 1968.

I am about to enter into a part of this biography which will set forth to all readers the true and authentic picture of 'The Great Defender'.

In the ensuing chapters, I will do my very best to record in depth, the greatness of this priest, his fight in the defence of the Church and Magisterium, his profound and total loyalty to the Sovereign Pontiff, his fearlessness in the face of bitter opposition from modernists and progressives – even if members of these groups came from within the confines of the church, or were those in high places, Father Flanagan left no stone unturned to bring them to task.

As already stated, Father carried the cross of persistent illness, overcame it when death had almost claimed him in 1966, and lived for another eleven years, years which were to prove that the **Hand of God** was guiding the **man of God.**

I will now take you through those last eleven years of Father Flanagan's life, during which, I will be recording direct from his *Catholic Priests Association Newsletter,* his own personal and militant defence of the Church, using verbatim, his own words, dates, etc., etc., thus allowing for the complete truth of his life to be recorded.

It was during the year 1967, while still convalescing at his presbytery at St George's, Polegate, Sussex, that Father Flanagan became aware of the havoc that already had descended upon the Church, with no visible defence against the invading enemy, namely Neo-Modernism. What had overcome the Shepherds of the Flock? Were they asleep, or just paralysed in the face of such danger? How could they sit back on their episcopal thrones and watch such destruction take place and do nothing?

These questions must be answered, cried Father Flanagan daily. The stone must be rolled back, and soon. So something would have to be done to stem the tide, and indeed Father Flanagan lost no time in bringing this to full fruition.

Consultation with other priests from different parts of the country took place. A meeting was arranged at St Wilfrid's Church Hall, Hailsham, and so a new Association of Priests initiated. Priests, in union with their fellow priests, would stand up and be counted in their efforts to combat and refute New Modernism.

A manifesto was drawn up, the contents of which will be given.

The Manifesto was drawn up as follows:

'Founded on February 20, 1968 to invite all Catholic Priests to collaborate in defence of the Pope and official teaching of the church.

'The Association of Priests is to combat and refute Neo-Modernism which is eating at the very vitals of the Church and destroying the faith of the people of our country. Our hope and purpose is to sustain and uphold, in the face of all difficulties, the teaching of the Pope in matters of faith and morals, and in important issues of ecclesiastical discipline such as celibacy. We affirm our devotion to the Catholic doctrine of the Holy Eucharist, and fidelity to the Sacred Scriptures as interpreted by the Magisterium of the Church.

'No other link joins the members of the Association than the common purpose of defending the Church and Papacy. Members receive a *Newsletter* which is published approximately every two or three months. Lay associate members may also receive a newsletter. We earnestly ask all Catholics devoted to their Church, to help us in any way possible.

'At a time, when the Church is in a terrible crisis, possibly the worst in its long history, priests must surely realise that they can help the Church they love best by collaborating with fellow priests.

'We exhort all priests to join our Association.'

The Association, thus formally established, received its title, and would be known as *'Cephas'*. This title was soon to be changed to *'The Catholic Priests' Association'* (reasons to follow) and in years to come, due to its international involvement and readership, to be finally known as *'The International Catholic Priests' Association'*.

Certainly no 'Myth', as a certain priest i.e., Father John Sullivan of

Eastbourne, defined it, when writing a report to the Sacred Congregation of Clergy at the Vatican following the death of Father Flanagan (more on this later) in 1977.

Reasons for change of title   By Father Flanagan
From CPA NEWSLETTER
25th March 1969 (Page 1)

Six weeks after the manifesto was signed and accepted by the Fathers who formed the Association, a small group, headed by a non-founder member, and without the approval of those who had joined and submitted to the first manifesto (120 members in all) introduced an anaemic substitute.

This latter group, now known as *'Cephas'* has recently issued its first journal in the same name. Three Cheers for any group or person who defends the Papacy today, and we wish the publication every success. We would, however, raise a number of points of criticism:-

1. It is regrettable that this 'splinter group' should have started in the first place, without being prepared to submit their point of view to the judgment of all members through a postal vote.

The offer was made more than once, and not even acknowledged.

2. When the separation of this group took place, the Association's total membership was 334 and all but sixteen of this number signed the manifesto.

3. Priests who will be more than surprised by this separation into groups should know, that the 'Catholic Priest's Association' is an 'Association' not only in name, but in reality; in fact, it would be better described as a 'movement', as we believe very much in the personal freedom of the priest, and that, being a mature person he is best positioned to know what he can do in the best interests of the Church.

4. Members of the 'Catholic Priests' Association' must be left free to criticise (always with respect and with a sense of responsibility) **anyone who deviates from loyalty and obedience to the**

Pope. Bishops or even Cardinals are not excepted. CPA members are not 'mitre conscious' and not influenced by the call of ecclesiastical preferments, and so, are in the best position to offer an objective and true assessment of the problems that face the Church in this tragic hour.

We give unstinted loyalty, respect and obedience to our respective Bishop and to the Hierarchy as long as they conform in turn, to the obedience and loyalty they owe to the Roman Pontiff.

We think it sad and pathetic that a journal with the name of *'Cephas'* and purporting to support the Holy Father, should quibble on the 'grade' of assent that is due to *'Humanae Vitae'* and consider that solemn document as not containing infallible doctrine (*'Cephas'* P.4 – 5). No genuine theologian questions the infallibility and irreformability of what has always been the traditional teaching of the Church on this vital subject.

Father Flanagan's account of 'Splinter Group'
(CPA 'Newsletter' May 1969)

'Our first duty is to express our congratulations to Monsignor A. Clark, Chairman of the breakaway group, on his appointment as Auxiliary Bishop of Northampton. We wish him *'ad multos et faustos annos'*. Within hours of the appointment being made public, people made contact with this office, asking how we knew, when the last *Newsletter* went to press (March 25) that a 'mitre' was in the offing, and reference was made to the editorial of that particular issue.

'The editor of this *Newsletter* has no comment to make, except to commend the accuracy of his source of information. It was regrettable that the *Catholic Herald* in the issue of April 4, should refer to members of the 'Catholic Priests' Association' as 'extremists' and give an entirely untrue report on what brought about the formation of a 'splinter group' in the original Association. Several indirect approaches have been make since the appointment of Monsignor Clark, in favour of this separate group returning to the original. That is an issue which individual members of that section, can alone decide. Dedication to upholding the authority of the Pope and ordinary Magisterium of the Church, as outlined in our first manifesto, is all that we require of members.

'The bringing into being of this Association of Catholic Priests, is as clear in my memory today, as to the day of its founding and formation.' Father L Whatmore, Chairman, Father Flanagan – Secretary. Entering on this important era, for this biography, Catholic readers, true to the Church's teaching, will learn of the courage and stamina emulating from this soldier of Christ about to embark on a fight to death (and that is how it finally turned out to be) against the innovations of Neo-Modernism. Faith of our fathers, living still, in spite of dungeon fire and sword, would be the banner carried and defended all the way by this newly formed Association, right up to the day of Father's death on 27 March 1977. I know, for I was there, all through those now historic years of the Church's battle for survival. I watched the efforts to stem the tide, being made by this association of priests, and I witnessed too, the quick reactions from those within the confines of the Church, those from whom we expected leadership and guidance in such gruelling times, namely the Hierarchy. It did not come. Instead came a marked and visible onslaught of anger and antipathy, especially from the (now late) Bishop Cashman of our diocese of Arundel and Brighton.

With his photograph, in full episcopal garb, occupying the top half front page of a Catholic Weekly Newspaper, he stated openly and emphatically, that he disowned such an Organisation in his diocese, and no priest of his diocese had his 'approval'. Father Flanagan quickly corrected this reprimand by informing the Bishop, that, as an 'Association', no approval was required. Only when it is an 'Organisation' is 'approval' sought.

Again, with reference to this 'Splinter-group', readers will decipher later on, from Father Flanagan's Articles, recorded for this biography, the true meaning behind the move to break up this newly formed Association, by another newly formed group, under its chairman Monsignor Alan Clarke, now the Bishop of East Anglia. For the present, I will continue with the Father's immense task to get this Association off the ground.

Work of Association Commenced

Immediately on return to his presbytery, with the minutes of this inaugural meeting to hand, and a clear format in mind as to the immediate preparation required to launch this vital and sorely needed Association, Father Flanagan, as its Secretary, lost no time in setting the 'wheels' in motion.

It was a very heavy task for one priest. Father Whatmore, as chairman, helped as far as was possible, by contributing articles etc., for the

'Newsletter' soon to follow, but Father Flanagan took upon his own shoulders the actual physical burden involved.

A request for help was later made which would have been answered immediately by all priests concerned, but the problem was, these priests, in their respective parishes were placed in different parts of the country. It was at this point, that I became fully involved in this great work. Father Flanagan had asked for my help which I felt so privileged to give. I left myself 'open' to do anything and everything within my capacity as a lay person, of that, I assured Father Flanagan and so, we were ready to begin.

While Father Flanagan formally prepared the Manifesto for subsequent duplication, the first work load for me, was as follows.

From the *Catholic Directory of England and Wales,* the names and addresses of all clergy, in all parishes of each diocese, plus all clergy at every college and seminary throughout the country had to be found and written on envelopes ready for the manifesto.

This was certainly a time-consuming task. It took myself, with the help of Father Whatmore, who covered a few dioceses, many hours of the following weeks to complete.

Once completed, and with all manifestoes safely in the post, Father Flanagan eagerly awaited the result. His own words to me were, 'Our efforts will disintegrate or snowball, according to the Will of God'. Father Flanagan did not have long to wait, it snowballed and so the first real fight, in opposition to Neo-Modernism was on.

The financing of this work to start with came from very close friends of Father Flanagan, Mr and Mrs Beech (now deceased), and also from myself.

The immediate influx of correspondence through the letter box marked the first sign of the urgent need for this new Association.

Here were Catholics, true to the Church's Magisterium, in fear of where the 'new set' within the Church was finally going to lead them. 'Priests too (as Father Flanagan so often informed us), were in a dreadful state, not knowing which way to turn', for the disagreement could mean a prolonged attitude of 'cold' treatment from those in charge, and so for many good holy priests, life in their parish, or in their seat of academic studies became almost unbearable, and for one priest, to the actual point of death, which I will relate and record for this book, when writing Father Flanagan's exposition of what happened to 'The Good Shepherd of Shepherd's Bush'.

Therefore
1. To defend the one true Church, with all the power, determination and knowledge at his command.

2. To help and encourage priests to stand up firm, in face of persecution.
3. To give heart and hope to the Catholic laity, was to be, and proved later, to be, the three hallmarks in Father Flanagan's life for the next eleven years.

Having now given a general synopsis of the work involved in the launching of the Catholic Priests' Association, as I personally witnessed it, I will, from here onwards, be recording fully, Father Flanagan's articles and editorials direct from the CPA *Newsletter,* where fearlessly, he exposes and names those concerned in the revolt against the Church and Magisterium.

I will commence with the first article namely, 'The Worship of Man' and will record it in full – Parts I, II and III, as it sets out from the very start to end, the post conciliar disaster that befell the Church, and those who caused it to happen.

Other articles will follow, equally important, in defining the pattern emerging in this country by progressives and renewalists, whom Father Flanagan refused to spare at all times, irrespective of name or position.

Also for inclusion, Father Flanagan's work for the Holy Shroud of Turin.

III

THE WORSHIP OF MAN
PART ONE By Father Flanagan DCL, STL
CPA *Newsletter 25 March 1969*

IT WOULD BE a very inobservant person indeed, who would not notice in the post-conciliar Church, the shift of emphasis from God to man, from moral evil to social evil, from theology to sociology, from scholasticism to the empty jargon of secularism and pseudo progress.

On all sides one hears reference to the 'Spirit of Vatican II' and to the outmoded ideas and systems that this Council is alleged to have discarded.

Vatican II would appear to many, as the first Council which was aided by the Holy Spirit, which prompted the conciliar fathers to visualise renewal, which involved the rejection of even the most basic concepts of the Church's structure and dogmas.

Pope John XXIII on October 11, 1962, in his opening speech to the Council, had a very different idea in his mind when he said 'The greatest concern of the Ecumenical Council was, that the Sacred Deposit of Christian Doctrine should be guarded and taught more efficaciously. This doctrine must be transmitted pure and integral without any attenuation or distortion.' (Documents of Vatican II, by Walter Abbot, S.J., p.715).

But the good intentions of Pope John were not enough to keep in check the pressure from intellectuals who were temporarily restrained by Pius XII in *'Humani Generis'*, and on the death of Pius XII, it is an open fact, that while the Catholic world at large mourned the passing of a great Pontiff, the renewalists and modernists rejoiced in the firm conviction that their day had come at last.

(*World Trend Sydney* 1968)

Pope John's well known optimism had little place for 'the apostles of doom' to use his own words in his address to the Council. He did not see in the fact that Pius X, in 1914, Pius XI in 1939, and Pius XII, in 1940, had referred to the wickedness of the world 'as the beginning of miseries' which was foretold by Christ as a forerunner to the end of the world. 'Men must prepare themselves to meet disasters such as mankind has never known before,' said Pius XII in 1947, and the context is not necessarily linked with the possible use of the atomic or hydrogen bomb. (That the Papal statements referred to in this paragraph interpret the miseries of mankind with the end of the world, as foretold in the Scriptures, is not just a deduction of the writer of this article – the texts of the Popes (Pius X, XI, XII) statements are explicit on this point.)

On the death of Pius XII the advocates within the Church of strange and dangerous philosophies, pushed forward to their goal.

Existentialism, Situation Ethics, and a cluster of other spurious modes of thought suddenly developed, endangering the whole fabric and life of the Church. The deification of *De Chardinism* by the advocates of the new theology, gave a big impetus to the 'progressive' movement. The ranks of the 'periti' and various 'commissions' working in conjunction with the Council, became easy prey to the subtle infiltration methods of the new '*avant-garde'*.

The realm of liturgy received their immediate attention. If *'lex orandi est lex credendi'* holds good, it should not be too difficult to change and modify our notions of 'prayer through anew approach to the concept of 'liturgy'. 'Involvement of the people of God', 'meaningful experience' and a host of other human twitterings preached by dedicated zealots and presented as approved by Vatican II, have produced the desire results.

Prayer, public prayer at least, becomes the clamour of the social unit or community, and not at all the cry of the human heart to God in *'Et clamor Meus ad Te Veniat'*.

While the 'involvement' argument wins the support of some of God's people for whom the noise of the 'beat drums' hue an appeal, the ruthless dismantling of the most sacred structures of the church goes on with unabated fury, and in spheres of religion where the reasons alleged by the reformers can have no possible application. Many such instances come before our mind the many Churches, while the 'President's Chair' stands out as the focal point in the Church, the very reversal of Vatican Council teaching.

The servant has replaced his Master and usurped his place could we call it by the name of 'Liturgical Communism'.

We think of the frightful disrespect to the Holy Eucharist – a practice now becoming widespread in this country in colleges and universities, when the blessed sacrament is pushed into filthy unwashed hands of dedicated contraceptionists who are told that there is no reason for confession before communion by some pill preaching priests. (For first hand information on what is happening in Holland we refer the reader to articles by Douglas Brown in the *Sunday Telegraph* 9 March 1969 and by the same writer in the *Catholic Herald,* March 14, 1969).

'He was delivered into the hands of sinful men' to quote the words of Sacred Scripture, now take on a new and frightening meaning.

Right through the whole field of Sacred Liturgy, an abysmal difference has been deliberately created between the authentic teaching of the Church and actual observance. One factor which emerges quite clearly, is the refusal or failure on the part of the liturgical scholars, to follow established rules. They 'get around them' on any pretext; 'the laws are being misunderstood', or 'they do not apply to the local pastoral requirements' are only two examples of escape attitudes, adopted by the liturgical experts in this matter. There is always a title to justify deviation from the norms established by the Holy See.

Father Gerald Sigler, the Executive Secretary of the International Committee for English in the Liturgy, was one of the group of priests in Washington, U.S.A., to be disciplined for his opposition to *'Humane Vitae',* and his writings in *Worship* on liturgical matters connected with Holy Mass, have been described as 'scandalous' and deserving of discipline. (Triumph, Jan 23, 1969).

The small 'Mass group' which started on the continent some eighteen months ago, is now becoming a danger to the whole church.

It started in an heretical environment and with the concept of the 'Priesthood of the laity' for its basis. Mass is celebrated on the breakfast table using bread and wine, as an ordinary meal. After all, those who originated this concept of the Mass, consider that it is 'an ordinary commemorative meal'.

Mass of this type will be said in every home, by the head of the family, male or female. Traditional church buildings will in twenty years be 'out'. The church building of the future will be a 'Dialogue Room' with other adjacent meeting rooms attached. One such church has already been built at Leiterhofen, near Augsburg, according to *Suddeutsche Zeitung* (Dec. 10, 1968).

A liturgy moulded by men whose faith and theology were unquestionably sound, could not go far wrong. But that is not the case.

De Chardin and Sartre have many dedicated followers in the inner circle of the Liturgical experts, and it is only to be expected, that their pantheistic (where De Chardin is concerned) and existentialistic ideas will spill out into the Liturgy that they produce.

The sheep of the flock of Christ are in real danger from these unscrupulous reformers. Of course the analogy of sheep in the scriptures to the docile faithful, is hardly relevant any longer, as the 'involvement' which the innovators insist should characterise the people of God, in the new liturgy and the new church, would make them more like 'rampaging rams' than 'docile sheep' that listen to their Shepherd's call, and follow a safe path to pastures that are fit to graze.

Most Catholic Priests today are acquainted with the names of Father Schillebeeck, O.P., the Flemish theologian and Father Schoonenburg S.J., who with Hans, Kung and Father Karl Rahner formed a well known quartet of *'periti'* connected with the Vatican Council. *'Peritus'* is a term that all of us have become very familiar with since the last Council, because to a great extent, they (the *'periti'*) have continued to speak and write, after the Council, as if they were commissioned in some special way, to spread their personal views, as the views of the council, and as part of the Magisterium of the Church.

We think of St Augustine in his confessions when he wrote: *Garriebam quasi peritus* (I chattered away like one in the know) and he was referring to his days when he was enthralled by the Manichean heresy and was teaching (as he thought it) the whole world the truth. Many of our Vatican Council *'periti'* could learn a lesson from St Augustine. They continue to chatter their own views, which so often are in direct conflict with the Magisterium of the Church. By divine will and ordinance, the power of teaching, ruling and sanctifying, in the church, was committed by Christ to St Peter and the Apostles or, to the Church of our day, to Pope Paul VI and the Bishops of the Catholic Church, who teach in harmony with him. But our age has seen a tremendous upheaval it has seen whole hierarchies failing to give complete obedience to the one, who alone can confirm them, and keep them in office.

It is with this atmosphere that the theological and liturgical background of the present day Church, can be understood.

In these adverse circumstances, can the rapid deterioration of the Church in almost every sphere, be explained?

Man is an ensemble of his acts, says Sarte. It is by 'body actions' that self and others are 'realised'. Hence the importance of bodily self-expression, according to the Existentialists an idea which explains the emphasis which

Liturgists put on 'involvement in the liturgy', also explains our modern craze for 'marching demonstrations' in the streets.

For the Catholic, Holy Mass is a public act of worship of God; for the Existentialist theologian, it is an 'encounter with God' by means of words, signs, preaching, singing – it is an acknowledgement that Christ is already present in the community, and this 'realisation' is now stirred up. External objects are only real, says the Existentialist, from the item a subject projects his personality into them. Applied to the Holy Eucharist this means that Christ projects himself into the bread and wine, and through those gifts He becomes **present** to the faithful. Christ's **presents** is not Christ's **PRESENCE** . . . The Eucharist becomes a mere keepsake or souvenir of Christ, left to his people. (Triumph, Jan 1969, p.21).

From what has been said, the reader will realise that the Existentialist theologian (and alas most of the big names in theology today are of this school) will not admit analogical change in the bread and wine after consecration; for them **'Transubstantiation'** is **'OUT'** and **'Transignification'** is 'in'. De Chardin held, that Christ is truly, physically present, not merely in the Eucharist, but in all men and in all matter. (*The Future of Man*, 137). De Chardin was a pantheist and yet he is canonised by some Catholics!

From the weird and heretical doctrines just enunciated, emanate many of the equally heretical doctrines connected with the Mass and the Eucharist, which one finds spreading in all directions, even in this country.

Charles Davis considered the Eucharist as a Commemorative meal only. In *The Word In History*, pp156-157, he wrote the Sacrament of Christ's Sacrifice is a sacred 'commemorative meal'. The meal is the sacrifice, not something which follows it.

Father Louis Bouyer identifies Christ's body with the community. (*Liturgical Piety*, p.161). For others again, following closer to De Chardin, the 'real presence' of Christ in the Eucharist is not in any way different from his presence in people. Father Godric Young, O.F.M., writing in *The New Franciscan,* July 1968, p.157, has this to say of the real presence.

'When we think about the Real Presence in this context we will be so at a loss, if we find a Church in which the tabernacle is not the focal point.

When we see more clearly how Christ is present in His people, in us, we shall not feel that something is missing even in a Church in which the Real Presence is not there.'

(The writer of this article wrote three letters to the Superior of the Franciscans, complaining about the publication of this article in *The New Franciscan*. There was no reply in all three cases).

You may be shocked, dear reader, such statements as are given in this article, but be assured that it is not a question of picking out the most sensational, or the most absurd writings from papers and magazines etc. today. It is no exaggeration to state, that there is no doctrine of the Church which is not rejected by some priests today. ('Is it the same Church', by F.J. Sheed, P.31) and there is no statement too absurd for Catholic writers to put on paper.

All of them, no doubt, believe that truth is on their side, all of them rejecting the infallibility of the Pope, which they claim for themselves.

Sister Mary Collins, a Professor of Catholic Theology in America, believes that the Church lost the true words of consecration and remembered one brief phrase of interpretation – 'This is my Body: This is my Blood' (Triumph, Jan 1969, p.23). Father Schillbeeckx wonders if the words of Institution are really essential for the consecration of the Lords Supper. (Liturgical Piety, p.137).

We have now reached the final paragraph of this first section of this article. The question may well be asked – is the Holy Mass in peril?

As Catholics, we know that Christ promised to be with His Church to the end of time and that the gates of hell will not prevail against it. We also know, that the Mass and the Eucharist is at the very core of the Catholic Faith. But it is only this Divine Guarantee that can give us security and assurance.

Were it not for this, it would be natural for us to experience extreme anxiety as we would ask ourselves the question, what happens when perhaps Bishops will believe that Mass is not a Sacrifice, how can they have the intention of conferring the 'Sacrificing priesthood' on those to be ordained? What would be the result if validly ordained priests should now believe that the words 'This is my Body' (Father Bouyer's theory) refers to the community present, we know that a Bishop in ordaining, and a priest in consecrating, must have at least the intention of doing what the Church does, but we also know, that this general intention of conferring the Sacrament CAN BE vitiated by the positive and deliberate act of the minister, and this will affect validity.

We need the steady hand of Peter on the tiller, to guide the barque of the Church safely to its destination.

Oremus pro Papa et Ecclesia Sancta Dei.

IV

THE WORSHIP OF MAN
PART TWO

THE KIND READER will have noticed by now, that in Part I of this article, the theological and philosophical trends, which have influenced the growth of so many false theories and practices connected with Holy Mass and the Blessed Sacrament, were dealt with. In this second section, I should like to cover in a general way, the many manifestations of subversion and falsification within the Church, but, in operating in spheres, other than the Mass and the Eucharist.

I entitled the article *'THE WORSHIP OF MAN'* and I hope that by now the reader will have understood my reason. As we push God more and more out of His lawful place in the Church, and fail to listen to His only authentic voice in this world – THE VOICE OF THE POPE – we set up MAN in GOD'S place. We deify Him. We want a God of our own making, who will be more concerned with poverty and disease, than with the supernatural life and the moral laws.

We hope that the following paragraphs will help our readers to assess, the extent to which secularism and humanism have made their inroads into the Church's life and practice, and set up man in God's place.

Belief in the Divinity of Jesus Christ is looked upon by some Catholic writers, as either doubtful, or as a theory which should be rejected. In a very subtle way, some of our 'progressive theologians', first gently insinuate the idea, or downgrade the prerogatives of Christ's Divinity, in the first step towards utter rejection. Father Sebastian Moore in his work *God is a New Language,* p. 119 speaks of 'Christ's point of view, and our point of view', though no one would imply that Father Moore questions seriously the Divinity of Our Saviour, but it is an unfortunate expression on his part. Father Mainberger of Lucerne writes that the death of Jesus Christ on the cross has no sense. 'If God the Father accepted the sacrifice of His own son, then He was a sadist', and further on, he states, 'The Kingdom of God must be replaced by a kingdom of thIs world'. (*Que' Pasa?'* 18-1-1969).

The restrictions once in force, which protected the innocent and the unwary from imbibing heretical doctrines, are now almost universally ignored. *THE GRAVE OF GOD* (Father Adolf) and *Honest to GOD* (Robinson) are now found in the libraries of schools and even convents.

The indisolubility of marriage which the Church has always upheld, as of Divine Law, is now being challenged in some countries, particularly in Holland, the Dutch Bishops have demanded the whole case to be examined.

Some Dutch 'research' theologians have already discovered, that the Church's teaching was based on a myth. The Dutch Pastoral Council has already demanded at its meeting (Jan 5 to Jan 8 1969), that the remarriage of divorced persons should be blessed in the Catholic Church with Nuptial blessings. The practice has already been started in some places in Holland. *La Croix* (9 Jan 1969).

The same Dutch Pastoral Council, according to *Le Monde* (8 Jan 1969), clamoured for the canonisation of Che Guevra, 'while Cardinal Alfrink sat in silence smoking his cigar.' The clamour for the canonisation of Che Guevara, should not surprise anyone, familiar with the influence of Father Schillebeeckx, in the Netherlands or elsewhere, for according to *Revue de Press Internationale* (Jan 1969 p.28) the good Domincan Priest considers 'Revolution in the Church, and rebellion against its dogmas and institutions, as AUTHENTIC CHRISTIANITY'. Someone opened the Vatican Windows too wide!

The ecumenical spirit, when not kept within the just limits, outlined by the Holy See, in its *Ecumenical Directory*, has also brought disastrous practices into the Church in many countries.

Bishops in many cases, seem to assume, that they are authorised to admit non-Catholics to Holy Communion. The downgrading of the importance of dogmas in the Catholic Church as also brought terrible consequences, and these are not just a few isolated cases, but wide trends of actin. The Bishop of Nanterre, Monsignor Delarue, recently wrote in his diocesan paper, according to *Revue de la Presse Internationale* (Jan 1969 p.8) 'That it is not at all certain, that the Catholic Church has preserved all Revealed Truths and for that reason alone, there is reason for reunion with the separated brethren, so that full revealed truth may be rediscovered'.

Clerical celibacy is the principle object of attack at the moment, from the followers of the new theology in most countries. We find extreme pressure being exerted in Holland, and in many parts of France and Germany, to force the Pope to surrender on this issue.

Some advocates of a married clergy, are not content to leave it to individual priests to ask it as a favour, but believe in exerting such pressure, that the hands of the Pope will be forced to grant it. Father Hoefnagels, S.J., Professor of Theology in the University of Amsterdam, encourages priests to exert such pressure on the Pope, that he will have no option but to yield on the matter.

One parish in Utrecht, sent an ultimatum to the Bishop, to have the law of celibacy removed within six months, and this took place shortly after Cardinal Alfrink had declared that there was 'no question of modifying celibacy without the approval of the Universal Church' – *La Croix* (Jan. 23, 1969).

The Belgian Paper *De Standard* (Jan. 16, 1969) declares, that between 1964 and 1966, the Holy See gave 4,000 dispensations to Priests to marry, and be reduced to lay state, and in Holland alone, during that period more than 600 priests (out of a total of 6,000) abandoned the priesthood.

The universal degradation of faith and morals continues to gather new momentum, as each day passes. No section of the Church is immune from this virus (aptly called *Bacille Hollandais,* by a writer of the Italian paper *Il Messaggero* [Jan. 15, 1969]). It has infected every dogma and moral principle in the Church, and in every country and in every community. Cardinal McCarthy, reporting in the *Revue de las Presse Internatinale* gives the case of a Trappist monk (Anselm Atkins) giving a reception in the Mayflower Hotel in Washington, and states, that incredible changes have taken place, even in the Trappist Monasteries, where radio and T.V. and cinemas are now installed, and the monks indulge in all kinds of recreation and entertainment. Many such monks have left their monasteries, some to marry.

What has happened to the Church, we have tried to explain, in the various paragraphs of this article. Where and when will it all end? That is the burning question of the hour.

One writer in *Figaro Litteraire* (Jan. 26, 1969) holds the view, that continuous concessions by the Pope, to demanding clerics, together with the profanation of the Sacred Liturgy, and a democratisation of the Church, at most levels, are the three principal causes (immediate causes) of our present plight, but that the total wave will have to be rolled back from next October, when the synod of Bishops meet in Rome and will receive final warnings from Pope Paul VI. *Dominus Conservet eum*.

If this article, dear reader, presents a depressing scene, it is only because it tries to give a genuine picture of the situation.

Unless we know the evils, we cannot effectively eradicate them.

V

THE WORSHIP OF MAN
PART THREE

AS EXPLAINED IN the previous issue of this *Newsletter,* a revolution instead of a renewal, a lowering of our concept of God and things Divine to the level of man and society. Man and society have replaced God, as sociology has replaced theology; the authoritative teaching Church is being replaced by the 'democratic Church'. This whole movement is aptly called 'Horizontalism', which may be described as seeing God on the level with man 'horizontal' to the exclusion of the 'vertical' dimension which should also be there.

The 'New Theology' is one dimensional, in which all is reduced to the love of the neighbour, to a function of a social service. Horizontalists in the Church, empty the church of the sense of God; faith, becomes service to our neighbour and becomes banal and sentimental.

The characteristic of Christianity is the primacy of the **Vertical dimension** – the love and worship of God, from which the **horizontal** alone can have meaning, if the Christian religion is not to be reduced to pure humanism. There is no other world than this – for the horizontalist; the 'next world' for him is, paradoxically – this world. The material world in which we live, can satisfy all man's aspiration, if only man will live for this world and forget the next. For the horizontalist, sin is a frustration, conversion is revolution, virtue is a social service, the Church is the state, the parish the local community, the Magisterium is to be found in the press, public relations and television. Do not laugh, dear reader but the strangest thing about all this, is the fact, that the dedicated horizontalist will be furious if you declare that he is outside the Church, by his beliefs and actions, and that he should cease to speak of himself as a Catholic. He would classify himself as a 'committed Catholic' – committed to what, is a different matter!

It was our divine Lord Himself who said 'By their fruits you shall know them. Do men gather grapes off thorns, or figs off thistles?' The massive defections of priests, nuns, and ordinary faithful from the church, particularly in those areas of the world where the 'new theology' has got root, are convincing proofs of the rottenness and decay from which these heresies blossom.

As printed out in Part II, the most sacred institutions of the Catholic faith are in peril. Our Sacred Liturgy is being moulded to fit a false and heretical doctrine, which is being moulded to fit a false and heretical doctrine, which is being constantly pushed forward by the innovators. The *'Lex Orandi'* will determine and fashion the *'Lex Credendi'*. It is not surprising that prayer, penance, mortification etc., are ugly words to the horizontalist, or as Maritain puts it – 'Three things that an 'up to date' Christian should never mention – (1) the other world – as there is no such thing, (2) the Cross – only, symbolic of sacrifices demanded by progress, and (3) Holiness (*The Trojan Horse in the City of God*, p.112).

Every Catholic has a responsibility in the present crisis which is existing in the Church and which endangers its structure and mission.

It cannot be overemphasised, that the passive attitude of so many, enables a small minority to produce enormous havoc in our midst. How often have we seen the exception suddenly turned into the principle, owing to the pressure of the rabid minority claiming that they speak for the people. How often have we seen innovations, introduced into our Liturgy, and later discovered that it was 'on request of many'. Who are 'the many'? Who are those faceless ones that determine what the rank and file of the people 'demand'? It is time that the majority of priests and people made themselves felt in favour of orthodoxy and traditionalism.

Let us now come to some particular cases, which manifest the attempts of the progressives to dethrone the divine and substitute of human.

As mentioned in Part II, Father Gerald Sigler, Executive Secretary of the International Committee for English in the Liturgy ('IECL') has written some scandalous doctrines on the very nature of Holy Mass. With Father Robert W. Hovda, another 'liturgical expert' and editor of liturgical conference publications, he has contributed articles to the well known American Liturgical periodical *Worship* which are downright heretical.

Yet these two men are permitted to mould our liturgical thinking, and ultimately our doctrinal beliefs. In the November issue (1967) of *Worship*, Father Hovda writes as follows:-

    1. 'Presiders must become familiar with current writing on

Eucharist Theology, if they would do justice to the canon (the new canons) for their own sake, and for the sake of the catechesim they owe to community.
2. 'The Presider is the one who preaches, sums up the prayers of the faithful, proclaims the canon initiates the peace greeting, and makes sure that all the faithful present are served at the holy table.
3. 'To attend to anything, even the book or bread and wine without attending to the persons present, is the opposite of the style we seek'.
4. Father Sigler concludes 'When the "Presider" proclaims 'that the bread and wine are consecrated, he merely means that the bread and the wine, and the people who provide them, have been accepted by God as pleasing offerings'.

The above quotations unmistakably show the heretical doctrine espoused by these expert Liturgists. A 'Presider' is one who receives his mandate from the people and depends on the people.

This is borne out by another statement of Father Hovda in the same article in which he states 'We must provide and soon, a less arduous method of resigning from the episcopal or priestly function. '

The idea of being a 'priest for ever' is now out dated; the new approach is the 'Presider' – the community he serves will have a say in his selection. He will do what they tell him, not what the Church teaches.

In quote (2) above, the idea of the canon being a prayer is out. It is a proclamation. Note how communion is practically compulsory; no mention is made of making sure, those approaching the holy table, have the spiritual dispositions – this is all fossilised theology of the pre-Vatican II era, before the Holy Spirit ever visited the Church. Note, dear reader, in quote (3) how important 'people' have become in this new theology.

The reason for this shift of emphasis is not far to seek it is explicitly given to us by Father Hovda's right hand man, Father Sigler, who following the doctrine of Father Louis Bouyer, (*Liturgical Piety*, p.161) identifies Christ's body with the community.

Father Sigler has no hesitation in accepting this heretical doctrine when he writes in the same *Worship* (November 1967) 'When the Presider proclaims that the bread and wine are consecrated, he simply means that the bread and the wine and the people who provided them, have been accepted by God as pleasing offerings'.

After this piece of open heresy, the Architect of our new liturgy goes on to make his ideas clearer still – 'The Body of Christ is in the community'. Gone is the doctrine of the Mass as a 'Sacrifice' – it is a meal, which can only be celebrated with the community and with their implicit approval.

Every age has had its heretics, but they found themselves outside the Church as soon as their heresy was externalised by word or deed. Past centuries offered us no example of heretics fashioning our liturgy to fit their force doctrines.

We hear today on many sides, people saying why does not the Church expel them, as in the past? Why do they continue to destroy the Church from within? The Swiss theologian, Father Hans Urs von Balthasar, quoted in the *Osservatore Romano* (4 April 69) writes that 'those who challenge the authority of the Pope and the Church, should leave the Church . . . corrosive acids which today are poured into the hearts of millions of persons through the press and radio and come even from the pulpit, under the pretext of clarifications . . . have not been prepared by persons who love God'.

I would suggest that the good Swiss theologian is far too lenient. Cessation of membership of the Church may take place in either of two ways – (a) by public heresy, which by its very nature, terminates membership of the Church, independently of any incurring of excommunication, and (b) by excommunication in accordance with canon 2314. These *'periti'* are **NOT** members of the Church – they have lost membership through their public heresy, but through weakness and diplomacy, which can only be called criminal, they are permitted to savage the faith of our Catholic people. Judas Iscariot betrayed Christ, though he was divinely selected. But he did leave the Church and hanged himself with a halter.

We are not suggesting our heretical *'periti'* should destroy their own lives, but we are suggesting that they be treated as apostates in so far as the Church is concerned.

After all, it was Christ Himself, who gave the warning about 'plucking out the eye' and 'cutting off the arm' that give scandal.

Elsewhere in the world, we see many examples of the great apostacy, strangling the Church under the pretext of development.

Who can have any doubt, that it was to the Church in Holland, that Pope Paul VI on two successive days of Holy week (1969) applied the word 'Schism'?

Who can doubt the accuracy of Pope Paul's assertion?

Our national papers have given much publicity to two priests of Holland who were finally suspended but only for a few days.

'*Schism* over my dead body,' cries Bishop Zwartkruis of Harlem, but words mean nothing when openly contradicted by deeds.

Let us spotlight this unhappy country for a moment, caught up in the vortex of the liturgical maelstrom now pounding northern Europe and sending its chilling shock waves into Britain.

The good Bishop of Harlem has more than tulip bulbs growing in his diocese. Recently, according to the *Revue de la Presse Internationale,* (Feb 1969 p.21), he consecrated a Church in the suburbs of Amsterdam, rectangular in shape and 'multi-functional' in purpose. Thanks to its thoughtful designer, the Church can quickly be transformed into a 'pub' and recreational centre or youth.

In this Church the local Lutheran Minister reads the lessons during Catholic Service. A similar 'church' was opened and blessed dedicated to St Thomas Acquinas, with 'pub' and 'dialogue room' adjacent, and the consecration (on Dec 27 1968) was carried out by the Bishop, following a form of consecration, drawn up by the local community. Holy Communion was distributed (into the hand) by the priest who celebrated mass, dressed as a lay person, and while hundreds of young people loudly discussed the topics of the day. A priest (Father Klappe, O.P.) solemnised marriage in the church, between a Dutch girl, a convert from Lutheranism to Mahomedanism, and a Musulman.

The Catholic Church took the place of the mosque in this case. The newspaper *De Telegraaf* (22 Feb 1969) published an article on the new 'MIXED MONASTERIES' which are now becoming popular in Holland.

In one such 'monastery' at Nijmegen, the community consists of six persons in all, three religious (two Jesuits and a Carmelite) and three women (two ex-sisters of different convents and a student).

The 'monastery' consists of three bedrooms, one lounge and one bathroom. The superior of this community is a Father Thuring S.J., who a year ago, announced his intention of founding a new type of 'monastery' more adapted to personality problems! The members of this community teach catechism to children and youths nearby.

While Cardinal Alfrink declares that a 'married clergy can only be considered with the universal church' (*Le Monde,* 15 Feb 1969) Monsignor Ernest, Bishop of Breda declares that 'The Dutch Bishops will do everything possible to introduce a married clergy *Revue de la Presse Internationale,* (Feb 1969 p.22) and one Dutch Radio Station even announced the identity of priests who had already taken the matrimonial step.

Le Figaro (13 Feb 1969) confirmed that the Dutch Bishops were demanding research into the question of celibacy, and the 'approval for some functions to be exercised by married priests and their wives.'

The campaign to abolish priestly celibacy in Holland is only a part of the greater campaign in that country, to establish absolute sexual liberty between all classes of the community, homosexuality not excluded. (*Revue de la Presse* Inter nationale).

Where will our liturgical reforms lead us to?

When will our liturgical *'periti'* say 'Thus far and no further ?' What are the limits of liturgical absurdity, beyond which even our darling liturgists may not go? No one knows the answer.

If they should dream of borrowing from their counterparts in another ecclesiastical community (The Episcopalian Church, New York) our tribulations are only commencing. The use of the cloaca with flushing water to symbolise that we are being washed from our sins, may appear like a kindergarten play, but when it becomes a reality, as in the case just mentioned, it is time for us to man the barricades in defence of our faith – and our common sense.

The 'sharp practice' of the liturgical experts to create the *'fait accompli'* situation, following by the announcement that 'Local pastoral considerations demanded such' and were 'enthusiastically received by the people of God and has characterised much of the liturgical changes throughout the world, is not unknown here in Britain. A letter from one of the Hierarchy, in reply to a query, why the ancient title of the Blessed Virgin *'Genetricis dei'* was dropped from the Canon of the Mass without objections to the 'ICEL' (International Commission for English in the Liturgy) brought a strange response. It declared that he (the Bishop) was not given any text of the new translation beforehand, but he merely heard a tape recording being played of the new text of the Canon.

Other members of the Hierarchy seem to have been treated in the same way, but all were assured that the omission of the title was only for a short time and 'as an experiment'.

Can one experiment with such matters? It was not ineptly called an 'experiment with heresy' by one publication.

J.W. Flanagan,
Polegate, Sussex.

VI

ARTICLES II-IV
ARTICLE II From C.P.A. *Newsletter* June/July 1969.
REFORMATION OR REVOLUTION

TO EVEN THE casual observer of the world situation, it is clear, that the crisis in the Church today, has reached proportions, that would be just incredible even three years ago. The spiritual renewal of man and society, the safeguarding at all costs of the deposit of faith and Christian morality, which Pope John XXIII set before the council, in his opening address of October 11, 1962, have not been fulfiled – far from it. Not since the Lutheran Revolution of the 16 Century, has the Church suffered more, than it does today, in almost every country in the world. It is not surprising that some writers (*the Universe* May 16, 1969) could refer to Vatican II as the greatest *fiasco* in the last two hundred years. The writer of this article does not agree with this conclusion – on the contrary, the fruits of the council were poisoned by unscrupulous hirelings, for their own advantage.

These hirelings were from many stages in the ecclesiastical life of the church – from Catholic publishers, who, in the hope of sordid gain, fed heretical novelties to the reading public, to the ambitious *periti,* Bishops and even Cardinals who should never have been advanced to the positions they held.

Long before Vatican II, the rule of advancing the *dignissimus* to the vacant seat of authority, was, in practice, thrown to the winds; it was not what you are, but, who you are, that became the determining criterion for ecclesiastical preferment.

The crime of simony was not at all exceptional, but it was covered up by those who indulged in it as something which could not happen – a *Nec nominentur in vobis.* The Church is now paying the penalty for corruption in its human element.

If there is any facet of the new revolution which is more obvious in this country, it is twisting of the purpose of the Church, from a supernatural mission, to one, of serving the social needs of man.

This aspect of the new theology has bitten deep into the life of many of the pastoral clergy, who in their genuine desire to help their people, and assuming that the theological lead which they have received from higher authority, is in fact the wish of Vatican II, have unwillingly become the teachers of an heretical doctrine.

It is not at all uncommon to hear purely natural and social problems, which either arise from the weakness of nature, or from the faults of a social system, put forward, **to prove the untruth of a supernatural religion.** It is pathetic how many good people, including priests, continuously confuse 'Revealed Religion' with 'Natural Religion', arguing from the latter, to reject the former. As the Pope pointed out (Jan 15, 1969) the 'renewal' visualised by the Council – 'a moral, personal, and interior renewal' is forgotten, and in its place, man 'filled with a frenzy, exalted by a dizziness, and at times a madness, overturns everything, in blind hope that a new order, a new world, a fully predictable *palingenesis* (rebirth) will inevitably come about'.

The Church of order and dignity, in a few years, has been turned into one of confusion – bordering on chaos. No wonder some think, that communists and anarchists have caused this turmoil – and this belief would not be without some foundation.

But if communists and anarchists never existed, much of the present chaos would still be there. There is a marked similarity between the Church of today and the sixteenth century.

Luther in Germany and King Henry VIII in England, claimed that they sought to reform the Church; they would reform it, by destroying it, as they wanted a Church – not of Christ's making but of their own. The very same thing is happening today with numerous Luthers and Henrys.

Luther had little time for 'spiritual reform', as he wrote to a friend – 'I have seldom time for reciting the Divine office or for saying Mass'. He was more interested in the social needs of people – just what the innovators of today manifest.

One has only to read such classical works as *The Life of Luther* by Grisai, to see how much he advocated nuns and priests should get married – just as the reformers today. Luther rejected the Sacraments, with the exception of Baptism which the laity could administer – we have it all back again in 1969, just the same heresies, but dressed up, to make the doctrine more attractive to 'committed' Catholics.

A peculiar characteristic of both revolutions, is the importance that the reformers give 'sex' — man is of course, being freed from the slavery which subjected him, the reformers would have us believe. Hence, the opposition to *Humana Vitae* in our time. Hence the insistence by the innovators on compulsory sex instruction in school. The approach is subtle.

It is based on the ageless fact, that when moral restraints come to an end, it is much easier to convince the intellect of the victim. Henry VIII was a perfect example of this principle. We recall his excellent 'Defence of the Seven Sacraments' against Luther, for which he received the Papal Title of 'Defender of the Faith', but we know how his intellectual convictions were soon shattered when his moral fibre was weakened.

In this country, we may not yet have experienced the full blast of this 'compulsory sex education' for our children in school, but with the hurricane raging around us, on the continent and in America, our immunity will not last too long. Parents should now be warned of the onset of this ugly storm. The 'sex education' which these zealots advocate, is not the wholesome parental-cum-teacher instruction which the young need — far from it. It is a spiritual and emotional rape of the children through various and devious methods of mind manipulation. This new tool is a powerful weapon in the hands of the liberals, to break down moral values in the individual. Let us take an example of this new approach, as reported in the *Wanderer* April 17, 1969:-

Dr Mary Calderone, speaking to three hundred and twenty boys of the Blair academy in New Jersey, declared: 'What is sex for? It is for fun . . . for wonderful sensations. Sex is not something you turn off like a tap — if you do, it is unhealthy'. When asked by a student what she thought of pre-marital sex, she snapped back — 'What do you think? Nobody from on high (God) determines this. You determine it. I don't believe that the old 'thou shalt not' applies any more.' Be it known dear reader, that our friend Dr Calderone, does not claim to be an agnostic or an atheist,but a 'religious person'. Dr Kirkendell (the founder of the society *SIECUS* to which Dr Calderone belongs) states, 'The purpose of sex education is not to control and suppress sex expression, as in the past, but to indicate the immense possibilities for human fulfilment that human sexuality offers . . . It is not moral indoctrination.' (*The Wanderer* l.c).

In the February issue of this *Newsletter* the writer of this article put forward the belief, that if contraception were justified, the logical step would be, to justify pre-marital and extra-marital sex. This opinion becomes more certain as time passes. The 'population explosion' so vehemently put forward by the advocates of contraception, has become a 'copulation explosion' through the breakdown of morals at every level.

There is worldwide conspiracy against clerical celibacy, a conspiracy very similar again to the attacks mounted by the 'Progressives' of the sixteenth century, against this noble virtue. Only in April of this year (1969) the Pope, realising the insidious and universal nature of this evil 'grand design', repeated more than once, that the Church would not consider its abrogation, and he called upon the Bishops of the world to uphold support for this ancient practice of the Church. Few Bishops have responded so far.

The spirit of non-co-operation with his Holiness, by many Bishops of the world, which has characterised the last few years, is still very much in evidence.

Sadder still, are the overt efforts of even members of the College of Cardinals to manacle the Primacy, by subjecting it to the whims and fancies of a democratically acting Church. Cardinal Suenen's mammoth article, as published in *The Tablet* May 17, 1969, is just such an example. Careful analysis of this article discloses, that every single point of his thesis, can be found in the doctrines of the Modernists, condemned by the saintly Pope Pius X in the early years of this century.

The reader will notice how Cardinal Suenen manipulates arguments and even texts of Scripture, to prove his points.

He stretches to the limit, Acts of Apostles, C2, V14 and C4, V14, to show (what he believes) that Peter acted with the other Apostles and did what the other Apostles told him, while nothing is said about the crushing weight of evidence from Sacred Scripture, that Peter also acted 'alone' and was recognised by the others as the official spokesman of the Apostolic College and the Church. This is but one of a score of carefully planned tactics to deceive the unsuspecting.

The Cardinal wants his hands on the 'Keys' entrusted to St Peter and his successors, and a say in when they should be turned to lock, or unlock. History is repeating itself almost in detail. The violent outbursts of the 'progressives' of the sixteenth century against celibacy, was linked with even more violent efforts to snatch the keys of authority from the hands of Peter and transfer them to 'popular decision'. We think of Pope Clement VII in his letter to the Emperor Charles, how he was even prepared to surrender to the 'progressives' and permit the clergy in Germany to marry, in order to preserve the Catholic Faith in Northern Europe.

On completion of the foregoing chapters, a reader will easily discern for her or himself, the steady and disastrous decline the Church is being plunged into, and sad to relate – by the very men within its confines – history repeating itself.

Also, certain groups of lay dissidents, played a major part in this onslaught for reformation. The battle for the safeguard of the Church and Magisterium is now on our own doorstep – and must be won.

Father Flanagan's words were correct and to the point, when saying that this decline would soon reach our own shores.

It is here! And in no small way.

As I enter the 1970's for this biography, one can follow closely the force of evil in its endeavour to strip the Church of its Sacred Nature and Deposit of faith – thus making the one Holy Catholic and Apostolic Church, a common denominator with other Churches outside the fold.

The evil, and those participating in it were soon to be dragged out into the open – for all to see. I will proceed, once again, from Father Flanagan's Editorials – articles, and open letters to the Hierarchy of England and Wales, verbatim.

ARTICLE III

From I.C.P.A. *Newsletter* Sept/Oct 1969.

The *Missa Normativa*

As every member of the Catholic Priests Association is aware, the new liturgy of the Mass becomes obligatory on Sunday November 30, 1969. Will this date set off explosive elements in the Church, but for a change – within the ranks of the traditional or conservative Catholics? Some, who up to the present have been the staunch supporters of Pope Paul VI, are now threatening open rejection of this new liturgy, and have sent demands to the Holy Father for permission to continue the use of the Roman Missal of Pope Pius V (See *Courrier de Rome* June and July 1969).

It will be a calamity if the *Missa Normativa* should do for the Church what *Humanae Vitae* failed to produce – disloyalty – among those dedicated to the Roman Pontiff and faithful to the teaching authority of the Church. There is much evidence that the disobedience shown to the Papal ruling on contraception came, to a great extent, from those whose faith was already weak. The example of no less than seventeen of the forty-one dissident priests in the archdiocese of Washington, entering the state of matrimony, and without dispensation from their vows, and often under circumstances that can only be described as diabolical, is proof of the 'conscience' that motivated so many of them to disobey.

Before the publication of the *Ordo Missae* of the new liturgy, approved by the Congregation of Rites, three days after his Holiness Pope Paul VI had given his approval (April 3, 1969), there was considerable agitation among priests and laity, as to the three new Canons, which with the old Canon, now forms the central core of the *Missa Normativa*. Some Catholic priests allege invalidity of Consecration, according to the new Canons, while other opponents declare them illicit, and that a priest cannot in conscience celebrate Mass according to the new Canons, while other opponents declare that a priest cannot in conscience celebrate Mass according to them (*Courrier de Rome*, l.c.).

To reconcile their conclusions with Papal approval of the texts, they introduce such allegations as 'The Pope is a prisoner of the Progressives,' 'he has surrendered to the liberals and Protestants, reducing the mass to a meal,' etc. Those who claim that he is a prisoner of the progressive, will have some explaining to do when *Humanae Vitae* is considered, or how is it, that almost every week that has passed in the last few years, Pope Paul has fearlessly and energetically, re-affirmed the Church's traditional teaching on many points both of faith and morals.

In this present article, we will be content to examine some of the objections raised against the new Canons, leaving to a later issue, a liturgical criticism of the new rules that surround the August Sacrifice of the Mass. May we say in passing, and as referred to in an incidental manner in the Editorial of this *Newsletter* there will be some points in the new liturgy that will displease and disappoint, even the most charitable of Pope Paul's dedicated followers. We have all read in the national papers of the resignations of some outstanding priests, who feel that they could not wholeheartedly join with their congregations in the new *Missa Normativa*. Some new elements introduced into the liturgy, will prompt some to ask, how they are in anyway, an improvement on what they replaced.

At this stage of our discussion, it is only fair to say that in some cases, at least, it is the translation of the new text that gives the shock. Here again, it is not being declared that the ICEL (The International Commission for English in the Liturgy) has given us a wholly unsatisfactory translation of the new Canons, but that in some cases the translations give not only an inaccurate expression of the approved Latin text, but that there are cases, where the translations are so bad as to convey a different sense to the words – even to the extent of affecting the theological implications.

Anyone who has studied the constitution on the Sacred Liturgy issued by Vatican II, and the encyclical *Mediator Dei* of Pope Pius XII, must be made aware of the awesome nature of the Sacred Liturgy. 'Liturgy' states the encyclical just mentioned, 'is the public worship Our Redeemer, as Head of the church gives to the Father, and the worship, which the society of believers gives to its Head, and through Him, to the external Father; in a word, the integral worship of the mystical Body of Jesus Christ'.

'Every liturgical celebration, because it is an action of Christ, the priest, and of his Body, which is the Church, is a sacred action surpassing all other.' (*Sacred Liturgy*, n.7) Is it surprising then, that Pope Paul, speaking on February 7, 1969, to 300 members of the Italian Liturgical Commissions, went to the utmost pains, to repeat again and again, that 'Liturgical texts must be translated to perfection – we emphasise to perfection'. Pope Paul tied the necessity of 'absolute perfection in translation to the supreme sacredness of the Eucharist . . . the august, austere, sacred, venerable, tremendous limits of Eucharistic prayers, which in ancient times the *disciplina arcani* long sought to protect from indiscretion and profane gaze'. Could a Pope make it more emphatic, that nothing but the best in translation, will do? Yet, we get translations that are in face new versions – they may satisfy some of the Latin approved text.

It is not an irrational fear that some have, that certain texts have been deliberately twisted, in their translation, to fit 'new approaches' in theology. Some weird concepts on theological matters are not unknown among the experts of the ICEL.

Nevertheless, we return to the approved new Canons (a later issue will deal with certain aspects of the *Ordo Missae* and of the *Missa Normativa*).

It is entirely inconceivable that the Roman Pontiff would give his approval to anything which could be remotely linked with the accusations brought forward by 'extreme' traditionalists – I use the word 'extreme' in all charity, and for the want of a better word.

All of us uphold the ancient Roman Canon, and many of us will regret that some priests, may from now on, seldom use it, preferring one or other of the new Canons. But we must remember that we only know that the Roman Canon is genuine and authentic – because it has received the approval of the supreme authority of the Roman Pontiff. It was to Peter and his successors that this prerogative was given by Christ, and a successor of Peter has now approved the new *Missa Normativa*. Loyal Catholics have only one option – whatever their personal likes and dislikes may be – to accept the new *Missa Normativa*.

Objections have also been raised, and not without good reason, to the omission of certain things, which the Holy See has insisted should be observed in all published texts of the Mass.

Let us take a few examples:-

1. The Holy See declared that the words of Consecration should be printed in a way, different to the rest of the text, 'in order that they may stand out more clearly' (Eucharistic Worship 1967 n.21). The official and copyrighted English version fails to do this.
2. Ant. 57 of the 'Instruction for the proper implementation of the constitution of the Sacred Liturgy' (September 26, 1964) required that the Latin and Vernacular texts be printed in parallel columns in all Liturgical Missals. This ruling has been widely ignored.
3. In the first translation of the Roman Canon, we were given 'We honour Mary, the Virgin Mother of Jesus Christ Our Lord' as a substitute for 'The glorious Mary, ever Virgin, Mother of God and Lord Jesus Christ'.

This translation from the experts, and which is still found in English versions, deliberately omitted three defined articles of faith – the Divinity of Christ (*Nicea, 324*), the Divine Maternity of Mary (*Ephsus 431*) and the perpetual virginity of Our Lady – before, during, and after the birth of Christ (*Lateran, 649*). It is a translation, such as this one, given us by the experts, and now revised and corrected by the Holy See, which has caused a loss of confidence among Catholics, in the ICEL.

The revised translation became operative from January 1, 1969, but even still, more than nine months later, we find the defective text widely used. (*Cf. Notitiae,* May – June 1968).

Some extreme traditionalists allege that the new Canons do not preserve a valid Consecration, as they are changed in essentials in the Consecration formula. Others question their validity under the heading of a denial of the sacrificial nature of the Mass. Apart from the inconceivable situation of the Pope approving such a formula of Consecration, the changes in the new Canons from the old, do not modify the concept of the sacrificial nature of the Mass, but rather emphasise it.

If the words of Consecration of the bread, as found in the old Roman Canon, are compared with those of the new, it will be found that the new ones merely add the words *Quod pro Vobis tradetur* ('Which will be given up for you') to the old. These words which are found in Luke 22 v.19 and 1 Cor. 11, 24, are SACRIFICIAL in character, and bring out into relief, at the very moment of Consecration the SACRIFICIAL NATURE of the Mass. The fact that these words were missing for centuries from the formula of Consecration, shows that the Church has always believed that

TRANSUBSTANTIATION is accomplished by the words 'this is my Body' alone.

Yet again it is objected that the words of Consecration of the chalice are perverted, as the approved text in Latin reads 'pro multis effendetur' and the vernacular reads '(shed) for ALL men'. There is nothing in this objection. The New Testament uses the words 'many' and 'all' interchangeably. The Mass is a renewal of the Sacrifice of the Cross, and Sacred Scripture makes it clear that Christ died for all, for the whole world, for all mankind – See II Cor. 5, 14; Tim. 2, 5-6, 1 John, 2,2. The whole context of the Roman Canon makes it beyond question, that the Mass is a sacrifice for all. See the prayer that accompanies the Offertory Offering of the Chalice, and the *Agnus Dei qui tollis peccata mundi*.

The Catechism of the Council of Trent in its chapter on 'The Eucharist' points out this distinction between 'many' and 'all'. It states – 'Looking at the efficacy of the Passion, we believe the Redeemer shed His blood for the salvation of ALL MEN; but looking at the advantages which mankind derive from this efficacy, we find they are not extended to the whole, but to a large proportion of the human race.' In other words, while the death of Christ was for all, some men will in fact, not profit by Christ's death.

People question the omission of the words *Mysteruim Fidei* (Mystery of Faith) from the second Consecration as, in the new Canons these words are only found after the Consecration. The words were not spoken by Christ at the Last Supper. They are taken from St. Paul – 1 Tim. 3, 9, and were used in the early days of the Church, by the deacon, to announce to the people, that the Consecration had been accomplished, as the congregation were shut away (still so in the Greek Church) from view of the altar. When the promulgation by the deacon dropped out, the words found themselves into the formula of Consecration, but in parentheses.

In the three new Canons, the words *Mysterium Fiedei* have been restored to their proper place in the liturgy.

To proclaim openly 'We will refuse to follow the *New Ordo Missae*' as those who support *Courier de Rome,* 25 July 1969, do and to reject the *Missa Normativa* as a 'shadow of Luther' *(Courier p.5)* is to repudiate the authority of the Vicar of Christ, and to claim for themselves a guidance from on high and an immunity from error, which in practice they deny to the only one the Sacred Scriptures testify as re-echoing the words of Jesus Christ Himself.

Needless to say the Roman Canon, because of its antiquity, (it existed at the beginning of the fifth century) its dignity, its great spiritual richness and sublimity, will maintain its supremacy among the other Canons for centuries to come.

Priests will not, we feel sure, fall for the fallacy put forward by some 'Ultra' traditionalists, that the Bull *Quo Primum* of Pope Pius V, issued 19 July 1570, in which he strictly forbids any change, modification or any alteration whatsoever, to take place in the liturgy of the Roman Missal, under the penalty of automatic excommunication and incurring the indignation of Almighty God and the Blessed Apostles Peter and Paul, could only be changed by another Pope. The view is put forward by some, that Pope Pius V restricted the authority of his successor – Pope Paul VI. This is a fallacious argument, as no Pope can limit or restrict in any way, any successor of his, in matters which are of ecclesiastical origin – such as the liturgy of the Mass. A certain Father Lawrence S. Brey in a pamphlet *An Answer to the Defenders of the New Canons* (no date given) argues at length on the insufficiency of the new Canons for a valid and licit Consecration, and finally falls back on Pope Pius V's prohibitions to change the Missal. His arguments, with all due respect to him, are entirely worthless.

ARTICLE IV

By Father Flanagan. From the ICPA *Newsletter* summer 1970.

The Mass or the Pope

In the *Newsletter* of September 1969, we expressed our opinion, that while certain features of the *Missa Normativa* would disappoint 'even the most ardent of Pope Paul's dedicated followers . . . it was entirely inconceivable that the Roman Pontiff would give his approval to anything even remotely linked with (accusations brought forward by 'extreme traditionalists') unorthodoxy of doctrine.'

The seriousness of the situation created in some places, by opposition to the new liturgy, prompts the writing of this article, and we hope it will be of some little use to counteract in time, the deviations of otherwise good Catholics.

What we write about is, of course, based on the approved Latin Text of the *Missa Normativa* – the only text which received with the Italian, the personal approval o the Vicar of Christ. Translations, which are not strictly in harmony with this personally approved text, are not the prayer of the Church, and have no binding value as to their observance. Let it not be said – as one hears from time to time – that those translations are approved by the Sacred Congregation of Divine Worship to such an extent, that defective or erroneous concepts introduced into the translation, are given a kind of *Sanatio in Radice* (for laity a 'validation of the defect') which removes the error, or accepts it, as part of the Church's official liturgy. It is nothing of the kind. The approval of the Congregation has no such power wrapped up in its sanction; it is only approval, based on the presumption, that the translation is true, and is free from error. The Congregation of Divine Worship is not an authority on the vernacular of another country, and has to assume, that the approval given by the Hierarchy of this country to the English text, before it was sent to Rome for congregational sanction, was given, because the text in English does, in fact, faithfully re-echo the Latin text.

When this is not the case – and we are not referring to words and phrases, with just optional shades of meaning – then the Congregation's approval does not cover the errors nor render them acceptable to the Church. Pope Paul has, time and time again, insisted on an 'absolutely perfect translation' (7 February 1969) but he has been let down by the experts in the Commission (ICEL) and by the Hierarchy that approved of the ICEL translation.

More about this, later, in this article.

Lay Catholics are to be forgiven, who, building and depending upon our English translation, are in revolt against certain passages of the script. They cannot reconcile what they read, with what they have always held as part of their Catholic Faith. These people need instruction and a true translation of the Latin text. It is a different story with other groups who reject the *Missa Normativa* as it is, and see in the new liturgy, and even in its true translation, a violation by the Pope of solemn warning of Pope Pius V (1570) and the introduction of error, even of heresy. To them, the problem in the church today is 'THE MASS OR THE POPE'.

They feel that they must make a choice between one or the other; they cannot be loyal to the Mass and loyal to the Pope, and so they opt for the Mass, rather than the Pope. There is no such choice existing. The Mass and the Papacy are the very warp and weft of the Catholic Faith, the targets for attack by heretics down the centuries of the church's history, and the very pledge and seal of true Catholicism. It is said by Catholics who oppose the *Missa Normativa,* that the Papal approval is certainly not 'infallible', and so can be disregarded. It is strange to hear this objection coming from those who condemn our present day Modernists for saying that *Humanae Vitae* is not 'infallible', and so can be disregarded.

But this is not the answer. Those who reason like this, should however remember, that Pius V Approval of the *Missale Romanum* was not 'infallible', and so, no title exists under the heading to give the decree of Pope Pius V a greater certainty than that of Pope Paul VI.

The Mass is the very centre of our Catholic Faith. Its very core is just not something that is Catholic, but Christ himself.

One is not obliged to see in the new liturgy, something of great liturgical beauty, that existed in the old; one may even hold, that aesthetically considered, the new liturgy is a disaster. Catholic faith and membership of the Church, does not bind us to accept Papal judgments on such matters, though we should respect them. It is an entirely different matter where DOCTRINE is concerned. That the New Liturgy (may I repeat that I am speaking of its Latin text) contains false doctrine is completely unacceptable, as it contradicts the assurance given to St Peter and his successors, by Christ, that the 'Gates of Hell' would not prevail against the 'Church'. It would have prevailed if error, or even danger of false doctrine succeeded through Papal Approval in entering into the very heart of the Catholic Church – the Eucharist. Hence, the importance of getting our vernacular texts properly translated, and the insistence of his Holiness, that nothing short of an 'Absolutely perfect translation' will do. False expression in a faulty translation can undoubtedly affect the sacerdotal intention of offering sacrifice as the Church intends, though a wide scale or massive invalid consecrations are not conceivable. The Divine guarantee of protection from error would see to that.

Much of the misunderstanding about the *Ordo Missae* is due to the fact that the innovators of this century, through their members in, or associated with the ICEL, feel that the new liturgy is Heterodox in its principles, and leaves more room for accommodation of the new 'insights' than did the old Roman Missal. True it is, that some of them are disappointed in the new liturgy, which did not go far enough to fade out such ideas as 'transubstantiation', an ugly word in the theology of the modernists. The Protestant, Max Thurian, writing in *La Croix*, 30 May 1969, says: 'Non-Catholic communities could celebrate the Holly Supper with the same prayers as the Catholic Church. Theologically, this is now possible'.

At this stage of our discussion, it might be useful to see, what the earliest known description of the mass was like, and see if it corresponds more accurately with the *Missa Normativa* than the Tridentine Mass. The earliest description of the Eucharist service is that given by Justin, the Martyr, who died A.D.152. He speaks of it twice – once in reference to the newly baptised, and later in regard to Sunday Worship. The first text reads as follows:-

> 'As for us, when we have baptised the one who believes, and joined him to us, we conduct him in turn to that place, where those who are called the brethren, are assembled.
> Then we pray fervently together for ourselves, and for the baptised and for all others everywhere, in order to obtain through

knowledge of truth, the grace to do good and keep the commandments so as to attain eternal salvation. We give one another the kiss of peace and conclude the prayers.

Then, the bread and chalice of water and wine are brought to be president of the assembly of the brethren. He takes them and gives praise to the Father of the Universe, in the name of the Son and the Holy Spirit; he makes a lengthy thanksgiving for the blessing which God has deigned to give us.

When he has concluded the prayers and the thanksgiving, all people exclaim – Amen.'

Justin specifies that the consecration takes place 'through the prayers formed from the words of Christ.'

In the second reference we read; 'On the day called Sunday all who live in the cities or country, assemble in one place.

'The Acts of the Apostles are read, or the writings of the prophets. When the reading has ended, the president instructs by word and exhorts us to imitate these good things . . . Bread and wine are brought in, the president offers prayers and thanksgiving.. and the people respond by acclaiming Amen . . . The *oblata* are brought in, and the president pronounces the great prayer which consecrates the offerings'. In the words of the Eucharist, the praise of Christ is proclaimed: 'Who has taken flesh and blood for our salvation, for the passion he endured, for he is still suffering by his own will. 'The great High Priest is crucified'.' (*Studia Liturgica*, 2 1963), p.8-28: '*The Mass*' – *Ancient Liturgies and Patristic Texts*, edited by Andre Hamman, O.F.M., pp. 17 – 18).

Anyone reading through these earliest descriptions, will be struck by the close similarity between them and the *Missa Normativa*.

Indeed by the fourth century many of the features which we rediscovered in the new liturgy were clearly defined. The separate consecration of bread and wine with words drawn from the scriptural account of the Last Supper, formed the very kernel, of the early Mass, in which 'Christ, the High Priest,' was crucified. The sacrificial nature of the act of worship was clearly manifest in the early centuries, and it was the sacrifice of Christ on the Cross, that was being re-enacted.

The 'Apostolic Tradition' (about the year 220 or 250) testifies to a common liturgy in East and West, and while a century later, the essentials remaining the same, two liturgies developed – that of the East and of the West. There was no question of the 'sacrifices' which the faithful made in connection with the worship of God in the Mass, being identified with the sacrifice 'par excellence' of Christ. This is the kernel of the trouble today in the church.

Our modernists have seized on a genuine effort to recover the ancient liturgy and restore it to the Mass, as a good opportunity to fade out the sacrifice of Christ, and replace it with the 'sacrifice' of the people. Recall the words taken from 'the new Mass' (living Parish Series); 'The Mass is a sacrifice, if we understand 'sacrifice' as the Jews understood it – an act by which we seek the fellowship of God.'

Our Modernists are using this weapon to bring the downfall of otherwise good and faithful Catholics, by trying to insinuate, that not only has the *Missa Normativa* introduced a new liturgy, it has introduced a new doctrine on the nature of the Mass itself. Hence, Catholics are faced with the dilemma – the 'MASS OR THE POPE', and many of them, feeling that their first allegiance is to the Mass, weaken in their allegiance to the Pope. This alternative, 'Mass or the Pope', conflicting alternatives as some see it, is an illusion. It is brought about by the deliberate and subtle efforts of our Modernists to alleviate from obedience to the supreme pontiff, those whose attachment to the See of Peter is nearly as strong as their love for the Mass. It is gratifying to see that Cardinal Ottaviani repudiated the distortion of the opinions he exposed in a private letter to the Holy Father, a letter which appeared as a preface to a booklet entitled *A Critical Study of the New Order of the Mass* by a group of Roman theologians.

The *Critical Study* which is to be found in many parts of this country, was first published in French in January 1970, and it was immediately refuted by a monk of St Wandrille Abbey, in Normandy, Dom Marie – Gerard Lafond. Dom Lafond, in February of this year, received from Cardinal Ottaviani a letter dated 17 February, in which this Cardinal congratulated the monk on his defence of the new liturgy, and deeply regretted that his name was 'misused, by the unauthorised publication of a private letter to the Holy Father' and the Cardinal concluded that after the 'The discourses of the Holy Father on the 19 and 26 November, no one could sincerely find fault with the New Order henceforth.' (Paul Poitevin, reporting from Paris in *The Wanderer*, 19 March 1970).

Let us hope, in the light of this letter from Cardinal Ottaviani, that we have heard the last of the Cardinal's supposed opposition to the *Missa Normativa*.

Our support for the *Missa Normataiva*, we would like to make plain, is not any official attitude of the Catholic Priests' Association. Individual members must make up their minds on that. But rejection of the new liturgy is incompatible with our allegiance to the Pope and to Papal authority. We are not under any obligation to try to convince ourselves that it is the best possible liturgy, or that it is free from defects. Few, if any, would take up this attitude. It is entirely inconceivable that the Pope would, or even could, approve a liturgy that is heretical in its content, or positively dangerous.

This is the ground on which the author of this article stands – and it does not, as already said – commit other members of the Association to this view. We are entirely sympathetic to those priests and lay people, who were shocked to realise that certain priests, noted for their liberalistic views in the realm of Catholic theology, understand and accept the decision of his Holiness to give representatives of liberalistic views an intimate place in the moulding of our liturgy.

Several of those whom he appointed to the commission of experts to study contraception were well known, *ab initio* for their views that contraception was not immoral. Failure on the part of the Pope to appoint such members of these bodies, would bring more harm than good. He would be accused of stifling without hearing views contrary to the traditional Catholic trend.

In the March 1969 issue of *Newsletter,* we spent considerable time and space spotlighting some of those whose views were so alien to the Church, particularly to the Holy Mass and the Eucharist (See *Worship of Man,* March 1969) and who still have played such a big part in our present liturgy.

Since writing this article many priests have written to me to indicate how accurately the article in question, summed up the developing crises in the Church.

Father Sigler of the ICEL, has resigned since the article was written, but not before he played a big part in aesthetically ruining, and after having doctrinally muddied the Church's sacred liturgy.

The burning question of today is: why are so many parts of the liturgy approved by the Pope, so twisted in their English version? We prefer to call it a 'version', though it should be 'translation'. Many of the laity judge the whole new liturgy, on the strength of this English version, and it is understandable that they (thinking the Pope has approved it) wonder what is wrong with His Holiness. The Catholic Priests' Association has sent a letter to all members of the Hierarchy of this country, and to the Catholic press, begging them to intervene and give us a true and proper translation.

Only one Bishop, His Lordship of Nottingham, acknowledged this letter for which we express our gratitude and thanks. We all know what a staunch and true shepherd of his flock the Bishop of Nottingham is. *The Universe and Catholic Herald* gave a brief summary of our letter to the public, but the *Tablet*, which publishes the full manifesto of every group, opposed to orthodoxy and the Pope, gave it no reference. It was what was to be expected.

In the first paragraph of this article we mentioned that we would return to the question of our English version, and why the Hierarchies of the English speaking countries approved of such erroneous translation. Many explanations are given, including one from South Africa, that the ICEL had acquired great sums of money from the Hierarchies of the English speaking countries to finance the publication of the text, as approved by the ICEL, and these sums could not be paid back, if any changes were to be insisted upon, as the vernacular texts had gone into mass production. One Bishop wrote that he approved of the text, after hearing a tape recording of a small portion of the text version. The best explanation, seems to be that given by Father Giese, who is a member of the ICEL, and who, writing in the New Freeman (Canada), 31 January, 1970, states the policy of the ICEL. It was, according to him – 'to develop an ecumenical text or texts, argued upon, for common use by the major Christian Churches throughout the English-Speaking world.'

The new prayer texts (still quoting Father Giese) were prepaid by a group called THE INTERNATIONAL CONSULTATION COMMITTEE ON ENGLISH TEXTS, and participating, were members of the International Committee on English in the Liturgy (ICEL) representing Catholics in twenty English speaking countries, representatives from the Anglican Church in England, Ireland, Scotland and Wales, of the Episcopal church in the U.S.A., the Inter Lutheran Worship commission of North America and representatives of the Methodists, Congregationalists and Baptists Churches.

Here is the key problem. Is there any wonder that our English version has so many false doctrines introduced no doubt by heretics, whose ideas and theology on the Holy Mass, are completely alien to ours!

Is there any wonder, that we find so many cases, where the translation is quite clearly perverted to fit into Protestant theology?

It is one of the greatest tragedies of the Church in the 20th century, that the Bishops, who voted into effect the Constitution on the Sacred liturgy, with the insistence on the preservation of the Church's tradition and doctrinal orthodoxy, are now permitting this most sacred element of the Church of Christ, to be defiled by heretics, and presented to the people of God, when, in fact, it is diluted Catholicism at the best. Oh, for many more like Cardinal Bengsch, of Berlin, who warned his fellow Bishops of the world (*L'Osservatore Romano*, 5 February 1970) that the Church 'can suffer a most serious set back, if within four years after the Ecumenical Council, the Bishops who took part in it . . . no longer abide by the Council's decisions.' Articles 23, 3s, 54, and 11s of the Constitution on the Sacred Liturgy, which the Bishops helped to frame and promulgate, are being cast into the waste paper basket, as long as our so-called English translation as permitted to be used. No priest can in conscience follow some of the translations given us, and a priest not only may, but should, make the necessary adjustments himself, if the Hierarchy see that manifest errors are in our English texts – errors that involve change of Catholic doctrine, or whittling down of them – and fail to give a corrected version.

It is not within the scope of this article to enumerate all the erroneous points in the English translation – that, we hope will be covered in a later article – but we would like to refer to the one that gives most grounds for anxiety, the translation of *'pro multis effundetur'* as 'that will be shed for ALL MEN.'

Some writers, pin the invalidity of the consecration, on to this change (see *Questioning the validity of the Mass, using the English translation* by Patrick Henry Omlor (1969) and *Interdum*, 24 Feb 1970, by the same author) holding, that the English text when used, leaves the consecration of the wine invalid, or at least of dubious validity. Many scholarly arguments are advanced by those who hold contrary views on this point, but the weight of opinion always seemed to be in favour of a valid consecration .

Indeed, the use of the form 'Shed for ALL MEN, etc.' was in the opinion of the writer, sufficient for the validity of the consecration. It may not be generally known, that recently *Notitiae* (No. 50, 1970) the official publication of the Congregation for Divine Worship answered the following questions, dealing with this very point. For example the Italian text, which received personal approval of the Pope, just in the same way as the Latin, has the words *'Per Tutti'* (for all men) and the Spanish text has *'Por Todos'* (for all men) and so the following questions were asked of the Congregation of Divine Worship.

1. Is there a reason to justify this variation (in 'ALL for *Pro multis*)?

Answer: The said variation is fully justified. According to exegetes, the Aramaic word which was rendered by 'pro multis' in Latin is 'pro omnibus'. The multitude for whom Christ died is without limitation . . . Christ died for all men.

2. Is the doctrine concerning this subject to be found in the Roman Catechism edited by Pope Pius V, henceforth to be considered obsolete?

Answer: In no way is the doctrine obsolete. Its distinction between Christ's death, sufficient for all, but efficacious only for many, retains its force.

3. Are all the renderings of the said text to be considered less relevant?

Answer: In giving approval to these vernacular variations of liturgical texts, nothing less correct has been introduced which demands correction or amendment.

We hope the text of this decision, will put at rest, the turmoil in the minds of some priests as to the validity of this English form of Consecration.

EDITORIAL
By Father Flanagan (From the ICPA *Newsletter* Summer 1970)

Throughout the Catholic world, pressure mounts against the Church of Christ, to accommodate itself in its doctrines, morals and government, to the needs of the twentieth century materialistic world. The old principles and ideas of modernism, so ruthlessly condemned by Pope St. Pius X, are reappearing, sometimes in new dress, but often, less covered in their stark reality, than in the days of the Saintly Pontiff. Modernists of today, have learned much, from the failure of half a century ago, and their new weapons of war are used to the limit, and with every dexterity that modern man can muster. Radio, television, and the press, are under the control of dedicated modernists, known in many parts of the world as members of the IDOC, With allegiance to Amsterdam rather than Rome, with Kung, Schillbeeckx, Haring and a host of other innovators, replacing the divinely established and protected Papacy, it is only to be expected that Catholicism should now be in the vortex of doctrinal, liturgical and moral uncertainty, such as she has never seen before in her long history. The effect of this situation on priests and laity is immense. Devout priests and laity for whom the certainty of the Church's teaching, the dignity of her worship, and her uncompromising attitude to the immoral, together with her unique and glorious system of government from the apex of authority (precious indeed priceless – stones in this great edifice not made by human hands) have now been shocked into a realisation almost overnight, that the pillar and the ground of truth is shaking under the pressure from the new reformers. Not all poor souls can see amidst the tumult now being created by self-appointed prophets, the continuity of the Christian message and the same Church as founded by the Divine Master nearly two thousand years ago.

The casualty list is heavy. Priests and nuns become disollusioned – not in the sense that they have lost faith in Christ and his Church – but in the sense that those prelates to whom they looked up, as musclemen of the Church, have proved in so many instances, to be made with feet of clay.

Pseudo Renewalists and fellow travellers have launched a most vicious attack on Catholicism in this country. In the face of assaults on the Pope and on official Church teaching, these hardy Renewalists have pushed their tentacles out in all directions feeling, influencing, twisting, distorting, manipulating public opinion and 'the demands of the people of God'. One often wonders, if some of the readers of the movement were trained – not in Moscow but in the capital of modernism – Nijmegen, the University town of the Netherlands. There is no doubt that schismatic Holland has its agent in this country – The Dutch Pastoral Council, which has loomed so prominently in recent months, and which has publicly boasted, that it was sending its Agents into most countries. Hardly has some new aspect of the war against the Church, shown itself in the land of the tulips, then it appears to blossom on British soil. Holland is busy exporting her heretical and schismatical products to this and other countries, and there seems to be no sign of tariff barriers going up from our episcopal customs and excise officers. The people of the dams seem intent on flooding our country with their modernistic slush, and assume, that we are already in a common market, where rejection of the Holy See is concerned.

There must be few priests in Britain today who have not received by post the pamphlet, *On the Road to Damascus*, with its subtitle *Lord, what will thou have me do*, published by Stitching In De Rechte Straat, Velp, Netherlands, and telling the poor innocent priests of this country, the glories of the married state.

One wonders if the subtitle of the pamphlet is intended to impress the priest reader, that the discarding of celibacy comes to him, as the direct result of prayer to the Holy Ghost, the inspiration of the *Paraclete*. Many priests that I have heard from, were of the opinion, that this pamphlet came from some Protestant Church in Holland or some group of Jehovah's Witnesses known for their hostility to the Church of Rome, but inquiries make it quite clear that the Dutch Catholic Church Reformers have nothing to learn from the rabid innovators of previous times.

Perhaps those readers of this newsletter who saw the BBC2 programme, MAN ALIVE, on Wednesday 22 April at 8pm., depicting the Church in Holland today, will have no doubt as to the extent of Church demolition reached in that unfortunate country. This documentary showed the Lenten Pageant in Amsterdam at the start of Lent, 1970, and with the mockery of the sacerdotal and religious life on the streets of the capital city. Actresses playing the part of nuns exposed their naked breasts at the Church thus caricatured.

Bishop Zwartkruis, of Haarlam, will have to do better if he expects viewers of the programme to believe that Holland is not going into schism. Indeed, it is not, it has already gone into paganism, judging by the evidence of this documentary film. It was at least refreshing to see the police force move into the streets of Amsterdam, when the sexual exposures got out of hand. If the Church in Holland have less sense of decency than the state police, it would indeed be erroneous to apply the word 'Schism' to the situation. Perhaps this is what the Bishop of Haarlem means when he says, 'Schism over my dead body'.

At the time writing this Editorial, no reply has come from the Hierarchy, to our request that celibacy should not be permitted for discussion at the Priests' conference at Wood Hall on the 21 June. Everything indicates that certain groups of priests, apart from the revolutionary element from the Archdiocese of Liverpool, will make a determined effort to force a discussion on celibacy. His Holiness last November asked the Bishops of the world not to permit this topic to be discussed in view of possible removal.

We hope that our Hierarchy will insist with those who control the agenda at Wood Hall, that celibacy is not for debate.

The *Motu Proprio* of Pope Paul reorganising the Church's legislation on mixed marriage, may solve or diminish some of the human problems connected with contemplated marriages of Catholic and non-Catholic. To the writer of this editorial, it would appear that the greatest hazard to faith, may well arise, out of the manner in which the Hierarchy of this country or of any other, uses its power to dispense in certain cases, from the canonical form of marriage. Are we going to see in our parishes many cases of Catholics who, to all appearances, have only contracted a civil marriage, and when later, they appear at the communion rails and we assess that they are not validly married and should be refused Communion, we may discover to our horror that they received a dispensation from the canonical form of marriage, from the Bishop of the diocese. How these dispensing powers of the Bishops will be used, is a matter of vital importance to the good of the whole community. We also hope that the faithful will not be able to point the finger to the exceptions made, and say: 'Oh, she received this dispensation to marry in a non-Catholic church, because of her family's social position', *Ad Scandalum praecavendum* is now almost obsolete in practice and the sooner it is brought back into the life of the Church the better.

Lip service and obedience of Papal authority is undoubtedly a basic cause in the Church's turmoil today. One after another, Papal directives are ignored – sometimes contemptuously – and as nothing succeeds like success, if opponents of Papal authority can point the successor of Christ, and give examples of their want of obedience, the argument against the claims of the Papacy increases in cogency. This is particularly applicable to the sphere of the Sacred liturgy.

Vatican II and the Pope (on many occasions) have spelt out in unmistakable language, the necessity of preserving the Latin Liturgy. Most diocesan regulations faithfully re-echo this ruling of the supreme authority, and yet, there are vast areas of this country where a Latin Mass is never celebrated even when diocesan regulations impose a certain number of Masses in the Latin Liturgy each week, these regulations are discarded. No one is underestimating the value of the vernacular liturgy – thank God it has come – but whatever we may think of the pastoral value of some Latin Masses, the obligation still rests on us to preserve it, and to be faithful to diocesan requirements in this matter. The writer of this Editorial is aware of the exaggerations made by those who over stress the pastoral advantages.

The wish of the Church and the clear insistence of Vatican II and his Holiness the Pope, that the Latin Liturgy must not be permitted to die out, must surely be a factor to be considered.

In a few years time, if the strangulation of the Latin Liturgy continues, it will be dead liturgy indeed. The progressives are using this sphere of Church interest, to press home the emptiness of Papal ruling – they point to the widespread disregard of the Pope's authority to legislate in this matter. If his authority can be rejected – or, at least, neglected – in this matter, why not the same when the 'Old man' upholds the Church's teaching on contraception, or on celibacy for the clergy? It is increasingly difficult to acquire a copy of the *Missa Normative* in Latin, and the old *Roman Canon* which the Church has cherished for so long, is not even being printed in English. One can acquire in some book shops, the English version of the New Canons, but the progressive title is a reminder that our Church was once subject to the See of Rome. So better forget all about it.

Monsignor Tomlinson, co-Editor of the magazine, *Sunday*, tells us in the

March issue of that publication (Vol 5, No. 3) that during the years of the Latin Liturgy 'the treasures of Scripture were closed to the ordinary Catholic who never heard the word of God'. (p.14).

When I first read these words, I thought that the must have been written by the Reverend Ian Paisley, but I was mistaken. In my many years as priest and as a student, the Epistles and Gospels were always read to the people in English, though they had been read in Latin. Monsignor Tomlinson had another strange statement in the same journal when he writes describing the *Missa Normative* – 'After Communion, all sit in silent thanksgiving, perhaps the most significant change of all, and so realise their unity in Christ'.

I find it difficult to grasp how 'sitting' more than any other bodily posture, can bring about the 'realisation of unity with Christ', particularly as the Church does not make it ('sitting') the rule, but only an option – *ad sedem redire potest.*

One of the greatest dangers to the Church in this country today arises from a movement known as 'The Renewalists'. Their policy is to renew the Church adapted to the world, and this can only be done by destroying it. Their Publications and Manifesto clearly outline their policy, and how much they are out of step with the Church is plain for anyone to see. In their *Bulletin,* No. 8, March 1970, we read of Father Keane (a dissident and suspended priest of Nottingham Diocese) – rejecting infant Baptism, but being prepared to give the present practice 'a trial' up to the age of 18, when a personal and formal decision would be made. The really only 'deadly sin' is hardness of heart. This latter target for modernists' attack is now well known. A priest writing in *The Tablet,* 4 April 1970, under the heading of *New Approaches to confession* derides the element of 'humiliation and shame' in auricular confession, which according to him 'have nothing to do with the divine Law', and he concludes by 'rejecting the necessity of confessing serious sin before receiving Communion'. He hastens to add that the 'arguments and theological considerations behind this, have roots deep in scripture'. We are not of course, given those 'Scriptural roots or theological considerations' as we would be unable to follow them. The Council of Trent was, of course, wrong when it declared in the most solemn manner, that anyone who should presume to defend, teach or hold, etc., such an opinion was anathema and under excommunication *(Session XIII, chap V, s 11, 155).* How quickly do our Modernists dispose of the accumulated wisdom and teaching of the Church – how quickly do they claim in practice for themselves, the infallibility which they deny the Roman Pontiff!

THE NEW MASS is the name of a pamphlet of the *Living Parish* series. Bishop Worlock, Oliver Pratt and others, are give as the, joint authors.

It has an *Imprimatur* from Bishop Casey, and we are even told that a book with an *Imprimatur* is 'considered free from doctrinal and moral error'.

Many parts of the pamphlet show how free it is from error. Let us quote but a few:

1. 'The most obvious thing about the Mass is that it is something done by a group of people, and it is an action that they consider important.' (Page 1)
   Comment: No wonder the English text (it is not a translation) of the *Orate fratres* reads 'Our Sacrifice' instead of 'My sacrifice and yours'.
2. 'In the Mass we open ourselves . . . to the wonder and realism of God's presence amongst us'.
3. 'In the Mass we say "yes" to reality as the Christian knows it to be, and the material in which we can help bring to birth God's presence amongst us. The material in which this comes about is, of course, the people . . . God is amongst them through the human community.' (page 5).'
   Comment: There is obviously, no place for the Consecrated priesthood in this theology – the priesthood of the laity suffices. But hold on – there are more insights to come.
4. Sin affects our relationship with our environment – God is dead. (Page 7).
5. 'The New Testament accounts of the Last Supper make it clear what the signs are . . . a community takes food and drink, bless it with a Eucharistic prayer, share it and consume it . . . We have been describing a meal. This is what the Mass says it is about – the celebration and fostering of fellowship. A eucharist was contact with God in all his historical reality' (Page 13).
6. 'The Mass is both a SACRIFICE AND A MEAL, if we understand sacrifice as the Jews understood it – an act by which we see fellowship with God. The meal is this act; It is the sacrifice and seeking of fellowship (page 14).
7. The Communion is not a separate action to that of the eucharistic prayer. It is the meal over which the prayer is said (page 17).

In another pamphlet, *You and the world,* in the same series as the one already referred to, and with Bishop Worlock, Oliver Pratt and others as authors and with the same *Imprimatur* that it contains no doctrinal or moral error, we find several enticements for Catholics and others, to take part in revolution (disclaiming it as a 'bloody one') against the social and economical set up in the world.

Addresses of international agencies for such 'revolution' are also given. It was then, Oliver Pratt goes on to tell us, that the Papal encyclical on 'This Great Social Problem' *(Progressu Populorum)* is the one that expresses the consensus of the Catholic world, not the encyclical *Humanae Vitae,* that he reaches the depths of his ignorance on the nature of the Church and its mission. We hope that Bishop Worlock will dissociate himself from Oliver Pratt's 'New Theology', for it was he, who only last year, spoke of the pre-council Church as a 'former faith' (*The New Christian* April 1969).

The words of the Protestant theologian and critic, Martin Marty, writing in the guest column of a National United States Catholic weekly last autumn, are very applicable to Oliver Pratt and his fellow 'Renewalists in Britain today. The American columnist said. 'Since 1965, observers have detected few signs of a spiritual renewal. The present Church problems arise from a lack of faith and belief in the authority of the Church . . . the young liberal Catholic who tried a bit of guitar-cum-Teilhard', but soon gave up because, as he described it, the whole Jesus thing meant very little to him.' Renewalism, in destruction if the church's most sacred structure, is easy and appealing, but the practice of prayer and self-mortification is a different matter, and has no appeal to the humanistic renewalist.

I give herewith the substance of a letter written to me, by a distracted mother, after she had heard a lecture given at the school attended by her son - dealing with the New Liturgy of the Mass.

The good woman asked me to give her name and address if I were publishing this letter, and to designate the school, so that no one can be under any illusions. The lady is Mrs D P Hurst, 40 Purley Oaks Road, Sanderstead, Surrey, and the school is St. Joseph's, Blackheath, London SE5. Here are quotations from the letter:- 'We were invited by the parents' association of my son's school to attend this unique opportunity to learn about the new liturgy. To say that we were enlightened would be an under-statement. On the panel were two priests, one Anglican priest and two members of the laity – Dr Oliver and Mrs Pratt (authors of *Liturgy is what we make it*). The attitude of both Catholic priests was one of flippancy. The Anglican Priests gave us fifteen minutes lecture on Cramer's Mass. Mrs Pratt complained that the churches were too big and formal for Mass. Mrs Brown and Mrs Jones cannot have their little chat! It is better to have Mass in the house or in a small hall. Let the kiddies get the Altar ready, write the prayers, and crowd around. Doctor Oliver Pratt followed, and assured us, that we would all understand things much better, if we would forget the word 'transubstantiation'. It is a difficult word to explain and understand. Besides, Christ is in the bread, before it is consecrated, just as much as after Consecration. It all depends on what you think. If you want to think Christ is really present, then he really is. Doctor Pratt also likes to think that Mass is sacrament, rather than a sacrifice. 'The Sacrifice bit', he added, only comes in, by first going to make peace with your brother, before coming to offer your gift.' Mrs Hurst concluded, that not one of the priests (and one was a Monsignor of the Archdiocese of Southwark) had a word of criticism, let alone of contradiction to the blatantly heretical views. So this is Renewalism!

It is time that ecclesiastical authority made it perfectly clear to all those who reject or question doctrines of Faith in the Church. That by this very fact, they are placing themselves outside the Church. The promulgation of a penalty of excommunication is not necessary for the cessation of membership of the Church, when such truths of faith are rejected.

We can soon expect in this country, what is already existing in others – priests in lay garb at the Altar, and in the Confessional, smoking their cigarettes – condemned by Cardinal Cerejeira in Lisbon 16 April 1970, or worse still, the consecrated bread thrown down the toilet, about which the laity in South Africa had to complain of recently in a letter to the Holy Father (*The Keys,* May 1970, Page 106).

It must be one of the most extraordinary phenomena of human history which future historians will have to assess accurately, to see how the many persecutions against the Church in past centuries, failed so miserably, compared to the efforts of our present-day Modernists to destroy the Church. We recall in particular the Iconoclasts persecution when in the 'flea market' in Rome's Porta Portese are found today the Church's statues and precious ornaments being sold as 'junk'. The clergy, indoctrinated with the virus of the *pseudo aggiornamento,* with authors such as Kung, Schillebeeckx, Haring and others, delivering the deadly dose, become almost overnight obsessed with the hatred of religious objects, that only weeks before, they professed, helped them in their devotions.

The *Irish Catholic,* 30 April 1970, reports the sale every Saturday evening at the flea-market in the Eternal City, of chalices, ciboria, mutilated statues of saints, crucifixes, broken tabernacles, gilded altar pieces, vestments for cushion covers, monstrances etc., all adapted or adaptable for uses that are not only profane but 'irreverent' and sacrilegious.

The *Vatican City Daily* said: 'Liturgical implements must remain an ornament of the Church of God, and the priests to whom they have been entrusted, have a sacrosanct duty not to tamper with them, sell them, or disperse them'.

We remember the bloody days of the Spanish Civil War, when hell was let loose on Catholics in that country, but now, we have the sons and daughters of the Church infatuated with the word *aggiornamento* which becomes the magic word to set in motion the fiendish forces of the lower world.

VII

WHO IS JUDAS?

SOMEWHERE IN, OR connected with, the Vatican is an utterly disloyal person. The last year or more has witnessed case after case of matters which the Pope insisted must be kept secret and confidential, being leaked out to the public.

We recall the discussion and votes among members of the Commission set up to give their opinions of contraception – leaked to the public by unauthorised sources, and causing embarrassment to His Holiness. Again the discussions that took place at the Roman Synod last October (1969) were leaked out within days to press reporters by certain prelates 'working for certain Cardinals'.

More recently, we had the disclosure of the text of parts of the envisaged *NEW CANON LAW,* and yet again the regulations on Mixed Marriages.

Cardinal Lorenz of Panderborn, told a Catholic Protestant meeting on 3 March, held at Loccum near Hanover, that the Church will, under certain conditions recognise the validity of a Catholic's marriage before a non-Catholic minister and Cardinal Jaegar told representatives of the German Bishops' Conference, that the permission to marry before a non Catholic minister will fall within the competency of the Bishop of the Diocese.

These disclosures on the Mixed Marriage problem were made, nearly two months before the Papal *Motu Proprio* was made public and the points in question are accurate. There is someone out to embarrass the Pope, at every step, and we hope that His Holiness will, one day, take action against the betrayers of his trust.

Readers may recall, how last July, the notorious Father Schillebeeckx was to appear before the Congregation of the Doctrine of the Faith, to answer certain charges of heresy and false doctrine alleged against him.

Suddenly it was announced in our Catholic papers, that this was not now taking place.

Information at our disposal, states that the dossier on the Father Schillebeeckx case mysteriously 'disappeared' the day before the hearing.

It is not surprising that so many should believe, that those who are out to destroy the Church, received Kremlin-like training for war on the Church.

VIII

THE ENCYCLICAL *HUMANAE VITAE* STILL UNDER ATTACK
By Father Flanagan ICPA *Newsletter* February 1969

WHAT A DIFFERENCE there is between the Church of the Apostles and the Church of today! Liberal theologians who claim it is their desire to restore the Church to its primitive condition and simplicity – would do well to follow the example of the early Christians, when the first Pope gave the two big decisions of his pontificate. The acts of the Apostles (C.11, v.18 and C.15, v.12) tells us of the 'silence which fell upon the multitude' when Peter spoke on the controversial matters of his day. It would be wonderful to return to the primitive obedience and respect of the early Christians for their Pope. Not content with undermining the Divinely establish authority of the Papacy, our 'instant theologians' of today fling mud and abuse at his very person. When a Catholic could write of Pope Paul VI 'That doleful spaniel-eyed, self-deprecating, self-commiserating Pontiff ejaculating anguish ad *urbem et orbem*', and refer to the 'rock upon which Christ built His Church' as a Montini cocktail – extra dry (one part absinth, three parts *lacrimae Christi* and a dash of bitters) always served with ice', – it is time for Catholics to sit up and take stock. The quotation just given is from the magazine *Commonwealth* (Sept. 1968). In writings of this nature one can almost audibly detect the slithering movement of the serpent.

It is interesting to watch the trends of Catholic thought on moral matters, on those who oppose the encyclical so vehemently; it is understandable from their point of view, that they would wish the Pope 'to keep his hands off the Church and stop interfering' (as one French Seminarian wrote last summer). Some writers hold that matters of morals do not belong to the competency of the Church . . . others state that the Church has only the right to give general directions. After that, it belongs to conscience. It is to be expected that these sinister view emanate from the same schools of thought as advocate 'trial marriages' or 'love apprenticeship' as they prefer to call them. These unions are not forbidden by the Gospel story, we are told. Others against, advocate a theory that a 'child should only be legally considered born when it is two days old' – useful for destroying the deformed and unwanted. At the other end of the scale, it is held, that life should be legally over on the completion of one's 85th birthday. These ideas come from a Catholic Doctor and a Nobel Prize Winner.

It convinces one more and more, that the need of a Divinely appointed Head of the Church is an absolute 'must', otherwise we will have *Tot sententiae quot capita*. However, the two main targets for attack from the liberal-minded opponents of *Humanae Vitae* are in the area of the certainty of the document, and the extent to which it can force itself on conscience. These, we should like to consider specifically.

THE CERTAINTY OF HUMANAE VITAE

No Catholic apologist contends that the Encyclical is a formal *ex-cathedra* definition – this point is not in dispute. It is extraordinary however, how many present day Catholics immediately conclude that the Church's teaching is then **NOT CERTAIN,** or in other words, is reformable, hence it is argued, that the faithful cannot be strictly bound in conscience to accept what is not guaranteed certainty.

LUMEN GENTIUM (par.25) imposes obedience – submission of mind and will even to non *ex-cathedra* definitions.

But can it be argued that the encyclical is infallible and irreformable, under another heading? The answer must be in the affirmative. Let us see why this is so.

Christ's promise to be with His church to the end of time, has never been understood as only referring to the occasions when the Church would exercise its Solemn *Magisterium*, which has only been used some 20 times in almost 2000 years. The promise of Christ was, that He would be with His Church 'All days even to the consummation of the world'.

Dogmatic theologians have already understood this promise as verified when the Pope as Head of the Church, recalls to all the faithful, the great teachings and great obligations, the great invitations to sanctity of Divine Revelations as contained in Scripture and Tradition. This constitutes the Ordinary *Magisterium* of the Church; it is the daily feeding of the faithful, with the spiritual food of God's revealed truths.

THE ORDINARY *MAGISTERIUM* OF THE CHURCH is infallible, and consequently irreformable, just as much is the solemn *ex-cathedra* definition. This is not a new doctrine to support a weak *Humanae Vitae*, but rather it is the constant and universal teaching of theologians down the centuries.

The few years of disquiet and unrest, during which a new and special study was being given to contraception, was not at all sufficient to break the long unbroken traditional teaching of the Church, and even during those few years, there was no uncertainty in the mind of the Pope or the Church, only in the minds of a small minority who insisted on taking a change in the doctrine for granted. It is indeed remarkable how many commentators today – since the promulgations of *Humanae Vitae* succeed in avoiding at all cost, any mention of the vital aspect of the question.

An indirect approach to destroy the certainty of the Papal teaching, comes from those, – some of whom are Bishops of the Catholic Church – who try to show that one or other of the reasons or arguments given in the encyclical is false or uncertain.

The encyclical is looked upon as coming from a purely human or scientific *magisterium*, and its strength or values rests on the validity of the rational arguments in the encyclical can be discussed and re-examined, weighed and debated, convincing some, and not others. They have no purpose than to prepare the mind for the conclusion, which is **NOT** based on them. The doctrine of the objective immoral nature of contraception if founded on a certainty of a spiritual and evangelical order, and it is not affected by any subsequent discovery that a particular argument is no longer rationally convincing.

As a study of the arguments of the Papal Commission shows, reason alone could not possibly reach a definite conclusion on this profound question, as reason alone, could only study man, in the transient nature of his earthly pilgrimage.

The doctrine enunciated in *Humanae Vitae* is true, and truth is certain. A truth of the Ordinary Magisterum is as certain and as irreformable as a truth guaranteed by the special charisma of an *ex-cathedra* definition.

Any difference is theoretical and legalistic – and it is strange how our progressive theologians should give this form of 'legalism' the right to survival, when they are so keen on destroying all other manifestation of it.

The doctrine of *Humanae Vitae* is a certain as that of COLLEGIALITY, and here again, we have the illogical position assumed by those, who wish to reject the Papal Encyclical and retain collegiality. It is objected that certainty of doctrine, must come from the Church as a whole and not just from the Pope, and the Pope's failure to submit the vexed question to a vote of Council Fathers leaves certainty obscured.

Any student of theology should know, that the last Vatican Council supplied the background and indeed inspired the immediate principles which govern the question of contraception.

The Constitution *Gaudium et Spes* warns parents about birth control that they must not proceed arbitrarily 'but must be governed always according to a conscience conformed to the Divine Law, and submissive to the Church's teaching' (No.50).

In the same section it states – 'Sons of the Church may not undertake methods of birth control which are found blameworthy by the teaching Authority of the Church in its unfolding of the Divine Law'. By remitting the decision to the Pope, the Council merely carried out the practice of the ancient Church down the centuries of its life, in conformity with the doctrine of Papal supremacy of jurisdiction and his personal charisma by which his teaching to the whole Church is divinely protected from error. 'We must', writes St Thomas Aquinas 'abide by the Pope's judgment, rather than the opinion of any theologian, however well versed he may be in the Divine Scriptures. Against his authority, neither Jerome or Augustine, nor any others of the Holy Doctors, defends his own personal views'. (Summa 11A LIAE QUODI.1X a, 16). The Council's decision, to leave the decision on contraception specifically to personal judgment of the Holy Father, is an open admission of its recognition of his personal and awesome responsibility.

To conclude then this section of the article on the Certitude of the Encyclical, it is only necessary to state emphatically that there is no doubt, no objective doubt that contraception is a moral evil. This truth is as certain as any other truth taught as part of the Ordinary *Magisterium* of the Church e.g. the immorality of abortion, fornication, infanticide. If our progressive theologians reject the sinfulness of contraception, they must logically reject the immoral nature of abortion and infantide. The opinion put forward by even certain Episcopal Conferences that *Humanae Vitae* also sets an IDEAL for the faithful, leaving them free to deviate from its norm in difficult situations is utterly baseless – as is admitted even by liberal writers who support it. 'Theologically, of course' (writes 'HERDER CORRESPONDENCE' Jan.1969) 'this is bluff.' But it is no more bluff than the attempt put forward by many, even in this country, to leave the moral impact of the encyclical to conscience – a matter which we will deal with in the following paragraphs.

HUMANAE VITAE AND THE PLACE OF CONSCIENCE

Amongst the many attempts to create a loophole through which the dissident cleric or lay person endeavours to escape from the moral obligation of accepting the Papal decision on birth control, recourse to (pseudo) conscience, is the most widespread and deceptive. It is an escape hatch through which Bishops, priests and lay folk still try to come to the top from their sunken hopes that the law against contraception would be changed. Hence, it deserves careful and accurate assessment as to its place in accepted theology.

Experts in Christian Ethics and Catholic Moralists are in perfect agreement that **CONSCIENCE** is the human intellect assessing the moral nature of an action; with it, there is a human impulse to 'do what is good and avoid what is evil', Kant's *Categorical Imperative*. Conscience is not a different faculty from the intellect – it is exactly the same. There is nothing infallible about the human conscience – other than its impulse to do good and avoid evil. Its faculty to acquire knowledge of the first or primary precepts of the natural law – know as *synderesis* gives man almost an instinctive knowledge of basic precepts of nature – but these are of a most general kind and need refinement through education of conscience – *conscientia formata* or 'formed conscience' in the English language.

From the basic summary of the 'theology' of conscience, it is evident that the faculty of intellect which has to learn truth, which lies outside itself, be it in the order of mathematics, history or astronomy, has also to learn the moral principles, the objective precepts of the laws that govern it. A conscience, is 'true or correct' only in so far as it conforms with the objective norms or morality.

If it does not conform with those objective norms, it is an erroneous conscience. As the constitution *Gaudium et Spes,* No.16, points out, it is only with an 'invincibly erroneous conscience that man can act without losing his dignity' – a doctrine which enshrines the traditional teaching of Catholic Moralists on this point. But when is a conscience labouring under 'invincible error?' Here again, there has always been perfect unanimity of teaching among Moralists – only in recent years can one discover attempts to change the accepted principle.

Moralists have given two kinds of an invincibly erroneous conscience;

1. Where the thought or even suspicion, that a contemplated action was morally wrong, never entered the human mind.

2. Where the thought or suspicion did arise, where the use of moral diligence to acquire the necessary information, has failed to dispel the ignorance.

No one who is *sui compos* can claim that *Humanae Vitae* can be the object of invincible error in the sense in which these words have always been understood. But some liberal writers give a typical 'twist' to the point at issue and introduce a new definition of 'invincible error', to cover the case of conscience that is unprepared to accept a clear authoritative precept.

We find this meaning given to 'invincible error' in many periodicals today, and sometimes from writers who seem carried away with the idea that the last Vatican Council has given a new primacy to conscience, heretofore not enjoyed. Nothing could be further from the truth. Vatican II has emphasised in the clearest manner, that the traditional teaching on the sphere of conscience remains entirely unchanged. It is a well known fact, that some liberal theologians and even some Bishops endeavoured to have inserted in the original draft of the decree on 'Religious Freedom', a clause, asserting the supremacy of everyone's point of view on moral matters; the proposed draft was most emphatically rejected by the Commission, which pointed out, that conscience could not override the normative teaching authority of the *Magisterium* of the Church. To make sure that this error could not creep into Catholic thought, the Decree *Guadium et Spes* incorporated the rejection into its text, by giving us the crystal clear teaching of the Church, down the centuries. The decree reads, (and it is dealing with this very point of birth control) 'Spouse should be aware that they cannot proceed arbitrarily, but must always be governed by a conscience dutifully conformed to the Divine Law itself, and should be submissive to the Church's teaching office which authentically interprets that law in the light of the Gospel' (No.50).

His Eminence Cardinal Felici, in his treatment of this whole question in the *Observatore Romano* (Oct. 24 1968) gives a detailed study of the care and thought that went into the words quoted above from *Guadium et Spes* and he concludes – 'The conscience of husband and wife must be formed according to the objective standards or morality . . . these are constituted by the law of God, of which the *Magisterium* of the Church is the faithful interpreter'. Those who try to persuade themselves and others that any subjective conviction of theirs, contrary to the teaching of the Church, can be followed, delude themselves and deceive others. Such people labour under 'affected ignorance' which as all Moralists teach us, increases the guilt, instead of lessening it.

Bishop Butler in *The Tablet* (21 Sept. 1968)

(Conscious and Authority) goes out of his way to defend the position of a conscience, that rejects the teaching of a non-infallible decision – such as *Humanae Vitae*. He holds, that in this sphere – 'the ultimate resolution is always to be left to conscience'.

This opinion of the Bishop's (which he also defended in a broadcast on January 26, 1969, Radio 3) that outside the realm of infallible decisions of the Pope, conscience must freely decide, is utterly opposed to the traditional teaching of the Church – opposed to the explicit teaching of Vatican II, *Lumen Gentium* n.25 and contradicts many affirmations made by the present Pope in recent years in his weekly allocutions in the Vatican. Its errors even go deeper as the Bishop fails to recognise *Humanae Vitae* as an infallible doctrine, not indeed as an *ex-cathedra* definition, but because it repeats the unbroken traditional teaching of the Church in Her ordinary *magisterium* – which is, according to all Dogmatic theologians -infallible. To offset the requirement that the ordinary *magisterium* must be traditional before it can be considered as infallible, Bishop Butler, (in his radio broadcast 26 Jan. 1969) declared that it was of doubtful traditional nature – it was merely a question of individual Christian writers being influenced by the cultural surroundings in which they lived. If Bishop Butler is right in his contention, then the Pope is wrong, when he claims in *Humanae Vitae* that it is, and always has been the traditional teaching of the Church.

On this point, we conclude with the telling words of Von Hilderbrand when he writes, 'One might conceivably argue as follows – This document imposes on me, something which my conscience tells me is morally evil – something which God Himself prohibits. I must follow God and not His Vicar.'

In the realm of the non-infallible, there is a possibility of what God **prohibits** may be **commanded** by His Vicar. In this case, I can tremblingly act in defence of the Pope appealing to conscience in its **strict** and **true sense**. But is this applicable to *Humanae Vitae*?

Are defiant Catholics sure that their conscience prohibits them from conforming their lives to the encyclical? In a word, do they fear, that putting away contraceptive practices constitutes a sin? If so, they can tremblingly appeal to conscience against a non-infallible decision. If, however, they mean THAT THEY SEE NO SIN IN USING CONTRACEPTIVES, then, it is not their conscience, but their desires which move them and they have no possible justification for their defiance' (*The Wanderer*, October 24 1968).

Undoubtedly, it is in this last sentence of Von Hilderbrand's statement, that practical cases in every day life will be verified; dissidents will see contraception as permissible (not as 'mandatory') and this cannot be the voice of God.

It must not be forgotten that the author is visualising the theoretical case if *Humanae Vitae* were not infallible, but it is as already pointed out, an infallible doctrine guaranteed by the Ordinary *Magisterium* of the Church – hence even the imaginary case of a justifiable rejection, is out of question.

In the light of what has been said in the previous paragraphs, it should be evident that the English Hierarchy's statement on *Humanae Vitae* was, to say the least of it, most unfortunately worded. After asserting that the 'primacy of conscience is not in dispute' and that all are bound to make sure that 'conscience is truly informed', it lapses into a statement, which at its best, is ambiguous, and is in fact, still quoted by dissident priests and laity in their favour. The passage reads – 'Neither the encyclical nor any other document of the Church, takes away from us, our right and duty to follow our conscience'. A clear unequivocal statement from the Hierarchy on what is meant by this sentence, could go far to solve disturbed minds.

LEGAL CONSEQUENCES OR REJECTION OR REFUSAL TO OBSERVE *HUMANAE VITAE*

Over the last few months, we in this country have read with dismay, the attitude adopted by certain priests towards the Papal Encyclical. While some of them rejected right out, the encyclical's binding force, most of them declared, that their conscience could not accept its teaching. We read of some Bishops who endeavoured to preserve the faithful from being infected with this virus of Modernism and removed or suspended the priests from their priestly duties. Then came the outcry – 'This cannot be done. They have committed no crime, they are following their conscience'. A certain writer in one Catholic paper even declared that those Bishops who took action, could be prosecuted in civil courts. The same paper had a long article from a well-known writer, declaring, that as an ecclesiastical tribunal would be necessary to try such cases, for every witness brought by the prosecution, the defendant could bring more in his favour. Such theological poppycock! Such senseless drivel, as is being fed to the reading public for quick assimilation!

What are the consequences that could follow to a cleric who rejects the encyclical or refuses to observe its ruling? They are briefly as follows:-

1. A priest who in the circumstances, visualised by the Apostolic Constitution referred to in Canon 904, gives advice, etc., contrary to the ruling of *Humanae Vitae* where contraception is concerned could be considered as guilty of *Sollicitatio ad turpia* and hence subject to the same penalties as given in Canon 2368.
2. Pertinacious disobedience to the Roman Pontiff (or to one's own Ordinary) can be punished, with censure if necessary in conformity with Canon 2331, par.1.
3. The removal of a Parish Priest (or of an Assistant Priest) from his duties or office, if contemplated as a punishment for a crime must take place in accordance with the specific rules governing criminal procedure Canon 1933 to 1959. The ordinary is obliged in procedure to follow those exacting regulations before any penalty can be imposed.
4. A Parish Priest (or Assistant Priest) may not however have been guilty of a proved specific crime – in fact there may not be even the likelihood of an ecclesiastical crime – and yet the priest can be speedily removed. This summary or administrative process, is followed, not in punishment of crime, but in the protection of the faithful and in the interest of the Church. No court of enquiry is needed, no tribunal to examine the evidence for or against is demanded. All that is needed is the fact, that in the judgment of the ordinary, the spiritual interest of the faithful is better provided for, by the removal of the Priest of the Parish – whatever his status may be. The Canons governing this summary procedure, are given in Canons 2142 to 2194. Canon 2147 gives some of the reasons which would justify the use of this summary procedure, but all canonists admit that the list is not exclusive. Those given are 'lack of ability in running one's parish, old age, hatred of the priest by the people, even though it is unjust, loss of respect . . .'

In the light of this brief summary of the legal principles governing the removal of priests from their office, it is futile to allege that the hands of ecclesiastical authority are tied in the face of situations which have been created in recent months in this country. Church law has little time for scandal as can be seen by consulting Canon 2222, par.1, where almost any action which causes scandal (and it does not have to be universal scandal) becomes, potentially, a criminal law. The protection of the faithful against false doctrines and wrong principles of morality is given first place in the entire legal system of the Church. 'Salus Animarum Suprema Lex' runs tight through the Code of Cannon Law.

It is not to be wondered at, when one hears so many people say – 'How can the Bishops permit Priests who reject or disobey the encyclical to continue the celebration of Holy Mass?'.

What the enquirer has in mind of course is, the disposition of soul that all of us know one must have to receive Holy Communion or to celebrate Mass. Many Catholics are understandably scandalised by the situation.

They know that the encyclical calls upon Priests to set the example to the faithful by loyal obedience; the faithful know that this law must bind Priests under pain of mortal sin, to accept it as the true doctrine in a very serious matter.

You answer that the Priests in question do not consider its acceptance as something which binds them under mortal sin − this is the charitable interpretation. It does not satisfy the lay person, who will then ask you if any priest is free to think out the gravity of any law for himself.

Could a Priest consider abortion or infanticide as venially sinful in the same way? Could he consider the Recitation of his Divine Office as a light matter? These are questions which have no answer − no logical answer, if the law on contraception is not accepted as a grave matter, and if it is, how do dissident Priests continue to celebrate morning after morning, and how do the Ordinaries view the matter?

We pity the laity in their confusion and dismay, as we share in the same anguish of spirit.

AN OPEN LETTER TO THE BISHOPS
From *Newsletter,* Spring 1970

'Your Eminence, Your Grace, Your Lordship,

You are the official guides of your people, the official mouthpiece of the Church in your diocese, the guarding of your flock has been committed to your care by the successor of St. Peter. Your insignia of office indicates to all Catholics your duties and responsibilities they serve as reminders of the heavy task that is yours − to hand on the teaching of our Divine Master pure and unadulterated, under the supreme authority of the Holy Father, to the faithful of your diocese.

You, by virtue of your high office, are to be the bulwark against the inroads of erroneous doctrine within the fold, the champions to defend the innocent and pure of heart, from the corruption that the evil one has always tried to create within the Church, that souls may lose their faith.

But there is no need for me to detail your privileges and responsibilities − the last Vatican Council has done that in the clearest possible terms.

It is with great sadness of heart, and with great difficulty that I write this 'open letter', but with hundreds of Priests of this country, and with thousands of the bewildered faithful, I feel that the time has come when an outspoken appeal will not be out of place.

This is not a criticism, and still less, an attack but it is a cry of the heart to come to the aid of the afflicted, the bewildered, the despondent and even those who have already left the Church in a moment of dejection and utter despair.

Who the writer of this open letter is matters little, for there are thousands like me. Yes, thousands of heavy-hearted men and women who, not long ago, looked upon the Church as the firm bastion of truth and justice, of love and service to its divine Founder, Jesus Christ; men and women who gloried in the name of 'Catholic' and who lead a life to be wondered at, viewed by people of the world. Almost overnight, this is all gone.

The voice of Christ coming from the lips of Paul VI is ridiculed, reviled, questioned or contemptuously ignored. Self-appointed theologians, evolutionists, revolutionists, purveyors of sex, corrupters of doctrine, romancing priests, giddy mini-skirted Sanctuary intruders, a patch quilt of liturgical queers, go prancing, dancing by in dissenting and dissolute abandon.

While all this goes on, our Bishops observe a sphinx-like silence, watching over the self-destruction of the Kingdom of God on earth.

You cannot say that these statements (they are not attacks) are untrue or exaggerated, or that we have no patience with the 'Church developing' according to the designs of Vatican II. The things that horrify us Catholics, Priests and laity, are not and cannot be developments of anything – they are false doctrines and scandalous practices that are draining away the life blood of Catholics in this country. Look at the state of our Catechetical Centres, they are mass-producing heresy after heresy and feeding them into the minds and souls of our teachers and future teachers. Our schools for which our Catholic community made such sacrifices over the years (to keep them Catholic, and to hand on the faith to others), are now almost invariably in the hands of so-called progressives, for whom 'infallibility' belongs to Kueng, Schillesbeeckx, Davis and even Bishop Butler – but not to the successor of St. Peter.

Go into a Catholic bookshop and see the books that are on demand and which alone are kept in stock – books that reject Catholicism in whole or in part, and some coming from the pens of 'instant theologians' do not even keep a semblance of Christianity. Yet these are the books recommended and read, sold and given on loan and enjoying a most wide reading public. Ask for a book on orthodox Catholicity, ask for the books that follow the official teaching of the Church – ask for a Mass book that gives the Latin as well as the vernacular text, and you will be laughed at to scorn, as a relic of an age that is past, and gone forever. It is not long ago since certain 'Renewalists' openly referred to Catholicism of the pre-Vatican days as a 'past faith', yet the Renewalists were received and given approval by a high ecclesiastic of this land. Discover for yourself what books are more often found in the libraries of schools, convents, presbyteries (of the younger priests) and whose doctrines are imparted to others – you will find that these heretical authors mentioned above, are given pride of place – and the Dutch Catechism, not withstanding the many classifications of errors pointed out by the Papal Commission in 1968, is still extensively quoted in support of a downright heresy.

See the attitude to the Pope, the Vicar of Christ! Almost in every area where we have had dissenting Priests who were prepared to spew their own vile opinions on the people, in opposition to Papal teaching, the interests of the faithful who should be protected from scandal and from false doctrines, were hardly considered.

Priests who openly disobeyed the Papal Encyclical on birth control, and who still reject it – thereby committing grave sin (let us not humbug ourselves about this, by appealing to pseudo-conscience) are still permitted to celebrate Mass and administer the Sacraments – and even continue to spread their erroneous opinions to faithful souls.

The Pope is mocked, ridiculed and treated with contempt, even in so-called Catholic papers and magazines, but that perhaps is not surprising, since the same innovators treat the Real Presence of Christ in the Eucharist with contempt and with blasphemous behaviour.

Read week after week, the agonising appeal of the Holy Father to the Bishops and Pastors of the world, that the Church structure as Divinely established is unchangeable, or that celibacy must not be discussed in view of promoting its removal, or that Vatican II did not change in any way the traditional teachings of the Church.

Read the appeals of the same broken-hearted Pontiff to stem the tide of innovators rushing through the Church.

What have they produced from the Bishops of this country? Nothing, but stony silence! Nothing but blank apathy! A spiritual paralysis seems to have affected almost every Bishop in the country, which has turned his spinal cord into jelly, be-muted his faculty of speech, enlarged his ego, and given him feet of clay.

I say 'almost every Bishop' – thank God there are a few exceptions to the general principle; men who remember that their Pastoral staff symbolises

THE ENCYCLICAL *HUMANAE VITAE* STILL UNDER ATTACK   79

the care which the shepherd must exercise over his sheep, and is not to be identified mistakenly as symbolic of a crook.

May St. John Fisher, the only member of the Hierarchy of the sixteeenth century who was not afraid of fines, imprisonment or of death, and who died for Papal Supremacy, bless those few faithful Bishops and bring remorse of conscience to those others who jeopardise the faith of their flock because they are afraid of 'popular opinion'. May St. John Fisher who bent his neck for the axe, rather than accept the primacy of human authority, enable those weaklings, before it is too late, to be ashamed of bending their necks to popular demands.

In the midst of the Hierarchy stands Bishop Butler (yes, we will name him – it is time to do so) classed as the greatest English theologian, and yet, who week after week almost sells his Catholic Faith (if he ever had it) to encourage the rabid anti-Papalists. His attacks on the Papacy in recent times have been so appalling, so scandalous, that many have concluded, it was the priest who admitted him into the Church, and the Bishop who ordained him, who must take the blame.

Yet, notwithstanding his repeated efforts to cut down the Pope to his proper size (as seen by Bishop Butler) has this Bishop been rebuked by his fellow Bishops! Has he been rebuked by his own immediate Ordinary – the Cardinal!

If he has, it has been in private, and has brought no change of heart.

The writer of this 'open letter' calls upon the Cardinal of Westminster to have this man removed from office and assigned to a house of penance.

Bishops and Archbishops of England and Wales, do you know what it is to be unwanted, lonely and out of place in the Church into which you were born! Yes, that is happening in this country. Faithful Catholics because they are loyal to the Church and the Pope are unwanted in their own Parish Church where 'progressive' clergy have taken over. They are out of place in their Church because innovators have so taken the law into their own hands and put on a service (instead of Mass) that is repulsive and it is an unwarranted innovation. Do you know what it is to feel you are treated as an 'antique' because you defend the Primate of Rome, or believe in the existence of Original Sin, seeing it was erased by Father Peter de Rosa in the post Vatican years! Do you know what it is like to be sniggered at by some newly ordained Priest, a product of our 'new seminaries', because you believe in the existence of angels or in the Real Presence of Christ in the Eucharist! Do you feel the anguish when some child of ten or eleven or more tells you that 'Confession' is just 'out' until one is an adult, and quotes a Diocesan Inspector of Schools for the statement. You will not be the person to feel the embarrassment when a newly ordained priest tells his Parish Priest that 'dancing girls' in the Church service are now permitted, and as a proof, presents an article from a Catholic paper, on the opening of a new Catholic Cathedral in Liverpool, and moreover cites a few of the 'Liturgical experts' to clinch the argument, including the Professor of Liturgy of a certain seminary. You may not be the one to feel the exacerbation when a TV personality describes herself on a TV show as a 'Catholic theologian', and then goes on to demolish the Catholic belief in the Resurrection of Christ, which she describes as 'just a spiritual breakthrough'! When convent school girls return home and tell their parents and others that Mortal Sin no longer exists except on paper and quotes the teacher at school in support of their position, or when a Catholic school girl announces that 'one need not go to Confession any more as the general absolution before Mass, or the actual reception of Holy Communion cleanses the soul of all guilt', and again cites her Catholic teacher for her new ideas. Do you think that these and a thousand such incidents, happening all over the country, are best answered by impenetrable silence, or an attack of brushing off the complaint as if it just could not happen?

Yes – rosaries, statues, crucifixes, medals, pious pictures, which helped so often and so many, to keep their faith and morals in the past, are now believed to be almost condemned by the Church (Vatican) or at least frowned upon with utter disdain by the more enlightened of the faithful. To appeal to the Pope's most recent words on such subject, is to invite an outburst of either pity or sheer contempt sometimes answered with the words – 'Who listens to him anymore? Even the Bishops have no time for him anymore'. The attitude of certain Bishops, particularly a few of the English Hierarchy, to the Holy Father's teaching, is then shown by recourse to their statement on the Papal Encyclical on contraception.

The widespread belief among Catholics today that one is now, 'justified' in forming one's own conscience on any matter, setting aside any Law of God or of the Church, owes its momentum to a great extent to the Joint Statement of the Hierarchy on the Papal Encyclical already referred to. Teachers quote the words 'Neither this Encyclical or any other document of the Holy See, takes away from a person the right and duty to follow his conscience' to their children, and priests with more liberalism than Catholicism quote them to their parishioners; to help them find the Decalogue easy on their journey through life.

'Let conscience be your guide', is peddled about as if it were used by the Council (when in fact it is not even mentioned), as an easy escape from moral restraints; what Protestantism failed to foist on Catholics – the 'right of private judgment' is now welcomed by them under a new label of the 'right of conscience'. In the field of Ecumenism, the very first principle insisted upon by the Holy See in its 'Ecumenical Directory' is the safeguarding against scandal to the faithful; in practice, this is the last thing thought of or considered.

On a parochial level and even more so on a Chaplaincy level, younger Priests and nuns and laity ignore all conditions laid down for ecumenical gatherings, and contemptuously describe 'scandal' to the faithful as a want of charity on the part of those scandalised – 'A lacking in the charity of Christ' as one missioner described it to a man and wife who could not face the ordeal, that the final closing of the two weeks in mission in the parish was to take place in the local Baptist Church.

I am sure, Your Lordships, that you will say by now that all these cases are individual ones which can happen anywhere and are inevitable in any country. If you think so, then I would respectfully ask you to weigh those facts against the hard reality of an ever-increasing drop in sacerdotal and religious vocations in the country, an ever-increasing drop in Mass attendance in practically every parish a Diocesan Directories over the last three years have shown, an unprecedented drop in the number of priests and the religious who have abandoned their sacerdotal or religious life – often to marry. These cases I give you, are not isolated ones by any means – they are widespread cases all over the country.

Your Eminence, Your Grace, Your Lordship, this letter is written with only one purpose in view – the hope that it might be even a remote instrument to arouse you from the complacency that seems to have settled upon you since the Vatican Council.

We pray that noble St.John Fisher, the Bishop who was not afraid in the sixteenth century, even when imprisonment and dreadful death had to be faced for following the Pope rather than his monarch, will give you courage. You have only to face popular opinion among a certain small section of the community – the liberalistic-minded and so-called Renewalist.

To follow the Pope will not mean death or imprisonment for you – it will just mean that our pseudo-progressive will describe you as 'not with it'. Who wants to be 'with it' when 'IT' is out of harmony with the teaching of Christ's Church!

The 'IT' is the world that Christ said would hate you and all his followers. We pray that St.John Fisher may inspire you with wisdom and courage; wisdom to see that your 'prudent silence' may in fact be 'criminal silence' and no true Bishop can keep silent when heresy or false doctrine of any kind stalks the land. Be brave and place your trust in God. Lower not your heads to everlasting shame and ignominy, when the one you should aspire to imitate did not hesitate to lower his head before the axe – in defence of a truth not even then 'infallibly' declared. St. John Fisher did not quibble; surely you will not lose your life, by silent defence of theological drivel.

Those faithful Priests and laity – and their name is legion – look to you – appeal to you, to defend them energetically from the flood of false doctrines and practices rushing through the Church of this land. Will their appeals go in vain? Will the sheep have to defend themselves from the ravening wolves, while the Shepherds look on, in silence.

I'm asking every Priest member of the Catholic Priests' Association in this country, which now number over 550, to offer Holy Mass for the Bishops of the country during Holy Week 1970, and every lay associate member (which runs into thousands) to offer Holy Communion on Maundy Thursday for the intentions of the Hierarchy of this country, that they may be strong and stout of heart as 'DEFENDERS OF THE FAITH'.

Author's Note

In continuing this biography of Father Flanagan's life and work for the 'Church Suffering', the reader will appreciate the great pressure involved on an already sick man. Needless to relate, nothing daunted his firm courage and stand, in the defence of orthodoxy and the Papacy.

Attending to his pastoral duties in his lovely little Church of St. George, the needs of his people – especially the sick – held a very special place in the life of this priest.

He attended now to the vast influx of correspondence (CPA) twice daily arriving on his desk, from disturbed Catholics, not knowing which way to turn and thanking God for this breakthrough, and at last, someone to turn to, in this dreadful crisis in the Church, when Christ's words to His Shepherds 'FEED MY LAMBS – FEED MY SHEEP' appeared to have rested on deaf ears.

Also, to be noted here, the bitter revolt from those, who felt the first impact of intrusion being made upon their new updating of Vatican II. These progressives attacked Father Flanagan from all angles, and with all the force at their command. But, they had met their equal, and there would be 'NO SURRENDER'.

The long days of work at his desk, until late at night, were followed on retirement by a period of reading, then some hours of sleep. That period of sleep disturbed by an early morning 'phone call (between 1-2 a.m.).

Some 'crank' (although Father Flanagan felt sure it was the voice of a young priest) threatening him: – 'You stop this or . . .' followed by a few more sarcastic remarks, then silence.

Naturally, a sleepless night would follow, causing much anxiety, but by early morning, Father was up and out, preparing for his Mass – his pastoral duties – and immediately back to his desk, to begin another day in the defence of the Church and *Magisterium*.

Later on I will bring the reader up to the pressure which finally overtook him, when he suddenly collapsed and suffered a major coronary thrombosis.

As yet, Father fights the good fight, which I will again continue to record.

IX
SOME EXTRACTS FROM *NEWSLETTER* EDITORIALS
By Father Flanagan Spring 1970

1. WRITING AN EDITORIAL is not easy. There are so many points that one would wish to mention, but the sheer weight of numbers makes that just impossible. Hence, we have to be selective and publish the one which we think should receive priority.

On November 27, the Apostolic Delegate sent me, as secretary of the Association, a letter, expressing the gratitude of the Secretariat of State of the Vatican, for the messages of loyalty sent to the Holy Father, just prior to the Roman Synod. The Secretariat also expressed thanks on behalf of the Holy Father for the expression of loyalty to the Holy See that had been sent to Pope Paul at an earlier date. In this context, we feel we should also mention a letter received from the Archbishop of Dublin Most Reverend Dr.McQuaid who said (23 Nov. 1969) 'The Association can have only the unqualified assent of priests, in maintaining the teaching authority of the Church'. We are grateful to the Archbishop for his kind words. Yet another Archbishop has joined our Association – The Most Reverend Finbar Ryan, D.D. L.L.D., now living in retirement in Cork and a distinguished member of the Dominican Order.

Membership of the Association continues to grow in numbers and strength – it now numbers no less than 550 priests in Great Britain. One zealous new member, a Benedictine priest in Kingston, Jamaica, West Indies, is busy at work organising the Association among priests of his country.

It was very consoling to hear from him, that most of the priests working in that part of the world, are loyal to The Holy Father and the Church. This good priest's name is Father Friesen O.S.B., St. Michael's Seminary, Kingston.

SOME EXTRACTS FROM NEWSLETTER EDITORIALS 85

We will pray for the success of his undertaking and give him every support.

The last *Newsletter* brought many letters of thanks and appreciation. We are grateful to all those who have written letters of congratulations. Some called it 'strong meat' and referred to it as 'the most outspoken journal today'.

2. Few centuries of the Church's history can bear such scurrilous attacks on the Vicar of Christ as are now being witnessed. The fury of the evil one to spew out his foul and fiendish accusation against the Pope have now no limits. One could understand them coming from an avowed enemy of the Church, but when they come from those who claim to be Catholic and Renewalists, and who profess membership of the Church, it is another matter. It is worse still, when these vile charges are published in catholic publications and with the approval of ecclesiastical authority in some cases.

The Sunday Times, 14 December 1969, reviewing a pamphlet by Antony Spencer (described as 'one of the best known Catholic Sociologists') quotes Mr Spencer as follows: 'The Pope completely misunderstands modern society. You name it. He's attacked it. It is partly a question of personality, partly because he is prisoner of the Vatican. He is surrounded by a bureaucracy which feeds him with alarmist stories of what is going on'. *The Sunday Times* continues that 'Spencer made a mark in the Church, mainly as a Sociologist'. We could not agree with the *The Sunday Times* more. He has 'made a mark'. He has caused a wound to the mystical Body of Christ and his accusations against the Pope are as false as they are imaginative. The Editor of *Newsletter* sent a stinging rebuttal of this article to the *The Sunday Times,* but as would be expected, it was, not published.

It was with satisfaction, that one later read in the *Osservatore Romano,* that this paper had taken up the challenge.

But Anthony Spencer's insulting words about the Vicar of Christ, pale into insignificance, when we read (as published in *Approaches,* [Dec. 1969 p.43]) in *Catholic Eductation Today,* (Jan-Feb issue 1969), where a Dr Hubert Campbell accuses the Pope of being sexually disturbed when writing one paragraph (of *Humanae Vitae*) and then accused him of 'reckless calumnies which sin against, justice and charity, ending up by accusing him of 'sinning against the Holy Ghost'.

The first reaction on reading this type accusation against His Holiness is to ask 'Who does Dr Campbell think he is?' To make things worse, his journal is published in the Archdiocese of Westminster and with the permission of the Cardinal Archbishop. The Latin words *permissu*

Superiorum can have no other meaning. This *Newsletter* calls upon the Archbishop of Westminster to repudiate this charge against the Vicar of Christ, even though it is now a long standing one (since Jan-Feb 1969), and to take steps that no such vile accusations will be levied against St. Peter's successor in future, without serious sanctions being immediately put into effect. Our would be 'Renewalists' have reached the point, when they are prepared to stop at nothing – they are playing on the weakness of ecclesiastical authority.

The booklet *Catholic Education Today* in which this scandalous attack is made on the Pope is published by Catholic Teachers' Federation and the Catholic College of Education at Strawberry Hill, Twickenham, Middlesex.

We as Priests in parish work, who have to finance so heavily the Catholic Schools, have a right to demand that none of the cash we siphon into Diocesan Funds is used in producing such vile productions. What an encouragement it is for priests to continue collecting for his Catholic Schools when this is one of the end products!

3. Speaking shortly after he had delivered the severest criticism of his Pontificate to the Dutch Hierarchy on permitting clerical celibacy to be discussed by the Dutch Pastoral Council, His Holiness the Pope had a word of stricture also for those who were so conservative as to be 'rebellious' and appealed to them to 'follow his authority'.

The Pope had in mind the opponents of the *Missa Normative* who have condemned it as a betrayal of his office, by giving it his approval. We of the 'Catholic Priests' Association' have made no such mistake, and we will not make any such blunder. Our axiom will remain *Ubi Petrus ibi Ecclesia*.

We must pray that these whose love for the Church and the Mass has got misdirected, will have the good sense and the courage to correct any deviation from the one sure path – that of following Peter.

In Section 10 of our editorial in the last issue of *Newsletter*, we had some severe criticism to make of Father Clifford Howel, S.J. and his attempts to downgrade the validity of the ordination of the priest and to 'upgrade' the Priest as 'President' of the community. Several Priests have written to us that it was this weird theology which was accountable for the present experience, alas too common, of seeing the priest pay far more attention to who is in the congregation, than attention to the faithful pronunciation of the words of consecration. Priests have written to me, of fellow priests (not named) acting on the altar, as if they were chased around by a swarm of bees and making a laughing stock of themselves to non-Catholics who entered the Church to see the 'new liturgy'. In the December issue of the *Clergy Review,* Father Howell returns to the same old theme, that he had in the September issue. He writes as follows:-

'The president's responsibility for effectiveness in Liturgy, is rather like that of the conductor of a symphony . . . it is he who causes it to be 'put across' . . . He is as much a part of the Sacramental Sign as the bread and wine of the Mass or the oil and water of the Sacraments . . . The correct presidential attitude, namely, conscious preoccupation with the people . . . all the time he must be concerned for them and their needs. He must not forget them for a moment during the entire celebration.'

The above quotations could raise many points – since when did the person of the President become of equal importance to the validity of a Mass, as the wine and water to be consecrated? Is this entire mental preoccupation with the people, compatible with the existence of a true *actus humanus* required for a valid consecration – or perhaps it is that the latter does not count? The Editor of this *Newsletter* fails to see how one can be fully and entirely preoccupied with the people, and at all times, without running the risk of interfering with the human act required for a valid consecration. It is a pity that Father Howell has to turn the place of the president of the community during Mass into something it was not intended to be – obviously.

Our future text books of theology, will have to give, as the essential elements of a sacrament – matter, form, and 'the presidential capacity'. We, older Priests, however, need not worry about the validity of the Mass we 'presided at', nor the Sacraments we conferred. Father Howell's imagination does not suffice to create any probability, even when it does nothing but re-echo the words of Father R.W. Hovda, the Archpriest of the ICEL in his work – *Style and Presence in Celebration* who writes – 'Good presiding means an effort to solicit the attention of each person in the assembly with one's eyes, as well as with one's general demeanour – to attend to anything else, book, bread, without attending to the persons present, is the opposite to the style we seek'.

Not a word of what the Church expects and seeks.

One of our Association members, who is a Chaplain to the British Forces in Belgium, writes to inform us that a document *(A Bulletin for the Chaplains)* was in circulation towards the end of last year, which explicitly stated, that Catholics were no longer obliged under pain of mortal sin, to assist at Mass on Sundays. The 'new theology' came from the pen of Priests who boast that they are 'affiliated to the Westminster Liturgical Commission' and presumably as they are linked to this body, they should know the truth. The same opinion has boldly been put forward in the pages of the *Catholic Herald* (16 Jan. 1970) by the self-appointed lay theologian, the stout defender of *Lady Chatterley's Lover,* Norman St. John Stevas.

The same Army Chaplain tells us, from his own experience in Holland, that during the last few years, the Sunday Mass attendance in the Low Countries has dropped by over 50 per cent with the resultant drop in Church revenue.

To offset the cash deficiency,the intrepid Dutch Hierarchy has permitted Catholic Churches to be sold for other purposes, and even to be demolished, and the building sites sold to developers. It is an interesting study to compare the Mass attendance figures of the Churches in and around London between 1966 and 1969.

The drop in the Sunday Mass attendance during those years is frightening, and it is difficult to imagine that some of the areas at least, have suffered losses through redevelopment. We hope at a later date, to give a list taken from the Diocesan Directors of the Diocese concerned.

4. We are experiencing some of the aftermath of the Synod of Rome last October, which many of the media which are under the control of the I-DOC, would have us believe, was a resounding victory for the forces of 'progress and collegiality' over the despotism of outdated Papal Supremacy. As the dust of battle clears away, it is perfectly clear that the ambitious Cardinal Suenens, with his colleague Cardinal Alfrink, of Holland failed to impress their longed-for democratic principles on the Bishops representing the world. Defeat however, only gives ambitious prelates new fire to restart their lost campaigns, and it will be very surprising if the next Synod does not see yet another effort by the forces of democracy to topple the Pope from the Petrine Chair.

Some of the 'discussions' which went on outside the Synod among the *periti,* can serve as a useful indication as to the real source of the trouble within the Church.

I give herewith some extracts from the pen of that devout reporter, Frank Morris, the special reporter of *THE WANDERER* covering the Synod. In the issue of that paper dated 30 October 1969, he selects Cardinal John Heenan of England, as exemplifying the tendency of some of the Synod Bishops 'to blend oil and water' (Papal Primacy and Collegiality) leaving it to the Holy Spirit to make a homogeneous mixture. Referring

SOME EXTRACTS FROM *NEWSLETTER* EDITORIALS 89

to Cardinal Heenan, in his interview in the Vatican Press, building at the end of the Synod's first week, Mr Morris quotes him as saying 'that it is up to the Holy Spirit to straighten out the labyrinths and open the *cul-de-sac*, created by the meeting of cross currents of Papal Rule and Collegian Right.

'Cardinal Heenan' writes Frank Morris, 'whether conscientiously or not, in the interview, suggested some of the directly contradictory issues involved. On one hand, he admitted the surge of anarchy in the world, and on the other, he advised, that not only Bishops, but also Priests and laity, be admitted to the fullest operations of 'Collegiality'. In the same breath, the Cardinal admitted that no one had yet come close to saying, just what collegiality is'.

In other words, the Cardinal approves of the growing individuality in the world, and wants the people to be invited into the inner chambers of Church decisions – but hopes, that those same people in whom he sees the virus of anarchy, will not infect the Church with the disease. The Cardinal rightly rejected the idea, that the Synod would have deliberate voice (with a juridically binding voice in church affairs) arguing that Priests and lay Councils, would then claim the same at diocesan levels, and havoc would be created. He was content to have consultative voice given to the Synod, – but he must realise that 'consultative' voice degenerates into 'deliberative' unless there is a strong authority at the head to prevent this happening. Cardinal Heenan's statement which appeared in the Catholic Press in this country – 'No one wants to question the primacy of the Pope – this is part of the Deposit of Faith' – will find a re-echo in the heart of every true Catholic, but, is there not the tendency for the Bishops to aggrandise their own position and role, at the expense of some authority being lessened on the part of the Pope. Other points, which Mr Frank Morris gives from the press interview in the Vatican, makes startling reasoning. He quotes Cardinal Heenan as saying – 'Citizens of the City of God, no less than citizens of a modern nation, are prepared to submit to authority, only if they see it reasonable and responsible'. This sentence which the reporter quotes, was also given in our Catholic press in this country, and it creates an absurdity. If the efficiency and binding force of the exercise of authority over subjects, depends on the latter's perception of it as 'reasonable and responsible', it can only end in chaos – both in Church and State, a situation which the Cardinal has already deplored. It was, when the question of *Humanae Vitae* was raised, to continue quoting Frank Morris, that Cardinal Heenan made his biggest blunders. He declared that 'The laity feel quite able to discuss theology . . . 'and many excellent Catholics said about *Humanae Vitae,* 'We will not listen to the Pope'. The *WANDERER* special reporter, went on to say the following, about these sentences of the Cardinal – 'Laity feeling quite able to discuss theology is very different from, being able, in fact, having the competency to do so. If we have reached a state of things in which people can do this (reject Papal teaching) and still be considered as 'excellent Catholics' by a Prince of the Church, then the Papacy and its rightful power is in serious trouble. The possibility facing us is, that there will be a theoretical admission of the Pope's Supremacy and primacy, as the Synod delegates have all made, but in practice, an ignoring of that Supremacy and primacy.'

When Father Patrick O'Conner got to the heart of the matter, by asking the Cardinal two questions: 'Also are some Bishops saying, that they can teach doctrine independently of the Pope?' Are some Bishops saying, that they can disagree with the ordinary Magisterium of the Church?' Well, the Cardinal never really got round to answering these points directly, did hint, that this was the crux of the Synodal discussions. He pointed out that Bishops from 'developing countries' felt strongly, that Bishops from 'sick Europe' should not be issuing statements that seem to conflict with what the Pope had said, while Bishops from 'sophisticated' areas felt that they should not be restricted to what the Pope teaches in their pronouncements. He (the Cardinal) affirmed, that this was the disunity in response to *Humanae Vitae* that occasioned the Synod, and in the closing days of the Synod, the Bishops would be working out practicalities, so that future confusion, such as that which followed 'Humanae Vitae', can be avoided.

'The confusion will remain, if it is not made clear that 'excellent Catholics'; be they Bishops or otherwise, are not free to refuse the teaching of the Pope on faith and morals' – comments Frank Morris – a comment with which every true Catholic will wholeheartedly agree.

X

OCTOBER SYNOD IN ROME: REPORTS

AS WE ARE dealing with the October Synod in Rome, the exposal of the tactics of 'progressives' may help readers of *Newsletter* to understand how news is manufactured and packaged, distributed and consumed as it comes through the notorious I-DOC, which *Approaches* did so much to reveal to the public in one of their issues of 1968.

English-speaking journalists at the Synod's press coverage were given 'inside information' by a panel of well-known 'progressives' on the payment of twenty dollars. Not only were items of information released to them for that sum, but 'interpretations' and 'opinions' of experts on the various Synodal discussions were also handed out. The panel consisted of Father Bernard Haring, Father Francis X Murphy (widely reputed as Xavier Rynne – the author of *Council* stories), the Augustinian, Father Martin Nolan, and from time to time, Father Donald Campion S.J. (the editor of *America*) or Father Thomas Stansky, all of them 'progressives' and in varying degrees 'dissidents' where *Humanae Vitae* was concerned.

Readers of *The Tablet* will recall how Father Francis X. Murphy considered the Papal Encyclical as just 'an ideal' and the final arbiter of the morality of contraception was one's private conscience. Many of the reporters were also of the 'progressive school' and put suitable questions into the mouths of the news panel, e.g. 'Doesn't the Synod want deliberative, rather than consultative voice?' To which Father Haring answered with an emphatic 'YES', which proved to be false, but it went out as 'News from within the Synod' and was avidly consumed as truth by progressives all over the world.

When, in the final stages of the Synod, the Synod Father emphatically upheld the right and duty of the Pope alone, to teach freely for the universal Church and without restrictions from the Bishops, the many papers throughout the world that had published the contrary, before the Synod ended, did not have the honesty and courage to correct the blunders perpetrated at the expense of 'the people of God', whom they had deluded.

It is worth noting just a few of the 'questions' answered by this panel of experts. They answered with such authority and cocksureness that most reporters came to the conclusion that they had direct access to the synodal deliberations and were speaking with personal experience of its discussions still fresh in their minds. But, when finally, the blunt question was asked of Father Haring, if he were actually in the sessions of the Synod, he was forced to admit, that such was not the case – the Synod was secret.

How then, did he get his information? Father Haring's reply to the question is interesting – 'We work with some of the Cardinals'. This reply given to the *Wanderer* reporter, Frank Morris, causes a deep sense of disgust, as it means that certain people on the panel of 'progressives' have received information on the deliberations of the Synod, denied to others, who have to be content with the little information released by the officially approved channels. Some Cardinals in the Synod betrayed their trust, if Father Haring spoke the truth on this point, and we have no grounds for disbelief.

Are some of the Cardinals disloyal to the Pope, and betraying the confidence placed in them, doing this for a share in the twenty dollars, given by each journalist, so as to be 'in' on the latest! We shudder to think so!

We give here some of the statements made by one or other of the priests of this panel – they are not given verbatim, but in substance with some verbatim texts.

1. FATHER HARING in criticising the Roman Curia, had this to say when Luther 'spoke with the whole Church' for the new thinking. The Curia reacted in the wrong way. (So Luther spoke 'with the whole Church' – it was the Pope who was out of step). The Pope juridically can do anything, but the Pope is bound as a servant of the Church . . . he is bound before God to do what is the best possible to realise collegiality . . . the Synod wants a deliberative vote.

2. FATHER NOLAN The defensive attitude of the Curia was to blame when 'my confrere' (Luther was an Augustinian as Father Nolan) sought reform and then took off. The departure of great intellects in the days of nominalism put the Church on the defensive, and so the attitude arose that people must listen to the Pope. So, the voice of Luther finds an echo in the voice of Father Nolan – 'his confrere'!

3. FATHER MURPHY 'Theology is the reflection of what is happening in the Church — it must follow what is happening in the Church at any age.'

COMMENT So Father Murphy's theology, will be the theology of the people, with its principles measured by the yardstick of what the people want — the people want contraception, and so it is sound theology. Theology is to be bent to accommodate the world and man's appetite.

MISSA NORMATIVA – (FALSE TRANSLATIONS)

Many Priests of the country, will have received by this time, the vernacular text of the *Missa Normativa,* and will, no doubt, have discovered for themselves the many atrocious translations in the Latin approved text, that are being foisted upon us. In the last issue of this *Newsletter,* we stated that if the vernacular text was, as it was reported to me, a rough translation, tantamount to a new version issued by the ICEL, we would appeal to the Holy Father, for a better and truer text.

Our anxieties have been justified, and any priest can see for himself, the erroneous and frequent discrepancies between what the Pope approved (the Latin text) and what is now to be printed in this country.

The Holy Father has more than once insisted that only 'an absolutely perfect translation will do', a translation with 'no omissions' and with 'no changes'.

The ICEL text sins against Papal requirements in all ways — by omissions, by additions, by changes in the idiom, etc. This vernacular text was approved by the Hierarchy of this country, and sent to the Congregation for Divine Worship, for its stamp of approval. It was then sent to the printers, the 'Collegiality', in which the priest and laity of the country would well have proved a useful part, and which was so important in Cardinal Heenan's statement during the Roman Synod, was not observed in this country. The Cardinal got a wonderful chance to show what 'Collegiality' in this sense could have done if the text of the ICEL were first released to the priests of the country for their criticism. THE 'STAMP OF APPROVAL', which the Congregation has now given the vernacular text, does not give it the same specific approval, which is equivalent to 'PAPAL APPROVAL'. Consequently, the necessity of an 'absolutely perfect translation insisted upon by the Pope personally, is not satisfied by this type of approbation.

The ROMAN CONGREGATION is not an authority on any

vernacular translation, and cannot make an erroneous translation a true one. The Congregation of Worship's Approval, creates only a 'legal presumption', which, like any presumption, is offset by contrary proof. One has only to scan the vernacular text, even briefly, to see its scores of defects in translation.

XI

CAN CHRISTIANITY SURVIVE THE 20TH CENTURY?

By Father John Flanagan D.C.L.   ICPA *Newsletter* Jan.1970

SINCE VATICAN II, the Catholic Church has hovered on the brink of disintegration. Heresies and schisms of past ages took time – long periods of time to travel even to the nearest country, but today we are experiencing a sudden universal outburst of strange latent forces, which like rivers of lava running down the side of an active volcano, have percolated into every country, town and village of the world – almost overnight.

Every dogma of the Church is questioned, every aspect of Catholicism has *periti* to ridicule it. Anxiety broods over the Church like a great storm cloud, that at any moment can burst into torrents and sweep all before it.

Those who point to specific problems of the Church today – authority, celebacy of the clergy, contraception, as the factors which cause all the trouble, are confusing mere surface symptoms with what lies much deeper – at the very heart and core of Catholicism itself. Fear haunts us – some like to deny that fear exists and prefer to lull themselves into a persuasion that all will be right, as Christ has promised that he will be with His Church to the end of time.

No one doubts this promise and guarantee who accepts the Divinity of Jesus Christ, but this Scriptural promise does not tell us what kind the Church will be, that will remain until the end of time – will it be a Church of the Catacombs, or a Church so destructuralised that humanly speaking, it is lost in the world about us?

Many priests and laity are today asking – what is Christianity anyhow? This very question shows the depth of the problem; people as a rule do not ask this question unless they have already begun to fear that Christianity is nothing anyhow. Fear prevents basic questions being answered and faced – the questioner is often terrified to pass beyond peripheral questions – it is a mental escapism all of us know so well in our dealing with others and forget that it also applies to ourselves – the priests of Christ.

Humanly speaking we can put the questions which form the title of this article in another way. Are the forces seeking the dissolution of Christianity, more powerful than those who seek its continuity in the world? Again, can it survive the present century? Older priests are in trepidation; younger priests – very often – long for the day of the dissolution of the Church in its present form, believing that a more simple and more authentic form of Christianity will follow it – always believing this new form will be more in keeping with the primitive Church.

Many priests and nuns have left their vocations in the last few years 'to return to the world' as a traditional priest would see it, but for those left, in some cases at least, it was from a conviction that Christianity must be identified with the world.

The Church has gone wrong in the past, by drawing this line of demarcation between the Church and the world – they say. Even a superficial study of the Biblical texts of the New Testament will prove very conclusively that the Christianity of the early Church was a Christianity of belief in definite truths of Christ's revelations, as distinct from a vague uncommitted belief that 'God exists'.

The Christian must believe 'concretely'.

One who accepts the existence of God is a theist but not a Christian, unless his belief is positive and specific in Christ and in His Revelations. The God whom Christians worship in Christ, is the God of Revelation above all; natural religion can help and sustain Revealed Religion, but it cannot take its place.

Hence the Apostles' Creed, the Athanasian Creed and the Nicene Creed give the Christian's truth of belief; they are positive and definite and expressed in human language. After all, God revealed Himself and conveyed the truths of Faith expressed in human language. Catholic Faith must go all the way – accept all the truths of revelation – truths that are immutable, notwithstanding the imperfections of the human language in which they are expressed.

One specific truth of Faith which is under particular attack (not that exceptions are made by our Modernists) is the truth of the 'Catholic Church'. 'I believe in the Holy Catholic Church' says the Apostles' Creed. 'I believe in the one, Holy Catholic Church' says the Nicene Creed. The Church is then the object of 'belief' just as much as any other point in the Creeds concerned. **Christian belief must be motivated by the WORD OF GOD;** acceptance of the Church must be the result of an act of Faith.

Today this very point is overlooked in the strange frenzy that has beset men to 'rationalise' religion, down to the smallest detail.

If reason accepts something – well and good; if reason does not accept something – then it must go. The belief which we profess in the 'Catholic Church' is not just Her existence – indeed this aspect of the matter claims our rational acceptance. The Faith we express in the Church is the Faith in Her mission and teaching authority – faith in all that She puts forward for our acceptance; Faith in Her Divine Structure, Faith in Her Spiritual and Supernatural activities. Too often, particularly today, the Church is only seen as an historical and worldwide society of corrupt men and women. This aspect of it, is humanly discernible and is not an object of Catholic Faith.

When, as at the present time, the Church is undergoing so much criticism from within its members, we would expect that the Church, as the object of Catholic Faith, should escape censure and accusation, but it is not so. It is forgotten that the Christian is one who is sharing in the body of Christ, whatever the Christian's condition in life, or age, or sex may be. As St Paul says (Gal.3:28) 'There is neither Jew nor Greek, slave or freeman, male or female, for you are all one in Jesus Christ.' The degree of sharing will depend on the sanctity of life of the individual – Church structures. Church laws, Church practices, etc., so avidly attacked today, have no particular bearing in the Church that we accept through faith. 'Renewal' of the Church's external garment will play little part, if any, in the only renewal that counts, the renewal fostered by the Pope, V12., the renewal of our spiritual life in Christ.

Alas, today's 'Renewalists' in many lands, travelling under different names, give much energy and dangerous zest to patch up the outer fabric of what they see and consider as the Church.

Drastic recommendation, heated 'teach-ins', patience breading 'sit ins' interspersed with a symposium here, and a symposium there, are felt a factor that will contribute to a new era in the Church. In all of them, a common element is found – physical readjustment is considered as 'progress' but based on the false assumption that the Church in the twentieth century is the Church of the world.

Notice how often this point comes up in argument to justify contraception, to 'appeal' 'to modern man to make something 'understandable', to 'remove difficulties', 'to make it easier', 'to get people's co-operation', etc. Most, if not all of these are the adjustments that go on in any human society – they are necessary to some extent to preserve the interest of people.

But what bearing have they on something which one accepts on the motive of 'God Revealing'? Little or nothing – an indirect bearing at most.

It is not at all uncommon to hear priests and indeed laity express their disappointment, that in certain spheres, Vatican II did not tackle the problem that really mattered.

Liberalistic minded people would express the same disappointment for different reasons however – why didn't the Church decide to give away its wealth to help the poor? Why aren't Churches used as youth and social centres, etc.? For these, the Church should become an object of a Socialist's faith and receive his commendation and approval.

But this is not the Church of Christ, the Church of suffering, the Church of self-abnegation, the Church of self-conquest – the Church of the Spirit.

Reading through the various documents of Vatican II, one is not surprised that the great Council was followed by a wave of humanistic demands. One feels that more emphasis could have been given to the spiritual as in contrast to the social, more attention to the great virtues than to the great needs of the people of God. While it is true that God's interests lie in every page of the Council's voluminous documents, one cannot help feeling that the 'people of God' is given a rather emotional connotation. Indeed, it is this phrase which has supplied most of the ammunition to our progressives to fire at the Church; the words are twisted to convey the impression that the Church is THE people, with all the democratic privileges that THE people should enjoy.

No wonder there is such a mushroom growth of councils, committees, sub-committees, commissions, Synods, chapters, etc. The subordination to Christ in all things, the spiritual tonic to be derived from what the 'people of God' do not control and cannot control, is unmentioned or if so, far too vaguely. In brief we seem absolutely bent on knocking the mystery out of the mysterious – whether it be the Mass, the Sacraments, the Angels, or Christ's own life, passion and death.

No one who is conversant with present-day trends in the Church can escape the conviction that with this harmonising of the mystery of the Church with sociological beliefs of what every day society should be, there is also going *pari passu* the demysterisation of all that the Church holds and teaches. Commissions and Synods, Committees and Councils, now apply mundane yardsticks to the Church's most sacrosanct contents – The Mass, The Real Presence, Indulgences – the lot. What does not square with humanistic worldly measurements must be left over, is superfluous and should be 'out'. We recall the story of the definition of a camel – the animal that was made by a commission. Hence the hump to contain the irreconcilables. It looks unsightly, but solves other problems.

CAN CHRISTIANITY SURVIVE THE 20TH CENTURY?

So it is, with our trends in the Church today. Our Commissions and Councils are rationalising to make the mystery acceptable – little is said of the only thing that can make a mystery 'rational', acceptance on the WORD OF GOD. It is strange how all generations have tried to make men 'new' in his outlook, and to see 'fresh horizons' that will eventually liberate him from the things he considers as enslaving him.

Much of this may spring from man's own restless spirit – never really happy, never really satisfied. This, in a human society if perfectly normal, but in a society such as the Church, whose members know, or are supposed to know, that man will always be the same, it makes very surprising reading to peruse the writings of some of our Catholic theologians today. An *ecclesial euthopia* could be realised, if such and such a change took place in the Church's doctrine, we are told. Contraception is justified, it would fill our Churches again and increase enormously those receiving the Sacraments – what a dream! A vernacular liturgy would make unprecedented Mass attendance possible – were told.

So far, Mass attendance has dropped very considerably all over the country since vernacularism was introduced.

The writer is not saying that one is the cause and the other is the effect, but in the same short time both events have materialised and one could suspect a link between them.

The 'new man' that we are expected to become with the changes we have seen taking place in the Church, may well be only a dream, as the 'renewal' as it is being worked out at grass roots level, is striking only at man's outer life, his social life, his dealings with others, and with the Church.

There is little evidence that it goes deeper. The loss of faith among so many, the mass defections – comparatively speaking – from the ranks of the clergy and from convent life, is unquestionable evidence that spiritual renewal has lost its momentum (if it ever had any) in the post Council days. Love of dialogue is no substitute for the love of the Decalogue – and after all this is, by Christ's own terms, the proof of the love of God – If you Love Me, you will keep My Commandments.

It is strange how the 'elimination' of evil – physical and social – from the world, to which so many of the younger generation are dedicated, has been caught up with the belief that even moral evil must not exist. Living as we are, in the era of 'love' on the Catholic Church, some believe that moral evil can only be eliminated by denying its very existence. The old objection, that the 'God of Love' cannot really create hell or purgatory, has taken on a new life in recent days. Sin must be, as was advanced before, a residue of some social taboo, that in some strange way got mixed up with Christianity. Change the definition of sin — make it an 'offence against society' and not against God, and the problem will be solved. Of course, it could be conceived that God is displeased if we offer society — the community in which we live. This would make sense, and this is how our progressive theologians now see it. This, of course, means that 'reconciliation' (without penance or confession as we know it) and 'atonement' by Christ must be discarded. But, of course, Christ was a 'Revolutionary' fighting for freedom of his people from Roman slavery, as the Catholic Church of the West today fights for its freedom from the slavery of the Church of Rome.

These ideas all tie up in a fairly logical sequence, and leading to the rejection of the Divinity of Christ, the whole Christian Religion, that millions of 'the people of God' died for, becomes a great — indeed the greatest mass deception the world has ever known.

Some Catholic writers labour under the erroneous impression that one or other of the Church's doctrines can be dropped, forgotten, even possibly rejected, without in any way bringing the whole edifice of the Church into a heap of dust and ashes.

This is impossible. The Church's edifice may seem to the unsuspecting as only a loose-knit fabric in which 'outmoded' ideas of the past can be relegated to the ecclesiastical rubbish heap, and the Church will thus be improved by this pruning.

This is impossible. The doctrines of the Church are linked together by spiritual bonds, and all of them rest on the teaching authority of the Church and finally on the Divinity of Christ. Every attempt to create a crack in this Divine edifice will have spiritual repercussions all through; it is comparatively easy to create a man-made form of Christianity, but the spurious is easily detected.

The Church of Christ must be genuine in its entirety — as it comes from the Divine Hands that moulded it.

Nothing less will do.

One would have thought that highly placed ecclesiastics, who have learned in their seminaries and school of experience, that the Church of Christ is not of this world, and of necessity will be not just tolerated, but hated by the world.

Our Divine Lord has assured us of this truth in St John XV, vv.18-19.

Human efforts to 'adapt' the Church to 'meet the twentieth century', which we read about so much today, is being carried to the point when it is not just the external clothing of the Church — the portion that is not a mystery — but the Church as an object of Faith, is being relegated to the plane of the rational and the human. 'If you were of the world, the world would love what is its own, but, because you are not of the world, but I have chosen you out of the world, therefore the world hates you' (St John, XV v.19). These words of Christ according to Biblical exegetes, are not to be understood as restricted to the time of Christ alone, but are applicable to the Church because of the nature of the Divine Mission. Yet so many of our high prelates are more keen to 'democratise' the Church than they are to exemplify the Christian message and virtues in their own lives, and in that entrusted to their care.

Which of us in not aware today of some Bishop or Bishops, who in their efforts to avoid offending so-called 'Renewalists' and others, are prepared to let the most scandalous happenings take place in their diocese, and when their attention is drawn to it, the invariable reply is, that they prefer the faithful to resist such attacks on their faith? The sheep themselves, have to defend themselves and their lambs (the children) from the merciless fangs of the ravening wolves that romp at will through the sheepfold, unmolested, unopposed in their evil designs.

Reform, or if you wish *aggiornamento* of all our institutions in the Church can, and in fact has already, created a most dangerous situation where man is concerned. There is a proneness in every man to point the finger at something, or even some person, outside himself, as the cause of his interior weakness. It is the story of Adam and Eve again — Adam blames Eve, and Eve blames the serpent. This *aggiornamento* in institutions and things outside ourselves, can accentuate the radical weakness in man, unless with the adaptions in his environment there is also a new spiritual upsurge created.

If man blames his former environment for his past weakness and failure, he will quickly find the changed one just as deserving of his criticism and condemnation. The whole time it is his inner self, in his inborn weakness arising from original sin, that lies in the heart of his trouble, and soon he will be seeking new horizons, and still more distant ones — pursuing the cause that never existed.

If Vatican II gave a new emphasis to the Holy Scripture in the life of the Church, and in the individual, this stress on its importance has to a great extent been lost through the same media has twisted and distorted many of the Council's messages. Note how much is written today about a 'return' to the simplicity of the early Church, to put it briefly, but this principle is only developed when it is useful as an instrument of destruction of the Church's institutions and practices. Apart from His Holiness the Pope in his constant call for a spiritual revival in our lives and a new emphasis on the virtues of the Christian, practically no literature appears expressing that a return to the early Church must be a return to it in every aspect - penance – self-denial – love of poverty – the entire moral law respected – dedication to the successor of Christ, dedication to the Church, etc. Holy Scripture and the writings of the early Fathers – so much despised today – give us all we need to know about the early Church, and if we return to the 'Primitive simplicity' which we find therein, all will be well.

The points which I have been discussing in this article are only a few aspects of the Church and her crisis today, but we priests cannot ignore a question which affects us all.

'Is the priesthood relevant today?' This question is being discussed by priests and laity, and in a tone that must shock the unshockable. 'Is Christ relevant today?' is only the next step away as the priest is an *Alter Christus*.

Demolish the need for one, and it will hold for the other. Turn the priest into a social worker – which is the 'new approach', and then, of course, he is **NOT** relevant to this century. The trained and highly skilled social worker, coming from a local authority will have much to teach the priest-cum-social worker. Indeed, the priest in this context will be redundant. If our progressive writers continue to cloud the whole concept of Christianity, the Church, the Supernatural life of grace, the Divinity of Jesus Christ, etc., then of course, the priest must be given a new assignment or sink into oblivion, and be a relic of the past. Many priests are upset and bewildered with the advance of those hideous ideas to the very door of their presbytery; parishioners discussing in some pastoral Council, whether the time has come to replace the Father by one of themselves – one who can read better, speak better, carry himself better, and one who is abreast of the times!

The idle speculation on the priesthood has not just remained in the fanciful imagination of some sick mentality. It is being discussed in his parish Council, with its meeting in his parish – often next door to his presbytery; and with the Council following an 'agenda' approved by his Bishop. These circumstances lift the whole problem from the speculative into the world of reality – hence, the priest is anxious, indeed alarmed.

The violent attack on priestly celibacy, by our present-day innovators, strikes deep into the heart of the priesthood today.

Indirect assaults form the usual plan of campaign of the so-called 'Renewalist'. The outflanking movement of military strategy, gives the best results very often, with the least loss to the attackers.

To identify the priesthood more and more with the man in the world and the other arm of the pincer movement – the priesthood of the laity – closes the gap, and surrender is inevitable. The relevancy of the priesthood in the twentieth century becomes as much a part of history as the chariots that rolled down the Appian Way in the days of Caesar.

'Renewalists' do not worry too much about logic. The pseudo-argument of the 'population explosion', so much insisted upon in the rational efforts to justify contraception, becomes lost, when, in the same breath, our hardy 'Renewalists' want another population explosion through the removal of priestly celibacy.

XII

FURTHER EXTRACTS FROM THE *NEWSLETTER*

Newsletter Jan 1971

SINCE THE LAST issue of this *Newsletter*, the canonisation of the 40 Holy Martyrs of England and Wales has taken place. There were many expressions of regret that ecumenism should monopolise so many of the hymns sung on the solemn occasion. A few days before the event, the *Daily Telegraph* published a very brief report that Pope Paul would be expressing his reverence for the Protestant martyrs who died under Mary, as part of the ecumenism of today.

This report disturbed many Catholics. They could understand him expressing his admiration for their bravery in dying for their beliefs, but to express reverence for the cause for which they died, is a different thing. A considerable number of these Protestant Martyrs were women who married renegades from the Catholic Faith into which they were born.

So many people inquired by telephone at this office, as to what the report in the *Daily Telegraph* could have meant, that I telephoned the Apostolic Delegate. The Apostolic Delegate himself was not available, but his secretary answered and was annoyed that such a question should be asked.

He pointed out that it was for the Pope to decide what to do (which no one disputed) and in the most emphatic language rejected the idea of 'renegades' from the Faith, etc.

His answer was most disappointing, seeing that the whole purpose of the telephone call was to enquire if the press report was true. A subsequent telephone call to Mr Miles Board of the Catholic Information Office stated that the report as published in the *Daily Telegraph* could hardly be true. In fact, the Pope, during the Canonisation Ceremony, made no mention whatever of the Protestant Martyrs, as *The Times* was not slow to mention in its edition for Monday 26 October. Acquiring accurate Catholic information is a difficult task today, as *fait accompli* tactics are quite common, in order to establish a precedent.

Let us recall the case of Miss La Olsen, who married a Catholic in a Catholic Church a few years ago. We all read in the Catholic and National papers how the Pope had personally given his permission for her to receive Communion, though she remained a non-Catholic. We were told that she believed in the 'Real Presence' just as Catholics do, and this was the title for the special privilege. Extensive enquiries made, have shown, that this was yet another example of the *fait accompli* approach. Instead of the Pope granting this permission personally he was 'absolutely furious' (to quote one source close to the Holy See) to hear of it when it was all over. In the meantime, the alleged permission is being used by Modernists, to advance the practice of inter-Communion between the Churches. We reported one such case in the last issue of this *Newsletter* (Autumn issue) where at Coloma College, Kent, it was stated by a representative of an ecumenical group, that 'loyal Catholics' were in fact taking part in inter-communion, as 'they had discovered a unity in Christ, which the Churches had not yet found.'

So we have an ever widening practice in this country, based on something which never took place, and purporting to be approved and legitimate.

The twisting of Catholic truth to fit the demands of the Modernists goes on without a blush. Have you read in the papers at the time of the Canonisation, how the martyrs 'died for their conscience' or for 'freedom of conscience', and of course, it was only natural, to then insist that the Protestant martyrs should be canonised? It is understandable for Modernists to behave like this, but when a Canon of a southern diocese could end his lecture on the 40 Holy Martyrs with the words: 'I do not see why the Protestants should not be canonised, since they too suffered heroically for their conscience sake' and this Canon's Curate could say in sermon; 'The Martyrs died for conscience and freedom. We do not want any more of old Sectarianism', it is time to ask ourselves what has happened to the theological knowledge of many of our priests today. Our text books of theology have always taught us, that only death, endured in defence of a Truth of Catholic Faith, gave the title of Martyrdom, but even this now seems supplanted by the Modernists and swallowed by the gullible. The trust which many of us clergy, permitted to settle on our lines as priests, seems to have left us in a dreadful muddle.

Perhaps we are not entirely to blame. The life of a priest in England is not an easy one, with the Bishop demanding more and more cash for his Diocesan Development fund, we have found ourselves taken up in a vortex of pools, bazaars, whist and jumble sales, until these words flashed across our Breviaries or perhaps invaded the very Canon of the Mass, and we had no time left, to reflect on our own theological days.

Cardinal Suenens, having trampled on the Roman Curia since the Vatican Council, has now become a world commuter, selling his wares to all who are prepared to open their doors to him. If any man in the world today can give onlookers the impression that he has the Chair of Peter as the object of his ambition, it is the sturdy Cardinal from Belgium. Brussels sprouts more than cabbages since Lenon Joseph became Cardinal Primate of the city in 1962. His indefatigable efforts to export the Belgian brand of Modernism to the world, proves not only his zest, but his efforts to replace Catholicism as the world has known it from the beginning, with a vast collection of small pseudo-Christian units, believing what they like, acting as they like, and owing no more than nominal respect and honour to the See of Peter.

If one studies the recurring theme of the Cardinals lectures and writings, it is the See of Rome that receives his constant attention.

With suaveness and urbanity, that could deceive many, the Cardinal invariably pronounces the importance of the Holy See, The Primacy of the successors of the Apostle Peter, Papal infallibility, etc., as untouchable doctrines in the theology which he advocates. But one does not have to read much further, or listen much longer, to discern the gradual and systematic dismantling of the whole structure of the Church, as it has come down to us through the ages. The Cardinal does, of course, make frequent references to 'the early Church' to impress on his listeners or readers, that he is 'only returning to the Church of Apostolic times'. Be not deceived. The grand design in the Cardinal's plans involves changes no less radical and ruthless than those openly introduced in past history, by the great innovators and ecclesiastical revolutionaries.

To achieve his ambitions, the power of the Pope must be shackled. Providence often works in strange ways, and it is not without reason, that Leon Joseph Suenens was given, as his titular Church in Rome 1962, that ancient Church known as 'St Peter in Chains'. The Cardinal is living up to the title of his Church.

Let us look a little deeper into the activities of the Belgian Cardinal. The Catholic Press of this country, hailed the recent Brussels Conference as a milestone on the road to modernisation of the Church, and attributed the success of its deliberations (admitting of course, there were some problems) to the ability of those who organised it, presided over it, and under whose patronage it was sponsored. Some reporters were, however, more discerning. *The Atlantic* (Sept. 1970) characterises in this context Cardinal Suenens as a 'Symbol of opposition to Pope Paul in the Church' and *Newsweek* (28 Sept. 1970) considers the theological Conference as a political congress.

The notorious theological journal *Concilium* with the equally notorious Edward Schillebeeckx, as editor, was instrumental in convoking this meeting point of way out theologians. Professor Langdon Gilkey, a Baptist minister of the University of Chicago, who was present as an observer, accurately summarised the theological content of the Congress, when at its termination he said: 'There is little that has been said at this congress, that a Protestant would not agree with. I could have written Hans Kung's speech if I had his talent' (*Remnant*, 30 Sept. 1970).

Newsweek (28 Sept.) gave some interesting insights into the discussions among the theologians present. The democratic election of the Pope for a limited time – the brain child of Cardinal Suenens – the election of Bishops, was pushed forward with ruthless determination, but thanks to the valiant opposition of some half dozen theologians, who took an opposite view, and with clamour steadily increasing from the floor of the Conference Room, the assembly had to be content with speech making, and general resolutions.

The proceedings were televised throughout Europe. The Cardinal stated that 'someone had to take the initiative and what better group than the *Councillium?*'. One would like to ask at this point, why should the Church over which he presides be the one to take the initiative?

Has the Cardinal entirely rejected the principles discussed and accepted by the last Vatican Council, which reaffirmed in unmistakable language, the Primacy of the See of Peter?

The Church has had two Roman Synods since the termination of Vatican II, in which, matters arising from the Council and subsequent to it, have been discussed in the presence of the Supreme Pontiff, and yet Cardinal Suenens thinks it fit, to promote a conference of left wing theologians to decide issues which vitally concern the whole Church. Who is he, to have such matters discussed, without the approval of the Holy Father? Are the Bishops of the world to stand by and see the centre of Catholicism shifted from Rome to Brussels?

Have no illusions as to what the Cardinal meant – it is plain for all to see.

The report in *Remnant* (30 Sept.) fits the picture when it says — 'The Assembly voted overwhelmingly to grind out its resolutions, which left not a shadow of doubt as to the target — the Primacy of Peter . . . Suenens wants the Pope to be a limited monarch!! This *Newsletter* of the Catholic Priests' Association calls upon Bishops faithful to the successor of Peter, to make it clear to the Cardinal of Brussels, that in so far as they are concerned, he will find himself in complete isolation, in his endeavours to shackle the divinely established Primacy of Peter's See.

If our post-Council days show an ever increasing desire to return to the word of the Scriptures, and to the simplicity of the early Church, let Cardinal Suenens set the example by showing unqualified submission to the Holy Father, or failing which, let him have the common decency to resign his See.

One of the most heated debates of the five-day congress arose when our American theologians (Father Raymond Brown) clashed with the heretical Father Hans Kung over the bodily resurrection of Jesus Christ. The words of St Paul 'If Christ has not risen, then our Faith is in vain and your Faith is also in vain,' have, of course, lost all meaning for our Modernists. Our own Rosemary Haughton on a T.V. programme last year, contemptuously dismissed the physical resurrection of Christ's body, which she described as a 'break through'. To return to Father Hans Kung exposition of Catholic Truth at the Brussels' Conference, Father Hans Kung argued that 'If there had been television coverage of the tomb, they would have seen nothing.'

Against this, Father Brown declared that 'for anyone to deny the supernatural element of the New Testament, would be, to deny Christianity itself'.

One cannot help feeling that this argument would be lost on Father Hans Kung, who has already denied Christianity as the Church has taught it, anyhow.

Cardinal Suenen's appeal at the congress for a new ecumenical Council representing all Christian Churches, to be held at Jerusalem, the birthplace of Christianity, must have put some scholars thinking. Are we today, not only in Holland and Belgium, but throughout the Catholic world, heading for that humanistic, atheistic counter-Church, the Ape of God, such as Feodor Dostoeviski and Wladimir Soloviev predicted a century ago? To put it bluntly: Cardinal Suenen's call for a Second Council of Jerusalem is startling in the amazing parallel it seems to suggest, between precisely such a projected event, and the one predicted by Soloviev, when he wrote about the great Humanitarian World Emperor, who would, one day, convoke such a World Council, in Jerusalem, but in final analysis he would be exposed by Pope Peter II, as the Great Impostor, the Father of Lies, – the Antichrist.

As this *Newsletter* is read by many lay people, the Editor of this magazine hastens to assure them, that the previous paragraph is not put forward to frighten them that the Antichrist has come, but one cannot escape the ominous sounding parallel, between Cardinal Suenen's suggestions and his destructive ideas, on one hand, and the words of Soloviev on the other, particularly as the letter (often referred to as 'Russian Newman') who was outstanding for his deep Christian mysticism and his extraordinary theological insights.

Theological Conferences, such as those that took place at Chur and now at Brussels, with other ones less known in many parts of the world, go to indicate the extent to which much of the modern theology broke loose from its moorings and can no longer be called 'Catholic Theology'.

The Conference at Brussels would not have been complete without some effort being made, to see the abuse of sex as no longer sin. This three lettered word is no longer acceptable in the humanistic society of today, and a Church (such as Suenens visualises) which is trying to come to grips with the world, by accepting its axioms, must sooner or later abolish 'sin' from the regular vocabulary, and assign it to the relics of past ages – the ages of pre-Council days when unenlightenment was universal. Hence it was to be expected that a priestly champion of sex would arise in the Brussels congress, and proclaim to the world through television that 'The Church must now come to terms with eroticism as a legitimate expression of present day society.' (*Remnant,* 30 Sept. 1970).

Father A. Vergote, a Belgium priest under the jurisdiction of Cardinal Suenens, became that champion. The Catholic Church forsaken by the Holy Spirit until our own age, erroneously taught that the abuse of sex was sinful, and in principle, a serious matter.

Yes this is what our theological experts would have us believe.

The Brussels conference, notwithstanding its pretensions, was not a success. Even its authors and inspirers were bewildered by the sheer 'claptrap' intellectualism that crisscrossed the floor of the assembly.

Father Yves Congar, the French Dominican, was forced to say, 'If I had known earlier, all I have learned in the past three days, I'd have written a much different paper. What I have heard, is a sufficient justification for a review of all our theological views . . . we have been too much immersed in the study of theology.'

Quoting the same source, the Cardinal stated 'that he could not quite grasp the texts put forward by the congress organisers . . . I understand every line, but when I've finished, I don't remember what has been said.' (*St Louis Review*, 25 Sept., quoted by *Remnant*, 30 Sept.).

Obviously, the spirit that directed and guided the deliberations of the congress, was not the Holy Spirit that enlightens with its wisdom. The Holy Spirit can hardly be where the Vicar of the Second Person of the Blessed Trinity, is disobeyed and even contemptuously spoken of.

The recently promulgated Instruction of the Congregation for Divine Worship has hit hard at bizarre experiments in the liturgy and innovations which are arbitrary, and endanger the sacredness of the sites and ceremonies of Mass, in particular. This instruction is indeed welcome, as no one else who is acquainted with the rapid trend of liturgical novelties in the Catholic world today, can be other than horrified at the practices to be found all over the country, and parading under the name 'Liturgical Adaptations in conformity with Vatican II.'

Vatican II – what crimes have been committed in thy name! It would take many issues of this *Newsletter* even to list the aberrations of an appealing nature, now characterising the liturgy of this country.

The electrician sent to repair a fuse box in a certain Church, was not to blame, when opening it he found it was the 'tabernacle with the Sacrament'.

The young priest of the southern English diocese, who finding the weather warm in the month of August, announced to the congregation present on Sunday, that 'it was too warm to put on Vestments' and so, celebrated in short jacket and stole. The 'banjo' Masses that set the feet of the youngsters to dance, moving their limbs, instead of their minds and souls, and a multiplicity of other horrific and scandalous activities, will come under the ban, but it will all be in vain unless the Hierarchy decides to adopt a strict line of taking immediate action against those who destroy liturgy and shock the faithful.

In assessing what should remain and what must cease, they would be well advised to leave many of the 'Liturgical Experts' out of it, and seek the opinion of the ordinary decent and practising Catholics. Experts and 'Commissions' have contributed enormously to befoul the sacred ceremonies, and one can find an 'expert' to approve of anything. There were 'experts' who approved of 'Pop Masses' and from then on, some experts approved of the 'Pot Masses' – as one expert said 'The Pot helps with charism'.

The liturgy has gone to such limits in Britain, that nothing other than a complete ban on everything, not explicitly approved by the Church will suffice to clean up an incredible situation.

FURTHER EXTRACTS FROM THE *NEWSLETTER* 111

We pray that the Bishops may have the moral courage to take this step before it is too late, before the fast dwindling Mass attendance turns into empty Church benches. The Bishops can hardly stand by in apathy, while diocesan statistics show, year after year since 1966, a nationwide substantial drop in Sunday Mass attendance.

The lady who said – 'Father, I left the Baptist Church, believing the Catholic Church to be the one true Church, and I am wondering why I left', no doubt expresses the minds of thousands of Catholics in this country today. Unless something is done, it will be 'every man, to his own liturgy' in Britain before too long.

CHURCHES STRIPPED OF TREASURES BY PRIESTS

In a previous issue of this *Newsletter* (Spring 1970) in an article entitled 'Churches stripped of treasures by Priests', this *Newsletter* pointed out that the extent of vandalism perpetrated on the Church by Priests and Bishops in a frenzy of some pseudo-*aggiornomento*. In fact this news item brought many letters from horror-stricken readers, asking if this report was true. I take this opportunity once more to repeat that this *Newsletter* does not go to print, without a special screening of all reports that come through to the Editor's desk. Our reporters as a rule, are conscientious priests scattered all over the world, who testify only what they know to be true. We give here- with a report from Doctor Elizabeth Gertsner (Bensberg/Immekepps) from her 'Diary of the March to Rome' a Retrospective View! The report states that in the 'Flea Market' in Rome at the Porta Portese, one can buy every- thing from a Monstrance, Chalice Altar, Communion Rails, etc., anything that the ecclesiastical vandals bulldozed from the Sanctuaries of the Churches. The writer describes, how one 'old golden Monstrance' had become a photograph frame with the laughing face of Claudia Cardinale looking out. The author knelt down and kissed the Monstrance out of love and reverence for **HIM WHOM** it once contained. The salesman understood and removed the picture of the film star.

This was the Real Presence of a decadent humanity. The ultimate in degradation of the Blessed Sacrament. Yet this Victory of the Devil will leave so many untouched, in their peace and complacency! It will seem to Bishops and Priests as a matter which is not their concern.

The words addressed to Judas Escariot by the Pharisees, will well up in their hearts – 'What is that to us, look thou to it.'

The Times (22 Sept. 1970) in a short article on the Vandalism of the Catholic Church in Britain, has this to say – 'Victorian Gothic Churches with elaborate rood screen or reredos, are particularly vulnerable. In St

Chad's Cathedral, Birmingham, the rood screen installed by Pugin (some say, brought by him from Flanders) has been removed, only to be snapped up by the Anglican Church of the Holy Trinity at Reading. In the Church of Our Lady of the Holy Saints in Kensal New Town, (Bentley, Architect of Westminster Cathedral) the changes are more extensive and include some, more apparently fashionable, than liturgical: not just rood screen, but the reredos covered by a velvet curtain, the titles by red vinyl, the sanctuary floor by plastic marble and by white paint.

Austin Winkley, a Catholic architect is at work on the Jesuit Church at Farm Street, which has an elaborate Pugin altarpiece. He has designed Churches of the new pattern, but still appreciates the old.' I accept the principle of the rood screen and the reredos have to go,' he said, 'and that the high altar must be either removed, or put out of sight. If you have the two visible it is the sign of disunity.'

The Lord deliver us from the experts in liturgy.

INCREDIBLIA
by Father John W. Flanagan   From C.P.A. *Newsletter*, (Jan. 1970)

This feature of our *Newsletter* will deal with matters of the gravest importance in the life of the Church, and which call for the united efforts of priests and laity alike, to see that those wrongs are rectified.

THE TEACHER'S COURSE OF LECTURES AT NOTRE DAME DE FRANCE
Catholic teachers living in the London area, have been invited to attend a course of lectures, at Notre dame de France, Leicester Square, London, from October 1969, to May 1970.

This course will undoubtedly shape and mould the minds and outlook of our future teachers all their lives of thousands of children, who will be taught by them, in many parts of the country, in the years to come.

A teacher's course is not then, something to be taken lightly, something which can only affect themselves – repercussion from it, for good or for bad, will be widespread, for a long time to come. A teacher moulds the souls and minds of the pupils, and these, in turn, will be, what they have got in their student days. One would think then, that for a course intended to benefit Catholic teachers, the lecturers would be hand picked men and women, where Catholicity is concerned.

Looking through the names of the lecturers as advertised in the *Herald*, the Catholic reader gets one shock after another, and ends up with the only conclusion possible, that this course must be intended to indoctrinate our

Catholic teachers with the weirdest possible collection of ideas, covering the whole range of Catholic life and thought.

One thinks of the good parents who have made such heroic sacrifices to make possible the sending of their sons and daughters to a level of education that, in turn, makes admission to the teaching career within their grasp. One thinks of the parents in the years ahead who will make such sacrifices, to enable their children to receive education in a Catholic school, where, as they presume, Catholicism will be upheld. What a shock it will be for them when they realise, that instead of Catholicism, principles ranging from humanism to rank Protestantism will be engrafted in their children's' lives.

Let us examine the credentials of some of the lecturers under the heading of sound Catholicism. Catholicism, after all, by its nature, demands acceptance of Papal teaching, be it a solemn *ex-cathedra* doctrine, or the teaching of the Pope, as the Chief Teacher and a Shepherd of the whole flock. Subtle distinction between the type of obedience due to one or other of the Pope's teachings, is of little importance to the teacher that belongs to the theologian. In every case, respect and obedience to the Successor of St Peter, is part of Catholicism, and the Catholic's way of life.

But let us see some of the lecturers under this heading.

1. Bishop Butler the Auxiliary Bishop of Westminster has been described (by the progressive school of thought) as the 'best English theologian'. He may well be a man of genius in the realm of speculative theology, but in fact, he has caused great pain to millions of Catholics of this and other countries, by his attitude to the Papal Encyclical *Humanae Vitae*. His efforts to get his doctrine subordinated to the whims of a so-called conscience, his many subtle attacks (in *The Tablet* and on radio and television) to undermine its true impact on conscience and his sensational article in the *Sunday Times* have classified him, among many, as an outstanding 'liberal' theologian, whose principles put him fairly and squarely outside the border line of Catholicism. The many appeals of his Holiness to return to sanity of doctrine and acceptance of the Church's teaching on *Humanae Vitae* occasioned attacks on the paper itself.

   No Catholic parent can feel safe, if the Bishop is a lecturer on Church matters to their children. He is a theological hazard that one is not justified in facing.

   Father Richards – Former Head of *Corpus Christi* (now closed) has left the Priesthood and married a nun.

   Father De Rosa – Laicised – and married.

2. Father Peter de Rosa one of the signatories of the notorious *Humanae Vitae* letter to *The Times*, and later reprinted in *The Tablet,* 5 October 1968, guest speaker at many 'Teach Ins' up and down the country. Notorious for his doctrines on Original Sin, Baptism, etc., which cannot be reconciled with the official teaching of the Catholic Church.
3. Father Peter Harris. Distinguished by being co-author with other liberal thinkers, of a book opposed to *Humanae Vitae* – the very first anti-encyclical book published in this country.
4. Father Nicholas Lash an 'ultra progressive' writer and lecturer on many doctrines of the Church. Author of *His Presence in the World* – a book on the Eucharist full of inspired insights of the author, into the great mystery of the Eucharist – insights, however inspired, which do not reconcile with the teaching of the Catholic Church.
5. Norman St John Stevas the ubiquitous Pope Norman of *The Catholic Herald,* needs no introduction to readers, but he could well do with an introduction into the first principles of Catholic theology, a sphere in which he has set himself up as an expert, possessing a complete dossier on every movement of the Holy Spirit, and in fact, controlling the Holy Spirit's outpourings, which are only directed towards 'Progressives'. Norman's anti-papal attitude is as strong as the Reverend Ian Paisley's. In fact, it is surprising that this self styled Reverend gentlemen, is not also named, as one of the lecturers of Catholic teachers.

Other lecturers for the course are: Father Hubert Richards, principal of Corpus Christi College, Derek Lance, Jack Dominian etc.

We ask His Eminence the Cardinal, how tacit approval, which at least he must give in this matter, can be justified and how it can square with the primacy of teaching of the Pope, which he, the Cardinal as he declared on his return from the Roman Synod, he upholds, indeed, has never questioned.

Surely acceptance of the primacy of teaching from the lips of the Successor of Peter, must not be allowed to remain on paper. Let us see if proved in practice. Failure to act now, will mean the further escalation of error, which will annihilate the Catholic Faith in the hearts of many of our teachers, and cripple it in many others. Why continue to build so many schools, supposedly for Catholics, and under ever-increasing strain, and all we will get is the dead ashes of humanism and protestantism for our sacrifices.

THE MONSTER OF 'SENSITIVITY TRAINING' HAS REACHED OUR SHORES

The people of this country on opening their national newspapers on 28 October 1969 read, what to many of them must have appeared as a silly statement from the news reporters, that the BBC was to introduce 'SEX EDUCATION programmes for children of ten.'

Some papers seem to have taken it as a joke – 'Sex, but no love, for children at ten' read the heading of one national paper.

Next day the papers had letters, some for, some against, but none of the writers seemed to be aware, that the planned programmes, are not just education as we know it, in the matter of sex. The monster of 'Sensitivity Training' has crept into many countries, parading as an innocent form of education, that could be even taken by the innocent babes, without any harm to their minds or emotions. Let us see a little more about this new creation of evil men to lure to moral decadence and depravity the coming generation of men and women.

'Sensitivity Training' is known under several scores of names throughout the world, many of them innocent and apparently limited in their scope, so as to remove any suspicion from the minds of those interested. We find such titles as 'Group Dynamics', 'Group Confession', 'Group Discussion', 'Basic Encounter Groups', 'Self-Honest Sessions', 'Self-Evaluation Courses', 'Prayer Therapy', 'Auto-Criticism Groups', etc. , as just so many other names for what it is in principle, a BRAINWASHING SYSTEM evolved from the Brainwashing System practised by the Communists as early as 1919 and highly developed after the last war. It claims that it is intended to bring love, trust, openness of character, feeling for others and personal and social responsibility into the lives of people who are hedged about the accumulation of ages which prevent one from being oneself, and playing a part in bringing joy and happiness to others.

'Sensitivity Training' can, and in fact frequently does, link itself with Christian ideals and ways of life, in order to infiltrate, unsuspectingly, into the inner defences of the individual and society. It is at this time presented as something which gives 'depth' to our Catholicism, and which has a special appeal for Catholics who believe that the life of a Catholic should be an active one.

In Ireland, a movement known as the *CORSILLA MOVEMENT* started recently – attractive to the Irish temperament and character, and ostensibly, devoutly Catholic in its ideals, but its hidden nature cannot be concealed.

It is, as *Regina Notes,* July 1969, rightly points out 'just another form of 'Sensitivity Training', indeed, an insidious one, with the aim of creating secret apostasy, but parading under the guise of Catholicism that needs renewal, and a return to the true Catholicism that past ages had adulterated.' (*Revue de la Internaitornale,* p.21, August 1969.)

The full range of 'Sensitivity Training' cannot be described in this short article. Suffice it to say, that there is no part of a man's life that is too sacred for its intrusion.

As a political weapon, it is more dangerous than the hydrogen bomb, as it enslaves man from within himself. In his social, educational, emotional, political and religious life, this devilish service takes over every personal secret, every fear, every worry, every respected desire, every act for which one is ashamed, which must be trotted out, handled and pawed, by a group acting through its tyrannical dictator.

Man becomes in his entire life, down to the very depths of his soul, the utter slave of this monster from HADES.

We are only concerned with 'Sensitivity Training' now being imported to this country under the label of 'Sex Education', one of the group's most successful exports. It is a course that is mushrooming all over the world and is being swallowed wholesale by gullible educationalists and politicians, doctors and health visitors, lawyers and clergymen – as the greatest discovery of the age. Let us see something of the principles and practice in this new science.

What is to follow may seem like a dialogue from within the walls of an asylum for the insane, but, unfortunately, it is coming from the writings, talks, lectures, etc., of organisations and individuals, dedicated to spread this nightmare far and wide in the world.

Picture one of the classical scenes which are identified with the workings of this 'Group Dynamics', a 'mini-form' of which is now being prepared for our British schools once the 'softening up' campaign has been completed by the BBC in its coming radio and television programmes.

'Imagine the hefty body of a big man jumping about the room like a ballet dancer . . . A nun describing her daily battle with her sexual desires . . . A business executive is dissolved into tears . . . A Church member with a group of fifteen men and women in a circle, who touch hands and close their eyes.

Soon they begin to sway, and movements get hectic and basic. Bodies writhe against each other, hands explore the roughness of jeans, the softness of the female face, the coarseness of the masculine face . . . In half an hour, the group collapses in a heap . . . No one is agreed on what they got out of the experience, but all are sure — that whatever it was — it was exhilarating, joyful, renewing — and religious in nature.'

The above description (*Sensitivity Training,* by Gary Allen) is only a mild example of what happens in the 'Group Dynamics' after long training under their leader. They feel 'renewed and religious' after the event!

The conversation and chatter among the group (which is generally about fifteen in number) which goes on during and after the groups meetings is not that which one associates with adults who are supposedly seeking self-improvement and desires of bringing relief to mankind. In a letter paragraph of this article, the reader will be given some examples taken from real life of this movement.

During the 'Confession Group' seance, a member is not permitted to defend, excuse or conceal his or her most secret self, in any way. Coming at a time when our liberal theologians and writers are advocating the urgent need to abolish auricular confession to a priest, and replace it all with the general acknowledgement of guilt before the community — such as is contained in the *Confiteor* — this new movement with its insistence on the absolute need of nakedness of soul (and body) to all and sundry, is not setting an example of logic.

The importance of bodily nakedness in the 'groups' search for truth, self expression, and dedication to the service of others, is not just something which remains on paper as a requirement. Complete dissolving of male and female members contributes much, according to the advocates of 'Sensitivity Training', to the necessary stripping away of the veneer that surrounds the real identity of each person.

The many personal and social 'taboos' which have covered the genuine person, and which prevents him from knowing himself as he is, and from realising his duties to society, must be ruthlessly removed. Nakedness of body without shame or self-consciousness if the first step in the search for discovery of self.

It is to be expected that in a philosophy of this kind, the sacredness and intimacy of sex life could not be tolerated — it must go, and go quickly. Hence the need to indoctrinate the children at the earliest age with the new ideas on sexuality. Capture the soul and mind of the young — as early as possible — subject to its demands of 'modern research' and 'new insights in human behaviour — and the battle for the souls of men will be war. Did not Lenin or Trotsky, as early as 1919, insist the corruption of the young — getting them away from religion, fixating them with sex and making them superficial — were the first steps to the creation of a 'new society', a new world, a 'utopia'! Many writers who view the international situation today, where the undermining of morals and the destruction of religion are concerned, believe that the red hand of Communism is to be found in all those turmoils. Who knows? Perhaps those writers such as George Schuyler, Gerry Allen, and Father Francis Fenton, etc., are right when they declare this universal moral decadence as engineered by Communist Russia, in her efforts to destroy Christianity and Western civilisation.

If anyone thinks that the 'Sex Instruction for Children' idea which has now manifested itself in this country, and which the BBC is so anxious to publicise, through the medium of radio and television, is an innocuous and necessary matter, they have a lot to learn. The 'Instruction Course' starting at ten years of age ('far too late to start' – write two Health Visitors, in the *Daily Telegraph,* 29 October 1969) and containing a full description of everything connected with sex, is not something which is native to this country.

Our children do not reach puberty at 10 or 12 as they do in some countries (e.g. Egypt) and so one gets suspicious of the course, from this very fact. It is well known, that advocates of early sex education from the infamous American society known as SIECUS (Sex Information and Education Council of the United States) have long been pressing for a similar establishment in this country, and indeed, every country.

It looks like their efforts have met with success – if popular opinion and the influence of the Christian Churches in Britain fail to prevent the promised BBC programme. At this stage some extracts from the statements and writings of SIECUS may help to give members of the Catholic Priests Association in this country, some idea of what is in store for their young parishioners.

The director of SIECUS (Dr Mary Calderone) speaking to 320 boys in an American school some months ago, said 'What is sex for? It is for fun . . . for wonderful sensations . . . Sex is not something you turn off like a tap – if you do it is unhealthy'.

When a student asked, what the doctor thought of pre-marital intercourse between teenagers? she replied, 'What do you think of it? Nobody from on high (God) determines this. You determine it. I do not believe the old "Thou shalt not anymore"'. Doctor Calderone believes that 'sex instruction should start for children at the age of three. Around this age, the kiddies should assimilate this knowledge, and with the right terminology'.

As this *Newsletter* is read by many lay people, I prefer to put in Latin what Doctor Calderone said: '*Pueri-infantes, instrui debeant de modo que spermatozoa patus in vaginam matris injiciuntur permembrum virile*'. *Sex Education Problems,* by Gary Allen.

So, nothing is hidden from the child of three years, nothing is concealed. Dr Calderone leaves decisions, on pre-marital intercourse between teenagers to the glands of her young listeners — God must have no say in the conduct of His creatures, as the moral law is 'out'.

The technique of the advocates of the 'New Morality' to get into schools and institutions is very simple — it is the old *fait accompli* move of 'do it first, and explain later' if necessary. Dr Kirkendall writes on this point — 'Don't say you are going to start a sex education course. Always move first. Say, you are going to enrich, expand and make better, to parents and others, who might object. Bypass them'. Parents who object are 'sexual deviants . . . who do not think rationally'. (*Triumph*, p.p. 12-13 Oct. 1969).

Some of their methods employed by *Sensitivity Training* experts in children and teenagers' groups are so disgusting and revolting, that it would be offensive to pious eyes to read about them. At the same time, priests need to be aware of the extent to which this so-called education has gone, in view of protecting their own flock against this monster of immorality, rightly called the *Manichaeism of the Twentieth Century* (*Triumph* Oct. 1969). (Hence a few crude examples *In lingua latina pro Sacerdotibus* may not be out of place.)

Children are not just taught the facts of life in a manner becoming their age and degree of maturity they may have acquired. *Sex Skill* is incalculated as most important, and four letter words are unscrupulously used by the devotees of this system. I quote from a photostatic copy of a student's notes from the Christian Family Living and Sexuality Course given at the Immaculate Heart of Mary School, St Louis, U.S.A., where fifth grade children were instructed in the meaning of terms that are certainly not clinical. (*Pro Sacerdotibus* — Instructor *studentibus proponit quadrum verba organis sexualibus connexa, et explicit singnificationem verborum*, e.g., 'f . . k', 's . . k' *(anglice); in in hoc ultimo instrucot dixit Puella labiis suis sugit organa sexualia pueri, et hic sugit organa puella).* Just imagine what a victory for Satan in a Catholic School dedicated to the Immaculate Heart of Mary!

Yes, it is not just a question of knowledge, but of practical skill as well.

Many incidents are reported from the home of 'Sensitivity Training' of parents discovering their children or the children next door, trying out their newly acquired knowledge in a practical way.

No wonder that the *Daily Telegraph* (4 Nov. 1969) gives a news item, quoting a member of Birmingham Education committee as saying in reference to the coming BBC Sex Programmes — 'When we teach children in the schools to read and do arithmetic, you tell them, "Now go and practise it". When you give the children sex instruction, do you say "Don't practice it?" 'And what happens if you don't tell them that?'

Children are not just taught the facts of life, but every possible sex perversion, many of them too shuddering to human conscience, even to outline, are given in all their crudeness, to children of both sexes. Are they taught that these perversions are immoral and to be avoided like a plague? Oh certainly not! On the contrary, they are taught that they are 'natural' 'unavoidable', 'harmless', etc. Again it is not knowledge that is left on paper or on the school blackboard. It is imparted as a 'skill'. Several American papers and journals refer to 'life-sized plastic *phallus*' that boys and girls take home from school for their homework. Solitary sexual activities and the indulgence in mutual sex offences, are not only condoned, but encouraged 'for the relief of tensions . . . they are almost a universal practice among healthy boys and girls', writes one of SIECUS (pronounced Seek Us) principle sexologists. *(Sex Education Problem,* p.p. 10-11 by Gary Allen.)

The desensitisation programmes have only one purpose in Catholic schools – to kill conscience and make the sex act, an act of raw instinct, as natural and as common as to eat, drink and sleep.

SHARED CHURCH

by Father John W. Flanagan   From *Newsletter,* (Sept./Dec. 1970)

On June 20 of this year, there was televised (BBC 1) a Mass from the 'Shared Church' near Slough, Bucks. , which must have brought tears to those who watched it.

Father Woodard was the celebrant and much of the liturgy was 'instant manufacture', that is, not found in any text book of Sacred Liturgy. Communion was given in the hand – though this practice is not as yet approved by the Holy See for this country. Children licked the 'lolly-pop' particles, before chewing them. Perhaps it is, that I am all wrong in describing this as a Mass, as I failed to see any Consecration, and others who also watched it, had the same report to give. I sent a strongly worded letter of protest to Bishop Grant of Northampton diocese, but received no acknowledgement.

I sent a copy of the same letter to Father Woodard and received a courteous reply, in which he stated that the Bishop had given full approval to this same ceremony, which he rehearsed before him, previous to the televising of it. Mass without Consecration is becoming more prevalent in recent months - I have heard of other such cases and have documented evidence of this happening outside Britain. It is supposed to be 'more ecumenical' and overcomes the 'problems of inter-communion'. One may ask the question – what of those people who think they are assisting at a true Mass, to satisfy their Sunday obligation, and who worship the bread they receive as Communion?

Is not someone guilty of not only permitting, but fostering sacrilege and idolatry?

THE CLERGY REVIEW

Once a reliable and orthodox monthly publication for the clergy, this continues to sink below the level that one expects of such a publication. The scholarly articles which once characterised it, and made it a review of world repute, have long vanished, and have been replaced by the 'new theology' of the progressives. The July issue of the *Review* has an Editorial entitled 'On Not Contemplating Our Navels', in which it is stated – 'If the Catholic Priests Association and the *Pro Fide* Movement were more interested in correcting the errors of the unbelievers, than in accusing other Catholics of heresy, they would be doing us all a real service, instead of providing a tiresome distraction'. That is precisely, Father Richards, what the Catholic Priests Association and *Pro Fide* Movement are trying to do – trying to correct the errors of unbelievers' who, as Archbishop Murphy pointed out in the *Universe*, 2 July, continue to stay within the church and 'eat it'. Father Richards should know, if he is awake to the present age, that unlike former times, many Catholics today insist on staying within the Church, though rejecting its doctrines which are essential for membership.

In the same Editorial, Father Richards has no censure for the 'Renewalists' Movement, who if it continues to 'give renewal to the world, and is not for improving other Catholics all is well and good.'

What rubbish to have published in any paper!

Is Father Richards not aware that the 'Renewalists' reject many of the fundamental doctrines of the Catholic Church; and emphasise the urgency of getting rid of many of the moral laws which inhibit the sexual life of man?

It is the 'Renewalists' who contemplate the navels, and yet, the Editor of the *Clergy Review* has no censure for them.

The sooner the clergy of Britain have a new and sound monthly publication, the better for the preservation of the Catholic Church in our country.

CATECHETICAL CENTRES & TEACHERS' TRAINING COLLEGES

Several appeals have been sent by the Secretary of the Catholic Priests' Association to Cardinal Heenan, asking if he would kindly establish a competent tribunal of priests, to investigate the many changes of unorthodoxy of doctrine emanating from our Catechetical Centres and Teachers' Training Colleges. He has been assured that abundant evidence would be supplied to such a tribunal, that the charges recently published in the Catholic Press and the pages of this Newsletter, were not without foundation.

The Cardinal has not replied to these requests, but has, as readers will recall, given a statement to the press, that the trouble is not one of unorthodoxy in doctrine, but only new expressions for old doctrines, that people are not accustomed to, as yet, or which some resent.

As Secretary of the Association I sent the following case to the Cardinal, asking him if this would be an example of 'new expressions'. The quotation is from the booklet *Preparing Our Children For The Sacraments* by Peggy Janiwreck, and is of *The Living Parish Series* with a *Nihil Obslat* from Monsignor Barton of the Westminster diocese and an *Imprimatur* from the then Auxiliary Bishop Casey (now Bishop of Brentwood). On page 12 we read the following:-

'But we still come to the central question for the child who has already accepted that the bread and wine will change into the body and blood of Christ, and then asks – 'But why do we want to eat Jesus?' One answer is fairly acceptable – how often a loved small child has been hugged and heard his parent say – 'You are so nice I could eat you.' The other answer lies in the fact, that as Baptism points towards the Last Anointing, Holy Communion points forward not only and obviously, towards Holy Order, but also to matrimony. The sex act of love is when human beings attempt to penetrate each others bodies, in order to signify their oneness. It is not surprising that the married Communicant may find woven into his or her thanksgiving, the very phrases he uses at the height of the sexual act of love.'

I pointed out to the Cardinal that if words mean anything, this book means that the best way to prepare children for Holy Communion is to teach them the sex act and what it means, and that this doctrine is supported by the ecclesiastics of his diocese, who give it the *Nihil Obstat* and the subsequent *Imprimatur*.

The Cardinal replied that I had misunderstood the matter, as the book was written for adults and not for children.

What an extraordinary conclusion!

Do words mean anything anymore? So it is all right to instruct adults on Holy Communion by referring to the sex act.

TRAGIC STORY OF FATHER DURYEA

He was a Vatican II priest, no question; Folk Masses, a strong parish Council . . . Last week the rest of the country found out, what some of his parishioners had known for months – that the pretty woman and five-year old-boy, who occasionally worshipped at the Father's Mass, were none other than his wife and son. (*Time,* 26 April, 1971.)

This tragic and sickening story of Father Duryea, the American priest who continued to exercise his ministry for five years after his marriage and who called his son Paul because he was born on the day that Pope Paul arrived in the United States, is referred to in the following account.

The account tells of the factors that lead to his marriage – his constant ecumenical activities with ministers of other religions who were married, the strong support he received from laity who were greatly influenced by the results of findings of various commissions and 'opinion polls' as to the burden of celibacy, etc., etc.

The said case of Father Duryea has its re-echoes all over the world.' Commissions', 'Councils', 'experts', 'Pastoral Councils' and a multiplicity of other groupings of priests and laity continue the democratisation of a Church, that by its origin and nature, was never intended to be such.

How often has Pope Paul insisted that Revealed Religion comes to us from above – from on high and not from the ranks of the Faithful. *Collegiality* between the Pope and Bishops has now been extended to every sphere of Catholic life and activity. Parish priests have fettered themselves or successors, with chains of collectivism, and are often reduced to inertia, depending upon the whims of the Parish Council. Bishops, often depending on so-called expert advice, wind up by turning to men and groups of men, who are basically in sympathy with renewal in the 'modernistic' sense of the word.

The men and women who create position papers, plan *curricula,* conduct conferences and seminars, write text books, catechisms, teachers' manuals and the like, are almost invariably the product of progressive thinking and training schools, and before long, they control the Bishop's thoughts and decisions, directing them along the modernistic lines.

These are the men and women who are dedicated to force the Church to accept a change entirely incompatible with Her Divine nature and origin; these people will bend the Church to adapt itself to the maxims of the world.

Do not think for a moment that we have seen the worst years in the post-conciliar battle for the allegiance of men's hearts in the struggle between orthodoxy and modernism, nothing of the kind. The infamous *National Catholic Reporter* (11 Dec. 1970) which has been the instrument for spreading neo-modernisation in many parts of the world, has declared that there is 'nothing in sight that can stop further progress, except perhaps the unwillingness of Catholic Renewalists to see their opportunities, and shoulder the burden that opportunity brings'. Orthodoxy needs every human effort that can be used, together with prayer, sacrifice and alms deeds, if the EVIL ONE is to be cast out of the Church.

We are not living in a conflict of ideologies, but in a conflict between God and Satan. Many reflective people think that Antichrist may well be on the earth, conducting the campaign for the destruction of the Church.

May we remind all Catholics of the words of the Saviour – 'He that is not with me, is against me.'

INDIRECT ASSAULT ON MASS AND HOLY COMMUNION

It is remarkable how swiftly the progressives are winning the battle for the desacralisation of the Mass and Holy Communion. No frontal assaults – these only create unnecessary opposition. No – the plan is indirect assault, downgrade the Mass and The Eucharist, give Communion in the hand, give endless concessions to the faithful, where Mass and the Sacrament are concerned. If a person receives the Host frequently enough into his or her own hand, before long, it will be considered as common bread; if the priest is enticed to cut down or cut out the reverences to the Eucharist, time will create in his mind the doubt as to what it is he handles.

Two good people have just returned from a 'fact finding' tour of Europe, and what they experienced makes nightmarish reading. In West Germany, a man from the congregation in his lay garb distributes Communion in the hand; in another instance common loaves are consecrated and devoured by all present, after being pulled to bits by dirty hands.

There was no effort made to show any respect for the large crumbs which fell to the floor. They became part of the next floor sweepings to be put in the dustbin.

In many dioceses of the UK., Pastoral Councils have voted for the introduction of Communion in the hand, and Bishops have taken their votes as representing that of the people.

These Pastoral Councils are packed with Renewalists and their fellow travellers, and any other result would not be expected.

FURTHER EXTRACTS FROM THE *NEWSLETTER* 125

PUBLISHED DOCUMENT BY HIERARCHY
on ACCEPTANCE
of BAPTISM WHEN CONFERRED in OTHER CHURCHES

The recently published document by the Hierarchy on the acceptance of Baptism when conferred in other Christian Churches, has caused much anxiety. One cannot help feeling that it creates in Britain, at least, too strong a presumption that Baptism conferred by the generality of Christian ministers, is valid.

No doubt a conscientious Catholic priest, in dealing with an individual case, will take no risks, and will rebaptise *sub-conditione*, if any reasonable doubt remains.

But living as we are in an ecumenical atmosphere, where so many priests seem to be bending over backwards in an effort to justify everything that is done in other Churches, one cannot help feeling that this document on Baptism has gone too far. One can bend over so much to facilitate other Churches, that theological ruptures take place, endangering the purity of Catholic Doctrine, and where Baptism is concerned the whole Sacramental life of one received into the Church. To illustrate our point we give the following cases:-

Mrs X. , the widow of the late Canon X. and Anglican Vicar for over 40 years, wrote to me, on reading the Hierarchial decision on Baptism and said *inter alia*, that her late husband never used water for Baptism on cold days, as he believed it gave a chill to the child. He blesses the one to be baptised instead, tracing the sign of the cross on its forehead with his thumb. Mr Y. an ex-Anglican minister and later convert, wrote to say, that for many years of his ministry, he did not pour the baptismal water, but signed the childs head with a moist finger.

These are only two cases, but they must be multiplied very many times throughout the country, by ministers who did not believe baptism was a Sacrament or who did not believe that water should be poured.

Of course, our advocates of the 'new theology' will tell us that we are falling back on senseless hairsplitting theology of the past which is now discredited.

If Christ established Sacraments – and what Catholic can doubt it – then what he instituted must be observed under penalty of invalidity, if essentials are not observed.

It is not a question of hairsplitting, but of observing what Christ instituted.

THE RIGHT REVEREND D. WORLOCK
The Bishop of Portsmouth, sent me, through the Bishop of Arundel and

Brighton, the following correction to a report which appeared in April – June issue of this *Newsletter,* p.70, under the heading of Sacrilegious Desecration.

'In the place of a temporary wooden altar in the Cathedral, a stone altar is being erected for the main sanctuary, and a further stone altar in the Blessed Sacrament Chapel. Stations of the cross have not been removed, but have been cleaned and are now in position. Thousands of pounds given to the Church by the sacrifices of the faithful have not been used to turn the Cathedral into a Social Centre; there is a social centre next door which serves the many social needs of the city. The money being spent on the Cathedral is money that has been raised specifically for the purpose of renovating the Cathedral.'

The Cathedral referred to, is, of course, St John's Cathedral, Portsmouth. The report published in the April – June issue of the *Newsletter* came from our Social Correspondent who visited the Cathedral in the process of reconstruction.

Before going to publication, the report was confirmed by more than one priest of the Portsmouth Diocese, as an accurate account. No doubt, a report published in the *Portsmouth News,* Thursday 28 January, 1971, as to the extent and nature of the work of renovation may have been misleading, though the material of it, was supplied by the Administrator of the Cathedral, Father David Mahy. This press report states, quoting Father Mahy that – the project is aimed at giving the Church an atmosphere and a design appropriate to modern worship and outlook. A Church building should be a 'home'. A home should be a place where we are proud to bring our friends. It must be lived-in, as comfortable and attractive as our circumstances allow us to make it.'

The Editor of *Newsletter* can only conclude, that if the above words mean anything, convey the impression that the Cathedral was being turned into a 'home' where one is proud to bring one's friends – and where one lives.

On receiving this corrected report from the Bishop of Portsmouth I asked our Special Correspondent to revisit the Cathedral and report again. His second report stated, 'Some change of heart seems to have come over those responsible, and the Stations of the Cross are back again. The Cathedral still shows its disharmony, by an effort to modernise the interior, that is a neo-Gothic building. One cannot see the Tabernacle from the body of the Cathedral – it is tucked away in the Canon's Chapel. It offends my sense of what a place or worship should be – and this is not just my opinion.'

THE *PRO FIDE MOVEMENT*
by Father John W. Flanagan   From *Newsletter*, (Jan. 1970)

History repeats itself. We may witness again in the Church of our time, the laity, being the instrument used by God to protect His Church from dangerous doctrines, as happened during the Arian heresy of the fourth century. The laity through the Sacrament of Confirmation are 'Soldiers of Christ' and hence, must be ready to fight for the Church. The author of an article *The Church in Travail*, (Church Publishers, Ramsgate 1970) rightly states:-

> Loyal Catholics everywhere should make up and rise in wrath against these destroyers of the Faith. How can the Holy Father know the loyalty of these countless Catholics the world over, if they remain mute, when loyalty demands that they should speak out?'

For that reason we welcome the formation of the *PRO FIDE MOVEMENT* – an Association of lay people, formed to defend orthodoxy within the Church, against the inroads of those who claim to be within the Church, but whose activities and doctrines are in conflict with Papal teaching.

The movement is not opposed to legitimate change and development, sanctioned by the Authority of the Church, but to the unwarranted innovations in doctrine and practice, introduced by those of whatever school of thought they belong, who are advancing unbridled individualism in the Church and causing great harm to souls.

The *PRO FIDE MOVEMENT* deserves the complete support of all Catholics loyal to the Holy Father and to orthodoxy. The time has come when every Catholic has a duty to abandon indifference and apathy and come out strongly and firmly on the side of the Church's teaching and practice. Away with the excuse of being 'divisive' and 'extremists' – these are handy and useful excuses for those who wish to advance Modernism in the Church, or who are obviously deficient in moral courage.

The *PRO FIDE MOVEMENT* can be helped to grow in strength by every priest in our Association giving it support in every possible way – the formation of a group in your parish, linking up with other groups in nearby area, etc., etc.

Contact the Chairman Major Patrick Wall M.P., 92 Cheyne Walk, London SW10. Those who would be prepared actively to help in organising the Movement locally, make contact as soon as possible. As the Catholic Priests' Association has 'associate members' from the laity, so too, the PRO FIDE MOVEMENT has 'associated members' from the ranks of the clergy.

With a solid front of priests and laity spread throughout every part of the land, the defence of the Church in the stormy days of our life, should negate to a great extent, the attacks of the enemies of the Church. We must never forget however, that this work can only come from us, as a result of our own efforts to be spiritually perfect. Hence, no defence of the Church is conceivable, unless it comes from those whose hearts and minds are dedicated to the service of God.

The pursuit of our own spiritual perfection, must always be the first step in our defence of the Church. Hence, the need of constant prayer, meditation, spiritual exercises, visit to the Blessed Sacrament, and frequent confession, to build up our own resistance against the evil one, lest while we indulge in much activity for the Church, the Citadel of our Soul should fall to the cunning devices of the Devil. Make no mistake, the universal attack on the Church today has originated in some Mastermind and it would be stretching credulity too much, to ask anyone to believe, that the mind is purely human. We must face the moment of truth. If the PRO FIDE MOVEMENT is not quickly built up into a strong and active body of men and women, prepared to sacrifice something for the Church of God, the prospects of the Church surviving as an organised body of the faithful in this country, are gloomy indeed.

IT IS NOW OR NEVER!

THE KEYS OF PETER

The magazine of the PRO FIDE MOVEMENT will have to sell thousand more copies if it is to survive – it must not be permitted to perish. I ask you, I beg of you, to initiate the PRO FIDE in your parish as soon as possible. Like the Priests' Association the PRO FIDE MOVEMENT is merely the voluntary collaboration of loyal Catholics among themselves, in defence of orthodoxy.

It does not need Episcopal approval, as it seeks no status in the Church. No Bishop's permission is needed to join with fellow

Catholics (or with fellow priests) in defence of the Church – this right and duty comes to us all from the Sacrament of Confirmation, by which we become 'Soldiers of Christ'.

Please give immediate attention to this pressing need. The faithful need to be strengthened by mutual collaboration.

Please act quickly – every week counts in our warfare with evil.

For *KEYS OF PETER* – Contact MR RONALD KING
4 BOSCOMBE AVENUE
LONDON E10

We recommend to our readers, to read the work of John Epstein *Has the Catholic Church Gone Mad, The Papal Magisterium and Humanae Vitae* by Father Joseph Costanzo, S. J., and a *Dossier on Catechetics* by Michael Davies – and *Approaches* a study document from Approaches, 1 Waverley Place, Saltcoats, Ayrshire, Scotland.

Still obtainable from *Newsletter* is 'The Evolution and Crisis Catholicism in the Netherlands' by Father Van der Ploeg, O. P.

HANDS KEUNG'S NOTORIOUS BOOK *INFALLIBLE*
by Father John W. Flanagan   From C.P.A. *Newsletter,* (Sept./Dec. 1970)

Rejected by several of the continental Hierarchies (e.g. French and German, etc.) this is being sold in the bookshop run by the Sisters of St Paul in Liverpool.

So states *The Catholic Pictorial,* 11 July, 1971. It adds, moreover that the sale of the book is being done 'with permission of Archbishop Beck.' The book was sold for some period of time, inside the doors of Westminster Cathedral, until pressure from laity forced its withdrawal. It was the Sisters of St Paul who were asked to sell Father Van der Ploeg's *Evolution and Crisis in Catholicism in the Netherlands* written by one of the Catholic Church's most learned and loyal sons, and with 100 per cent profit on every booklet. Every one of these letters sent to their convents or attached to their bookstalls in this country, failed to bring even a courteous acknowledgment.

We do not blame the good sisters, who are so often 'pawns in the hands of ecclesiastics who have sold themselves to Modernism'. This is where the blame must lie.

It must also lie on the shoulders of the Archbishop of Liverpool, if the report published in the *Catholic Pictorial* is true, and there has been no refutation of it to the best of my knowledge.

Elsewhere in this *Newsletter* a review will be published of this appalling book by Hans Keung, and a text of our letter to the Hierarchy of Britain, asking them to make sure that it receives no circulation in this country.

Received also, is Norman St John Stevas' book *The Agonising Choice'* dedicated to 'Hans Keung for his courageous Christian witness and fidelity to the Catholic and Roman Church.'

What a prostitution of truth!

Readers of *Newsletter* cannot be unaware, that Norman St John Stevas, hailed by so many as the champion of the Catholic Church in its condemnation of abortion, and privileged to 'read a lesson' at the installation of Bishop Casey, as Bishop of Brentwood, because of his 'defence of the unborn', is in fact in conflict with the official teaching of the Church on abortion and sterilisation, as he is on contraception.

His views on abortion are summarised on page 319 of his book, where he writes – 'The rights of a foetus should only be taken away, when they cause a conflict with other rights, such as those of the mother, or for some over-riding reason, such as the likelihood of the child being deformed.'

This Doctrine is in violent conflict with the Church's official teaching, that any 'direct action' which tends to destroy the uterine life is sinful and criminal.

Norman St John Stevas' defence of the Catholic Church teaching on abortion, is very limited indeed, and his justification for interference with the uterine life of the child that may be born deformed, as clearly stated in the above reference, is directly contrary to the Church's interpretation of the law of God on the sanctity of human life.

Mr Stevas has not modified in any way, the interpretation he gave *Humanae Vitae* in the pages of the 'Catholic Herald' following the publication of the Encyclical. As stated in the Introduction (p. 9) of the *Agonising Choice*, 'the view on birth control which informs this book, sometimes explicitly, but more often implicitly, is, that Catholics should be free to decide according to their own conscience, what method of birth control to employ.'

So, Mr Norman St John Stevas rejects the *Magisterium* of the Church in its ruling on this vitally important matter.

He rejects, what more and more unbiased theologians are coming to recognise as an infallible doctrine taught by the Ordinary Magisterium of the Church. *(Papal Magisterium and Humanae Vitae* – by Father Joseph Constanzo S. J., p. 140). Even this fact was rejected, and one denied its infallible nature, it is still the authentic teaching of the Church, through the Vicar of Christ, and consequently the 'religious submission of mind and will' which the constitution on the Church of Vatican II demanded for such a decision – should be given. Mr St John Stevas – who so often reminds his readers in the pages of the *Catholic Herald* that Vatican II had reformed the Church and rejoices in it being 'The Council' – throws to the winds the very same Council's explicit teaching, that on matters of birth control, as on any other – 'Spouses must be aware, that they cannot proceed arbitrarily, but must always be governed according to a conscience, dutifully confined to the divine law, and submissive to the Church's teaching office, authentically interpreting that law, in the light of the Gospel'. (*Church in the Modern World*, par. 50.)

It is clear from what has been said, that Norman St John Stevas does not accept Vatican II, except when its teachings agree with his. This is not the behaviour of a Catholic, and in the light of Pope Paul's statement (Nov. 14 1968) that 'No one is entitled to accept the label of a 'Catholic', without its contents – this would not be honest.'

To be a Catholic, means the sincere and total profession of the Faith, of which She has the deposit, and the joyful acceptance of the living *Magisterium* which Christ conferred on Her.' It follows that Mr Norman St John Stevas has no title to be considered a Catholic. One who teaches at variance with the Church in such basic moral matters as contraception, abortion and sterilisation, cannot be the possessor of orthodox Catholicism.

How two such books as Keung's *Infallible* and Stevas *The Agonising Choice* can be sold and distributed in Catholic shops, is difficult to explain. Still more difficult is it to explain the failure, (up to the time of going to print of this *Newsletter*) of the Bishops to intervene and issue a statement, that these books may not be read by Catholics, notwithstanding the last Apostolic Appeal by the Holy Father (8 December 1970) to the Bishops of the world to, 'defend the orthodoxy of doctrine in this diocese'. Keung's book incidentally, is not just a denial of the doctrine of Papal Infallibility, but of practically every doctrine of the Church.

CORPUS CHRISTI CATECHETICAL CENTRE

The announcement through the Catholic Information Office (2.8.1971) that Cardinal Heenan has disclosed the unsatisfactory situation existing in Corpus Christi Catechetical Centre, and that so many parents and priests were critical of the modern methods of religious education, brought one ray of hope.

The statement also disclosed that Father Peter de Rosa and Father Perry of the College Staff, signatories of the letter published in *The Times*, against the Papal Encyclical on birth control, has resigned from the college, before July 1, when the Cardinal had a full discussion with the staff, will of necessity, bring much speculation and not a little satisfaction. Corpus Christi has been from the beginning a centre of 'New theology', and the indoctrination of young teachers and nuns over the years past, with Modernism at its worst, has been outstanding feature of this college.

We hope that the Cardinal has at last come to realise, that it was not just 'new expressions' or 'new methods' in teaching, that was at stake. We also hope that the Cardinal and other Churchmen will take appropriate steps to undo some of the spiritual harm caused to so many, during their studies at Corpus Christi.

EXIT FATHER DE ROSA

Within a few weeks of Cardinal Heenan declaring the reorganisation of Corpus Christi and the wish of Father de Rosa and Perry to take up other appointments, has come the news, that Father de Rosa is leaving the priesthood. The *Daily Telegraph* in fact informs us, that the decision to leave the priesthood was given to Cardinal Heenan, as early as June 11, and of course American and Canadian papers had the news of return to the lay state, weeks before it was announced here.

The departure of any priest from the priesthood, is a sad and depressing event, particularly in Father de Rosa's case. The reason for his departure was his unpreparedness to accept the teaching of the Papal Encyclical *Humanae Vitae*.

It is not surprising that many of the original 55 signatories to the infamous letter to *The Times*, declaring their dissent, have now abandoned the priesthood, and some of them, according to reports, have abandoned their Catholic faith, or substituted a Catholicism of their own making.

One often wonders, if the blame for these priestly defections, should not be fairly and squarely placed on the shoulders of ecclesiastics in higher positions, who quibbled and shuffled in their acceptance of this ancient teaching of the Church.

The great mistake was made, in far too many cases, of creating for those priests an atmosphere where a dual priestly personality seems to have been encouraged. As long as they refrained from openly teaching or propounding doctrine contrary to *Humanae Vitae*, they were permitted by their Bishops to continue the ministry and retain their office in the Church. How could such priests be honest with themselves in this situation? How could they be honest, with God in the exercise of their Godly Ministry?

The Church's law, dealing with such a situation was ignored by the Bishops, but the Church's law is still in force, and it makes it mandatory on Bishops, to remove such priests from their office (Can.2317) and such priests should be punished with suitable penalties (Can.2331).

The Church has the accumulated wisdom of centuries and knows how to deal with dissidents.

As a consequence of permitting Father de Rosa to continue as the theologian of Corpus Christi College – where he was the source not only of doctrine contrary to the Church's teaching on contraception, but also the authority behind many of the strange doctrines on other matters emanating from this college – numerous teachers, including Religious Sisters, will continue for a long time to carry his errors into the classrooms of our Catholic schools. It is a tragedy that so many young people who entered the college with souls aglow for the work of the Church on earth, should leave it, with minds full of ideas and doctrines contrary to the teachings of the Church, to which they had dedicated their lives. Someone, somewhere, must take the blame for the spread of this Modernism among the young – and we know what Christ Himself has said to those, who shall scandalise the little ones.

It is too late to ask all Bishops to put the Church's law into practice, which demands of them the removal from office of priests, who refuse to accept the teachings of the Church or the Pope. Until they do so, we can expect constant recurrence of the tragedy of Corpus Christi.

A VERY IMPORTANT AND INFORMATIVE EDITORIAL
by Father John W. Flanagan   *Newsletter,* (Jan.-Mar. 1972)

Since the last issue of this *Newsletter* was sent to its readers there have been some signs of improvement on the horizon.

The firm stand by Pope Paul to uphold obligatory celibacy at the Roman Synod, and the strong support he received from the Bishops present, has given heart to those who are fighting against Modernism in the Church. But the war is not over, as is clear from the immediate reactions of the liberals to the decision on celibacy.

Our own Catholic papers referred to the 'Silent Synod' and depicted the brokenhearted Bishops returning to their dioceses with nothing for their people. The *Tablet* in particular followed its usual trend during and after the Synod, of giving much space to well-known 'left wing' elements in the Church. The outpourings of this section of the Community can always be traced to the IDO-C offices in the Hotel Alicorni, very near St Peter's Basilica in Rome.

In this office, a panel of 'experts' gave a daily comment on the latest information coming from the Synod.

As could be expected, the 'experts' seldom found anything with which they could agree, but this is not surprising considering that three of these 'leading experts' were Abbe Rene Laurentin, Father Francis Xavier Murphy C.S.S.R. and Father Bernard Haering, C.S.S.R. How St Alphonsus Ligouri must turn in his grave, with such priests in congregation!

Father Peter Hepplewaite*, S.J., Editor of the *Month* was never far away, anxious to gather up any fragments of news that could be jigsawed together, to give a picture of hope to the Modernists.

Father Peter has long been obsessed with an *identity crisis* where the priesthood is concerned.

With nearly 2000 years having elapsed since the Institution of the Priesthood, he still seems to be unable to make up his mind, whether the priesthood today is for carrying out the Christ-given Divine Command – 'Do ye this in commemoration of Me' – or, whether the priesthood's charter is to be found in the words of St Paul, 'All things to all men.'

In an article written by him for the *Pittsburgh Catholic,* 22 October 71, he laments, that the author of the words 'Identity Crisis', Eric Erikson, was not quoted by the Fathers of the Synod in their discussions. We find no reference to Father Peter Hepplewaite, lamenting the drift away, from quoting St Peter's successor, as to the nature and function of the Sacred Priesthood.

The IDO-C cell, operating from the Hotel Alicorni during the Synod, and which continues, even outside the time of Synods, to spread its poison into the World's press, has one main purpose – to destroy the Roman Catholic Church and all it stands for. This fact is incontestable. The sooner that the IDO-C is condemned for its evil designs by the highest authority in the Church, the sooner will orthodoxy be restored to its rightful position in the Church, and respect for, and obedience to, the Holy See be restored.

Total war on obligatory celibacy was launched by the IDO-C, before and during the Synod. There is much evidence that it is the IDO-C which continues to feed the various National Conferences of Priests with all kinds of aids and support to continue their struggle to force the Pope to surrender on celibacy.

The disastrous 'Resolutions' of our own Second National Conference of Priests held in Liverpool (6-10 Sept.) is no exception. If this Conference did not 'reject' obligatory celibacy, it was due to the excellent men, elected

* Father Hepplewaite S.J. – Laicised & Married

by some dioceses, to represent the Clergy, and by which their wisdom and loyalty to the Holy See, prevented the worst happening. We will be returning to this conference later in this *Newsletter*

To return however, to the IDO-C in the light of the established fact that this organisation is now entirely an instrument, in the hands of the Dutch Church, to subvert the official teaching of the Catholic Church, and bring down the Papacy and all that it stands for. It is deplorable that of the group of Bishops giving it financial support to make its nefarious activities possible, one Bishop should be from England.

This fact was disclosed by a member of the organisation and published in the American Catholic paper the *Wanderer*, (Oct. 14 1971).

Who is this English Bishop? Is he using diocesan funds which come from the taxation imposed on the parishes of his dioceses, and which in turn, come from the pockets of the faithful, to enable the IDO-C to continue its work? We say **SHAME!** to the Bishop concerned, whoever he may be, and suggest that he resigns his See as soon as possible.

It is interesting to note – a fact which has been pointed out in the pages of this *Newsletter* in a previous issue – that the ID0-C is not just an instrument for infiltrating Modernism into the whole Church, but it would seem to be intent on spreading the 'Dutch Church' type of Modernism universally.

When asked, were members of the IDO-C Catholics, it is now quite common to hear the reply 'Yes, they are Dutch Catholics', obviously in contrast to Roman Catholics. It is hardly a coincidence, that so many Dutch girls are to be found as Secretaries and Press Officers, in Cardinals' Residences, Information Officers and Bishops' Curia in so many countries, and all of them 'Catholics of the Dutch Church', as they describe themselves, on being asked their religion.

It is interesting to note two other points, which the same member of the IDO-C stated in the interview already referred to. He declared that 'In Africa and Asia, Bishops are being appointed, who are so far 'left', that if the truth were known, they would not be appointed . . . one was appointed, who was associated with arming a Liberation Movement' *Wanderer*, (14 Oct. 1971). One wonders if this only happens in Africa and Asia!

The second point speaks for itself. On the question of the 'Lex Fundamentals' the official of the IDO-C stated that 'All we have to do, is to state that the conservatives in the Church are behind it, and right away, the papers will stir up a huge tide of public opinion against it.'

We have seen many examples of this in the Church in recent years, – the capacity of the IDO-C to mount public opinion almost overnight, against anything that is opposed to the new 'Dutch Catholic Church'.

THE SECOND NATIONAL CONFERENCE OF PRIESTS OF ENGLAND AND WALES

The second National Conference of Priests of England and Wales took place in Liverpool from the 6-10 Sept. 1971.

Some of the points discussed at this conference were a disgrace to the Priesthood of the country. It will be recalled, that before the First National Conference last year (1970) signs made it evident, that this grouping of priests was already controlled by a small number of individuals who did not believe in the freedom they preached. Priests of 15 or more years after ordination, were to have no vote in the election of delegates; sacerdotal experience and wisdom are of little value to the individuals who would democratise the Church with their system of 'democracy'. Thanks to the intervention of the Bishops, this age limit was finally removed, much to the discomfort of the leaders of the party. Celibacy was discussed last year, notwithstanding the Pope's request that it was not a matter for discussion. Because of this flagrant disregard for the Papal instruction, the Catholic Priests' Association refused to collaborate with the Conference in any way, as it was feared that celibacy would again be brought up this year. As a last appeal, the Chairman of the C.P.A. and the secretary sent a joint letter to the Chairman of the Conference, Father Sean Kearney, begging him to omit any discussion of celibacy, and thus show the Conference as a 'shining light' to the world and as an example of true obedience to the Pope. This letter is briefly referred to, in the published *Official Report* on the Conference, but silence is kept on its contents.

Reading the *Official Report* one is struck by the amount of time that must have been consumed in discussing and voting on celibacy, compared to any other subject on the 'Agenda'.

One cannot help noticing the subtle manner of approach to the question of celibacy observed by those who guided the doctrines of this conference. There was first the 'inestimable value' of celibacy established, but it is only an 'inestimable value' on paper as the Resolutions then went on to disconnect it from its proper setting in the Church. Its theological, legal, and ecclesiastical links with the Church's priesthood, were one by one severed. Celibacy could be construed, as creating a 'false opposition with the charism of marriage' (Resolution 37). Once isolated from its proper moorings, the Conference moved in for the kill – a vote was taken that 'Every priest should have the right to marry' (Resolution 38, No.5). Thank God, that enough men of integrity were present, to vote this audacious Resolution 'out', though 23 priests voted for the Resolution and four abstained.

The abrogation of celibacy was obviously one of the principal objects of the Conference, and in case it did not receive the required majority from the assembled Fathers (which in fact it did not), the Conference Steering committee took two further steps – it passed a Resolution (No.33) that a National Survey on obligatory celibacy should be taken, with every priest and member of the laity having a vote, and carried out in conformity with the infamous 'Greeley Survey' in the U.S.A.

Only 14 priests voted against this Resolution, which was carried by a huge majority (71 votes for).

That 31 priests could vote, for the restoration to the priesthood of priests who had married (Resolution 38 No.4) is just incomprehensible, but not more so, than that 17 priests could vote against the Resolution (quoted from Vatican II) that there is a difference, both in essence and in degree, between the Sacred Priesthood and the Priesthood of the laity (Resolution No.2).

Resolution No.1 of the Conference stated that 'Since the Standing Committee is elected by the elected representatives of the clergy of the country, and is therefore, representative of the clergy in general, it be considered competent, during its term of office, to represent the clergy of the country at any International Conference, or to choose from its own members, an individual representative, when one is needed for a particular purpose, without any further election being necessary.'

The Catholic Priests' Association repudiates the claim that any such representative represents their members in this country.

The apathy shown by the clergy of most of the diocese, to take part in the election of delegates for the Second National Conference, and the fact that in some dioceses, delegates only received a few votes give a refutation of this claim as well.

The Catholic Priests' Association with its 1,300 members in England and Wales, if far more representative of the generality of clergy, than was the Liverpool Conference; but it would not presume to represent the general body of the clergy, nor would it have the boldness to assert that any of its members should be considered competent to act on behalf of the Priests of the country at any International gathering.

May we emphasise once more, that our opposition is not of the Priest members of the Conference, most of whom saved that gathering from falling into utter disgrace by their refusal to sanction many of the Resolutions with a two thirds majority. We do, however, oppose those who steered the Conference into discussions which should never have taken place, and who permitted votes to be taken on Resolutions which should never have been on the agenda, if respect for and obedience to the Holy Father were genuine.

XIII

THE INTERNATIONAL CATECHETICAL CONGRESS (ROME)
AND OTHER REPORTS

THE INTERNATIONAL CATECHETICAL CONGRESS held in Rome from 20-24 September 1971 will not be easily forgotten by those who attended it because of the scandalous example given by certain ecclesiastics to kill once and for all the *Catechetical Directory* edited and approved by the Holy See under the personal sanction of the Holy Father himself.

The report on the efforts of 'progressives' to smear the Directory as an inept publication for catechetics in our time can be studied in a special brochure edited by the *Pro Fide* Movement and produced by Hamish Frazer.

We would like to bring the notice of our readers certain points which are of the utmost importance in the field of Catechetics. The *Appendum* or the *Appendix* at the end of this General Catechetical Directory repudiates the growing practice in many parts of the world of not permitting children to make their first Confession before their first Communion. The Holy See declares, that the traditional practice is to be observed, and no departure should take place from this rule, unless with prior consultation with itself. The document tells the Bishops that 'They (the Bishops) should not permit parish priests or teachers, or religious institutions, to abandon the established usage, or go on ignoring it.' We hope our Bishops will see that this is the case.

With incredible audacity, a priest spokesman for combined delegations of England, Scotland, Ireland and Wales, told Cardinal Wright before the full assembly of representatives that the Appendums ruling on Confession before Communion was 'Totally out of accord with the consensus of this congress, and with the views of the parents, as we in our work, are in the position to know'. What a deceptive tactic! Did this priest receive the votes of Catholic parents in England, Ireland, Scotland and Wales, to speak like this on their behalf! It is time that *Father David Konstant of the Westminster Archdiocese, was relieved of his position as Director of Schools Chaplains and Chief Advisor on Religious Education.

His behaviour at the Roman Catechetical Conference was scandalous. His opposition to the 'Penny Catechism' approved by the Hierarchy, and his determined efforts that it should not be used in schools, are other titles to justify his immediate removal from the position which he holds in his own archdiocese.

Let us hope the Cardinal will show his loyalty to the Holy Father in a practical manner, and at the same time preserve his people from the danger of losing their precious Faith.

CONSCIENCE BOOM

'We are in a Conscience Boom', wrote a friend to me recently, 'I have never heard the word 'conscience' used to often – priests cannot accept *Humanae Vitae* in conscience, parents cannot in conscience accept the need of moral restraint for the children, and I heard of one woman who said she could not accept in conscience 'the immoral nature of abortion'. Yes, we are indeed, living in the midst of a 'conscience boom', but it is a counterfeit conscience, one that is deluding its owner and bringing him to destruction. I wonder, if the employer of the parent, who could not accept in conscience the immoral nature of abortion, told her at the end of the week, that he could not in conscience give her her pay packet, or if the Bishop told his Encyclical rejecting priests, that he could not 'in conscience' permit them to go on annual vacation, would the conscience addicts be happy, and logically accept the consequence of their own statement? So many priests have written to me on this point – has Vatican II upheld the 'freedom of conscience?'

'Freedom of Conscience' are not words that you will find in any of the documents of Vatican II, or any other council for that matter. 'Freedom of Conscience' as used by our innovators today, is a self-made spiritual drug, to numb the pangs of true conscience, which is disturbed by sin or by moral dangers. It is a rational absurdity of the greatest magnitude, incapable of deceiving any reflecting person. When coming from the lips of a priest, it is a *non-serviam* flung at God. A few reflections on this common use of the word 'conscience' may be useful.

A priest cannot in 'conscience' accept *Humanae Vitae*. What does this

*Father David Konstant is today, Bishop of the Archdiocese of Westminster.

mean? It means NOTHING. It is an ABSURDITY. It is a remark devoid of semantic significance.

He might as well say that 'He cannot in his boots accept *Humanae Vitae*'. The last statement is an absurdity, but not greater than the first. Between a man's conscience, and the morals or sins of another, there is no real connection. Conscience is only for the guidance of its owner – it is not for loan, it is not transferable. It is identical with one's own intellect, and this latter is exclusively personal property. Vicarious sin or guilt does not exist, neither does vicarious conscience. To say 'I cannot in conscience accept *Humanae Vitae*' is a semantic absurdity, completely meaningless, only to be expected in a lunatic asylum.

A priest, who would indulge sexually with a woman, and whose guilty conscience urges him to use contraception, would be a sad, deplorable and scandalous case, but it would not be an absurdity. His own conscience, in this case, has a meaning.

What a priest MEANS when he states 'He cannot in conscience, etc.' is another matter. He means that, the doctrine of the encyclical does not harmonise with his own personal opinion, and his own preferences, and so he rejects it, but this is NOT A REJECTION OF HIS CONSCIENCE. Conscience has just nothing to do with it.

The absurdity becomes more pronounced, when we visualise that it is (in the statement above) the conscience of a celibate that is rejecting the doctrine. By what stretch of the imagination can personal conscience reject acts which can never come from its owner? Be it remembered that conscience's place, is always the concrete act, never a doctrine or a principle.

Perhaps the best lesson for the priest, with the so-called conscience rejecting mania, can come from his Bishop, who cannot in 'conscience', permit him to continue the exercise of his ministry.

This could quickly solve the 'conscience' problem of the dissident priest. Let him be honest about it, and say that 'he just does not accept the encyclical', and we will understand him better.

DAMAGE TO POST-CONCILIAR CHURCH FROM WRITINGS, STATEMENTS etc

The post-conciliar Church has been much damaged by writings, statements etc., coming from priests and laity who are members of some 'commission' or other. Their position gives some degree of respectability and unfortunately of credibility to their outpourings.

We had far too many examples of that in recent months, one of which is referred to in this Editorial.

Father Arthur McColrmack's pamphlet *Population Explosion – a Christian Concern* published during October by the 'Justice and Peace Commission' of Hierarchies of England and Wales, and which received so much prominence in the pages of the pro-contraception press, is yet another example. The pamphlet to most readers – as it was to the Reviewers in the National Press – seemed to advocate contraception, and it stressed the point, that people should not be expected to follow a moral principle which they found impossible – the reference being – for those whom the 'rhythm method' was not satisfactory.

It is refreshing to read the *Catholic Herald*, (19 Nov. 1971) that Cardinal Wright has protested at some of the views expressed in this pamphlet, which just cut across the application of *Humanae Vitae*.

We cannot help wondering why the Bishops of England and Wales did not refuse approval for this pamphlet. We hope that the words of *Confiteor* as they recite it for Mass, 'That I have sinned through my fault, in what I have failed to do' will stir their conscience, as to their obligation to protect their flock from false doctrine.

We have yet another example, in the case of another Auxiliary Bishop, who, in the pages of the *Catholic Herald* (5 Nov. 1971) puts forward his beliefs, that there is a 'Eucharistic Presence' in non-Catholic Churches. As this ecclesiastic is one of those on the 'commission' (with Father Barnabas Ahern and Bishop Butler) representing the Catholic Church in this country in its discussions with Anglicans on the Eucharist, and which recently issued a statement, that 'substantial identity' of views had been reached, it is natural, that so many priests and laity should be profoundly disturbed. Acceptance of a Eucharistic Presence in non-Catholic Churches is linked with the Church's Solemn teaching on the invalidity of Anglican Orders. If the Bishops point is, that Christ is present in the reading of the WORD OF GOD, and where two or three are gathered in His name, may it be pointed out, that this form of presence is not a Eucharistic presence, and has never been accepted as such by the Church.

The **National Catholic Fund** of the Bishops of England and Wales, created by the special collections in Parish Churches for this purpose, is used in substantial amounts to subsidise the 'Commissions', as it was used in the current year to subsidise the 'Second National Conference of Priests' to the tune of £248.00.

Priests will naturally be disturbed to know that the collections taken from their people, and often with great sacrifice, are being used to spread false doctrines in the Church, and even to put forward ideas in conflict with Papal teaching.

As we look on the Church today, the Mystical Body of Christ, being lacerated by its faithless sons and daughters we cannot help considering the numerous alleged manifestations of Our Lady in recent years throughout the world. Only the Holy See can give final judgment on the authenticity of these alleged events.

One thing they all seem to have in common, and that is in their call to penance and return to God.

The spiritual message of Lourdes and Fatima is repeated in certain other places on the earth's surface. God has always been in direct contact with His Saints and mystics, and one would be foolish to ignore the message they bring, particularly when there are other signs and circumstances to give corroborating support. I would like to quote here, the words given in that absorbing book, *The Life of the Venerable Catherine Emmerick*, Vol.IV, p.356, which reads as follows:-

> 'I heard that Lucifer (if I do not mistake) will be freed again for a while, 50 or 60 years before the year 2000 A.D. I have forgotten many other dates that were told me. Some other demons are to be freed before Lucifer, in order to chastise and tempt mankind. I think that some are let loose now, in our own day, and others will be freed shortly after our own time.'

In Mexico, during 1969, two nuns of different convents, received by way of locutions, some extraordinary communication from Our Lord – so it is alleged. One of these nuns was granted Episcopal permission to publish her experience, and the aptness of the alleged event, to our time, makes it compelling reading. It is given in Ernst Knatzer's book 'Wir Durchleben Die Letzte Sekunden Vor Der Katastrophe', and the English translation reads as follows:-

> One man on earth, is My Representative: the successor of Peter. Paul VI must be recognised as My Representative. He must be freed from his enemies, and obeyed. There must be no earthly ambition in the governing of the Church . . . There must be no new meanings given to, no alterations made in doctrines laid down and approved in other centuries. Paul VI must declare the TRUTH before the world, and must acknowledge that pressure has been brought to bear on him, and that he has been forced into hasty

decisions of which he has not yet approved in his heart . . . Paul VI shares My feelings in his soul. He carries My overflowing love in his own heart; no one who fails to support him will be blessed, and accursed is he, who stands against him . . . I repeat to you – let a great cry go up to him, a great cry up to Paul VI. You must be among these who strive to be faithful to My teaching. He, Paul VI, must proclaim before the whole world, the truth which he has learned during his long martyrdom. I shall be with him, and I shall give him the palm that he has earned . . . Do not be deceived by false shepherds . . . No one, who does not support My own Representative, who does not follow him, can please Me.'

The passage above speaks for itself. Whether we accept the event experienced by the Holy nun, or not is immaterial to the issue involved; the alleged spiritual message is in conformity with Sound Theology.

On September 22, The Catholic Priests Association sent a letter to His Holiness the Pope, pledging our full support for his uncompromising attitude to obligatory celibacy.

We begged His Holiness to retain this precious jewel of the Priesthood at all costs.

On 25 October we received the following letter from the Apostolic Delegate in London:-

'The request of the Secretariat of State of His Holiness, I write to acknowledge with thanks, the letter of 22 September, to His Holiness, and signed by the Chairman and Secretary of The Association.

Your assurance of prayers for His Holiness and the expression of loyalty to his person, are much appreciated.

Yours sincerely in Christ

Archbishop D. Ennici
Apostolic Delegate.'

XIV

A PERISCOPE ON TEILHARD DE CHARDIN

by Father John W. Flanagan *Newsletter*, (Jan.-Mar. 1970)A
Secretary of C.P.A.

(IN A RECENT issue of *Newsletter*. We published certain points connected with de Chardin and his ecclesiastical and religious superior. In view of the many requests for another summary of how this case stands in the Church today, we give our reader the following:- Editor of *Newsletter*).

PART I

1926 Father de Chardin's Superiors in the Jesuit Order, forbade him to teach any longer.
1927 Holy See refused the *Imprimatur* for his book *Le Milieu Divin*.
1933 Rome ordered him to give up his post in Paris.
1939 Rome banned his work *L'Energie Humaine*.
1941 Father de Chardin submitted to Rome his most important work *Le Phenomene Humaine*.
1947 Rome forbade him to write or teach on Philosophical subjects.
1948 Father de Chardin was called to Rome by the Superior General of the Jesuits, who hoped to acquire permission from the Holy See for the publication of his most important work *Le Phenomene Humaine*. But the prohibition to publish it, issued in 1944 was again renewed. Father de Chardin was also forbidden to take a teaching post in the 'College de France'.
1949 Permission to publish *Le groupe Zoologique* was refused.
1955 Father de Chardin, forbidden by his Superiors to attend the International Congress of Paleontology. Father de Chardin died suddenly this year.
1957 The Supreme Authority of the Holy Office in a decree dated 15

November, forbade the works of Father de Chardin to be retained in libraries, including those of Religious Institutions, His books were not to be sold in Catholic book shops, and were not to be translated in other languages.

1958 In April of this year, all Jesuit publications in Spain, (*Razon Y FR., Sal Terrae, Estudios de Deusto,* etc.,) carried a notice from the Spanish without previous ecclesiastical examination, and in defiance of the decrees of the Holy See.

1962 A decree of the Holy Office dated June 30, under the authority of Pope John XXIII warned that . . . 'it is obvious that in philosophical and theological matters, the said works (Father de Chardin's) are replete with ambiguities or rather with serious errors which offend Catholics doctrine. That is why . . . the Rev. Fathers of the Holy Office urge all Ordinaries, Superiors and Rectors . . . to effectively protect, especially the minds of the young, against the dangers of the works of Father Teilhard de Chardin and his followers'.

1963 The Vicarate of Rome (a diocese ruled in the name of Pope Paul VI by his Cardinal Vicar) in a decree dated 30 September, required that Catholic booksellers in Rome, should withdraw from circulation the works of Father de Chardin, together with those books which favour his erroneous doctrines. The text of this document was published in daily *L'Aurore,* of Paris dated 2 October 1963, and was reproduced in *Nouvelles de Chretiente,* 10 October 1963, p.35.

Conclusion

Popes Pius XI, Pius XII, John XXIII and Paul VI endeavoured to prevent the spread of the modernistic errors of this pseudo-scholar, who, as he himself confessed in a letter to a priest friend, had aspostatized, deliberately remained within the Church to spread more easily his errors. (See *The Strange Faith of Father Teilhard de Chardin,* by Henri Rambaud).

PART II

The above paragraphs give an outline of the attitude of the Holy See and Father de Chardin's own religious Superiors to his doctrine and to his books.

We will now see, what in fact has happened on diocesan parish levels. To neutralise the decrees of the Holy See and the prohibitions of Father Teilhard de Chardin's writings, and to facilitate the spread of his erroneous doctrines into seminaries, schools colleges, convents, etc., a systematic campaign was set in motion by the Modernists in the Church. They hinged their movement around three points:-

1 that the *Monitum* (Warning) of the Holy Office, 30 November 1957 and the repeated *Monitum*, 30 June 1962, have been misunderstood, and in fact are now disregarded by the Holy See itself.
2 That His Holiness, Pope Paul VI has made a statement, praising the works of 'Father de Chardin' as 'indispensable'; and
3 that while certain points of Father de Chardin's works are perfectly reconcilable with the Church's teaching, and in fact, give new, deep, and 'exciting insight' into Catholic theology. He is hailed as the Thomas Acquinas of the 'enlightened age' of the Church.

Before refuting those three contentions of the Modernists, readers of this *Newsletter* may wonder how his works came to be published after his death, considering that both the Holy See, and his own Religious Superiors forbade their publication. The answer to this problem is simple. Father de Chardin made a will, appointing his one-time Secretary, Mile Jeanne Mortier, as his Executrix, a will which he could only have made in conflict with his own vow of poverty.

Within weeks of his sudden death on April 19 1955, Progressive elements within the Church, and some outside it, had taken steps to publish his works. So in an act of disobedience to his Superiors and the Holy See, and in violation of his vows of poverty, was born the *Vade-me-Cum* of the Neo-modernists, and a new and all embracing undermining of Catholic theology we perpetrated.

Now, to answer those points referred to in that second last paragraph.

1. The *Monitum* of the Holy Office, 1957, and the new *Monitum*, 1962, have been misunderstood. This is an absurd statement, as both *Monitum* made it crystal clear what they are intended to convey – a solemn warning to all the faithful and clergy, of the dangers inherent in the works of Father de Chardin. That the *Monitum* made specific reference to certain categories of people and institutions – seminaries and religious communities – had only one meaning, viz., that they above all, must be protected from the poison of Father de Chardin's works. It is just ludicrous, to read in the paper, published by the 'Father Teilhard de Chardin Association of America', that, 'Nothing whatever is said, to forbid seminarians and religious novices from reading Father de Chardin's work, or having them in their personal library . . . nor any laymen outside seminaries warned against Father de Chardin.'

When the Liberalistic minded 'progressives' indulge in the very type of distinctions for which they so ruthlessly condemn Catholic theology and Canon Law, it is time to say to them, 'We have had enough'. It is lamentable to find this same 'Father Teilhard de Chardin Association of America' leaflet being sent out to supporters of the 'Catholic Truth Society' of England and Wales, who object to the open sale of Father de Chardin's works in our own Catholic Truth Society.

Yet I possess one, with the signature of the General Secretary C.T.S. London dated 27 August 1971.

The *Monita* have not been disregarded by the Holy See. The Modernists have only their own statement to support this contention. In refutation, we have the following:-

1. A query sent to the Sacred Congregation for the 'Doctrine of the Faith' asking this precise question, was answered by the same Congregation through the Apostolic Delegate in Washington, that 'THE JUDGMENT AND DISPOSITIONS MADE BY THE CONGREGATION, CONCERNING THE WRITINGS OF FATHER TEILHARD DE CHARDIN HAVE NOT BEEN CHANGED, THUS THE *MONITUM* OF JUNE 30, 1962, CONTINUES IN EFFECT'. 8 MARCH 1967.

2. Further reaffirmations (20 October 1967; 23 March 1970 and 4 August 1971) coming from Apostolic Delegations but on the instructions of the Congregation of the Doctrine of Faith, removes all possibility of doubt on this matter.

Pope Paul VI, is quoted in the leaflet issued by the 'Father Teilhard de Chardin Association of America', as saying to Cardinal Feltin in the fall of 1963, *Le Pere Teilhard est indispensable à notre temps; son apologetique est 'nécessaire'* (Father Teilhard is indispensable for our time, his apologetics are necessary – English).

It will be noted that no date is given for this alleged statement, other than the 'fall of 1963'. If true, it would mean that what Pope Pius XII described as a 'cesspool of errors' in reference to Father de Chardin's works now, in the days of Paul VI, becomes indispensable.

To clear away any doubt as to the credibility of this 1963 statement, the question was asked of the Congregation for the Doctrine of Faith, and in the same reply mentioned already in this article (8 March, 1967) the following reply was given by the Congregation, through the Apostolic Delegate in Washington:-

I CAN AUTHORITATIVELY INFORM YOU THAT THE

HOLY FATHER HAS NEVER, IN PUBLIC OR PRIVATE, MADE THIS STATEMENT THAT FATHER DE CHARDIN IS GOOD AND VERY NECESSARY FOR OUR TIMES'.

We hope in the light of this reply, that our own Catholic Truth Society for England and Wales, will discontinue sending out justifications which have no basis, for their action of having the works of Father de Chardin on sale in the C.T.S. shops.

3. It is contended, that while certain points of Father de Chardin's works may be questioned, on the whole, his works are perfectly reconcilable with the Church's teaching, and in fact, give a new, deep and 'exciting insight' into Catholic Theology.

This statement is a figment of the imagination. Whatever may be said of Father de Chardin's work, its logical coherency into one whole, cannot be disputed. One of the greatest scholars on Father de Chardin, and one who has retained the Catholic Faith (so necessary, if one is to judge what is deviating from it) is Cardinal Journet. His verdict on the works of Father de Chardin is follows: 'Father de Chardin's works are disastrous . . . his synthesis is logical, and it must be rejected or accepted as a whole, but it contradicts Christianity . . . If one accepts Father de Chardin's explanation, one must reject the Christian notion of Creation, Spirit, God, Evil, Original Sin, The Cross, The Resurrection, Divine Love, etc., (*Nova at Vetera*, Oct-Dec 1962). Vatican II, in its constitutions *Lumen Gentium, Dei Verbum, Gaudium at Spes* has reaffirmed the traditional Catholic Church teaching, and it follows, that what is incompatible with the Church's doctrine, must be rejected.

Final Conclusion

The Faithful have no option, but to consider Father de Chardin's works as dangerous to their Faith, and hence, have a moral duty to avoid them. Priests and clerical students can only study them, so as to be armed against false doctrine. No clerical student is justified in considering Father de Chardin as a second St. Thomas Acquinas – he is a false prophet.

The *Monita* of the Holy See still continue, and there is a moral duty to respect and obey them. Father de Chardin tried to found a new religion. He wrote to a friend – 'His dominant interest and pre-occupation was to establish and diffuse a new Religion – call it a better Christianity, if you will, in which the persona God ceases to be the great Neolithic proprietor of former days, and becomes the soul of the world that our religion and cultural stage calls for (private letter, 26 January 1936).

Father de Chardin was a 'Monist', that is, one who holds that there is, only One being, and that being is in MOTION (Evolution).

Father de Chardin was a 'Pantheist', that is, God and Creation are identical. Father de Chardin was proud of his 'pantheistic' outlook, and boasted so.

Father de Chardin was a 'Collectivist' that is, man existed for Society, not vice versa. No wonder his works were welcomed by Communists.

Father de Chardin was a 'Secularist', that is, he identifies science with religion – there is no Supernatural, God is a 'cosmic force', ever evolving, and he is depending on man, more than upon God. To the scientist, Father de Chardin was a poet and a visionary; to the Catholic Theologian, he was an Anthropologist, and to the Modernist of our day, he was a Philosopher and Theologian, the Thomas Aquinas, of our age.

In last analysis of this man's philosophy, it is overlooked, that he is also the Founder of modern Racism, that is, his belief in the radical difference in the nature and potentialities of the diverse human 'races'. For Father de Chardin, the 'race' had not a common origin, and so, racial equality was precluded.

This aspect of Father de Chardin's life, seems deliberately to be concealed, as his liberalistic followers would fail to capture popular opinion, if his adhesion to racism was better known.

In the light of this periscope on Father de Chardin, and what it reveals, one can perhaps understand the unfortunate extremism of some groups at work in the United States of America, that recently petitioned Cardinal Cook for the disinterment of the mortal remains of the Jesuit from the consecrated soil of the Catholic cemetery where he lies buried.

Their argument is that it was the removal of the mortal remains of Wycliff from consecrated ground that finally brought home to the Church of his day the extent to which he had deviated from Catholic doctrine.

We can expect continuous praise for Father de Chardin from the ranks of the Modernists. Much of their intellectual prestige hinges on or around the claims they make on behalf of their idol. If he should fall from the place of honour and glory assigned to him by his supporters, it would mean a death blow to our Neo-Modernists.

We must be prepared for more alleged statements in his favour coming from the highest in the Church – it has succeeded in the future. Good Pope John XXIII so promptly cited for holding every doctrine in the Modernists' litany, is quoted by the 'Father de Chardin Association' as stating – that the *Monitum* of the Holy Office was 'regrettable', and some faceless member of the Bavarian Academy of Sciences was told to 'ignore it'. All efforts to substantiate this claim (so much at variance with Pope John's uncompromising attitude on doctrine) have completely failed, and we can conclude that it is like the statement put onto the lips of Pope Paul VI, that Father Teilhard was 'indispensable'.

XV

THEOLOGICAL COMMISSION
APPROVES OF THE AGREED STATEMENT OF ANGLICAN/CATHOLIC COMMISSION ON THE EUCHARIST

by Father John W. Flanagan J.C.D.   *Newsletter*, May/June/July 1972

PART I

The Catholic Information Office in its Document issued on March 1 1972, declared that the 'Theological Commission', the advisory body to the Bishops of England and Wales on questions of Doctrine and belief, has given 'warm welcome to the statement on the Eucharist, as an important advancement in the mutual understanding of the Eucharist, the Sacrament of Unity'. In view of the disgraceful betrayal which the Anglican/Catholic Commission has been guilty of in the compilation of the 'Agreed Statement', it is important to discuss how is it that the 'Theological Commission' can now support it.

One instinctively goes to the last page of the Theological Commission's Report to find out the identity of the persons who composed it. Here indeed is the key that unlocks the problem. The Theological Commission is composed of:-

Most Rev George P. Dwyer, Archbishop of Birmingham PRESIDENT.
Mr John Coulson, University of Bristol.
Rev J. Crehan, S.J., Farm Street, London.
Rev Cornelius Ernst, O.P. Blackfriars, Oxford.
Rev Nicholas Lash, St Edmund's House, Cambridge.
Rev John McHugh, Ushaw College, Durham.
Rev Robert Murray, S.J. Heythrop College, London University.
Rev Michael Richards, St Edmund's College, Ware.
Sister Romain, HHS, Holy Rood House, London.
Rev Francis Thomas, Oscott College, Sutton Coldfield.
Rev Patrick Kelly, Oscott College, Sutton Coldfield SECRETARY.

With only two or three exceptions, this list, is one of well-known Modernists, who have peddled their brand of Modernism in the various publications in this country. Some of them are notorious Liberals whose Theological lore is limited by the vision of Father de Chardin, Hans Keung, Bishop Butler or Cardinal Suenens. Others again, have no training whatsoever in Catholic theology, and yet, it is this group that form the Official Commission as advisers to the Hierarchy; it is their assessment to the 'Agreed Statement on the Eucharist' that is 'official'. Unfortunately what is 'official' is not always 'orthodox', and so we have a group of Liberals supporting a group of Liberals, and the last state is worse than the first.

One notices with satisfaction that the Theological Commission had some words of censure for parts of the Eucharistic Statement, but they were just not enough. These words of criticism we attribute to the few orthodox members of the Theological Commission, but they would have done a greater service to the Church if they had repudiated the whole document.

The Theological Commission's verdict on the 'Agreed Eucharist Statement' runs into five small paragraphs, the first paragraph merely stating that the Eucharistic Commission's Statement did not claim to be 'fully comprehensive', and it welcomes the efforts to find new patterns of thought and language.'

The second paragraph states: 'The Agreed Statement contains nothing contrary to Catholic Faith. A minority considered it inadequate on certain points in a way which could be misleading.' To say that 'nothing contrary to Catholic Faith' is contained in the Eucharistic commission's Statement is nothing short of nonsense. May it be said for a start that as Pius X pointed out in his letter to the Diocese of Venice and Mantua in 1894 – 'The Faith is threatened less by open denial, than by the subtlety and falsehood of those perfidious Liberal Catholics who are wolves in sheep's clothing.'

The Statement on the Eucharist sins more by omission that by commission. Its numerous deliberately created failures to express Catholic Doctrine when the doctrine should be expressed can have no justification. The faults are, however, not always one of omission – its reference to the sense in which 'Sacrifice' was understood by the Jews as a 'traditional means of communication with God,' clearly, by implication, if language means anything, involves a denial of the true Sacrificial nature of the Mass as solemnly defined by the Council of Trent.

On this point there can be no doubt whatsoever. It is absurd therefore to declare, as the Theological Commission does, that there is nothing in the statement contrary to Catholic Faith, and under no heading can the Eucharistic Commission's statement be accepted by Catholics without a base betrayal of Catholic Faith.

The Hierarchy has only one duty – to condemn in the clearest terms the unacceptable nature of the statement, because of its numerous errors by implication, and its failure to declare openly Catholic Doctrine.

The affirmation that the Eucharistic Commission has 'clearly maintained the real and true presence of Christ' will not deceive anyone, even moderately skilled, in the Theology of the Eucharist. Luther accepted a 'real presence' of a spiritual nature, but which left unchanged the substance of bread and wine.

That the Anglican Catholic Commission went a little further towards true Catholic Doctrine may well be contended, but it is quite clear that its rejection of the 'doctrinal sense' of Transubstantiation and its quibbling over the connotation of the words, leads to only one conclusion, that the 'real presence' is anything but clearly maintained.

I use the words 'doctrinal sense', as transubstantiation in Eucharist theology must be taken not only as referring to the mode of Christ's presence, but to the fact that the whole reality of bread and wine no longer exist after the Consecration; the inner reality of what was there before the Consecration is changed into the reality of the Body and Blood of Jesus Christ . . . Nothing of the bread and wine remains save the accidents. To downgrade transubstantiation as the Anglican/Catholic Commission does is to fail to accept this basic doctrine of Eucharistic Theology, or at least, to leave it obscure and uncertain, when in fact the Church's teaching on this point is beyond quibbling.

In paragraph 4 the Theological Commission's states that as the 'change in the elements is unique, totally mysterious and supernatural in character, it cannot be adequately expressed in words.' No Catholic Theologian will dispute the inadequacy of human language to express any mystery of God, but the fact that it is a mystery means that we know something about it, otherwise the concept of 'mystery' would be impossible. It is this 'something we know' which we must accept as the Church, the Divine Custodian of God's Revealed Mysteries to man, has taught and still continues to teach.

The Theological Commission endeavours to confuse our thinking by appeal to the inadequacy of human language to express 'mystery' in this context; we must understand it and accept it as the Church teaches.

The Theological Commission refers to the need of further discussions on the *Black Rubric* which is printed at the end of the 'Order for administration of the Lord's Supper, or Holy Communion' in the 1662 Book of Common Prayer.

The *Black Rubric* is a useful reminder today for those who are now trying to introduce many Anglican practices into our Churches (Communion standing, or in the hand, etc.), that their practices surrounding their 'memorial meal' have in many cases a history of denial of our Catholic Doctrines. The *Black Rubric* reads as follows:

'Yet, lest the same kneeling should by any persons, either out of ignorance or infirmity, or out of malice and obstinacy, be misconstrued and depraved; It is here declared that thereby no Adoration is intended or ought to be done, either unto the Sacramental Bread and Wine there bodily received, or unto any Corporal Presence of Christ's natural Flesh and Blood. For the Sacramental Bread and Wine remain still in their very natural substances, and therefore may not be adored (for that were Idolatry, to be abhorred of all faithful Christians) and the natural Body and Blood of Our Saviour Christ are in Heaven, and not here; it being against the truth of Christ's natural body to be at one time in more places than one.'

The fact that the Anglican/Catholic Commissions did not 'agree' to repudiate the contents of this *Black Rubric* is indicative of the 'substantial agreement' reached by the would-be Theologians. Perhaps it is that the Catholic Bishops on the Eucharistic Commission are hoping that, with the increasing abuse and desecration now to be found in Catholic Churches, where Liberals are in control, Adoration of the Abiding Presence of Christ in the Eucharist will be extinct in practice by the time the Commission hopes to see the 'unity' which they visualise achieved.

Many Catholic Churches in the country have for some time past been administered as if the Church had changed its Doctrine on the Real Presence continuing after the Consecration of the Mass. With Communion in the hand and given standing and with no tabernacle visible from the body of the church; with all Devotions to the Blessed Sacrament – Benediction, Holy Hours, etc., extinct in so many Churches, the observance of the *Black Rubric* in our Churches is not very far off.

The Liturgical protestantisation of our Churches has speeded up the acceptance of heresy, for the rejection of which the Glorious Martyrs of England and Wales gave their lives.

It is confirmation once more of the words of Pius X that openly false doctrine is less dangerous than what is proposed in an indirect and subtle manner. Truly, it may be said that the 'Liturgical Experts' are the picked soldiers of Modernism, capturing the fortress of orthodoxy without firing a shot in anger.

It should not surprise us if the Hierarchy as a body will accept the false 'Agreed Statement' as compatible with Church Teaching, thus betraying their duty. It happened before. We can only hope that another John Fisher will arise.

P.S. We welcome Father Boyer, S.J.'s Criticism of the *Agreed Statement* published in *L'Osservatore Romana,* 16 March 1972. It substantially agrees with that issued by the CPA – Editor.

N.B. Reverend Nicholas Lash – married.

PART II

ANGLICAN/ROMAN CATHOLIC STATEMENT ON THE EUCHARIST
– CATHOLIC PRIESTS' ASSOCIATION REPLY

The Catholic Information Office in a press release on the work of the Anglican/Roman Catholic Commission, which has been studying the Theologies of both Churches on the The Eucharist, gave the following points as accepted by the representatives of both Churches. It pointed out that there was 'agreement on essential points of Eucharistic Doctrine reached', and that nothing essential has been omitted. The Commission stated that it will now turn its attention to the 'mutual recognition of each Church's Holy Orders.' Finally, the statement is signed by the Co-Chairman of the Commission, The Right Reverend H.R. McAdoo, Bishop of Ossary (Ireland) and Right Reverend Alan Clark, Auxiliary Bishop of Northampton.

We find the following points of the Commissions Statement entirely unacceptable, as they are contrary to the teaching of the Church on the points concerned. These points are as follows:-

1. The 'Sacrificial Nature' of the Mass as defined by Trent, is either downgraded if not rejected. 'Communal Meal' and 'partaking of the one loaf' as emphasised at the expense of 'sacrifice' which latter is given a wide meaning as referring to 'communication with God', which, we are told was the traditional Hebrew meaning of the word. This whittling down of the Mass as a 'Sacrifice' as understood by the Catholic Church, contrary to what the statement declares, is an omission of an essential in the Catholic Theology by the Eucharist. It is the surrender of an essential, which can only advance a false concept of Ecumenism, about which the Pope has issued several warnings.

2. Consistent with the false doctrine about the nature of the Mass, as explained in the previous paragraph, the Anglican/Roman Catholic Commission reduces the Sacred Priesthood to such an extent that the Priest

'Presides at the table' (Par.7 of Report) as it is 'through the action of The Holy Spirit' that the 'bread and wine becoming the heavenly *manna* and the new wine'.

This doctrine is contrary to the Church's teaching on the part played by the priest in bringing about the Real Presence. If such a perversion of Catholic Doctrine was accepted there would be no problem whatever in 'mutual Recognition of each Church's Holy Orders.'

3. While the commission admits a 'real presence' of Christ in the Eucharist – as did Martin Luther – it is clear that the Commissions theology of this 'Real Presence' does not conform to Catholic theology. It is a 'real presence', 'independent of what the congregation believe'. But no reference is made to acceptance of the Catholic Doctrine, that the entire substance of bread and wine ceases to exist after the consecration, hence the words of the Commission so given in the Report are consonant with *impanation*. 'Transubstantiation' we are told is 'an affirmation of Christ's presence . . . in the contemporary Roman Catholic theology it is not understood as explaining how the change takes place' (par.6, footnote).

This doctrine is in conflict with Trent, with Pope Paul's encyclical *Mysterium Fidei*, 1965, and with the *Credo of the People of God* of the same Roman Pontiff, 1968.

Evidently Papal teaching is to be excluded from 'contemporary Roman Catholic theology' in the Commission's view, or, it is considered unworthy of a second thought.

4. The Abiding Real Presence of Christ in the Eucharist apart from the moment of consecration, also seems to be placed in doubt by the Commission's statement. The emphasis in paras. 8 and 9 of the Report leads inevitably to this conclusion. Para. 8 of the statement reaffirms, that the gift of Christ to the Church in the Eucharist is not 'just a presence for the believer but a presence with him.' In para. 9 we are told that the words, 'Take and eat, this is my body' does not allow us to dissociate the gift of the presence and the act of sacramental eating.' If the Commission means by these words that Christ's presence is conditional for the believer by the Sacramental eating, the whole Doctrine is false and must be rejected.

5. The Commission declares that 'remaining points of disagreement can be resolved on the principles here established.' This statement cannot be sustained by any philosophical or theological principle. If fundamental principles are false and erroneous, as we contend when we compare them with the Church's teaching, it follows that secondary principles, deduced from them to solve less important difficulties, must be equally false.

6. The Report states that 'The Commission will now turn its attention

to the crucial question of Ministry – and to the problem of mutual recognition of each Church's Holy Orders.' The Anglican Church has never failed to recognise the Holy Orders of the Roman Catholic Church, as evinced by the fact that, when some Catholics priests defected to the Church of England, reordination was never insisted upon. Hence, any further attention to the

Ministry cannot be called a mutual recognition of each other's Orders. It can only be a recognition by the Catholic Church of the validity of Anglican Orders. This matter has already been solemnly declared by the Holy See, by Leo XIII'S *Apostolicae Curae*. There can be no reversing of this Papal decision.

Accordingly, we call upon the Hierarchy of England and Wales to officially reject the Commission's false principles which are irreconcilable with the Catholic belief and tradition, and which, if not clearly and emphatically repudiated, could do great harm to true ecumenism in the country and could diffuse doctrines in conflict with the Church and appertaining to the very heart of Catholicism.

The Commission's statement that we 'acknowledge a variety of theological approaches within both our Communities' (Par.12) and that the Commission's task was to find 'A way of advancing together beyond the doctrinal disagreements of the past' (Para.12) throw some light on the nature of the work of the representatives of both Churches, namely, to create a compromise solution. Even this compromise, we contend, is clearly marked in favour of the acceptance of the principles of Anglican theology, rather than Catholic.

We consider this statement of the Commission a serious blow to true ecumenism, from which it will not recover unless promptly rectified. Time is not on our side, and every day that passes with this Commission's statement un-repudiated, will mean terrible harm to souls.

The text of this letter was sent by the Catholic Priests' Association to the Bishops of the country, asking them to repudiate the Statement, as soon as possible. We are glad to be able to report that our letter was published in many countries of the world with warm approval. Catholic publications, faithful to the Holy See, in France, Malta, Ireland, Canada, New Zealand, Australia, Ceylon, the United States of America, Germany, etc., etc., gave the full text or a substantial amount of the letter concerned, and with their open approval. The 'cold reception' given by the Vatican to the Commission's statement is indicative of its contents, and as the Anglican paper *The English Churchman,* (7 Jan. 1972) states: 'Already widely different interpretations have been made by the Commission's members; the authority which it carries is questioned on all sides'. The *Church Times* carried a number of letters giving the Catholic Church's teaching on the Mass and Transubstantiation which brought a very heavy post of congratulatory messages from clergymen of the Church of England, some of whom accused the Catholic members of the Commission of heresy, by supporting and signing such a document as the one issued.

XVI

AN ACCOUNT OF A SUDDEN AND SEVERE ATTACK OF ILLNESS
WHICH STRUCK 21 AUGUST 1972

READERS WILL, BY this time, be amazed at the strength, character and stamina exuded by this priest, who notwithstanding the present and almost persistent cross of ill health fought the enemies of the Church with every ounce of strength in his body. His orthodox views are reflected in his every editorial and article.

In the defence of the Church's Doctrines, he single-handedly prepared all his articles and editorials for publication in the Catholic Priests' Association *Newsletter* and this was indeed no light task, as I witnessed. Strong and authentic articles kept arriving from many parts of the world, including some from members of Hierarchies, offering their support and gratitude for his strong and valiant stand against Modernism.

But it was clearly seen by all concerned that apart from a few of the English Hierarchy, the part played would be one of contempt, in the form of a block of silence.

Father's very polite (and he was known for possessing this trait of character from his Seminary days – Read Chapter I) but strong appeals to them landed on deaf ears! **NO ANSWER.**

This attitude towards Father on the part of the Hierarchy and their retinue, continued all through these critical years for the Church, right up to his death in March 1977.

From a physical and mental point of view one wondered how long this pressure of work could last. Something must give – and it did. Extra and severe pressure caused, in receiving a letter from a new parishioner demanding more rights in the running of the Parish (21 August 1972) etc., together with virulent letters coming continuously from Modernists from within and without the confines produced their toll on Father Flanagan's health.

On that same evening of the 20 August 1972 Father Flanagan had returned from his Church at 9.15 p.m., where he had prepared for his Mass of the following day and 'locked-up'. On entering the Presbytery, he sat down to watch the Television News. In a split second, he fell out of his chair, pressing hard on his chest. Severe coronary thrombosis had struck him down. In a brief space of time medical help arrived, a cardiograph was taken, and treatment as ordered carried out through the night. I was indeed thankful to God for the possession of my nursing qualification. I was determined that Father Flanagan would get the very best of what I could do and give.

By morning, the Father was removed to Esperance Nursing Home, where all medical and nursing care was at hand, and where he always felt so happy with those good nuns, who spared no kindness, and with his own Doctor Ashforth who was not only his doctor, but a good friend.

In this atmosphere, Father made continuous progress, *Deo Gratias*.

After a period of treatment and rest, Father was soon able to attend to his large mail, which I brought to him twice daily. After I had opened and handed each letter to him to read, he placed them in two different bundles. Matters of importance to the Church be allocated to the Reverend Chairman, Father Whatmor, (CPA); all others, I took charge of, and, according to instructions, carried out his daily desk work, making sure all correspondence was completely cleared each day. This procedure had to be adhered to, as the next morning again brought the same influx of mail, with a repetition of the former day's work to be carried out.

AT ST GEORGE'S

During these, difficult and anxious days for us a priest came in to celebrate Holy Mass twice weekly. Otherwise, we (the parishioners) carried out all the work of the Parish alone and, having had a large football pool established to pay huge debts of Church buildings and renovation, our work was certainly 'cut out' for us. Father Flanagan himself played an important part in this work at weekends, and so, his absence was deeply felt, nevertheless, thank God and His Holy Mother, we could see, each day, gradual change for the better, until it was arranged that Father Flanagan could be nursed at his presbytery, and so a period of convalescence and care soon put him back on his feet and returned him to normality. Father's best tonic was to be on the doorstep of his little Church of St. George, for indeed nothing was too good for St George's or St Joachim's, Hampden Park, already described in this book.

His loyal parishioners, who stood by him every trial and tribulation, were again at his side. I will mention here that the Father was plagued with the 'disloyals' – and what Parish hasn't got them!! We always felt we had got more than our fair share, for we were a small community (rural) where the absence of even one parishioner meant loss. But we carried the 'can' in other difficulties and would throw our weight fully into making the Father's recovery a very special affair – each of us in our own sphere did just that.

Father Flanagan always felt very close to his Doctor, Doctor Ashforth, (Eastbourne), and to Doctor Surtees, (Eastbourne) for their professional care in saving his life – way back in 1966 – when after years of illness, his case was finally diagnosed by Doctor Ashforth, who ordered immediate surgery resulting in a Nephrectomy being performed (kidney disintegrated), thus saving the Father's life.

Once again, Doctor Ashforth gave the 'all clear' and Father Flanagan resumed his pastoral duties and his defence of the Church from his desk. I shall, record his articles and editorials, as before, until I reach a few years hence, when illness again strikes blow.

SPECIAL ARTICLE WRITTEN FOR EDITORIAL OF THIS NEWSLETTER

By Father Flanagan   *Newsletter* Vol.I and II 1972

These Extracts and Articles written by Father Flanagan, will continue all through this biography to expose openly and with no preferments the declining trend on all that is sacred and holy to the Church. As will be noted by readers, Father Flanagan fears no one in this struggle for orthodoxy, and continues to name those, irrespective of person or position – who must take the full blame for the present state of the Church.

I will now continue with this work (*Verbatim* from *Newsletter*).

ABUSES AND SCANDALS IN THE CHURCH

1. Success and failure are characteristics of every human life, and editing the CPA *Newsletter* is not an exception. We have learned much from letters of our readers, but, obviously, we cannot follow every advice, nor can we publish every article or letter sent to us. It would mean a *Newsletter* of a thousand pages, if we did. The *Newsletter's* purpose is, to be content with lighting the match here and there – in a thousand places throughout the world; hoping that one day, it will cause a conflagration, in which Modernism, and all it stands for, will with enlightened minds and contrite hearts, return to listen to the voice of Peter echoed in our century, through the lips of a frail little man, known as Pope Paul VI.

It has been the policy of this *Newsletter* to disclose the sordid corruption into which man and man-made doctrines can descend, without the guiding hand of God, Who, through His Church, shows the way, the truth and the life. In our sad days many Churchmen have endeavoured to make themselves 'little Popes', and with horrible consequences. The suffering of the Mystical Body of Christ, His Church, through the wanton disregard by Bishops, priests and nuns, for what the Church teaches, substituting in its place, their own ideas, or the dreams of 'experts', is immense. Much of the incredible suffering of the Church could be offset, if only more and more of the good men and women would raise their voices in protest; far too many are content to leave to 'others' what is a burden on us all – the duty of defending our Catholic Faith. 'Silence is golden', but only for the Modernist, who must secretly laugh; how quickly he can reduce opposition to impotence, by hurling the charge of 'un-charity' against those who oppose him. We should recall what the great St Pius X had to say on this very point. As he was canonised, subsequent to writing this letter, obviously it cannot be considered as 'Uncharitableness', but rather a fearless expression of truth. Writing of the Liberal Catholics of his day, he stated:-

> 'They are wolves in sheep's clothing. No type is more dangerous. Priests must watch against that hypocrisy, which attempts to enter into the fold of Christ – preaching charity and prudence – as though it were charity to let the wolf tear the lamb to pieces, or a virtue to practice that prudence condemned by God.'

(Letter to clergy of Diocese of Venice and Mantua, September 1894).

Christianity was, humanly speaking, saved from extinction in the fourth century when Arianism was thrust upon the world, by the intrepid faith and dauntless courage of the laity.

We are now living in an age that, in many respects is much worse than the days of Arius. If Catholicism sinks into past history, the only semblance of an organised Church being a Pope in exile, a Bishop in hiding, and some poor peasant woman reciting the Rosary – to fulfil the words of Christ that the Church would remain unto the end of time – we must take the full blame for it. The guilt is ours! The destruction of the Divine Institution of the Church is our own doing! There is no use in putting the blame on those who have already lost their faith – though to all external appearances, they are still members of the Catholic Church. It is only in 'external appearances', that these people – and the word 'people' includes Cardinals, Bishops, priests, nuns and laity, who reject or doubt a single truth of Catholicism – can be considered members of our Church.

Far too often, is it forgotten or overlooked, that the imposition of the penalty of 'excommunication' is not necessary before a person ceases to be a Catholic. Once unity in faith is gone, membership of the Church *ipso facto* goes; the legal penalty is only a matter of form, and the promulgation of what has happened already.

Today, we have Cardinals, Bishops and priests, nuns and laity parading to the world that they are Catholics, when they have long ceased to be members. What hypocrisy! But to turn to the essential point – it is our own lack of moral courage, our own lack of conviction that something must be done about the crisis, that we must first consider. It serves little purpose moaning about the abuses in the sanctuaries, and the scandals in the pulpit in the realm of doctrinal orthodoxy, when one of us even hesitates to walk out. What a remedial tonic it would be if even 50 devout Catholics walked out of a church, where there was a circus in the Sanctuary, where man has replaced God, where we hear so much about the 'brotherhood of man' and nothing at all about the 'Fatherhood of God'! What a remedial tonic it would be if these same 50 were to write to their Bishop and call on their local priest that they were no longer prepared to finance desecrations of The Blessed Sacrament! Yet this will have to be done before those, whose duty it is to defend orthodoxy, awake to the realisation of what is happening in the Church.

This *Newsletter* has never advocated revolution, and never will, it will continue, however, to present to its readers the appalling conditions to which our beloved Church is reduced, both by the destroying 'reformer' and by the spineless type of Catholicism that too many are content to possess. We just cannot be idle spectators, while the tragedy of the 1970's is being enacted under our very eyes. There must have been sympathisers who were idle spectators at the 'rigged' trial of Christ, and who did nothing about it – perhaps in our meditation, we condemned them.

We must now condemn those who witness the crucifixion of the Church and say with regret 'It is not my concern.'

Occasionally one hears of exceptions to the rule, when some priests or members of the laity, are not prepared to sit back and view evil with complacency. We salute their courage and God will bless them for their efforts. One such case was that of Father Michael Nugent, Parish Priest of Christ the King Parish in Reading, Berks., England. His words to the Reading Council protesting against the costs of contraceptives being put on the rates deserve wide attention and for that reason we give them here – quoting from the *Reading Chronicle, 17* November, 1972) Father Nugent declared:-

'The multi-million pound interests who exploit and operate this highly profitable market, must be clapping their hands with glee. They have been trying for years to break into the public purse . . . Into what state has the intelligence and moral sense of our Town Councillors sunk, when 25 good men and women can justify such an obscenity . . . perhaps it is that they want to reassure themselves, whatever their natural distaste, that by involving others, particularly the young, they will rid their minds of any residual guilt, and bluff the rest of us into accepting this measure . . . It is a lunatic flight of fancy, shot down in flames, by experience throughout the ages, that the way to remedy human weakness, perversity and sinfulness is to pander to it. The old pagan Greeks knew of this 350 years, before Our Saviour came to teach us the real meaning and purpose of life.'

Cheers for Father Nugent! Cheers for everyone – priest or lay person – who will take such action. Contraception on the Rates, Vasectomy on the Rates, Abortion on the Rates. Euthanasia on the Rates – is there anything else sinful to impose on the Ratepayers? What about our Catholic M.P. in Parliament, raising the question that Catholics are conscientious objectors to such lustful pandering to the flesh?

The last issue of our *Newsletter* (Vol.3 and IV, 1972) was received enthusiastically in many parts of the world. There was a very heavy volume of mail from supporters in this country and abroad.

One Italian professor at one of Rome's Universities praised it as 'strong, sound, revealing and entirely orthodox' and asked for approval for translations of several of its articles into Italian.

Yet another Prelate of the Church declared that, '*Newsletter* has kept the Faith alive in us poor priests, and we know that we are not alone.' These are but two token samples. On the other hand, the CPA magazine has been condemned in parish Newsletters in the Archdiocese of Liverpool and it has been condemned from the pulpit in a Southern Diocese. In both the Archdiocese of Liverpool and in the Southern Diocese referred to, there has been no condemnation of the many doctrinal errors, including rank heresies being taught in the schools and colleges and in the 'Southern Diocese' the condemnation of the CPA magazine came from a pulpit that only a few years ago had condemned *Humanae Vitae*. So, we are in good company.

In the wave of secular humanism labelled *Aggiornamento* it is inevitable that our defence of orthodoxy should meet with ruthless condemnation – from Bishops who preside over unutterable debaucheries in the sanctuaries of their Churches, from priests (dressed, of course, as laymen), who have long ago lost the Faith, and whose conscience is disturbed by *Newsletter*, and from nuns and some lay people, who are the unfortunate victims of doctrinal brainwashing, so subtle and complex, that it must have been Satan at its source.

Those, who reading this *Editorial* become furious that such 'wild statements' should be made, had better read the words of Pope Paul VI first, when he spoke on 'The Smoke of Satan entering the Church' on 29 June, 1972. This statement from the Supreme Pontiff must be completely unprecedented, and elsewhere in this Editorial we will give the reader further evidence of the accuracy, being taught in churches and schools, of the Papal statement.

That the Pontiff's words are applicable to Britain, may be judged from the incontestable evidence of heresy, and above all in Catechetical Centres with few exceptions.

Father William Lawson, S.J., writing in *Christian Order*, April 1972 states:-

'Heresy is now being taught in the Church – about the nature of the Church, the priesthood and marriage, the virginal conception of Christ, His Resurrection, His Real Presence in the Eucharist, Original Sin, baptism – this is not a full list, but it will do. The teachers of heresy are mostly, in the first instance, priests, and then their pupils, many of them Religious Sisters. The teaching of heresy has often been in defiance of the *Magisterium* of the Church, and deliberately made public in letters to the press and in TV appearances. The heresies are all of them old, and have been many times condemned.'

The great tragedy is that the 'heresy teachers' have not been silenced by the Bishops of the country. We write this, with every respect for the Hierarchy but we would be failing in our duty, if we did not seize every opportunity to awake our Bishops to the critical situations. Silence on their part is not enough – silence is construed as consent – consent to errors the new Reformers propound.

The July 1972 issue of *The Sower*, the magazine edited by Father Somerville S.J., for Corpus Christi College, had heresy on every page – I repeat on 'every page', yet, other than a letter from Cardinal Heenan to a reader of this *Newsletter*, that it was a 'disgraceful' issue, nothing was done to tell the readers of the journal that it abounded in error.

Some people still believe the contents of this evil production. Its inner cover had the words 'With ecclesiastical approval', and the Apostolic Delegate when asked if this meant the Church no longer approved of this evil magazine, could only reply, that the articles were published '**Without** ecclesiastical approval.'

The sheep must be protected from the ravaging wolves – that is what Pope Pius X called the slick peddlers of Modernism of his day. Protection from error is a duty on the Bishops, and one they have sworn to give on their consecration day.

We can understand their reluctance to move from the attitude of silence – it will upset the Modernists who hold the key positions on Diocesan 'Commissions' and in the Diocesan *Curia*. These people must be removed from office if it is necessary to safeguard orthodoxy.

One of the greatest sources of evil in this country is the **Catholic Radio and TV Centre,** sponsored by the Bishops and financed by the hard earned money given by the faithful in their annual collection for the Mass Media. As pointed out in a special article in the last issue of this *Newsletter*, we are paying for the destruction of our Catholic Faith. It is time all this stopped. No more money to 'Commissions' that are a disgrace to Catholicism.

The Commission for the Laity is yet another example, still pushing to have optional celibacy introduced, still demanding 'Communion in the Hand'.

When a distinguished and zealous Catholic man offered his services to the **Commission for the Laity** recently, he was told that his views would not be acceptable to the Commission. Obviously, unless you are a Modernist, you have no place in the Commission, yet this group, who only represent themselves, speak and write as if they are representing the Catholic laity of the country.

Do not blame them – blame the otherwise 'good Catholics' who tolerate this effrontery, their silence. This is where the blame lies.

Perhaps we will be told that the ecumenical climate created by Vatican

II demands the watering down of dogmas, which have been obstacles to reunion. Anyone who read the *Decree on Ecumenism* even superficially, will come to the opposite conclusion. The heresies which abound in the Church today are the real obstacles to reunion. Let us hear what Greek Orthodox theologians writing in *Logos*, October 1970, have to say on this point:

> 'Today, the Roman Church is no longer the monolithic structure of watertight discipline which drew the admiration of Orthodox Catholics . . . Today, we witness the challenging of Papal Supremacy and the release of humanistic thinking, errors and heresies, which continue to gather momentum as they spring from every conceivable direction. The dogmas that were once shared with Orthodoxy are being jettisoned by none other that Roman theologians themselves . . . secular theology is making fast inroads. An Orthodox cannot help feeling than many Roman theologians have no feeling of oneness with the Church of history, no consciousness of identity with what is known as the Church of the Apostles, Fathers, Martyrs and Confessors . . . The historic common ground between the two Churches is steadily lessening, and chances of reunion are slimmer than ever before.'

The Patriarch Maximos V of the Melchite Greek Catholic Church and already declared that the Church he represents 'Dissociates itself from the doctrinal novelties not found in Apostolic and Patriotic Tradition' and accepts only one change *metanoia* (repentance) the transformation of sinners into the Mystical Body of Christ' (*Immaculata*, September 1972 p.45).

This preparedness of Churchmen to bend doctrines to accommodate the ideas of secular humanists, whether it be under the auspices of *ecumenism* or 'development of Doctrine' only brings contempt from anyone with sincerity in his heart. The rush to hijack the Church and hold its members to ransom, exists not only among half-educated Catholic laity in such organisations as the 'Catholic Renewal Movement' and the 'Laity Commission' but also among numerous members of the Hierarchies of the world.

We have seen the hotchpotch *Windsor Statement* or the supposed 'reconciliation' of Catholic and Protestant Theology on the Eucharist

In the *Newsletter* we have discussed various aspects of the 'Substantial agreement' and pointed out, that it was agreement at the cost of jettisoning some Catholic doctrine. Bishop Allen Clarke, one of the Chairmen of the special commission wrote the following to a Catholic of his diocese:-

ILLNESS AND ARTICLES FOR THE *NEWSLETTER* 169

'It would be quite wrong of us to apply that word sacrifice in the same way to Our Lord's death on Calvary, and the Mass we attend on Sunday' (14 Jan. 1972).

This doctrine is heretical, and it is clearly opposed to the most solemn teaching of the Council of Trent, *Sessio XXII,* Cap.2, that the Mass is the same sacrifice as Calvary, the same victim, the same principal Offerer, and only differs in the sense, that the Mass is an un-bloody sacrifice. It is an easy matter to reach 'substantial agreement' by removing the discordant doctrines of the Catholic Church, until they fit into the structure of Protestantism. What can be done in such a situation?

If the other Bishops of the country cannot act – and as Cardinal Seper pointed out (Easter, 1972) in his letter to Father Mikulich:
'The Bishops who obtained many powers for themselves at the Council are often to blame, because in this crisis they are not exercising their powers as they should – Rome is too far away to cope with every scandal and is not well obeyed,' then the faithful must unite together to express their rejection and abhorrence of doctrine in conflict with the Church's *Magisterium.* It was the faithful who saved Christianity before and it will assert its *Sensus Catholicus* again.

As Cardinal Seper, already referred to, stated on the same occasion, 'If all Bishops would deal decisively with aberrations as they occur, things would be different, but it is difficult for us in Rome, if we get no co-operation from the Bishops.'

It follows that the main bulwark of orthodoxy is, once again, the Catholic laity. Cardinal Newman in *The Arians of the Fourth Century,* London, 1883 p.445, points out, describing the period following the Council of Nicea, which condemned the heresy of Arius:-

'The episcopate, whose action was prompt and concordant at Nicea on the rise of Arianism, did not, as a class of men, play a good part in the troubles consequent to the Council; but the laity did. The Catholic people, the length and breadth of Christendom were the obstinate champion of Catholic Faith . . . Of course there were exceptions – Athanasius, Hilary, and later Basil and the two Gregories . . . But taking a wide view of history, we are obliged to say that the governing body fell short and the governed were prominent in faith, zeal, courage and constancy.'

Arianism is again in our midst and the faithful must arise from their sleep and take the sword of the Spirit.

1. 'If you follow Jesus Christ faithfully, you just can't have a code of morality of any sort.'

So stated Father Fabian, a monk of Ampleforth Abbey and Chaplain of York University, according to *The Yorkshire Evening Post*, Wednesday, 10 May, 1972, giving an interview to John Osmond, and speaking in favour of 'Christian Lib.' True indeed, Father Fabian does not go the 'whole way' with the ideals of Christian Lib.

The article in question refers to him as one of the Catholic priests who 'came out openly against the Pope's Encyclical on birth control and he is unwilling to say that sex outside marriage is always wrong.' The article states that he 'has been at York University for the last 18 months, specialising in student counselling.' Over the centuries states Father Fabian, 'There has developed in the established Churches, attitudes towards sexual morality that were never implicit in Christian teaching, partly the result of Greek influence on the *Judaic* tradition, out of which Christianity sprang.' Father Fabian gives us other insights into his discoveries. 'Modern psychology, biology, and sociology, have prompted new understanding of the nature of man and of the married state and sex – most intelligent people now accept, that the sex act does not just serve to procreate children, it has an important role in promoting love and preserving loving relationships.'

One is justified in asking the question, how this monk can be permitted to hold the Chaplaincy of the University of York? Does one have to be judged 'uncharitable' and coming to 'rash conclusions' if one concludes that the 'student counselling' given by Father Fabian to young boys and girls, will reflect his own views on sexual morality, and Catholic parents who have made such sacrifices for the proper upbringing of their children would be justly furious to see them morally corrupted as a result of false teaching? Apart from Father Fabian's doctrine in conflict with the *Magisterium* of the Church, he has rejected *Humanae Vitae*, and his removal from preaching, hearing Confessions and every teaching post, becomes mandatory for his legitimate superiors (Canon 2317 of the Code of Canon Law).

2. The Holy See has declared more than once in the last few years – and the Pope has even personally referred to it in March of 1972 – that the days of 'experimentation in the liturgy were over'. But the scandal continues, the scandal that drives the devoted Catholic to the point of breaking with what is seen in many of our sanctuaries. The 'indifferent' Catholic, who takes little or no interest in the Church, is not, generally speaking, affected, and very often this type could not care less what vandalism parades in the sanctuary, in the dress of 'up-dating' the liturgy.

At the time of writing this editorial the Sunday, Mass statistics for the year 1971 are not yet available, but for those Dioceses which have already published the figures, the rapid downward trend continues, which started towards the end of Vatican II, gathered momentum when the vernacular 'digest' of the new liturgy was introduced, and is now reaching disturbing proportions. Can it be wondered at, when all that is holy and traditionally linked with the Holy Sacrifice has been thrown to the winds, when – following the initiative in Holland – priests, (often assisted by nuns and laity) compose their own liturgy on a Saturday evening.

It is not unknown for priests to invite atheists and agnostics to compose the Liturgy, because they are 'artistic' and 'talented'! Let us take a few examples of the sacriligous profanations of the Holy Mass that are permitted in this country. Mass for Lower Juniors, composed by the Westminster Religious Education Centre, 209 Marylebone Road, London NW1, reads as follows: -

> Sharing
> Priest: If your friend is playing with you, and has a bar of chocolate, you hope that he or she will share it with you. If he does not, you feel somehow left out. When I have chocolate and I'm with a friend who hasn't any, if I keep it all to myself, I feel mean.
> 'I confess etc . . .'
>
> Priest: 'God Our Father, we are together now because we are hoping to share the Bread of Life. Help us to share it with the people we love.'
> Reader: 'The first Christians were famous for sharing. People who lived near them noticed how good they were to one another . . . Here is something written about how they lived.'

Then follows the supposed reading of the Acts, ch.2, vv 42-47. I say 'supposed' as there is no similarity between the Biblical text and what the Westminster Religious Education Centre composed. The text given the children is a development of only two verses of the text concerned – the early Christians holding all things in common – is presented in a way that would do justice to any Marxist At the end of this concocted 'Gospel' all children say 'Thanks be to God.'

> Priest: Jesus Christ was good at sharing. As soon as he saw someone in need, he shared whatever he had, even if he did not have much. The story you are going to hear now, tells about Jesus sharing.
> Luke, C.9., vv 11-17 are then read and all reply 'Praise to you Lord Jesus Christ'

COMMENT: It will be noted that nothing is given to the children to convey to them the idea of the Divinity of Christ – He is referred to throughout in small 'h' for 'He' and the whole text of the Gospel is developed to show that He was not just another man but a **Communist** to put it in short. The word **Communist** is not used but it is clearly implied. Nothing is said to instill into the child's mind the greatness of God. Of course, the children we must **accommodate;** so the Marxist's School will tell you that a child's mind is incapable of conceiving God. We are tired of hearing that reply, and it will no longer deceive anyone.

The 'experts' also tell us that the Mass must be made 'meaningful' for the children, we must 'accommodate' to the child's mentality.

In one sphere the experts seem to reverse the argument. Where **sex** is concerned, nothing must be concealed, they must be taught everything, even the perversions.

To return to the Mass for junior children, the liturgy continues as follows:-

> 'Bidding Prayers for Children'
> At the Offertory procession the children can bring bread and wine, and chalice and paten and things (sweets, toys, food parcels) that they might be able to share them with others.

> 'Prayer over the Gifts'
> Lord God, this bread and wine are a sign of all the good things you give us to share with people who are in need' AMEN.

Two Questions for the authors of this Liturgy.

1. By what authority does this homemade liturgy continue, after repeated declarations of the Holy See that all such experimentation is over?

2. How can children be expected to grow up with any knowledge of God or the Mass, when both are made just human commodities that we **share** with others?

It is rather significant, that the liturgical productions concerned are under the title of WREC (Westminster Religious Education Centre). Where is there a grain of 'religious education' in this fuzzy concoction which is most apt to indoctrinate young minds on the need for Communism?

It would be interesting to have a children's education 'expert's' advice on the religious education contained in the following hymn sung at Catholic schools. It runs into six verses.

It was a Friday morning,
That they took me from the cell,
And I saw they had a carpenter
To crucify as well.
You can blame it on Pilate,
You can blame it on the Jews,
You can blame it on the Devil,
It's God I accuse.

It's God they ought to crucify,
Instead of you and me
I said to the carpenter
A hanging on the tree.

You can blame it on Adam,
You can blame it on Eve,
You can blame it on the apple
But that I cannot believe.
It was God that made the Devil
And the woman and the man,
And there wouldn't be an apple
If it wasn't in the plan.

Now Barabbas was a killer,
And they let Barabbas go.
But you are being crucified,
For nothing here below,
And he doesn't do a thing:
With a million angels watching,
And they never move a wing.

To hell with Jehovah,
To the carpenter I said.
I wish that a carpenter,
Had made the world instead.
It is God they ought to crucify,
Instead of you and me,
I said to the carpenter,
A-hanging on the tree.

COMMENT: The words of this hymn, are the words of a hymn of hate – hatred of God. They are the words of disbelief and rejections of God's Divine ways; they are the words of disbelief in the Divinity of Christ. Isn't it time that Catholic parents arose and in their wrath took their children from such Catholic schools and gave them religious education in their own homes with the help of orthodox local clergy? How long can the systematic expulsion of God and introduction of Godlessness take place in our schools without the Bishops' consciences being so violently disturbed that they become victims of insomnia?

Do not think dear reader that this tampering with the approved liturgy of the Mass takes place unknown to the local Bishop – some incidents may do so, but many are made known to him (often by the Editor of this *Newsletter*) and some take place while he is present.

On November 16, 1972 at St Edmund's Catholic Church, Beckenham, Kent, during Confirmation conferred by Archbishop Cowderoy of Southwark, a truncated liturgy was observed as opposed to the Decrees of the Holy See, as anything yet stated in this Editorial. The Offertory song was worded as follows:-

'Let us break bread together on our knees,
Let us break bread together on our knees,

Chorus:
'When I fall on my knees with my face to the rising sun.
O Lord have mercy on me.
Let us drink wine together on our knees.
Let us praise God together on our knees.

COMMENT: What a help this hymn is to children expecting to receive the Body and Blood of Christ – the words of the Offertory hymn must re-echo in their minds that it is 'bread and wine' that they are receiving. The 'Our Father' of this truncated Mass runs as follows:-

'Our Father in heaven your praises we sing,
In awe of your name and what heaven will bring.
Help us to struggle for peace here until,
On earth as in heaven we follow your will,
Feed our bodies and minds and forgive all our sins.
So we open our hearts let our enemies in.
Please save us from evil forever – Amen.'

ILLNESS AND ARTICLES FOR THE *NEWSLETTER* 175

The final hymn was a nursery rhyme:-

'Wouldn't it be nice to know the language of the bees?
Wouldn't it be nice to say 'Good Morning to the trees?
Wouldn't it be nice to ask a sparrow in the snow,
Not what he is but what he knows.'

Examples of disgraceful interference in the approved liturgy abound in every diocese. Some, known to the Editor of this *Newsletter*, are so revolting that they would cause too much scandal to produce them in print. How many years will it be before we have empty Churches, and falling financial income to the Bishop's House will bring it home to our Chief Shepherds that the Church has been ablaze with indignation, while they permitted the 'Commissions' and 'experts' to fiddle about with the Sacred things of God; and now it is too late to control the disintegration of the Church of Christ?

The Catholic Press reported that while a majority of Bishops of the Country voted for 'Communion in the hand' a two third majority was not acquired, and so the traditional manner of Communion of the tongue remains in force. We have often in the pages of this *Newsletter* declared that the 'progressives' (more accurately – the Modernists) will not take 'NO' for an answer. We have seen time and time again, that once a decision unfavourable to the Modernists has been given, whether it be from the Pope or the Bishops, the Modernists go to their 'action stations' right away to reverse the decision or to undermine it. The November Issue of the *Parish Newsletter* of Beckenham, Kent contains on page 4 such an example. It reads:-

'Some objections were raised to Communion in the hand, on the grounds that it was disrespectful. Father Strand said, perhaps we were confusing respect with past tradition which was a different thing. Holy Communion is given us in the form of food and as we are adults we should not expect to be fed in the same way as though we were small children. In reply to a question, Father Strand said, that no permission had been given by the Hierarchy in this country for Communion to be received in the hand, but our Archbishop had said that anyone holding out their hand should not be refused Communion.'

One is justified in asking the question – where does obedience to the Holy See come in? Could the person holding out their hand not be told that they should receive Communion direct to the mouth? Could the same procedure not be observed as was observed in St Peter's Basilica in Rome and in St John Latern, during the November *Pro Fide* Pilgrimage, when an announcement was made over the loudspeaker that 'Communion in the hand' is forbidden?

Father Strand is head of the Liturgical Commission in the Archdiocese of Southwark and should know better and set a better example of obedience to the Holy See. The law is one of the Holy See. The law is one of the Holy See's – it is not a law of the Archbishop's – and so, it is to the Vatican that he should turn his attention, and from it, learn his responsibilities. It is beyond dispute that the words of Cardinal Seper to Father Mikulich (Easter 1972) are true – 'If Bishops would deal decisively with aberrations as they occur the situation would be different. It is very difficult for us in Rome, if we get no co-operation from the Bishops.'

DIGBY STUART TEACHERS' TRAINING COLLEGE, ROEHAMPTON, LONDON SW15

It is a sad state of affairs when one in Episcopal office (and I quote here, from a letter sent to a lay person, who wrote to one of the Hierarchy, over the pernicious and heretical doctrines allegedly being taught in Digby Stuart Teachers' Training School, Roehampton, SW15) objects to the accusations against the College on the grounds that they are 'not formal heresy'.

This journal has given in the past many instances of erroneous and dangerous doctrines being taught in the College, but nothing has been done to rectify the situation.

Archbishop Cowderoy has a heavy responsibility to clear his Archdiocese. We ask all our readers to pray that God may give the Archbishop strength and courage to fearlessly root out the infection that attacks his Archdiocese; and we ask our priest members to remember him in their Holy Mass.

Digby Stuart College has now replaced 'Corpus Christi' as the centre of the 'new theology' that is draining away vocations and emptying churches.

Bishops on the day of their consecration swore to defend the Church not only against 'heretical doctrine' but also against 'dangerous doctrines'. With so much 'smoke' (*The smoke of Satan*, words used by Pope Paul VI, 29 June 1972) appearing over the Digby Stuart College, it is hardly likely it is without fire.

FURTHER ACCOUNT OF ABUSES IN THE CHURCH

The following is a full and complete account of an Editorial Article written for the Catholic Priests' Association *Newsletter*, in which Father Flanagan continues fearlessly to expose further drastic abuses in the Church, and those, especially some of the Hierarchy of this country, for their flagrant neglect of their responsibilities – that of defending the Church against the onslaught of Neo-Modernism – staring straight at them.

For this very reason, he urges all faithful Catholics to the *Magisterium* to discontinue or curtail financing Diocesan projects, such as Commissions etc., for this and that, when, as Father so often stressed, the Commissions were used to further the Modernists' views and work, and so, putting the Church of Christ in peril. Financing Diocesan funds – to be used in this manner – was out. Father Flanagan would not relent. See what happens later! It will be recorded later – or towards end of this biography – the acid reaction to Father Flanagan personally and it will be worth noting that those whom he exposed, couldn't dare face him during life – for what he said of them was authentically visibly true and so 'they' awaited their Retaliation until his body rested in the grave. They were then sure of no 'comeback'. Perhaps they shouldn't have been so sure!!

I will now continue to give the Father's account in this article as follows:-

EDITORIAL VOL.1 1974

Dear Father Flanagan,
Please accept the enclosed small donation to the CPA funds. Your *Newsletter* gives strong encouragement to those of us who are striving to defend ourselves and our people against the evils of the Modernists, and to preserve Catholic Truth and the true teaching of Vatican II.

Keep at it! Preach the word of God, dwelling upon it continually, welcome or unwelcome; bring home wrong doing, comfort the waverer, rebuke the sinner with all the patience of a teacher.

I do not know what we would do without our Priests' Association – it keeps us going and keeps many of us in the Ministry. God bless your efforts and give you boundless strength to carry on the fight.

John J. Walsh

The previous short note was written by the late Canon John J. Walsh, D.D., Parish Priest of SS Peter and Paul, Ilford, Essex the day before he was killed in a car crash. We now have an Advocate in Heaven. God rest his brave soul.

Pray also for Father William Matte, S.F.M., who died on the 4 June in his parish in St Lucia, West Indies. Also remember Mrs Palmer and her daughter, of Herne Bay, Kent, associate members of the Association, both of whom were instantly killed in a car crash in June 1973. God rest them and reward them for their loyalty to the Church.

While preparing this Editorial, we have been shocked to hear of the sudden death in New York of Father P. Crosbie, one of our outstanding members and a fearless champion of orthodoxy – Pray for his eternal rest.

Our Catholic Priests' Association and its lay-associate branch continue to grow rapidly, so much so, that in so far as the lay branch is concerned, we must soon establish it as an organisation, in close conjunction with the Priests' Association.

The title *Athanasians* has been suggested for it, after the name of the great champion or orthodoxy against the Arians of the Fourth Century. We hope to get down to this whole sphere of work within the next few months.

The so-called Catholic papers, *The Herald* and *The Universe*, seemingly want to be put out of business, judging by their activities. The former in its issue of the 17 August, accused the CPA of putting out 'mendacious allegation of forgery' in the case of the *Choices in Sex* booklet.

Anyone who wishes can come to the Secretary's office and see for himself the continuous stream of correspondence from Monsignor Barton, written between 26 June and 8 August, in which he affirms no less than some fourteen times, that he never gave the *Nihil Obstat* to this scurillous and moral destroying publication. The Monsignor sent me also photostat copies to prove the forgery and copies of letters from his legal advisors, that he should not spare the culprit. If on or about the 9 August the Monsignor changed his tune, whether freely or not we do not know, and discovered that he did give the *Nihil Obstat,* that is his affair, but this is not justification for the so-called *Catholic Herald* to level such false accusations at the CPA.

As the case stands, we are hoping to be financially capable in the near future of bringing a libel action against the Editor, as he has pertinaciously refused to make any correction. In the meantime, we ask all priests and lay-associate members to refuse to purchase this paper, or to deal with those who advertise therein. We have a strict right to self-defence and if the Editor of the *Catholic Herald* refuses justice, then he must suffer for his misdeeds.

ILLNESS AND ARTICLES FOR THE *NEWSLETTER* 179

We also express our contempt at the *Universe,* which in its issue of 26 October, on the front cover in the middle (leader column) and on the back page, went out of its way to make sure that all its readers would see the supposed 'condemnation' of the Association, by the Hierarchy during the autumn meeting, when it declared that only associations of priests approved by the Hierarchy may use the title *Catholic.* This Ruling of Vatican II, is made for 'lay people' and has been misapplied to our Association. This fact was promptly brought to the notice of the Hierarchy. Pope Paul VI in an allocation given on the 14 November 1968, declared that the title *Catholic* could only be used by those who 'entirely accept the *Magisterium* of the Church, by a sincere and total profession of Catholic Faith'. Under this heading, the National conference of Priests whose resolutions and topics for the agenda of the annual meetings clearly show that they have forfeited the right to be called *Catholic* are nevertheless the ones approved by the Hierarchy at the autumn meeting. This raises many questions indeed – the application of *Catholic* to *The Herald,* to even the Hierarchy itself, seeing that so much doctrine and practice in direct conflict with the *Magisterium* of the Church are permitted in so many dioceses of this country.

It is time that we become more and more aware that sins of omission or crimes of omission – neglect of office on the part of those who are obliged to prevent evil – are just as imputable to those concerned as sins of commission.

When we are shocked by the statement of Hans Kueng and other luminaries of the Neo-Modernists' world, we should also think of the people whose duty it is to prevent such crime and scandal and who do not do so.

In Ireland the *Catholic Herald's* sister paper, *The Irish Standard,* which during the month of September 1973 gave such space to the outpourings of the Arch-heretics, Kueng and Schillebeeckx – described of course, as 'the outstanding Catholic theologians of the world' (*Standard,* 14 September), – poured abuse on the Catholic Priests' Association in its issue of the 10 August. Under the threat of libel action, the Editor reluctantly published some amendment in that paper on 14 September. We shall continue to put pressure on the *Catholic Herald* for its 'mendacious allegations of forgery' charge (17 August) until it is corrected.

It is interesting to note how our Modernist-controlled papers are so prompt to employ the most laudable expressions to the heretics of today. Whether it be 'outstanding theologians' or 'world's greatest authority on . . .' the idea is the same – to create in the minds of the readers of the papers concerned that the Church with whom these heretics are in conflict, is wrong. One *French Review* aptly expressed it recently, when it stated that to be 'an outstanding theologian' one must have debunked not just one, but a number of *de fide* doctrines of the Church, Papal infallibility in particular. 'Top Irish Theologian Marries' states the *Irish Press*, 9 September, referring to the Modernist, Father James MacKey, described as a 'Theologian of International repute' who on the 25 August married Noelle Quinlan, in a Catholic Church in Kilcock, the ceremony being performed by Father MacKey's admirer and Modernist fellow-traveller, Father Gerard Watson of Maynooth. 'Rebel Priest aged 50 weds girl of 25' states the *Express*, 2 September 1973, referring to the marriage of Father John Challoner to Sara Clethero; the ceremony took place in the Anglican Church of St George, Edgbaston, Birmingham. The press report states, that large numbers of priests and nuns were present in the congregation to witness John Challoner receive 'Anglican Communion with his bride'. He still claims that he is a 'Catholic priest' (no mention of any objection from the Hierarchy or has the Hierarchy 'approved' of his use of the title 'Catholic?') though he was married without reduction to the lay state.

No one rejoices at the act of betrayal by any priest; it is for all of us depressing news to know that one of our fellow-priests has abandoned the exercises of his priesthood. More depressing still is the realisation that the Bishops will not learn the lesson that every one of the priests who rejected '*Humanae Vitae* will fall by the wayside, but only after they have brought disaster to many. It would not be a rash conclusion if one concluded that there has been some handpicking of the Chaplains and Assistant Chaplains to the Universities of the country from among those clergy who refused to accept *Humanae Vitae*. And almost invariably these men, after destroying the faith and morals of the youth entrusted to their care, by teaching them that the Church doctrine on contraception is wrong, end up by their own nuptials. One can only shudder at the enormity of the responsibility on Bishops to remove these men from their key positions and indeed from the ministry, as is mandatory on the Bishop by virtue of Papal Law – Can.2317.

As we are on this subject of using the title 'Catholic' – forbidden to the 'Association' if we were to take the Hierarchy's ruling as valid, and it is not – it is interesting to note – that Father Adrian Hastings claims that he is a 'Catholic priest, with full faculties from the Archbishop of Birmingham' (letter to the Secretary, 29 September) though he admits that he 'recommended' a report to the Anglican Archbishops of Africa that 'polygamy alone should not be a reason for refusing Baptism' to those who sincerely ask for it. *The Times* (19 July 1973) reported Father Adrian Hastings as stating to the Anglican Consultative Council, which held its meeting in Dublin 17 July, 1973, that:-

'To end a polygamous marriage in the name of Christ, who said nothing explicit to condemn it, as the expense of effecting a divorce which Christ explicitly forbade, is to pay too high a price to achieve a theoretical conformity with one part of the Christian marriage pattern.'

Sunday Press, Dublin, 25 July 1973.

We have reminded Father Hastings, as we now also remind our readers, that the Council of Trent (Session XXIV, can. 2 Denzinger, 33rd Ed. No. 1802) has solemnly taught:-

'If anyone shall say that it is unlawful for Christians to have several wives at the same time, and that this is not forbidden by any Divine Law, let him be anathema.'

So while Father Hastings insists on being called a 'Catholic priest' (letter of 29 September) he still holds that Christ had 'nothing explicit' to say in condemnation of polygamy — notwithstanding Christ's words in St Matthew c. XIX, 5 – 'They shall be two in one flesh . . .' Father Hastings may call himself a 'Catholic priest, but his break with the doctrinal unity which is essential for Catholicity, places him outside the Church. We note that he teaches at the Anglican College of the Ascension, near Birmingham.

A communique issued by the 'Anglican/Roman Catholic International Commission' on Friday 7 September 1973, stated, that it was releasing an 'unanimously agreed' declaration to the press; one which would have the 'deepest importance for the future relations between the two Churches.' 'In the past', the statement reads, 'disagreement on these two issues (the doctrines of the Eucharist and the doctrine of the Ministry) obscured a large area of common belief and made it impossible for Roman Catholics to recognise Anglican Orders.' If words mean anything, this statement means that members of the Commission unanimously agreed on some doctrine which would now make it possible for Catholics to recognise Anglican Orders. Was this a recognition by the Catholic members of the Commission of the validity of Anglican Orders?

Bishop Alan Clarke hastened to issue a 'prepared statement' to the press a few days later, in which he said that it was 'the nature and purpose of the ministry' which was agreed upon.

Accustomed as we are to the continuous quibbling by this Commission (recall the infamous Windsor Statement 1971) this new display of polemics is not surprising.

If to restate Bishop Clark's words, it was 'the nature and purpose of the ministry' that was agreed upon – unanimously – then, either the non-Catholic members of the commission accepted the 'sacrificial nature' of the priesthood, or, the Catholic members abandoned the Catholic doctrine of the Mass being a true sacrifice and the priesthood being a sacrificial priesthood.

In view of the Windsor statement which preceded it and which went far to assign the element of 'sacrifice' to the theological dustbin, one can only conclude that 'unanimous agreement' was arrived at, by betrayal on the part of the Catholic members of the Commission.

Recognition of Anglican Orders as valid by Bishops, ecclesiastics, nuns and laity is now widespread throughout the country – now close to Holland in the advancement of Modernism (thanks to the Silent Bishops!) – Eucharistic happenings' are taking place in which Catholics receive the Eucharists from the hands of non-Catholics and vice versa. Hardy *aggiornamented'* priests and others fling theological obstacles to the wind (their Faith having already gone) and indulge in all kinds of so-called 'Eucharistic' festivities. *The Unitarian* for August 1973 described the scene which took place in the Benedictine Abbey at Worth, during Holy Week of 1973, in the following words:-

> 'At the Conventional Mass we stood around the altar together – monks, students and Unitarian Minister – and joyfully celebrated the Lord's Resurrection. "You shall see Jesus in Galilee" the cantor sung to a very catchy tune . . . but it was impossible not to feel his presence right there at the breaking of the bread' (Page 89).

The author of the Article (Tony Cross) then concludes:-

> 'Too often in the past, liberal moves within the Church (RC) have met with cruel and crushing repression . . . but now the liberalisation process has gathered a tremendous momentum and cannot be stopped short of disaster. Indeed it would not be going too far wrong to claim that we were celebrating not only the resurrection of Jesus but also that of the Roman Catholic Church.'

The Secretary of the Catholic Priests' Association has been given much documented evidence of 'inter-communion' being practised in many

ILLNESS AND ARTICLES FOR THE *NEWSLETTER* 183

dioceses, and in particular in Chapels and homes, where Catholic University Chaplains celebrate the Eucharistic rites.

General Absolution in place of auricular Confession and Absolution is quite widespread, and has been practised by the Chaplain of Pilgrimage groups at Lourdes.

When details of such abuse are offered to the Bishop they just refuse to accept the evidence. We give here a report from *Life and Work — A Record of the Church of Scotland*, September 1973. It reads:-

'Scots at Charismatic Conference. A hundred representatives from 18 countries met in the summer of 1973 at the Ecumenical Academy at Schloss Craheim, West Germany, for the second European Charismatic Leaders' Conference. A 'progress report' of the Roman Catholic Pentecostal Dialogue was given by the co-chairmen David du Plessis and Father Killlan McDonnell. Theological papers were given by the RC Professor Francis Sullivan of Rome who spoke on 'The Roman Catholic Interpretation of the Pentecostal experience'. Among the most moving moments were the early morning sacraments of Communion, the liturgies of the Roman Catholic, Lutheran, Dutch Reformed and Baptist Churches, following on successive days, each one partaking of bread and wine at each service. Here was real deep ecumenicity, the Sacrament blending so naturally with the gift of the Holy Spirit.'

Yet another source of disrupting the unity of the Church is the ever growing 'Private Revelations' that now mushroom up all over the world. It is not for us to pass judgment on whether these are genuine or not, but there are some which must be dismissed as fraudulent deceptions right away, those in which the recipients are told to disobey the Pope. A publication called *Twenty-six Particular and Private Messages* with an *Imprime Potest* of S.J. Gaudeze M.F., 1 June 1972, *Vergel*, Mexico, and described as a 'gift from the Franciscians Minims of Perpetual Help of Mary, 249, La Villa de Gaudalupe, Coloria Santa Isabel Tola, 14, D.F., Mexico', contains in vol.II, 'heavenly messages' that the present liturgy is not a 'Catholic Mass'; that the local shop must reject the *Missa Normativa,* and the Mass of Pius V must remain.

As in previous editions of this *Newsletter* we continue to refer to yet again to the satanical (there is no other word for it) profanation of the Most Blessed Sacrament which continues, with the fury of forest fire, to sweep all before it, and all of it under the label of 'Liturgical Experimentation'.

When open desecration of the Blessed Sacrament is at stake, it is time for even the most squeamish to pack up their definitions of charity and get out an open war, a 'Holy War', on the ecclesiastics, Commissions, nuns, laity – whoever they may be – who insult our intelligence and trample our faith under foot and ask us as the 'People of God' to continue financial support to the The Blessed Sacrament desecrater, are found in every diocese in this country befouling the awesome centre of Catholicism itself. T.V. viewers not so long ago saw one Sunday evening in one of our Catholic Cathedrals, a certain Auxiliary Bishop walking up the centre aisle to celebrate a 'folk Mass', while a dancing girl went ahead of him. What an insult to Our Divine Lord that one of His own consecrated Bishops with the fullness of the priesthood, a successor of the Apostles, should lower himself and all that he is supposed to stand for, to the level of the street girl.

Why do not such ecclesiastics have the common decency to tell the 'people of God' that they have not the guts to stand up to Modernism and gracefully retire from the Episcopacy?

What an insult to the Eucharistic Presence of Christ! I imagine one of the Apostles taking in from the streets of Jerusalem, some young slip of a girl to bounce and gyrate before the Apostles at the Last Supper! No doubt Peter would have cut off more than his ear, as he did in the case of *Malchus in the Garden*. Catholics of this and other countries where Modernism is permitted to run riot, have long ago reached the stage of being like St Paul, 'ablaze with indignation'.

This *Newsletter* will not endeavour to extinguish the blaze, but rather it will do everything possible to fan the flames of righteous indignation against those ecclesiastics whose office is meaningless if they do not use it to resist Modernism at every step. 'People of God' – to use the words so frequently used by Vatican II, show that you are the 'People of God' and not the 'People of Satan' who will permit the desecration of the Blessed Sacrament in our Churches, built and paid for by our saintly forbearers. Arise from the sleep of indifference, take the sword of the spirit and slay Modernism wherever its fiendish head appears.

Dealing with liturgical aberrations, one often wonders if those who seek new forms of worship, really understand what it is that they pursue. As Dr Bryan Wilson, Reader in Sociology at All Souls College, Oxford, points out (*The Times*, 27 October 1973), those who seek new forms of Worship see in the Church today 'ossified forms of Church organisation' which they wish to 'restructure', but the word 'restructure' means for them 'destructure' or 'destroy'. 'Man's religion', writes Professor Wilson 'is today, necessarily biological, essentially sexual . . . Hence there is folk-rock panel discussions, song contests and free expression' – the ideas are drawn from educational innovators and from the entertainment industry . . . with an undercurrent of contrived ecstasy . . . In London, a Roman Catholic Folk Mass with dancing recently advertised the promise that the unexpected and unavoidable may happen . . . the young want mystical experience; ecstasy, the orgy, the trip . . . Christianity in the past served to discipline the emotions confining the ecstasy to moments of recollection in tranquillity.

It is not certain that Christianity today can continue to serve secular society, it is much more evident that it has no future as the plaything of the leisure moments of the young in search of instant ecstasy.'

How wisely does Professor Wilson write, striking directly at the very heart of the 'liturgical aberrations' in the Church today. The young seek a sexual ecstasy which they find, but only for a time, in the rock of Folk Mass, but which quickly evaporates; old novelties cease to appeal, and the young must then turn to other 'happenings' to recover the last sexual ecstasy. Hence, the liturgical innovations never end, except when they finally extinguish 'faith', and the young must once more return to the purely secular for the 'kicks' for a time, experienced at what was thought as 'new forms of worship'. We reach the ultimate when faith itself is snuffed out by the very means, which should be an expression of itself. The wheel of liturgical innovations has made a complete revolution, and the 'non-young' are lost in the process.

An example of what has been started in the preceding paragraph is found in the *Newsletter of the Diocese of Arundel and Brighton,* Autumn 1973, p.p.45-46, under the title 'Liverpool '73', an article in which three youths describe their experiences in both the Catholic and Anglican Cathedrals of Liverpool. They describe, how, in the crypt of the Anglican Cathedral at midnight, they had 'non-verbal communication' and the events that followed:-

> 'A smooth voice directed us in what was one of the most unnerving experiences of the week. We were all encouraged to relax – and to be aware of self - and then get up and find a partner – all this happening with eyes closed. On finding another by touch only, we had to explore each other; expressing feeling without the aid of words or vision . . . In the darkness, we were able to communicate on the same level – to love each other because we were both God's creations.'

The culmination of the week was the experience at the new Catholic Metropolitan Cathedral of Liverpool, which is described as follows:-

'We ended the week in the Metropolitan Cathedral singing, praying, and dancing around the altar (literally, the altar is in the centre of this 'Mersey Funnel') praising God for what we had learned.'

This example from real life, bears out the point emphasised by Professor Wilson, in the article already quoted. The 'sexual ecstasy' experienced during the mutual 'exploration by touch' of each other's body, is considered as a new 'form of worship'.

No doubt it is worship, but with Satan on the receiving end. It is bad enough to have such blasphemy in the Catholic Cathedral ('thanking God for what was learned') but publishing such satanical swill in a Diocesan Newsletter which has on its cover a photograph of the Bishop with his coat of arms (*Quis ut Deus*) strains our confidence in ecclesiastical administration to breaking point — not to count the evil demoralising effects on other youth, and the strain and anxiety created for parents.

Liverpool's Cathedral opened with girls 'dancing' around the altar, and the continuance of the practice is not surprising. A complete clean up of the Archdiocese, from the Archbishop down would do much to restore lost Faith in the Church in that Archdiocese.

Let us hope that a future strong Pope will, through, Divine Providence, come on the throne of Peter, who will not hesitate to dispatch the unfaithful Shepherds.

That the God **Sex** is replacing, in the minds and hearts of men, the true concept and image of God is beyond question — and with ecclesiastical approval. We have seen the uproar caused in this country during June-August 1972 in connection with *Choices in Sex* with its *Nihil Obstat* and *Imprimatur,* when parents and others protested against the filth of this booklet. We have seen the strong encouragement given to this soul destroyer by Father Enda McDonagh, the Maynooth Pope of Modernism, and the support he in turn received from other professors of that College. We have seen the sphinx-like silence of the Irish Bishops, while the Church is being destroyed under their very gaze. We have seen the valiant efforts of the intrepid Hamish Frazer to expose in his *The Scandal of Maynooth the Modernism* that is ripe in Ireland's primary seminary, and the abuse to which he and the CPA have been subjected in some of the Irish papers. The fight must go on — too much is at stake to remain apathetic. The story of the *Nihil Obstat* and *Choices in Sex* is nothing new.

In Canada in 1971, two 'Catechetical text books' were out in circulation with the *Imprimatur* of Monsignor Gerard-Marie Coderre, Bishop of St Jean, Quebec. The books were called *Sexualite et Vie Quotidienne* (*Sex and Daily Life*) and *La Force des recontres* (*The Force of Casual Meetings*), and they have been judged by a reviewer (Vers Demain, September 1971) as 'Blasphemous, sacrilegious, obscene, pornographic and pernicious . . . ' and so impure, that the reviewer (aged 60) declared 'I cannot try to understand them without risking mortal sin.' These booklets were written for young children, the 'little ones' concerning whom Christ issued the special warning, that it would be better to be drowned in the depths of the sea with a millstone about your neck, than scandalise one of these. These words and warnings of Christ, however, no longer mean anything to very many of the Church's Bishops, as they have lost their faith long ago, and those who have not lost their faith, have lost their courage.

Amidst the endless 'insights' which the Modernistic seers of today claim to have, it is most revealing how so many of them concern the basic instinct of sex. The effects of original sin on the human person seems to be intensified and re-enkindled by every loosing of the moral control, which as a Christian he is expected to have over his passions. Sex, more than any other human matter, seems to be the pivot around which man becomes either superhuman or subhuman.

We have seen in the previous paragraph of this editorial, how the liturgical innovators have made sexual ecstasy the attraction for the young, and we have no doubt, that as time goes on, the 'experts' with the monopoly of 'insights' into education, will discover yet new techniques for using the lever of sex to move people deeper into pure secularism.

Obsessed by sex the 'Christian' sees not absurdity between being the 'spiritual leader' of others and being the instrument of Satan. The lady on the way to the Church to distribute Holy Communion in conformity with the Apostolic Document *Immensae Caritatis* as she was one of the Episcopally approved 'Distributors' in the diocese, saw nothing wrong in stopping off at the chemist shop to collect her prescribed contraceptive pills.

Future historians will have fearful judgments to pass on those educational experts in the post-Vatican II period, who destroyed every vestige of Christian civilisation in the minds of those who were entrusted to their care.

It will be difficult to find words to express the utter destruction of all that is noble, all that is wholesome, all that is in keeping with the dignity of man by the prophets of the new Pentecost. It is an unquestionable fact, that the Church is now suffering from the effects of appointments to Episcopal Sees throughout the world over the last 40 years, of men who were in most part entirely unfit for the responsible position of chief pastor of a diocese. In Britain another factor must be considered – not a few of the Hierarchy in the post-Vatican II period are Neophytes, with little depth in their Catholicism. St Paul pointed out the danger that arises from such appointments, and it was Newman, himself a convert, who declared that is only after three generations of Catholicism, that the faith is firmly embedded.

We end this Editorial by giving our readers an echo from the hill of Calvary – to show that hatred of Christ of a diabolical nature masquerades in Catholic Colleges to despoil the souls of the young. The French-Canadian paper *Vers Demain*, September 1971, reports that in a Catholic School at Val d'Or, Abitoba, Quebec, a school game was initiated for the boys which consisted in a competition in which boys tried to beat each other in spitting at the figure of Christ on the cross. The one who succeeded in covering the face of Christ Crucified with the biggest spit, won the competition.

What echoes of Golgotha!

What an unspeakable act of contempt for the Saviour of Mankind – and all in a Catholic School.

One could suspect the source from which this insight came.

XVII

CHRISTIAN ORDER AND THE OLD MASS
by Editor of *Newsletter*   Father John W. Flanagan
Vol. 1 1974

IN THE JANUARY 1974 issue of *Christian Order*, the editor of that esteemed publication has an Article on The Old Mass and in this regard has reached certain conclusions which we regret and which we hold are not correct.

In the pages of *Newsletter* we have openly recommended Father Paul Crane S.T., *Christian Order* as one of the best publications in circulation today, and it is because we admire it, that we should feel free to state when we disagree with it, particularly in a matter which intimately concerns all Catholics today.

Father Crane opens his article by stating, how in the beginning, he accepted the changes introduced by the new liturgy . . . some points of which he approved and others (e.g. omissions of genuflections, blessings, etc) which he did not like.

On these matters, the author of this article in *Newsletter* would go further, by saying that, few if any of the changes were pleasing. The old liturgy was the clothing in which the Mass had long come to be recognised as the greatest and most sublime event on the face of the Globe. It was the ceremonial or 'court etiquette' which surrounded the tremendous and awe-inspiring coming of Jesus Christ on our altars. The beauty, the grandeur, the dignity which clothed the Real Presence in the old liturgy, have been whipped away in a manner never visualised by Vatican II, when it decided upon the Revision and simplification of the Mass Liturgy (Decree on the Liturgy, par. 50).

The new liturgy has thrown the clothing away, and like the executioners of Christ on the hill of Calvary, He stands 'exposed to the gaze of the mocking multitude' to use the words of St Alphonsus in his meditations on 'The Way of the Cross'.

It is the same Christ, however, whether He be wrapped in swaddling clothes in a manger or naked on the Cross.

It is not the liturgy that makes the Mass, but the Mass that makes the liturgy. The liturgical 'experts' who produced the new liturgy have done immense harm to souls and have contributed no small amount to the loss of faith in the world today.

Nevertheless, if the old liturgy was never changed, Modernism would still be with us in all its savagery and fury – in fact it was with us even before the liturgical changes came about.

Undoubtedly, the Modernists used the weakness of the new liturgy to advance their case, not only by perverting the only Papally approved Latin text of the *Missa Normativa*, but also by the world-wide implementations' of the liturgy for which the *Novus Ordo* made room. The liturgy has been turned into jollification bordering on the cabaret and stage performance – as evinced in the televised Mass on Christmas Day from Harrogate, Yorkshire, with Monsignor Buckley of Wood Hall, as the laughing, grimacing, clown-like celebrant – all facilitated by the failure of the Hierarchy to observe the 'Third Instruction on the Liturgy' (5 September 1971) and to enforce its observance by penalty, if necessary.

The Church urgently needs a true translation of the *Missa Normativa* as much as it needs priests to observe the law, that the Latin Mass is still the rule and the vernacular the exception see (Decree on the Liturgy, par.150). The celebration of Mass in the Latin tongue (with lesson and Gospel in the vernacular), the regular use of the Roman Canon and the omission of undesirable 'options', such as lay people reading, processions at the *Offertory* with ill-clad females, etc., will do much to restore the liturgy of the Mass to its former dignity.

Father Paul Crane in his article in *Christian Order* endeavours to establish that the new liturgy did not abrogate or replace the previously existing one. In his arguments he leans heavily on an article that appeared last year in the French publication *Itineraires* written by Père Dulac in which the author contends that the Liturgy of Pope St Pius V (known as *The Trindentine Mass*) still may be used by every priest at his discretion, as the new Mass is only an extra option. Father Crane accepts this view and for the following arguments, which we hope to refute to the satisfaction of the reader.

1. 'Pope Paul never intended to abolish the Old Liturgy; he issued no legislation, specifically intended to have this effect, neither did he make the new Mass mandatory.'

COMMENT: Vatican II, The Decree of the Liturgy, par.50, decided on a 'Revision and simplification of the Mass Liturgy.' The Decree is dated 4 December 1963. It would be remarkably strange if after ten years, the decision of Vatican II were not implemented. The Council in its Decree did not mention an alternative liturgy for the Mass, as would be the case if Father Dulac and Crane had come to the right conclusion.

2. The privilege given by Pope St. Pius V to all priests and forever, has not been abrogated by the new Liturgy.' (*Christian Order* p.48.)

COMMENT: The promulgation of the *Novus Ordo* by Pope Paul VI made it crystal clear that the previous liturgy is abrogated, and may not be used, unless in the exceptional cases permitted by the Supreme Legislator. One had only to consult the Official Acts of the Apostolic See in which all laws of the Holy See are promulgated, to realise this fact. *The Acts of the Apostolic See* (AAS) Vol.63 (1971, pp.217, 710 and 749 respectively, contain the official promulgation by the Holy Father. The radical and irrevocable change of the liturgy was insisted upon by the Pope in two allocutions given at the Vatican on the 19 and 26 November 1969, in which the Pontiff demanded from all Catholics, prompt acceptance. (*Notitiae*, 1969, p.412, see also *Documentation Catholique*, 1969 p.1102ss.)

To state that the Pontiff did not intend to abrogate the previously existing liturgy, is a gratuitous statement in the light of the fact that the Decree promulgating the *Novous Ordo* has the words -

'We intend that the statutes and prescriptions which we have established, shall remain firm and efficacious, both in the present and in the future, notwithstanding those Constitutions and Apostolic Ordinances of our predecessors, including those which require special mention before they could be abrogated.'

If words mean anything, the Pontiff clearly and unmistakably has withdrawn the previous liturgy of Pope St. Pius V.

There are some who argue that Pope Pius V's *Quo Primum* threatened severe judgment on those who would dare to change its contents. No Pontiff can possibly restrict the exercise of the plenitude of power of any of his successors, and the emphatic words of *Quo Primum* have never (until recent years) been understood by anyone, as appertaining to a subsequent successor on the throne of Peter. May it be pointed out, moreover, that Canon 23 of the present Code of Canon Law, would, apart from any specific mention of abrogation, terminate the previous liturgy, as we know from this Canon that a 'subsequent law abrogates a previous one . . . if it rearranges the matter of the previous legislation.'

The new *Missa Normativa* permits the use of the previous liturgy in certain exceptional cases — for the aged and infirm priests who celebrate privately. Cardinal Heenan acquired a further concession for this country, which enables the Bishops to grant permission for the former Mass in certain exceptional cases. The document authorising the permission is in the name of the Holy See (as the author of this article possesses two of them).

If, as Fathers Dulac and Crane contend, the old liturgy may be used everywhere and by all priests, as a 'privilege granted by a Pope may not be abrogated even by officials of the Vatican, including Archbishop Bugnini' (page 48 of *Christian Order,*) it is more than extraordinary that the *Novus Ordo* unquestionably promulgated by Pope Paul, would refer to exceptional cases where the old liturgy may yet be followed. A 'perpetual privilege' as Father Crane calls it, that is the right of every priest and forever, is meaningless, if it can be only used by individuals in exceptional cases.

One is forced back on the situation and forced to ask oneself whether it is Father Dulac who is right, while Pope Paul has been dreaming.

The writer of this article sympathises very much with Father Crane's stand, and realises that his (Father Crane's) conviction emerges from the realisation that he has, of the many broken hearts, and lost faith, among once good Catholics, who have been sickened to death with the Liturgical aberrations in the sanctuary.

But in assessing the validity of the arguments upon which his conclusion rests, he cannot permit emotive elements to enter.

If Pope Paul is wrong in promulgating the *Missa Normativa*, and if Catholics are free to ignore that the *Novus Ordo* is obligatory, will not this mentality lead to much greater disasters in the Church? If the Pope is wrong, and can be disregarded, where can disobedience end? The whole edifice of Catholicism has been Divinely built on and around the Vicar of Christ, and we ignore this at our own peril, and that of our fellow Catholics.

Father Crane's final point is, that it is a *de facto* case, that observance of the *Novus Ordo* is not mandatory — the practice of the *Sacristan* of St. Peter's in Rome who permits the Tridentine Mass there, when asked, is cited as proof.

This is no argument. St. Peter's, Rome, liturgically speaking, has always been 'above the Law'; one could, down the years, celebrate any Mass there, whatever contrary feast it happened to be. The writer of this article is aware of five ecclesiastics who put the question directly to the Roman Pontiff, 'Whether he intended to abrogate the former liturgy by the promulgation of *Novus Ordo?*'

The answer has always been the same: 'in the Affirmative, apart from the exceptional cases designated.'

It is an accepted principle of canonical interpretation, that if it (an interpretation) leads to absurdity, then it is erroneous. An interpretation of the will of the Vicar of Christ as to the new liturgy, that can be considered as a 'perpetual privilege enjoyed by all priests forever' (*Christian Order* p.48) and yet, which can only be used with due permission from the Holy See and in exceptional situations – as the *Novus Ordo* regulates, are two propositions which are in direct conflict, and this is an absurdity.

'*Verba clara non indiqent interpretatione sed executione*' states the axiom, which manifestly applies to the case under consideration.

THE NEW LITURGY – CHOICE OR OBLIGATION?
by Father John W. Flanagan   C.P.A. *Newsletter,*
Vol. V No.1 1975

This article is written for Catholics, and therefore for those, who, if they are entitled to this title, must accept the doctrine of the Church, that every Pope has the plenitude of authority entrusted to Peter by the Church's Divine Founder. As a Catholic, he must also accept the doctrine of the Divine guarantee given by Christ, that error would not be permitted to prevail against the Church.

The article will have no meaning for those who claim to be Catholics, but who, in their hearts are not sure about the two basic propositions contained in the previous paragraph, nor will it have any value for those, who unconsciously or perhaps, subconsciously, are affected by the Modernists' doctrine, that the Church and not the Roman Pontiff is the recipient of Divine protection, and who take 'Church' as a democratically established and opinion poll functioning assembly of the 'people of God', with the Pontiff as the Chairman who is ultimately responsible to the people.

Again, this article should not be studied by so-called 'traditional' Catholics, who have already made up their minds that the new Mass is a 'forgery', which Pope Paul VI has forced on the Church, and that it is neither moral or legal, and to assist at it, is nothing short of sacrilege. (See *The Great Sacrilege*, Father James Wathen: on second thoughts, better not see it, but burn it) Catholic readers do not have to be reminded that conclusions reached by such people as Father Wathen, that the Mass is a blasphemy and a sacrilege, in time, would bring the whole edifice of Catholicism down. If the Pope is a heretic, he is not a Pope; one who is cut off from membership – as heresy does by its very nature – cannot be the head. It is as simple as that. Father Wathen's conclusions – and the same holds for those who follow him – are incompatible with belief in the Divinity of Christ.

This article is not out to compare the glories of the previous liturgy with the new; it is not out to compare the aesthetic or even musical advantages that the old liturgy had over the new.

It is not out to uncover the machinations which went on among certain Council Fathers, to get the Constitution on the Liturgy approved as quickly as possible, and still less, is it out to uncover the subtle intrigues and backstairs manipulations which went on among liturgical experts before and during the Council, to have a text approved by the Council Fathers that would give them a launching pad from which to fire their deadly missiles at the very heart of Catholic life and worship – the Mass. There was enough intrigue and subtle machinations behind scenes at Vatican II, to bring the collapse of any organisation, that had not the Hand of God to bring the evil schemes to nought. As the Bishops of the world today have surrendered, in practice, their authority to rule their dioceses, to groups of faceless men (and women) called 'Commissions', so too, at the Vatican Council, Bishops, profoundly ignorant of theology and liturgy were sitting ducks for the sharpshooter liturgists who abounded within and without the Grand Assembly of Bishops.

Crackpot liturgists, were accepted by many Bishops as 'men with wonderful insights' into the depths of liturgical development, when in fact, those same Bishops were being fed with the liturgical swill of physically sick men. Many Bishops voted in favour of the new liturgy on the recommendation of eccentric liturgists. One well-known Dutch author, Father Schillebeeckx, was heard to say, during a Council session, dealing with liturgy: 'Give us authorised alternatives in the liturgy and we will change its whole nature.'

While the work of the progressive liturgists went on unabated, it would be wrong to conclude that the liturgical scholars were all men of eccentricity and out to destroy the traditional liturgy of the Church. Since the early '20s, to the days of the Council, the rise of liturgical Conferences grew in volume from a mere trickle to a mighty tide. The great tide threw up, not only the flotsam and jetsam of progressive speculation but also

CHRISTIAN ORDER AND THE OLD MASS – A CHOICE... 195

some excellent and scholarly material produced by liturgists who had given much research to the origin and development of the early liturgies. The name *Bugnini* much associated with the new liturgy, and discredited so vehemently by extremists in the period following the promulgation of the new liturgy, received his first step towards notoriety from the hands of the traditional Pontiff, Pope Pius XII, whom he was made Secretary of the Liturgical Commission. If we notice much of the Constitution on the Sacred Liturgy of Vatican II, studded with select quotations and phrasing of the great Encyclical *Mediator Dei* of Pope Pius XII, much of the credit must go to Archbishop Bugnini. With this brief summary of the tensions being built up on the liturgical front, between those who advocated revolutionary ideas in the liturgy, and those who favoured conservative but researched changed and modifications, we are not in a position to understand, how the much needed Divine Guarantee of protection from error, was essential, if the Pope was to safeguard orthodoxy on one hand, and yet, meet the request for changes on the other.

It will of course be said, that the rank and file of the faithful were perfectly happy with the then existing liturgy of the Mass, and their opinions were never asked. This is perfectly true, but during this period of the pre-Council days, were the faithful asked to express their opinion? If they had been asked, would they be in a position to express their preferences in an intelligible manner?

They were the days when the Bishops, and perhaps a few priest advisors, alone, had any say in the course of ecclesiastical events. Let not the reader conclude that the writer of this article supports the democratisation of the Church which we witness today – it is entirely abhorrent.

In the pre-Council commissions, nothing can be found in their discussions that would indicate the introduction of an alternative liturgy, that is, one that would co-exist with the liturgy of Pope St. Pius V. The whole thrust of the arguments favoured a return to simplification, and re-emphasis on dialogue between celebrant and congregation, already existing in the Latin dialogue Mass which existed before the Council and which was the fruit of much liturgical research. A more active part to be played by the people was favoured all round. This point of the 'alternative liturgy' is important, as it destroys the ground on whom some endeavour to retain the co-existence of Tridentine and new liturgy, to be used at the discretion of the Priest.

Much of the doubt in circulation today, mostly, if not entirely, among Catholics who hold extreme views, as to the binding force of Pope Paul's new liturgy, arises from the writings of a certain Father James Wathen, who in his book *The Great Sacrilege* quotes Abbé Dulac and Abbé Georges de

Nantes, who claim that Pope Paul's liturgy, was never intended by him to be an obligatory liturgy, but merely an alternative, one which any priest could decide at will, not to use. Father Wathen quotes the two Abbés as claiming that they have discovered a wicked forgery, perpetrated by the *Vatican Press Bureau* (see Father Wathen's *The Great Sacrilege*, p.136) and a deliberate falsification of a translation worked into the French, English and Italian texts, so as to give the idea that the liturgy was not optional. As this is the very heart of the matter and an error so blatantly perpetrated by the 'three wise men' (Wathen, Dulac and de Nates) so as to deceive the unsuspecting, it is vital that we take Father Wathen's arguments (if they can be called by that name) and expose them for what they are.

Let us recall that Pope Paul's Apostolic Constitution *Missale Romanum* was to the *Novus Ordo Missae*, what Pope Pius V's Constitution and Pius V's *Quo Primum* were solemn declarations of Papal intent, viz, to introduce a new liturgy. The Roman *Missal* which followed some years later, was the implementation of the previously expressed Papal intention. As Pius V's liturgy could only be properly understood by co-relating the text of *Quo Primum* with his *Missale Romanum* so, too, Paul V's Constitution and his *Novus Ordo Missae* form one piece of legislative enactment, and must be studied together. To argue that the document of 'intent' and the document of 'realisation' or 'effect' do not agree, because one is silent on what the other expresses, it is to fail to study them as one.

Father Wathen's citation from Abbé Dulac and de Nantes, are so profoundly false, that it would be injustice to the reader of this *Newsletter*, not to give the pertinent passages in toto.

Let us see what the *Great Sacrilege* has to tell us. On page 136 we read Father Wathen citing de Nantes:-

'In the first paragraph of this conclusion of his discourse the Holy Father expresses his hope that the new *Missal* will be received by all, as a sign and instrument of unity; *Confidimus*.

It is through an unheard of act of violence — abuse No.1 — that the Press Bureau invented the false translation which I am now going to give you: 'In conclusion we wish to give the force of law to all that we have set forth concerning the new Roman Missal'. This conclusion with its formally legislative tone, is a fabrication, inserted in the place where the Pope had merely written, according to the faithful translation made by Abbé Dulac: 'Concerning all that we have just set forth, regarding the new Roman Missal we are pleased here to end by drawing a conclusion.'

And this conclusion refers to the confidence that all will find again in this Missal, their mutual unity. Whoever has transformed this 'confidence' in a law, has lied.

'Having made a good start, and while they were about it, they invented a second paragraph, which does not exist at all in the original Latin . . . Here then is the fraud; 'We order that the prescription of this Constitution go into effect 30 November of this year, the first Sunday of Advent.'

This is the essence of the text and its forgery. 'Here we have a simple statement of the wishes of Paul VI, a directive bereft of sanctions . . . the forged text issued by the Press Bureau imposes an obligation: that is as much as to say that the true text imposes nothing of the kind. That was the thing to be proved. The Constitution *Missale Romanum* in its authentic Latin text, does not impose an obligation to follow his *Ordo Missae* . . . There is nothing that can validly annul the Bull of St. Pius V. Paul VI in his Constitution does not formally abrogate it (p.137).

On pages 138-9 of his *Great Sacrilege*, Father Wathen continues his comments as follows. Giving the words of the *Actas Apostolicae Sedis* dealing with the new liturgy and which reads as follows, Father Wathen gives the true as distinct from the erroneous translation. We quote:

'*Ad extremum, ex iis quae hactenus de novo Missalli Romano exposuimus quiddam nunc cogere et efficere placet . . .* '

Father Wathen gives as the INCORRECT TRANSLATION, what in fact is the CORRECT ONE. The Latin words *cogere et efficere* used by the Pope, literally mean 'to compel and to effect' – no place for a 'Directive' in this terminology, so Father Wathen's only approach to it, would be to try barefacedly to deceive readers of his book who do not know Latin. Truth becomes falsity and falsity becomes truth – this is Father Wathen's solution – tell the BIG BOLD LIE. Well, let us be charitable about it, and give it another explanation.

He then gives the correct translation as follows: 'Concerning all that we have just set forth regarding the new *Roman Missal*, we are pleased here to end by drawing a conclusion.'

One can only ask if Father Wathen has even done the rudiments of Latin? No schoolboy even starting Latin would be guilty of such a blunder Father Wathen is guilty of in this comment of his.

Perhaps he was hoping that his 'translation' would not be read by anyone who knew Latin. Yet, this man has the effrontery to give as the correct translation, a sentence which has no similarity to the meaning of the Latin. His supposed true translation in the words – 'We are pleased here to end by drawing a conclusion' – no doubt will prompt many readers to the right conclusion, that Father Wathen is the master forger, a crime which he attributes to others in the Vatican, or he has not a clue to the Latin language. We are inclined to accept the latter interpretation, which is borne out by a passage of his book (p.139) where he uses the word *Confidimus* (we trust or we hope) to convey the impression that Pope Paul used this word to indicate a mere hope or desire that his *Missal* would be accepted by the faithful, when in fact, as the text clearly indicates, the Pope used it, to express his desire for prompt obedience to the new legislative enactment, a theme to which he returned more than once in the subsequent years. When one says 'I hope the faithful keep the Ten Commandments' it is surely not implied that the Decalogue is now merely a directive without binding force!

Father Wathen's other arguments stagger the imagination. Quoting once again the erratic Abbé de Nantes, he claims that the original Constitution on the Liturgy did not give a date on which it became operative to have the new liturgy and later editions of it referred to the 30 November as the day in question, the Abbé and Father Wathen, see in this another example of the hand of the forger. It does not seem to have struck them, that as the new *Missal* had to be translated into numerous vernacular languages, it was impossible to settle a date for its practical operation on a world wide basis. This could only be done at a later date, as was the case.

We now come to another category of writer, very different from the 'Wathen-Dulac-de Nates' combination, which supports the view that the new liturgy is optional. These writers subscribing such articles to publications such as *The Remnant* (USA), *Christian Order* (London), *La Pensee Catholique* (Paris), *Courrier de Rome* (Paris), *Itineraires* (Paris), etc., etc.

The names of these writers are probably familiar to readers of ' Newsletter':-
    FATHER CRANE S.J.
    LOUIS SALLERON (FRENCH LAYMAN)
    MICHAEL DAVIES (AN ENGLISHMAN AND LAYMAN)
    MONSIGNOR JEAN MADIRAN (A FRENCHMAN)
and many others in whose arguments we are more interested than in their names.

In general, most of the points, established by the writers referred to above, are valid objections to the vernacular (French or English) texts on which they build their criticism.

To build a criticism of a Papally approved text on manifestly false translations of the same, is certainly not a sound policy. In a distinct pamphlet *Fortes dans la Foi* (a Repudiation) I have shown how every argument advanced in the leaflet issued by the French organisation *Fortes in Fide* is unsustainable, for the simple reason, that the criticism of the liturgy is based entirely on a FALSE TRANSLATION from LATIN to FRENCH. The same is true where other translations are concerned. The deplorable text of the English liturgy, is not even a decent attempt to translate the Papal text; the vernacular has been changed deliberately to create either a false sense of the content of the *Missa Normativa*, or to give it such an ecumenical twist, as to cause people to ask – 'Is truth being sacrificed for a false ecumenism?' Those who revolt against the liturgical reform, could well be advised to direct their energies in acquiring a true translation and in promoting the use of the Latin liturgy as the general principle in conformity with Vatican II.

One notices in reading the arguments produced by those last writers, a pronounced tendency to accept earlier arguments put forward by Abbé Dulac, without questioning the validity of the arguments themselves. For example, we find Louis Salleron in *Pensée Catholique* (No.153, 1974) pp.46-47, falling back on the use of '. . . PEUT utiliser . . .' and '. . . on POURRA utiliser . . .', the verb *peut* and *pourra* proving, as the writer imagines, that the whole new liturgy is one which 'one MAY use', when in fact, the enactments quoted are merely giving priests the option of using the new *Ordo,* rather than the old Mass, before the arrival of the date on which the new liturgy becomes OBLIGATORY. We find this argument (and what a false one!) already used by Abbé Dulac.

We also find from Louis Salleron, the argument, that even if the *Quo Primum* Bull of Pope St. Pius V, was revoked by Paul VI's *Missale Romanum* a priest would still enjoy, unchanged and unchangeable, the 'privilege', which is 'immemorial and given in perpetuity' by Pope Pius V, of celebrating according to the old liturgy.

This has also come from Abbé Dulac, and one can only ask if the Abbé has forgotten that a privilege granted *per modum legis*, as was the case in question, ceases with the revocation of the law from which it arose (CANONS 71 and 60, CODE OF CANON LAW).

It does not convince anyone, to be told, as Louis Salleron tells his readers, that 'the whole legal system of the Church is in complete disarray . . . and in all departments of both faith and morals, the French Hierarchy encourage subversion . . . and hence the laity must manifest their opposition . . .' Disarray among the Hierarchy and even betrayal by them of the Church – which is all too true – is not a title for disloyalty and obedience to the Sovereign Pontiff. The demolition of the Churches and the altars of which Salleron writes, has, no doubt, as a proximate cause, the failure of the Hierarchy in France faithfully to defend orthodoxy; but the remote cause must be the failure on the part of the Hierarchy in turn to enforce Papal decrees.

It will not help if yet another decree of the Vicar of Christ, on the new liturgy, is cast aside. Disobedience by the Hierarchy is not cured by disobedience to the Hierarchy's Supreme Bishop.

Like Louis Salleron, both Father Crane and M. Davies, who defend the Church's doctrines so well in other spheres, fall back on pastoral problems (reactions of the faithful against the new Mass – but what kind of 'New Mass' are they witnessing?) and feelings that Pope Paul could not intend to revoke (the emotive ban is frequently used) a centuries old Mass with all its beauty and spirituality. The best judge of what the Pope intended is surely himself, and at the end of this article, we shall be examining his words. To give greater strength to Pope Pius V's Missal, both Abbé Dulac and Michael Davies (*Remnant,* 17 August 1974), declare that the Bull *Quo Primum* can 'rightly be regarded not simply as a personal decree of Pope St. Pius V, but an act of the Council of Trent'. A decree coming from a Pope alone (a personal one) is as strong and effective as when it comes from a Council and Pope.

Paul VI's *Missale Romanum* also came from a mandate of the Council (Decree on the Liturgy, No.50). One cannot, without jeopardising the whole concept of authority in the Church and its Divine Guarantee of protection from error, hold, that Trent was a 'true council', guided and protected by the Holy Spirit, while Vatican II was held *saudente diabolo.* The evils of our time have not arisen from the Council, but from 'experts' who used the Council and its decrees.

Abbé Dulac as quoted by Michael Davies (*Remnant,* 17 August 1974), holds that 'the right to use, the age-old liturgy, could not be withdrawn by legislation issued by the Congregation for Divine Worship, such as that of 20 October 1969, or even by the Pope himself in such Papal allocutions as those of 19 and 26 November.'

No Canonist worthy of the name, would write such a sentence. A Canonist would ask – how was the legislation of the Congregation approved. Was it *in forma communi* or *in forma applica*? The former is only a general approval and does not raise the status of the enactment. A document of a Congregation approved by the Pope in *forma communi* would not, as Abbé Dulac states withdraw a Bull of a previous Pontiff, but

CHRISTIAN ORDER AND THE OLD MASS – A CHOICE... 201

it could and would (according to intention expressed in terminology) withdraw it, if the document of Congregation received Papal approval in *forma Specifica*, as this latter elevates the enactment, to the status and authority of a legislative act of the Supreme Pontiff. As to the allocutions of Pope Paul VI's dated 19 and 26 November, and which will be referred to more specifically later, the Pope in his allocutions only reaffirms what has already been established.

That is the scope of allocutions – the Pope as Supreme teacher of the Church is expounding the Church's existing doctrine. While an allocution, then, does not create change there and then, in the Church's laws, it is the most certain and doubt-removing vehicle that one can imagine.

Abbé Dulac and Michael Davies (*Remnant,* 17 August 1974), apply Canon 23 of the Code of Laws to the situation that 'where doubt exists, the revocation of an early, already existing law is not presumed; rather subsequent legislation and previous legislation must be drawn together and reconciled as much as possible'. Canon 23 has no place in the matter under discussion; the subjective persuasion of certain people, who insist on holding their views, notwithstanding the clear words of the Pope, particularly when so often clearly expressed, is not sufficient for the existence of an objective doubt. It is Cannon 22 which should be applied, not Cannon 23. Cannon 22 gives the cases where a subsequent law replaces a previous one

(a) when it expressly states so;
(b) when it (the subsequent one) is contrary to the former,
(c) where the subsequent legislation reorganises the matter of the previous enactment.

The liturgy of Pope Pius V is revoked by virtue Canon 22 (apart from any other clause of Paul VI's Constitution) under the terms of points (a) and (c) above.

'Pope Paul VI does possess the legal power to forbid the celebration of the old Mass, but he certainly has no moral right to do so, as such an act would in fact be an unprecedented break with Catholic tradition and practice' states the *Remnant,* 17 August 1974. This is indeed an extraordinary statement coming from a traditionalist publication. Who is competent to tell the Pope what he may or may not do where matter is concerned which is not of the immutable Divine Law?

Who is competent to tell Christ's Vicar, that the words spoken to his predecessor by Christ himself – 'Whatsoever thou shalt lose on earth, shall be lost also in Heaven' does not include disciplinary laws?

It is quite extraordinary to find statements such as 'a legislator must make his intention known the clearest possible terms'. No Canonist will make such a statement, for the very fact, that no matter how clearly one may express one's intention, grounds can easily be found to declare – 'this is a clearer way' and so the legal enactment starts off with a crippling defect.

All Canonists hold that the legislator must 'clearly' express himself or communicate 'sufficiently clear terms' his intention. We find the same issue of *Remnant* already referred to the following statement: 'The establishment of a time coming into force of a law, is an essential condition for the validity of its promulgation'. The Church always provides for this in Canon 9 of her Code of Laws, which states that Church Laws exert their force three months from the date of publication in the AAS *(Acta Apostolicae Sedis)* unless by their nature they bind immediately or a longer or shorter term expressly and specially stated.

'The specific reference needed to abrogate immemorial custom, so clearly set forth in *Quo Primum* is totally absent from *Missale Romanum*. Anyone wishing to refute this point has only to indicate the passage in the *Missale Romanum* containing the specific reference and the argument would be settled at once, (*Remnant*, 17 August 1974).

COMMENT: The author of the above quoted passage, confuses 'abrogation' with 'derogation'. The old liturgy is NOT abrogated but derogated; abrogation is the total withdrawal of a previous legislative enactment; derogation is the 'partial' withdrawal.

Hence it is that Pope Paul's *Missale Romanum* uses the word in its final paragraph – *derogatione* not *abrogatione*.

The writer of the passage quoted, is also confused as to what 'express' derogation means. It does NOT mean, that only if Pope Paul's *Missale Romanum* would mention in name the *Quo Primum* Bull of Pius V, would the Tridentine liturgy be derogated.

Let me quote for him, one of the classical scholars, on this whole question: -

'The revocation of a law can be express or tacit. It is express, when it is done through manifest and clear words i.e., we abrogate, we derogate, or by the use of abrogatory or derogatory clauses, many of which are found in our Code of Laws but the principal ones are – 'All things to the contrary notwithstanding', NOT, withstanding things to the contrary even deserving special mention'.

Now let us refresh ourselves on the final words of Pope Paul's *Missale Romanum*. It reads:-

'It is Our Will, that these our statutes and prescriptions be and remain firm and efficacious, notwithstanding, in so far as is necessary, Constitutions and Apostolic Ordinances of our predecessors, and other prescriptions even needing special mention and derogation'.

To the impartial mind, seeking truth and truth alone, a study of the final paragraph of Paul VI's *Missale Romanum*, can leave no reasonable doubt whatsoever, that the Pope has and in fact, from the promulgation of the Constitution, intended the revocation in part *(derogation)* of the Mass Liturgy of Pope St. Pius V. The clauses which we have studied specifically have no other meaning.

May it be repeated again, that if this clause were not present, the *Quo Primum* liturgy of Pius V would still be revoked in part, by virtue of the operative effect of Canon 22 of the Code of Canon Laws.

We shall conclude this article by a few remarks on points not yet referred to.

We do not think it serves any useful purpose to discuss at length the objection raised by some (e.g. Father Wathen) that the strong condemnatory clauses of Pope Pius V's *Quo Primum* against subsequent change in the liturgy, restricts the competency of Paul VI to approve of any change. Such objections are too absurd to merit any serious comment. It would mean, if true, that the plentitude of authority which all Popes possess, was in fact restricted by Pope St. Pius V, for all future Pontiffs. This would in turn mean that Pius V had more authority from his office than subsequent Popes.

This is too absurd to develop any further.

Christian Order, December 1974, in its criticism of the new liturgy pointed out that the reformers of the sixteenth century, achieved their aims more by 'omissions' than by the inclusion of specifically heretical prayers. The writer of the article seems to see the same sinister purpose in the 'omissions' found in the new liturgy, and raises the question of whether the principle *Lex orandi Lex credendi* (prayer reflects belief) has been endangered if not betrayed?

If the title of his article *The Fort Betrayed,* taken from St. John Fisher's remarks about his apposite colleagues, is intended to convey the idea that

Pope Paul has betrayed the Church's sacred deposit of faith, then we just cannot agree with him and we are forced back on the fundamental doctrines enunciated in the opening paragraphs of this article. The Mass is the very centre of Catholic Faith, life and worship, and for a Pope to give his specific approval to a liturgy that contains falsity of doctrine is inconceivable and is irreconcilable with the Divine guarantee given by Christ to His Church in the person of Peter and his successors.

Such a conclusion is so monstrous, as to mean, that the Church today, is bereft of a Head, as one cannot be the Head, who has lost membership of the Church through heresy. It has always been the teaching of theologians and canonists, that heresy on the part of the Pope means his immediate cessation as Pope. If this conclusion can be accepted, then in turn, we must retrace our steps and start questioning the very Divinity of Christ, who made a promise to Peter and his successors that He could not keep.

St. Ambrose's dictum is still valid – *Ubi Petrus ibi Ecclesia* – 'Where Peter is, there is the Church'.

We can only hope that readers of this article referred to in *Christian Order* will understand it to apply only to the falsified transition of the Mass thrust upon us by the ICEL.

In which case, the words of St. John Fisher, used against his apostate fellow Bishops of his day, are fully applicable.

The Holy See's approval given to the ICEL translation is a general one *(approbatio in forma communi)* and it is based on the judgment given by the Hierarchy of this country, that it is a faithful and accurate translation of the Latin text. The approval does not make the translation correct, nor does it mean, where it is manifestly false, that it can be conscientiously followed.

We now come to papal declarations on the question whether the new liturgy is a 'must' or a 'may'. We have shown from an analysis of the dispositive part *(pars dispositiva)* of the Constitution, in which the will of the legislator is disclosed, that no reasonable doubt remains as to the obligatory nature of the *Missa Normativa*.

It is now time to see what the Pontiff himself, and the Congregations through which the Pope operates, thinks of the Constitution. On 19 November 1969, Pope Paul issued a lengthy and strongly worded exhortation to the entire Church, to give a prompt response to the introduction of the liturgy which would soon (30 November) become obligatory.

Because of the importance of this Papal announcement, we shall give its salient points verbatim and follow the paragraphs with a brief comment:-

'We wish to draw your attention' stated the Pontiff, 'to an event about to occur in the Latin Church: the introduction of the liturgy of the new rite of the Mass. It will become Obligatory in Italian dioceses from the first Sunday of Advent next, which this year falls on the 30 November.'

COMMENT: If the entire new liturgy was 'Optional' as to use, it would be difficult to see how the Pope would make it 'Obligatory' for the diocese of Italy.

'How could such a change be made?
Answer: It was due to the Will, expressed by the Ecumenical Council held not long ago. 'The Rite of Mass is to be revised in such a way, that the intrinsic nature and purpose of its several parts, as also the connection between them, can be more clearly manifested, and that devout and active participation by the faithful can be more easily accomplished.'

COMMENT: Note the words used by the Pontiff – The Rite of Mass is to be REVISED, etc., no mention, no indication that it was a second Rite of Mass, which would leave untouched the existing one. The Pontiff attributes the 'revision' to the 'express will' of the Council.

'The reform which is about to be brought into being is therefore, a response to an authoritative mandate from the Church. It is an act of obedience . . . It is a demonstration of fidelity and vitality to which ALL MUST GIVE PROMPT ASSENT.'

COMMENT: The words of the Sovereign Pontiff just quoted, mean nothing, if he was announcing the introduction of an OPTIONAL LITURGY, to be used or not used, at the discretion of the priest the whole idea of such an OPTIONAL LITURGY cannot possible be understood from any part of this allocation.
  If the revision is an AUTHORITATIVE MANDATE from the Council, and one to 'which we must ALL GIVE PROMPT ASSENT', it is inconceivable that the Vicar of Christ was referring to any alternative liturgy.

'It is not an arbitrary act. It is not a transitory or OPTIONAL EXPERIMENT. It is not some dilettante's improvisation. It is LAW . . . We shall do well to accept it with joyful interest, and put it into practice, punctually, unanimously and carefully.'

COMMENT: Could words be more clear and emphatic? Views put forward in such publications as *Christian Order* and 'The Remnant', that every priest may still use the Tridentine Liturgy, are completely unfounded. No 'option' is given, for it is a 'LAW', and as such binds 'all of us to give prompt assent.'

'Nothing has been changed of the substance of our traditional MASS. Perhaps some may allow themselves to be carried away by the impression made by some particular ceremony or additional rubric, and thus think, that they conceal some alteration of diminution of truths which were acquired by the Catholic faith forever, and are sanctioned by it. They might come to believe, that the equation between the law of prayer *lex orandi* and the law of faith, *lex credendi*, is compromised as a result.'

'It is NOT SO. ABSOLUTELY NOT. Above all, because the Rite and relevant rubric are not in themselves a dogmatic definition. Their theological qualification may vary in differing degrees according to the liturgical context to which they refer.'

COMMENT: Papal allocutions are not, as everyone knows, 'off the cuff' statements made by the Pope. They are carefully prepared — as the texts indicate — statements made by the Pope as Supreme Teacher of the whole Church, a point to which he is wont to refer from time to time. Here, in his capacity as Supreme Teacher, he emphasises that the 'substance of the traditional Mass has not changed.' He also anticipated the objection as found in *Christian Order* (December 1974) that the changes involved a compromise in the principle of *Lex oranddi est Lex credendi*. The Pope points out, that liturgical rubrics are not dogmatic definitions.

Moreover, it may be said, that the Council which gave the mandate for this 'revision', elsewhere in its own documents, clearly reaffirmed the very truths of faith, which critics of the liturgy ascribe to it as denying. The theology of the Council will have to be sought in the documents of the entire Council, and not in a single arrangement of liturgical procedure.

'The Mass of the new Rite is and remains the same Mass we have always had . . . The unity of the Lord's supper, of the sacrifice on the cross, of the representation and renewal of both, in the Mass, is inviolably affirmed and celebrated in the new rite, just as they were in the old . . . Do not think that the liturgical changes were aimed at altering the genuine and traditional essence of the Mass. It is

Christ's Will, it is the breath of the Holy Spirit which calls the Church to make this change' (26 November 1969.

COMMENT: These emphatic words of Pope VI, pose to all Catholics, the vital question, is it possible, that as Supreme Teacher of the Catholic World — and it is in that capacity that the allocutions are given — that the Pope is mistaken? If he is so emphatic that the new liturgy (in its Papally approved text, of course) is the 'Will of Christ', and that the traditional teaching of the Church as to the nature of the Mass, its links with the Supper of the Lord and with Calvary, remaining untouched, the critic who rejects this teaching either must show that he is better informed than the Pope, or he must remain silent.

If the Pope is right, then those who reject his teaching are in the wrong. It may be said here by some reader, that the question whether the Mass preserves orthodoxy, is a different issue from the one which we set out to discuss, whether the new liturgy MUST be used or MAY be used is it an obligation or a directive? This criticism would not be without foundation, but it should be realised that for not a few, the new liturgy is unacceptable, because they believe or suspect that it contains a betrayal of orthodoxy. The Pope's words can put their consciences at rest.

We now come to the final paragraphs of this article, in which we shall briefly summarise the weight of evidence, which is such, as to render the contrary opinion untenable in practice.

All Catholic moralists are unanimous in holding, that no probable opinion can be followed in practice, when it is specifically contrary to a Papal pronouncement. That the new liturgy is a mere directive, which may, or may not be used, is an entirely false doctrine, which has nothing to support it, other than perhaps, the tenacity of some, to persuade themselves, that the Pope is wrong and they are right. We respectfully ask such, to consider their position, and recall the words of St. Thomas Aquinas —

'We must abide by the authority of the Pope, rather than by any theologian, however well versed he may be in Sacred Scripture. AGAINST HIS WORD, neither Jerome nor Augustine, nor any other Holy Doctor defends his personal view.'

With the publication *Marchons Unis dans la foi et l'amour* July-August 1974), p.239, we conclude that there IS NO AMBIGUITY WHATSOEVER, NO UNCERTAINTY, that the Constitution *Missale Romanum* promulgating the revised liturgy, imposes an obligation to observe it, and not the previous liturgy, unless for particular cases, the Holy See permits the use of 'former liturgy'.

These words 'former liturgy' are in fact, the words contained in the document from the Holy See received through the local Bishop, when this permission to use the Tridentine Mass was permitted. The words 'former' indicates that in principle the Tridentine Liturgy has been derogated. Some half-dozen clerics, unsure of this conclusion, have on the suggestion of the writer of this article, appealed to Rome for a clarification of what they thought was a doubt. In all cases the reply reaffirmed the cessation of the liturgy of Pope Pius V.

What a pity that so much time and energy has to be spent, on reaffirming the obvious — time and energy which should be used in seeking, demanding, a TRUE AND ACCURATE TRANSLATION of the LATIN text.

What a pity too, that the *Missa Normativa* is not used in its LATIN text, as a principle, with the vernacular the exception.

THE NATIONAL CONFERENCE OF PRIESTS
Newsletter
Vol.V No.2 1975

A CONFERENCE OR A CIRCUS
by Father Flanagan

Every year in the early days of September, the Catholic community of the United Kingdom is given a very false image abroad. It is depicted either, as a Church in *schism,* or equally divided between allegiance to the Holy See and the Unholy See of Modernism, which surrounds our shores on every side.

Australian, American, South African and New Zealand papers carry banner headings such as 'Catholic Church in Britain divided on Contraception' (*Southern Cross,* in South Africa), or, 'British Catholics reject *Humanae Vitae* or 'Catholic Clergy in England want to marry' or 'Church in Britain to accept Anglican Orders'. These are but a few of the false conclusions arrived at by the editors of the world's press intended for English-speaking people, a falsity which is partially due to journalists exaggerations but a large part finds its explanation in the pitiable spectacle of the National Conference of Priests at its annual meeting.

This *Newsletter* over the years has drawn the attention of its readers to the drift towards revolutionary theology and left wing extremism, which has marked the advance of National Conferences both in this country and elsewhere. One has only to scan the annual *Report of the NCP* which is issued at the expense of the good Catholics of the country, who contribute generously to support financially this subversive group.

The thousands of hard earned pounds which the NCP receives, are being used to advance causes, diametrically opposed and indeed abhorrent to the generality of Catholics in Britain. If we look back over the past issues of the 'Annual Report' – we find the recurring theme is, the removal of obligatory celibacy – notwithstanding the fact, that the Holy Father has repeatedly declared it was 'NOT FOR DISCUSSION'. Birth Control, *(Humanae Vitae)* and how the *Magisterium* of the Church could be circumvented, received attention. It is deeply regrettable, that an organisation such as the NPC, which could have played such a useful part in forwarding suggestions and ideas (and that is the limit of any 'Consultative Body') to the Hierarchy, for the Bishop's authoritative decision, the Church would be the richer in this country.

But from the beginning the NPC, notwithstanding the presence of some excellent priests within its ranks, was taken over by priests dedicated to the advancement of modernism. The same experience has been registered in nearly every country, where institutions similar to the NPC exist.

Priests of the country have not been slow to assess the situation, and have answered with the only weapon available to many of them – a boycott in electing delegates. The paucity of voters in practically every diocese in electing delegates to the Conference, is not due to just human apathy, but must be construed as a sign of want of confidence on the part of priests to the institution under discussion.

In some dioceses, as few as four priests voted in 1973 for the election of their delegates. In another diocese only one in eight of the priests voted. In yet another, only one in twelve bothered to vote. It is not surprising that the NPC – though it has moaned as to the apathy, *(Report, 1972)* – has failed to publish the number of priests who voted in all the dioceses in the country.

The 1974 National Conference has made all previous Conferences look like a boy scouts' picnic or a 'bingo session'. The national press reports so far, indicates the good old 'free for all' that characterised the meeting, but some of the 'behind the scenes' or 'not for the press' discussions, were such as to make one conclude that many of the priest members of this Conference have long ago lost their Catholic faith.

When several priests can support the view that abortion can be justified in some cases – contraception in all cases, one can only ask the question: has the Conference become so ecumenical, that even clergy of the lowest Christian denomination, were present as delegates? Again, there were present, priests who in private conversation, supported the Marxists' line in political policy, and praised the revolutionary activities now evident in various parts of the world. There were even priests present who believed that the Bishop of each diocese should be submitted for re-election every five or ten years, as this would compel the Bishop, not merely to listen, but to put into practice the popular 'democratically expressed' party line of the National Conference of Priests.

One thing which emerges more clearly each year, is the fact, that the NPC, either does not know, or is not prepared to accept a mere consultative voice in ecclesiastical affairs. *The Catholic Herald,* 20 September, reporting the Birmingham Conference, mentions Father Sean Kearney, the Chairman of the NPC up to last year, proposing a motion rebuking the Hierarchy for their failure to set up conciliation machinery, despite four years of negotiation.'

Who does Father Sean Kearney think he is? What does the NPC think it is? No organisation within the Church can dictate to the Hierarchy what it should or should not do. It is audacious to say the least of it, that the NPC should even think on those lines! No doubt, the NPC, aware of the failure of the Hierarchy to uphold the teaching of the Pope in so many spheres, has logically concluded, that if the Bishops can be disobedient to the Pope, the NPC can be disobedient to the Bishops.

Another discussion point of the NPC, which deserves attention, is that 'Seventy, was the normal age at which priests must relinquish complete charge of a parish . . . and there was applause for the idea, that priests of fifty could have retired priests as their assistants.' It is quite clear that the NPC are bent on a course of divisiveness, between the age groups of the clergy. Everything except the ballot system for the election of candidates, has been geared to give the young priest, fresh from the seminary, a place and importance in the Church administration, for which he has neither the experience nor the knowledge.

Over the past few years, there has been a growing practice on every level, often with the tacit encouragement of the Bishops, to reject the experienced Priest and assign him to the ecclesiastical dustbin, if he has reached, or will soon reach the advanced age of fifty. If he is of this age group, he is presumed to have been educated in the days of the pre-Council's 'DARK AGES'.

He would know little of the new enlightenment which came into the world through the Dutch experts and the itinerant lecturers who suffer from verbal inflation. A priest ordained in the pre-Council days would be as inept to administer a parish, as Julius Caesar would be to navigate a space ship to the moon. Such a priest would believe in the Sacrificial nature of the Mass, the existence of the supernatural order, the Divinity of Christ, and would be even prepared to listen to the *Magisterium* of the Church – all so much junk of a forgotten age.

What is the Catholic Church in this country coming to? Catholicism in this country urgently needs a strong Head who will not be afraid to be smeared in the discharge of his duty.

To return to the NPC, it may well be asked if certain members of the governing body of this organisation are not also members of the 'Catholic Renewal Movement'. This is worth investigation.

The *Catholic Pictorial,* Liverpool's weekly Catholic paper, 22 September, states that 'Resolution No.5' dealing with married life, recommends its working party to give special consideration to the problems of married life, taking notice of the *Sensus fidelium,* covering contraception and divorce. It is not uncharitable to come to the conclusion, that, as has happened at other National Conferences in which Modernists have had control, the NPC in this Resolution, has been trying to evaluate the force of *Humanae Vitae* by popular rejection. We are familiar with this tactic, of attributing the words *sensus fidelium* to boost the rejection of the Church's official doctrine in many spheres. It has even been applied to interpretations of dogmas of faith, e.g. the **Real Presence, Papal Infallibility,** and even **Original Sin**. It is certainly a novel form of Christianity which would base **Revealed Truths** on whether and to what extent, the rank and file of people felt such doctrines acceptable. Yet this is the sense attributed by Modernists to the *sensus fidelium,* which can, in their view, be true and valid, even when the 'sense' is in direct conflict with the *Magisterium* of the Church. One young priest at the NPC was heard saying: 'The Pope should mind his own business, he knows nothing of contraception, and when the next Pope is elected, and he will be a young man, all this *Humanae Vitae* stuff will be assigned to the rubbish heap.' Perhaps, we can see in this young man's mind the evidence of the 'prophetic community', as he seems to have prophetic vision that the next Pope will be a 'young man', Bishop Worlock or perhaps even Father Sean Kearney.

It is most pathetic that certain Bishops should patronise the Conference of weirdy, beardy and trendy eccentrics, who represent only the smallest fraction of the priests of the country.

We congratulate Father Carey of Saltash, for his brave stand, and other priests who abstained from voting on certain motions. One can only ask if their message of dissent could be more effectively conveyed by walking out of the Conference and registering their protest

To date, we have not been told by the press, what action Bishop Worlock took, who was present all through the Conference, at hearing Father Sean Kearney rebuke the Hierarchy for dragging their feet.

If Bishop Worlock did not publicly rebuke Father Kearney, he can only by judged as an accomplice, at least by silence, in this disgraceful behaviour. One would expect Bishop Worlock to be loyal to his fellow Bishops. 'The Bishops are a great bag of frauds' – these words were written NOT by a member of the ICPA, but by one of America's most ardent Modernists (John C. White) one of the leading 'Catholic Educationalists' of our day, and of course Professor of Religion in the La Salle College, Philadelphia, (see *The Wanderer,* 22 August 1974).

Perhaps by next year, Father Sean Kearney will have more than a 'rebuke' for the leg-dragging Hierarchy, and who knows, maybe by then the Bishops will have awoke to a realisation as to who their real friends are!

The NPC in the United States of America, at their conference held in Florida from 9 to 13 March 1975, passed a resolution that divorced and remarried people should be admitted to Holy Communion.

The 200 delegates present, representing 102 of the country's 165 dioceses, believed that the 'primacy of conscience, . . . and the healing and forgiving nature of the Eucharist' demanded this policy.

Monsignor Tomlinson, Parish Priest of St. James, Spanish Place, London, in a Newsletter to his parishioners, states, that they can now receive Holy Communion in the state of mortal sin, if the Penitential Rite has taken place. No doubt this will be one of the resolutions of our own NPC before long, or perhaps it will be that, as Father Hubert McCabe wrote (*Catholic Herald,* 27 December, 1974 'MRS McALISKEY (Bernadette Devlin) should be the next Archbishop of Westminster.'

CRUSADE OF PRAYER, FOR PRIESTS
by Father Flanagan

MONTHLY HOLY HOUR FOR PRIESTS

'Could you not watch one hour with ME', Matthew, 26 v.40.The request of the Holy Father for prayers for priests of the World, received a prompt response at the Central Office of 'The International Catholic Priests' Association'.

We have started since the Feast of St. John Vianney 1972, a Holy Hour on the first Thursday of each month, with Rosary, Litany and other suitable prayers composing the first half hour and Holy Mass the second half hour.

This practice has now been taken up by some twenty million members of the 'Blue Army' throughout the world, and has been given an incredible impetus by the devoted work of Father Aurelius Maschio, editor of *Don Bosco Madonna* in Bombay – so reports *Fatima International* (8 January 1974).

XVIII

WE ASK . . .
WE BEG OUR BISHOPS
10 IMPORTANT POINTS

1. To take immediate and efficacious steps to repudiate false and dangerous doctrine in their diocese.

2. To take immediate and efficacious steps to stop the desacralisation of the Mass and Holy Eucharist, now increasing in every diocese in the country.

3. To see that the ruling of Vatican II on the Latin Liturgy be preserved.

4. To instigate an immediate enquiry into the doctrines and practices now being found in Seminaries, Colleges and Convents in their dioceses in order to implement No.1 above.

5. To see that every parish has restored to it, the Devotions sanctioned by the last Vatican Council, and which have done so much to preserve and strengthen the faith of the people.

6. To see that 'Commissions' are reduced in number, and in time spent in idle discussion with waste of Church funds.

7. To see that all parish and deanery Councils, wherever established, are not permitted to usurp the authority and duty of the parish priest.

8. To take immediate action to eradicate from Catholic Schools and Colleges, books and publications, that are unorthodox or dangerous to faith and morals.

9. To see that abuses, now growing so rapidly and in defiance of Papal Authority, are promptly suppressed.

10. To see that priests and nuns are always known as such, in public by their dress.

DECLARATION ON CERTAIN QUESTIONS CONCERNING SEXUAL ETHICS
Editorial from CPA *Newsletter*
Vol.VI 1976 (Nos.1-2)

Within four days of the Pope giving his approval to the Declaration on certain questions concerning sexual ethics, the sluice gates of Modernism were opened to befoul the minds and hearts of Catholics, and to cover the Church's teaching from the beginning with the muck and slush, characteristic of the pigsty, and which is accepted by the standards or morals of those who have lost their Christian Faith.

It is well known by now, that this document of the Sacred Congregation for the Doctrine of the Faith, but approved by the Holy Father, was a direct hit at the audacious teaching of those who endeavoured to uphold the lawfulness of pre-marriage sex, homosexuality and masturbation.

There was nothing new in the Declaration; it was a simple reaffirmation of the ordinary *magisterium* of the Church which is infallible, that these acts in themselves, are always gravely sinful.

How was the declaration received? Some national newspapers received it enthusiastically; some rejected it as outdated. All our Catholic weekly publications, other than the *Universe,* derided it. Many of the self-appointed Catholic spokesmen in the mass media, were engaged by it.

Mr Norman St. John Stevas writing in the *Catholic Herald,* accused the Holy See of giving a 'stone for bread', and then proceeded to fling everything he had at the outdated doctrine of the 'declaration'. This self-appointed 'expert' whose final letter of commendation for the appointment of Bishop Worlock to Liverpool, and Archbishop Hume to Westminster, brought by the Apostolic Delegate to Rome (*Guardian,* 20 February; *Sunday Telegraph,* 22 February) was the factor which weighed in their favour, and over which Norman 'had a little crow' (*Catholic Herald,* 27 February) in picking 'the Episcopal double' from among what other papers described as 'outsiders', has the effrontery to repudiate the Church's *Magisterium* as contained in the declaration. 'It was as though Freud and Jung had never been born' writes Pope Norman, *Catholic Herald,* 23 January 1976.

It is the homosexual, however, that received the greatest sympathy from the Member of Parliament for Chelmsford. He is indignant that the Vatican Declaration should use the word 'pathological' concerning them, and adds: 'As far as I have been able to observe, there is nothing pathological about them' (*Catholic Herald,* 23 February 1976).

Cheers for Norman's powers of observation!

In the same so-called *Catholic Herald,* 5 March, Norman expresses his fury over the Principal of Plater College, Oxford (a Catholic workers' College) refusing to give a platform to the 'Oxford Students' Gay Society'. The Principal is reported as saying that 'It is not the business of a Catholic College to provide a platform for these people. I don't invite lepers to come and expose their sores. Why should I give a platform for these people to expose their nastiness? Norman's retort was that 'these words would never have come from the ONE whom he is pledged to serve. Someone should suggest to Norman that he give us the Biblical texts both Old and New Testament, dealing with homosexuals, and show us how the scriptures view this evil. It will be difficult to find an evil that is more horrendous in the sight of God (remember Sodom and Gomorrah) and yet for Norman, the Principal of the Plater College 'was imposing his own ideas on morality on the students, and censoring discussion of views with which he does not agree.' Will some member of the Hierarchy have the courage to tell dear Norman, that the Church's teaching on homosexuality is not just a 'view', but a doctrine which everyone must accept as a condition of membership of the Church.

Future Catholic teachers studying at Christ's College of Education, Liverpool, rejected as 'deficient and divisive' by 94 votes to 10, with 32 abstentions, the Vatican Declaration on Sexual Ethics, according to the report on the debate in the Universe (20 February 1976).

This is not surprising, in view of the ever worsening condition of this college over the years since Vatican II. It was this college that had the honour of being the first in the country to have a 'Maoist Club' in which the *Little Red Book of Chairman Mao* was sedulously studied, while Catholic doctrine was assigned to the wastepaper basket. All appeals to Archbishop Beck to exercise his authority over this school fell on deaf ears.

We hope that Archbishop Worlock will now have the courage to sack all students there, other than the ten who voted in favour of the Vatican Declaration.

A Dominican priest, writing in the *Catholic Herald,* 23 January, described the statement as 'a disaster for the Church,' and a 'leading' ('leading those who listen to him stray') Irish priest described it as 'very negative.' What a blunder God committed in giving so many 'negative' commandments to Moses on Mount Sinai! The magazine for the 'Gay Homosexual Catholics' blasted it – as would be expected – as 'narrow, unenlightened and disappointing.' In the same weekly paper, which I prefer to call the 'Journalists Sewage', we have a monk of Ampleforth, Dom Fabian Cowper, condemning the Church's teaching on Sexual Ethics as 'an insult and a scandal' (20

February 1976). Now, be it known to you, readers of this *Newsletter*, that Dom Fabian is the Chaplain to the Catholic students at the University of York. How did the then Abbot, now the new Archbishop of Westminster, permit this appointment to continue, as the outrageous views of Dom Fabian have been known for a long time, and the editor of this *Newsletter* focused attention on him several years ago, but with no response from the Abbot. No wonder a letter writer in the same Catholic Herald (5 March) could write: 'Don't put your daughter in at York, Mrs Worthington.'

The report in *The Daily Telegraph* (19 January 1976) of the 'Homosexual Gay Christian Movement' holding a special meeting in London, following the Vatican Statement, makes interesting reading, and shows the extent of infiltration of pagan ideas among the clergy. The news item reads as follows:-

> 'More than 70 Clergymen and Churchgoers, gathered behind closed doors at a secret address in Central London, at the weekend, to form the 'Homosexual Gay Christian Movement'. The aims of the Movement are: (a) To encourage formation of, and support for, existing local fellowship of Gay Christians: (b) To provide and support Christian fellowship for isolated and lonely Christians who are homosexuals: (c) To put pressure on the Churches to examine their existing negative attitude to homosexual relationships. None of the clergymen present – they included Roman Catholic Priests, Anglican Vicars, and non-Conformist ministers, wore their dog-collars. All refused to be named 'because of the prejudice in our Churches'. A spokesman said afterwards: 'The Gay Christians present are ordinary men and women, some clergy some lay people, who happen to have, or are seeking, a loving fulfilling relationship with another person of the same sex.'

The 'closed doors' and 'secret address', even the discarding of the dog collars, were not sufficient to conceal entirely the identity of the Catholic priests present. The editor of this Newsletter is prepared to disclose the identity of the 'Catholic' priests who were present at this gay meeting, to their own Bishops, but only on condition that the Bishops ask for the same, and are prepared to take positive action against the culprits.

It would be an incomplete picture of the repercussions created by the publication of the Vatican *Declaration on Sexual Ethics*, if no mention was made of Peter Hebblethwaite, one-time member of the Jesuits, but still the quasi-official organ of the Catholic Church in Britain, who is summoned by the 'Mass Media' to pontificate on every Church affair today.

Peter on radio, T.V., and in several of the national papers for 15 January — the day of promulgation of the Declaration — ridiculed the teaching, stating, 'you don't help people in their moral perplexities by hitting them over the head with this sort of crowbar' (Radio 4 *Today*).

Peter's recently published book *The Runaway Church*, has been commented upon by Gerald Priestland (Radio 4, *Chapter and Verse*) as suitable for an apt subtitle 'The Runaway Jesuit'.

Mr Priestland having asked Peter Hebblethwaite what the title of his book meant, was told: 'I have to admit, I wanted a good title. But, then I had in mind the fact that the Church, in many respects seems to be out of control; orders and instructions given from Rome are not obeyed. There is the second sense of running away . . . and here I had in mind certain problems, notably birth control, where there is a gap between what is asserted and what is actually practised.'

One may ask, who has contributed more to disregarding decrees of Rome, and creating confusion on *Humanae Vitae*, than the same Peter Hebblethwaite.

A letter of appeal to Bishop Holland, President of the ecclesiastical commission for the Mass Media in this country, asking him to do something to prevent renegade priests from speaking so often on radio, as representing the Church, brought the reply that the 'Mass Media Commission did not enjoy any right to prevent anyone.' One can only wonder what the yearly Sunday Collection in our Churches for the Mass Media Commission is producing. One can easily think of better purposes for the spending of money.

The destruction of even the basic principles of Christian conduct is the ultimate aim of our Modernists, as they know only too well, that with Christian morals gone, faith in Catholic dogmas will soon vanish. History has too many examples to prove this point.

For the ordinary Catholic, the unfolding of dogmas is of little interest to him — he leaves all that to those whose duty it is to know it; for him or her, the ordinary test is how the Church's doctrine on morals — the sinfulness of fornication, the hideousness of homosexuality and masturbation, etc., is received and lived in everyday life.

Humanae Vitae and the 1976 *Declaration on Certain Questions Concerning Sexual Ethics* are two inspiring examples of the *Voice of Christ* re-echoing in our time, to a world that is sex sodden and pleasure loving, recalling to man his own true nature, the purpose of life and his eternal destiny. The frail Pontiff who is the successor of Him who founded the Church, raises his voice above the hiss of Hell and the demoniacal shrieks of those who wish to enjoy the pleasures derived from unnatural use of their own bodies, and in our age, those, who while calling themselves Catholics, offer the placebo of 'love is all you need' to dull and finally smother the consciences of the young.

The trendy priest who has already lost his faith, the world-loving nun, who has entirely or in part abandoned her religious life; the modern catechist prepared in one of our Catechetical centres, the special 'expert' with insights into new approaches to faith and morals, will continue to wreck the Church of Christ, often with the implicit or tacit approval of one of the Chief Shepherds, who has surrendered all his obligations to commissions of ecclesiastical knaves.

Pope Paul can expound the Church's unchangeable doctrines continuously, but no responses will be re-echoed in the minds and will of the great bulk of the Bishops of the world. They are too busy with the work of 'commissions', the 'third world' and other social problems, to worry much about the next one. The hoary old heresies of the past can be heard all over the land – from the pulpit, from the lecture hall, from the Conference room, and are consumed with extraordinary appetite and relish, as 'developments' in doctrine and 'insights' which have escaped the notice of St. Thomas Aquinas, St. Augustine, even the Church itself.

As one good reader of this *Newsletter* pointed out to me with tangible evidence: 'The experts are almost invariably those who as clerical students, have great trouble in passing the Seminary examinations'.

We address this final paragraph of the editorial to priests and laity faithful to the Church: the Catholic Herald is bought in bulk by priests (or their lay representatives) and paid for by them. It is NOT on a 'sale or return' basis. Many Churches including Westminster Cathedral, have, at the end of the week, many dozens of Catholic Heralds left unsold.

These then are paid for out of Church funds. It is inconceivable, that priests who love their Church, should have at the doors of their Church building, a weekly publication that, as Archbishop Murphy (Cardiff) stated in his Lenten Pastoral (1976) referring to the Catholic press:-

> 'It is becoming increasingly difficult to flip through the pages of our Catholic Newspapers, without encountering the phrase 'creeping infallibility', or the 'disapproving Church'. Critics using them, call up a vision of every Catholic trussed up in infallible moral decision and struggling for his freedom. A new fungus of private judgment, falsely claiming lineage from Vatican II, is now creeping over all the

authentic teaching of the Church, and questioning its authority. Because such teaching cannot be classified as infallible, they feel they are justified in refusing their assent.' *(Catholic Herald* 12 March 1976).

It is not surprising that the following week, this so-called *Catholic Herald* should give an editorial with the title 'Why the Clerical Rage at the Catholic Press' in which it is lamented and deplored that, 'Priests feel free to ban Catholic papers from their Church porches.'

It is a long time since the paper in question has a title to be called 'Catholic', and the sooner it is banned from being sold (and paid for out of the Church finance) in Church porches the better.

This weekly 'Journalists' Sewer' is an offence to the REAL PRESENCE, and a terrible proof of what apathy can produce.

'To quarrel with those who quarrel with the Pope is to be in good company' as Archbishop Murphy rightly stated.

P.S. Following the promulgation of the 'Vatican Declaration on certain *Questions Concerning Sexual Ethics'* – 15 January 1976 – Father Flanagan received a telephone call from the BBC, London, to discuss this 'Declaration' at their Studio in Shepherds Bush, London, for a programme going out after the *Evening News*.

Seemingly an Auxiliary Bishop of a northern diocese had been requested earlier, but his episcopal appointments did not allow for this, and so he declined this request. It was then that Father Flanagan came into the picture. The BBC telephoned Father Flanagan in the late morning – approximately noon, when he promptly agreed to go to London that afternoon. Personally, I wondered how this journey was to be undertaken, for at that particular time Father Flanagan was a very sick man. He asked me to accompany him which I did. I will now give a true picture of the happenings of that never-to-be forgotten afternoon. Father Flanagan and I left Polegate at 3.15 p.m. (by train) and during that journey to London (one hour twenty minutes) he seldom uttered a single word and appeared pensive and deep in thought.

On arrival at Victoria Station, and on alighting from the train, the loudspeaker system was blaring out the following message:- 'Will Father Flanagan please go to the Station Master's office at the front of the station – a message awaits him.' This message was repeated several times. Now, what could this message be? We were soon to learn.

The steep flight of stairs climbed (a trial for Father Flanagan in his poor condition) the message was as follows: 'Ask Father Flanagan to telephone BBC Studios, Shepherds Bush before proceeding any further.' This Father Flanagan did from a kiosk at the Station. A receptionist explained that there was no further need for his service, as the Auxiliary Bishop contacted earlier – had telephoned later – to ask if the BBC was suited . . . when told that Father Flanagan would be in the Studio, the Bishop asked if he could cover the discussion himself, through the local radio station. This was then arranged by the BBC. What a vindictive act for this Bishop to inflict – to supplant a priest whom many regarded in every way as his Bishop's superior, as verified later when comments of the discussion were made by people who listened to the BBC that evening.

So Father Flanagan returned to Polegate by the same train he had only just arrived by some 15-20 minutes earlier.

It did not weaken his spirit or will-power – indeed only strengthened it, to push ahead with the battle in hand, ever present at the scene of combat.

Nevertheless, readers will now have a clear picture of the treatment meted out to this 'Man of God' – this Doctor of the Church, whose qualifications would put members of the present Hierarchy in the shade.

Father Flanagan never spared them for their neglect in safeguarding the Church's *Magisterium* – and they didn't like it.

TO FOLLOW:-
A criticism by Father Flanagan, of an article, by Dr J. Dominian, entitled, *'An Outline of Contemporary Christian Marriage'*.

Also, to precede this criticism – a letter to 'All Catholics faithful to the Teaching of the Church.'

TO ALL CATHOLICS FAITHFUL TO THE TEACHING OF THE CHURCH
The attached criticism speaks for itself. The publication under review is that of *Contemporary Christian Marriage* by Dr Jack Dominian.

> This booklet cannot be purchased at any bookshop, as its circulation is restricted by the author and its publishers. By chance, a copy fell into the hands of a nun of the Archdiocese of Westminster, who became physically and mentally revolted at its contents, and sent it to me to warn others of its dangers. A copy of this criticism has been sent to Cardinal Hume. The author is a well-known opponent to the teaching of the Church as contained in *Humanae Vitae*. His documentary T.V. programme shown on BBC some months back, on 'Convent Life' disgusted many who saw it. In this programme,

the author tried to put into the mouth of a young nun, that she needed sex in the Convent. This was the verdict of many who saw it.

His publication is in open conflict with the Church quite frequently, and in a subtle manner, undermines the Church's *Magisterium* on this Sacrament repeatedly. It is for that very reason, a most dangerous publication.

It is absolutely deplorable that the author should be so often invited to lecture to priests and nuns and even Catholic laity, on a Sacrament such as Marriage, when his views on it are in conflict with the Church.

Rejecting the essential of *Humanae Vitae* and numerous other points of Catholic doctrine, Dr Dominian is not entitled to be classified as a Catholic.

This is the teaching of the Popes down through the ages, as it is today.

Sincerely Yours in Xto.,
(REV) FR J.W. Flanagan
St. George's Polegate, Sussex.

AN OUTLINE OF CONTEMPORARY CHRISTIAN MARRIAGE

Published on behalf of the Major Religious Superiors of ENGLAND and WALES by the Liverpool Institute of Socio-Religious Studies, July 1976.
Author – Dr J. Dominian.

A REVIEW AND CRITICISM *Newsletter*
Vol. VI 1976

GENERAL REMARKS. One has to read and re-read this publication, frequently reflecting on what one has read and the more he reads and reflects, the more one continues to ask oneself: – surely this is contemporary pagan marriage – not Christian marriage as the title indicates?

Why major Religious Superiors, particularly nuns should ask for a booklet of this kind, is just amazing, but perhaps the answer to this puzzle lies in the words given by its author on p.35, that 'Religious see their vocation and their vows in positive terms, not as the avoidance of sex, material goods, or the acceptance of immature compliance in the face of authority'. The author of this booklet, long noted for his opposition to *Humanae Vitae*, continues to expound his opposition to the Church's teaching on almost every aspect of marriage. True it is, that this opposition is not always open and explicit, but subtle and devious.

The reader unless he or she, is sufficiently grounded in faith and in Catholic Theology, will find doubt and uncertainty replacing the one time confidence and security about the TRUTH of the Catholic Church.

In brief, there are so many errors and misleading statements in this publication, that it would take as many pages as the booklet contains to refute them, and this would be outside the range of the criticism. Hence, we shall concentrate on some of the more fundamental errors in contains.

On page three, the author tells his readers that Marriage was only made a Sacrament by the Church in the Middle Ages, but it was always a secular reality. The world believes that the Church is obsessed with sex (which, strange to say, is the most frequent word used by the author in the publication) and the Church feeds this illusion by its negative attitude towards sexuality. The author obviously does not attempt the Church's teaching on certain things (including contraception) being 'intrinsically evil', because for him, 'it is not sex in itself, but the circumstances of its use and the type of relationship present' (p.4).

The Church's 'traditional view on contraception is basically erroneous because it is an utter denial of the way human beings really experience themselves, as opposed to the fantasy of what they are seeking in the course of sexual intercourse. The fantasy, both in secular and Christian society is that men and women seek ultimately the pinnacle of sexual excitement, the climax, and this is the principle drawing force behind their quest. Such a view is principally male orientated . . . it is not an accident that so much of the theology of sex and marriage has been formulated by men' (p.19).

ON CONTRACEPTION, the author writes, 'Given the traditional attitude towards *Humanae Vitae*, every sentence concept is mistaken' (p.20). From such a sentence, one can rightly conclude that Pope Paul's encyclical affirming that the doctrine is of the natural law, is just a huge error — for Pope Paul. Dr Dominian knows better. The author contemptuously dismisses the charge that a man who uses contraceptives makes his wife a mere instrument for satisfying his own desires; this view, as well as the one that fornication has increased with the advent of contraceptives are 'common sense views' for which there is 'not an iota of evidence' (p.20).

'Any use of marriage must retain its natural potential to procreate human life — is untenable because it reduces the principle of the sexual act to its biological dimension, and this is inconsistent with the hierarchies of values in it . . . of which love is the highest.' (p.23) This doctrine of Dr Dominian is in direct conflict with *Humanae Vitae*, and as the encyclical is an exercise of the ordinary *Magisterium* of the Church, the one who rejects it has no title to be called a Catholic. Dominian's only opposition to contraceptives, is, when they damage the quality of the sex act, or endanger the union, physically or psychologically'. (p.23).

Dr Dominian sides with the younger generation rebelling against the 'static, legal, unalterable convention of a social contract in which the spouses fulfil their prescribed role . . . the revolt is against the idea of faithfulness, which is negative in nature and directed to the avoidance of adultery' (p.26). The 'on-going' development of the theology of marriage must be dynamic which encompasses three principles, sustaining, healing and growth. The intimacy and openness of contemporary marriage lends itself to social and emotional healing . . . In the last two decades a fascinating array of alternatives have emerged. The plea of all of them is the pursuit of love . . . yet all of them would horrify Christian consciences.

These variations include – Threesomes, spouse exchanges, quartets, swinging and so on. In all these instances the married couples with the full knowledge of each other, have had sexual relationships with others, married or single, in each other's presence or alone.

The pleas have been that this is liberating, rewarding, honest and helpful to marriage; they are condemned, because adultery is concerned, with little thought of why adultery is needed, except on the inescapable explanation for everything – sexual greed (p.28).

It is impossible for any objective evaluation of this booklet to be made, without coming to the conclusion that Dr Dominian's views of *Contemporary Catholic Theology* are at complete variance with the Church's official teaching in almost every sphere of marriage and sexual ethics. His purpose seems to be, to include every sinful deviation in the use of marriage as an evolving element from the secular reality of marriage – which always belonged to marriage (p.3) and to look upon it as a natural element which the Church wrongly condemned in the past and in the present.

While the author does not explicitly state that he approves of 'threesomes', 'foursomes' and 'wife changing' as lawful, he leaves the reader under the impression, that the healing, sustaining and growth (p.26) which he sees in outrageous practices, can increase the all important element – LOVE – which is the very 'Be all and End all' of the Modernists' Code of Ethics. Dr Dominian's ethics are not Christian and certainly not Catholic. We feel that Dr Dominian recognises for himself, the enormous disparity between what he has written, and the Catholic Church's official teaching on the same matter, and hence the declaration by the Director of the Liverpool Institute of Studies, which accompanies the distribution of this work, that the publication is NOT FOR PUBLIC SALE, and the prohibition from the author of the work, that the publication may not be reproduced in any part or in any way, without the previous written approval of the author. Those moves will seem to others as protective techniques against the nature of this booklet being made known to Catholics.

The author of this criticism does not believe that the Catholic Faith should be damaged by the circulation of the booklet, without an outcry being raised, in the interest of unsuspecting souls.

For that reason he is prepared to flout Dr Dominians restrictions forbidding the use of the text of his publication without permission.

It is inconceivable that Dr Dominian should be invited to lecture to priests, nuns or Catholic laity, on any aspect of Catholic theology when his own views are so much in conflict with the Church.

SEX EDUCATION AND THE CORRUPTION OF YOUTH
by Father Flanagan *Newsletter*
(Vols III & IV 1973)

It is quite natural that parents should ask themselves, whether the numerous leaflets, pamphlets, books etc., now in circulation and masquerading under the guise of legitimate sex education, are in fact corrupting the morals of their sons and daughters. There is no shortage of material in this line of business – commercially, anything connected with sex sells well, and perhaps this is the explanation for the mountain of literature on this delicate matter.

Unfortunately, not all the dangerous literature perverting youth today comes from the press of the Humanists. There are 'Humanists' in clerical garb or hiding under clerical appearances who are just as dangerous to the morals of the youth as the dedicated sex seller. In view of helping (and warning parents) we give here just a few references which may be of help.

The 'Family Planning Association' has proposed to offer sex education courses for teachers in Training Schools, and the following are quotations from publications obtainable at the Association's headquarters. Quite recently (March-April 1973) the F.P.A. mounted a massive campaign called **Countdown** to raise £1,000,000 to promote 'family planning'. With an address at 27/35 Mortimer Street, London W1A 4QW., it invited readers of the national press to contribute to its work. But let us have a few quotes from the publications the F.P.A. produce. We are most reluctant to quote some of the passages, and do so only because we believe that the greater good of parents being informed of what is going on, must be given prime consideration, rather than causing hurt to the sensitivities of readers.

'We no longer believe in telling the young what to do, but if we were asked for advice on this topic (moral rules) we should say something like this. 'Make love if you both feel like it. But first make sure that you are safe. If you cannot be satisfied without reaching orgasm, there are many ways of doing this, without danger of conception, such as manual stimulation or oral or anal intercourse; but remember if the penis even touches the vagina, there is a slight risk of conception.'

You (girls) have the advantage of being able to masturbate rather more secretly than boys can, because of your physiology leaving no traces. Your masturbating is no one's business, but your own, so privacy is appropriate. Make the most of it. You might feel it useful to practice coming quickly in case you take your lover, a boy who has not been fortunate enough to read Maurice Hill and Michael Lloyd-Jones. If your lovers are to be girls, the need to hurry is one minor nuisance among several others which you will luckily avoid.'

(Taken from *Sex Education* – National Secular Society).

We will spare our readers even more disgusting and revolting reading – all, of course, being – *Sex Education*. What a perversion of the word **education**. But we do not expect any high ideas from humanists, we just expect pure brutish instincts. We do expect Christian ideals from Christians, however, when we get the same moral permissiveness wrapped up in fine language and all produced in booklet form, edited by 'The Living Parish Series' and 'The Pastoral Development Group', centred at Ealing's Benedictine Abbey, W.5. and published with the *Nihil Obstat* and the *Imprimatur* from Bishop Gauzzelli, Bishop of the Archdiocese of Westminster, it is time to sit up and take notice.

Such is the booklet *Choices in Sex*, by Quentin and Irene de la Bedoyere, costing 30p, and running into 56 pages. In many ways, this booklet is far more dangerous than any of those coming from the 'Family Planning Association' or the 'National Secular Society', because while this book mentions not infrequently, the Christian ideals and moral precepts of marriage and sex, in the final analysis, it leaves the judgment on morality to the 'teenagers' for whom it is written. It is interesting to note, that this booklet has been sent, free to very many teachers and Catholic Schools, at the cost to the sender – one of the 'Catechetical experts' who in turn is financed by the Hierarchy's 'Central Fund'. Let us take a few samples from this production to illustrate what a suitable text book it is for Catholic teenagers.

St. Thomas More's famous words at his trial, that he had studied his decision to die for his Faith for years, is given on page 2 as proof that the teenager's own judgment must be the final criterion of sexual morality.

On page 3 we find 'Wherever love is, God is; whether it is in the ecstasy of the mystic, or the concern of the prostitute to give her client good value for money.'

On page 9 we are told that while 'ministers of the Church of England are not only prepared to celebrate a second marriage of divorced people, but also, to admit them to full communion.

Although Roman Catholic thinking does not go as far as this, there are certainly a number of reputable Church men who would not be in a hurry to condemn such a development . . . it could be, that these are forerunners of a deeper understanding of Christian Morality which is deepening.'

It is wonderful how many times one meets in Modernistic publications the old battleaxe, that 'new approaches' to the 'deeper study of sacred scripture' have given us new light. On page 9 of this 'living parish series' we are told that the Biblical texts which condemn adultery and fornication, cannot always be taken as a 'universal condemnation' of the sins concerned. In fact, the authors of this piffle, ask the question 'if the ability to separate intercourse from conception through birth control alters the issue?'

On Page 10 the whole teaching of the Church on contraception (not a mention, of course, is made of the binding force of *Humanae Vitae*) is reduced to a 'controversy with many eminent men on both sides' and we are told by the 'expert authors' that, 'In marriage, intercourse would be used to express the love, proper to that state; in engagement, it could equally well be used to express the lesser relationship'.

On page 19 the enlightened authors hasten to attribute the 'permissive society' as the creation of 'Sunday Newspapers', and this is reaffirmed by the statement made by a friend of the authors whose job in life is 'the photographing of naked girls'. Not a word about contraception or abortion being evil. On page 19 the enlightened authors hasten to convince us that 'The main condemnation of masturbation is to be found in the Catholic Church, but that before long Dr Dominian's thoughts will be accepted:- 'That masturbation is an intrinsic part of human growth at this adolescent stage of human development.'

Dealing with sexual stimulants, the authors show the real depth of their Catholic faith and moral judgments. Referring to those who would condemn 'petting' outside marriage, the authors declare:-

'The contrary point of view would declare that petting and intercourse need not be connected even in marriage – and in a culture, with a long waiting period between puberty and economic independence, it is a good half-way house, where young people can explore sexual relationships and make a better choice of their partner.'

The author tells us, that some people 'experience various ills, such as backache, irritation and sleeplessness, as a result of prolonged petting.

This seems to be the result of congestion built up by excitement, which never reaches a point of fulfilment and relief.'

But the author hastens to give the cure for those ills of the young:-

'It can be avoided, by continuing the petting until climax (orgasm) is reached, and some champions of petting argue, that this is the best way to bring the session to an end.' (p.29).

'Whatever the rights and wrongs of intercourse outside marriage' write the authors, 'they do not seem to be very important, compared to the risk of conceiving a child under such (where the child is not wanted) circumstances'.

This sentence is bad enough, but when it is followed by such a blasphemous statement as:-

'When Christ said is was better to have a mill-stone tied around the neck and be thrown into the sea, than to scandalise a child, He wasn't referring to this particular question' (p.34).

On a previous page of this criticism of *Choices in Sex*, we drew attention to the fact, that the author of this disgraceful book, rejected the idea, that we are living in a 'permissive society' and mention was made that the authors could not see their way to the massive abortion rate now running in the country (150,000 per annum) as leading to the conclusion of a corrupt society.

The answer, of course, to this problem is given by the authors on pp.34-35, where they consider abortion, normally speaking, as a 'controversy' in which 'others' argue that you 'cannot call a creature in such an early stage of development' as a 'meaningful' human creature. 'Is it right to condemn the activities of many sincere doctors who practise this operation (abortion) for humanitarian motives?'

So much for the 'living parish series' of pamphlets, whose authors believe in murdering the innocent.

What an affront to Catholics, who have such institutions calling themselves Catholics.

We re-echo the words of Bishop Lucey, Cork, Ireland, as reported in The Universe (June 1 1973) who declared 'Beyond a doubt, I think, that not all who call themselves Catholics at present, are in fact so.'

CHOICES IN SEX

A LIVING PARISH PAMPHLET – A BOOKLET FOR YOUNG PEOPLE

Edited by Lawrence Bright
Authors: Quentin and Irene de la Bedoyere

Nihil Obstat: John M.T. Barton (CENSOR)
Imprimatur: + Victor Gauzzelli V.G.
Westminster, 24 Auguast, 1972

In a letter sent to the Archbishop and Bishop of Ireland on 5 June 1973, **The Catholic Priests' Association** complained that the above mentioned publication had a 'postscript' written by Rev Father Enda McDonagh, of St. Patrick's College, Maynooth, in which he strongly recommends *Choices in Sex*, particularly for 'those in the second half of their teens who take their religion seriously'. We deplored the recommendation of a booklet, based, as is *Choices in Sex* on 'situation ethics' and asked the Irish Hierarchy, to take appropriate action to counteract the scandal given – the removal of Father McDonagh from his post and even from his ministry, would not have been more than necessary to negative the scandal he created.

As a result of some Irish National papers giving our criticism full coverage, Father McDonagh's 'fellow traveller' at Maynooth, Father P. Hannon, demanded an apology from the editor of the *Sunday Independent*, which was duly given by the editor, Sunday 24 June 1973. Father Hannon considered our criticism as offensive to truth and justice, as the quotations we had taken from the booklet were 'selective' ones 'totally divorced' from the whole context.

The editor of the *Sunday Independent*, in expressing his public apology, declared that 'the booklet carried the 'Nihil Obstat' of the Archdiocese of Westminster.

This means, that the relevant Church authorities in Britain guarantee, that the booklet contains nothing contrary to the teaching of the Catholic Church.'

So there is nothing in *Choices in Sex* contrary to the teaching of the Catholic Church, and we have this on the guarantee of the ecclesiastical authorities of the Archdiocese of Westminster. Hence, Catholics in Britain, at least can now hold the following propositions as true – as they are affirmed in *Choices in Sex*.

1. 'Whenever love is given, God is present; whether it be in the ecstasy of mystic, of the concern of the prostitute to give her client good value for money.' (p.3).
2. 'Many Christians wonder about the morality of intercourse between couples seriously engaged, and close to the date of their marriage' (p.9).
3. 'Masturbation is an intrinsic part of human growth' (p.19).
4. 'It is not right to condemn the many sincere doctors who practice abortion for humanitarian motives.' (p.35).
5. 'Orgasm is the best way to bring petting to an end.' (p.29).
6. 'In engagements, it (intercourse) could be equally well used to express the lesser friendship' (p.10).
7. 'Petting is a good halfway house (between puberty and economic independence) where young people can explore sexual relationships, and make a better choice of permanent partner.' (p.28).

The above seven propositions are only a few of the many doctrinal errors contained in *Choices in Sex* but now on GUARANTEE from the 'relevant Church authorities in Britain' – to quote the words of the editor of *Sunday Independent*, 'the booklet contains nothing contrary to the teaching of the Catholic Church.'

So, in Britain, at least, intercourse before marriage, masturbation, petting ending in orgasm, abortion for humanitarian reasons are no longer ethically immoral. The 'guarantee' that the booklet if free from teaching contrary to the Catholic Church should be enough to settle the minds of many of the ordinary faithful. A new impetus given is to the advance of the 'permissive society' in Britain. The Catholic Church looked up to by millions outside its field, as the one surviving bastion in the world against moral corruption, has come tumbling down to pander to the desires and lowest instincts of man.

The 'PERMISSIVE SOCIETY' receives the Blessing of the 'PERMISSIVE CHURCH'.

The editor of one of Catholic Ireland's National Sunday papers (*The Sunday Independent* prostrates himself before Father Enda McDonagh, for daring to publish an article of news, that would even give the impression, that Father McDonagh would dream of supporting a doctrine at variance with Catholic teaching. Shades on our memory of *Humanae Vitae*!

As I pondered over the incredible, that the ecclesiastical authorities of Westminster Archdioceses would give a 'GUARANTEE' that 'Choices in Sex' was free from error, the thought struck me, that the 'Censor' of the Archdiocese, the 'Grand Old Man' whose Biblical and Theological love thrilled us in the past, was not likely to 'guarantee' anything, such as the editor of the *Sunday Independent* declared. I contacted Right Reverend Monsignor Canon Barton by letter, and by telephone and then light was thrown on the problem.

In a letter dated June 26 he wrote:- 'I am more and more convinced, that I never saw the great work, that is until after the publication . . . I may have signed the card inadvertently.'

In the course of the letter Monsignor Barton indicated his rapidly failing sight, since 1966. So this is the heart of the matter! The old 'fait accompli' tactics have been used by our charity loving Modernists. The 'guarantee' of orthodoxy has burst into the air, and the time has now come, when the editor of the *Sunday Independent* owes to the ecclesiastical authorities of the Archdiocese of Westminster, a public apology.

It is time that truth and justice so near to the heart of Father Enda McDonagh should be vindicated once more, the responsibility to remove the scandal from the Irish Church, falls heavily upon the Bishops.

'The Living Parish Series' of pamphlets edited by some monks of the Benedictine Monastery at Ealing Abbey, and including such well-known 'Liberal thinkers' as John Coventry, Rosemary Haughton, Bishop Butler, Bishop Worlock and others continue to pour out so much doctrinal waffle, some harmless, some not so harmless (e.g. Peggy Janiwrek in her 'Preparing our Children for the Sacraments', writing, (p.12) that 'Communion can be compared to the sex act, and hence 'married' people find woven into their thanksgiving, the very phrases used, at the height of the sexual act of love.')

What a 'preparation' for Holy Communion for 'our children'!

On behalf of the **Catholic Priests' Association,** a public apology is hereby demanded from the editor of the *Sunday Independent* to the ecclesiastical authorities of Westminster. How dare any paper leave the cause of moral rottenness at the door of Cardinal Heenan, his Auxiliary Bishop, and his revered and highly respected 'Censor Duputatus' – Monsignor Canon Barton.

Sincerely Yours

Rev FR L. Whatmore (Chairman)
Rev FR John W. Flanagan (Secretary)

XIX

THE SCANDAL OF 'HOLY COMMUNION IN THE HAND'
by Father Flanagan May 1976

A CRITICISM OF the Decision of the English and Welsh Hierarchies to introduce 'Communion in the Hand'.

The recent decisions of the Bishops of England and Wales, to request authorisation from the Holy See, to permit priests to distribute Holy communion into the hands of those who wish to receive in this manner, will be deplored by the vast majority of priests and laity of the country. It is yet another example of a small minority from both priests and laity, arbitrarily imposing on the Church, their views, as to what should the place in the Sacred liturgy. Not content with the uprooting of Holy Communion rails (often of great value) to force people to stand, to receive the Sacrament, notwithstanding the clear decision of the Holy See, that the Sacrament should be received 'Kneeling or standing, according to the custom of the Church' – and who will deny that the custom of the Church in Western Europe was to receive it KNEELING – a contrary practice, namely, standing, was promptly introduced. (See *Instruction on the Worship of the Eucharistic Mystery* CTS publication, No.385, par.34). Our churches, large and small, have witnessed unparalleled vandalism, in an idea that the Eucharist is the Body and Blood of Christ. We have seen yet another form of faith destroying 'Episcopal approvals', following the promulgation of Pope Paul's *Immense Caritatis* (AAS, 1973, p.264 SS) in which the Pope, in order to meet the real needs of a large number of Communicants, who could not be adequately served by the number of Priests available, permitted the Bishops to authorise some of the laity to distribute Communion after careful preparation for this office.

Simple convenience on the part of the Priests, became a substitute for real necessity on the party of the faithful. Great numbers of men and women in many dioceses were given approval, so that it is not an uncommon experience today, to see lay people distributing Communion at Sunday Mass, while some of the priests are having a 'lie in'. It is just another example of a Papal concession, being twisted and interpreted, as to be unrecognisable from the original.

Returning to the question of Holy Communion in the hand, the pamphlet of the CTS, *Reception of Holy Communion in the Hand* declares, 'The choice (between Communion in the hand or to the mouth) belongs to the individual communicant, not to the priest or other minister'. The author of the pamphlet (Father A.B. Boylan, Secretary of the Liturgical Commission) gravely errs in making this statement. The 'indult' granted by the Holy See, must be understood in the context of Pope Paul's *Memoriale Domini* (1969) as giving a *facultas Communionem recipiendi*.

In any *facultas Sacramentum administrandi*, the minister of the Sacrament is the final arbiter as to whether he will use the 'permission' or not. It is therefore the priest who must decide on his own judgment, whether one who presents his/her hand to receive the Sacrament will receive it to the mouth, or as requested – in the hand.

To hold that the majority of priests and laity of the country want Communion in the hand, is utterly false. One survey carried out by the Catholic Priests' Association in 1971-1972, and covering some 10,000 members of the laity, showed that 96 of them ABHORRED the idea. Over the years since *Memoriale Domini*, so much violated on every level of the Church in this country, small pressure groups, – e.g., 'National Conference of Priests', 'Pastoral Councils' and 'Deanery Councils' have contained their agitation for Communion in the hand. These organisations represent a very small minority of priests and people, and not a few of them were demanding with equal vehemence, that priests must be permitted to marry. Surrender by the Hierarchy to the ceaseless demands, is only a final proof of their own weakness, and the presence of so many nominal Catholics in key positions in the Church, where they continue the process of secularism and profanation even to the point of including the REAL PRESENCE.

This new abuse can only contribute, still more, to the destruction of Catholic faith in this country.

We pray that priests and people will stoutly resist this snare that endangers the priceless jewel of the Catholic Faith.

N.B: Father Flanagan has written a longer article on this important subject namely 'The Case Against Communion in the Hand.' It is in booklet form and can be had from the KEYS OF PETER, 4, BOSCOMBE AVENUE, LONDON E10. ('Dedicated to: The Shepherds who fell asleep, overcome by weakness').

Also from the above address the following booklets:-
1. *The War Against the Pope* (From *Newsletter* Vol.VI No.1 & 2, 1976).
2. The *'Good Shepherd' of Shepherd's Bush* – with the following FOREWARD – This article deals with the events that tragically terminated the life of Father Jeremiah Daly, Parish Priest of Shepherd's Bush. It is a documentary report. All letters used were the property of the deceased, who in July 1974, and again only four hours before his sudden death on 13 December 1974, gave the author of this article not only permission to use them but every encouragement to do so. Well worth reading!

The 'Good Shepherd of Shepherd's Bush' has been fully recorded for this biography, and can be found towards the end of this book.

SPECIAL EDITORIAL
Newsletter
Vol.VII No.1 1977

From author of this biography:-

I am now reaching the end of the last eleven years of Father Flanagan's life. I am about to record verbatim his very last editorial for the Catholic Priests' Association *Newsletter*. Father Flanagan marked it, 'SPECIAL' for that first, and last issue of 1977. Reading through it now, one feels, that Father Flanagan was aware of his end being near, for his last words were strong and telling, his fears for the Church, his exposition of the Great Betrayal and his own great and valiant defence of orthodoxy. This is how he will be remembered and this is what this book is about – a true priest – a gentle man – a gallant fighter for his Faith.

I will now continue to write this 'Special' editorial and also, his last effort to help Catholics anxious and disturbed about the Church. This effort, was by way of a letter from those concerned, to His Holiness Pope Paul VI. Father composed this letter, and requested that people should send it, so as to arrive in Holy Week 1977. This they did, when hundreds of these letters descended on the Vatican, but alas for us, we were a bereaved people, for

God had called this great churchman, God's own champion, to his eternal reward, where now, please God, he will be caring for us more than ever.

'SPECIAL' EDITORIAL

No adult, unless one mentally retarded, can, at this stage of the crisis now in the Church, continue to have doubts on the ultimate objective of the assault on the Church by the secular humanists, feverishly at work to bring about its collapse.

No excuse can be a motive for Bishops, priests, nuns and laity, continuing their indifference in the face of the most hostile forces ever let loose in the Church. No self-deception, that the replacement of Pope St Pius V's Liturgy, by the new Missal of Pope Paul VI, is the cause of the turmoil, and the cure can only be in its restoration, can hide the fact that the enemies within the Church would have pulverised the Tridentine Liturgy if it was not changed, as ultimately the sacred character of any liturgy will be polluted and desacralised, unless the protecting hand of Episcopal Authority is there to uphold it. This is what the Church is missing today, and in almost every diocese in the world.

Pope Paul is powerless to curtail and still more so, to expel from the Church, the Anti-Christs who sit in judgment on our commissions and direct our lives, unless with the full and willing co-operation of our local chief pastors.

Our Bishops with crook in hand, are bent on the establishment of a National Church, where they will be the supreme authority and the highest court of justice.

The documents of Vatican II, have been time and again, manipulated and interpreted, to convey the message that the Church's 20th century thrust is in this direction.

Bishop Alan Clarke of East Anglia could dare to write:-

> 'In the Roman Catholic Church there has begun a movement away from the model of a single centrally controlled worldwide Church, towards that of a communion of Churches (in the sense of dioceses, often regionally grouped), bound together by their union with the See of Rome' (The Roman Catholic Church in England and the Ten Propositions of the Church Unity Commission, p.1).

Only a dimwit will ascribe to the words 'in union with the See of Rome', a saving clause; it can only mean a union with the See of Rome's enjoying primacy of honour, as the 'movement' is 'away from the centrally controlled Church.'

Who are the people who form this 'movement away from the centrally controlled Church?'

They are those who have broken with the doctrinal unity of the Church already, and so have no title to be called **Catholic**. Bishop Clarke has contributed more than his share to this **movement** and Catholics are not going to take his views as representative of Catholic thought.

The depth of degradation to which our Bishops have permitted the Church in this country to sink, can be evaluated from the following quotation taken from an article by the Anglican Bishop, John A. Robinson, writing in the *Catholic Gazette*, November 1976:

'I virtually never meet a Roman Catholic who believes in the Pope, as he himself expects to be believed in . . . Inter-Communion simply happens, discreetly both ways – as does the (illegal) passing round of the elements in house celebrations, from hand to hand. It would never occur to me to think any of my married Roman Catholic friends are not simply using their own judgment (about the pill) which seems to be the advice of most Catholic theologians anyhow. The Curia playing Canute convinces no one.'

No discerning Catholic adult will doubt the truth of the Anglican Bishop's statement, but what a reflection it is on the safeguarding of faith and morals which is the duty of our own Bishops?

If we need any further evidence of the grand betrayal by the Bishops of the Church that raised them to their present position, we can reflect on Bishop Butler's recent remark, that the moral code of Humanists must not be criticised, and that 'Sunday evening Masses should be abolished and replaced by Ecumenical services.' We find no indication that he was rebuked for such outrageous statements by the Cardinal Archbishop of Westminster nor has anything come to light, that the Cardinal objected to the PUBLIC ANNOUNCEMENT *(Catholic Herald,* 26 Nov.) that Bishop Butler was attending the AGM of **Quest** that was being held in London. **Quest** endeavours to attribute to homosexuals, the status of normality and respectability. The Catholic Priests' Association is not an association of 'Bishop bashers' nor of 'Bishop booters', but of 'Bishop boosters'. Whatever the Bishops may think, we are the only organisation of priests in the country which gives unstinted loyalty to the Pope and the Church, and as the Bishops are an essential part of the Church, our loyalty to them IN THE LEGITIMATE DISCHARGE of their office, cannot be questioned.

A CRITIQUE AND OTHER CONCERNS 237

We are saddened, we are distressed, we feel obliged to express our dismay, objectively and realistically when our Bishops either actively promote or passively permit, doctrines and practices to grow and indeed flourish in their dioceses, that are manifestly opposed to the Bishop of Bishops – the reigning Pontiff.

We offer a boost to our Bishops in their difficulties and anxieties, but if they prefer to lean so much on the completely unrepresentative body known as the 'National Conference of Priests' or on 'Senates' and 'Commissions' which are riddled with Modernists, then they must take the consequences.

Our Association has hundreds of priests with the highest academic qualifications in the Church; yet they are debarred from any opportunity of using their expertise for the good of the Church.

P.S. To follow, an exact copy of the original letter, composed and sent out to all Catholics disturbed and anxious about the Church, January 1977. His own words, verbatim – 'If I can leave just a candle I will be happy' – Father Flanagan didn't leave just a candle – he left a bonfire lit for the greater honour and glory of God, and to show that light to others.

TO ALL CATHOLICS ANXIOUS AND DISTURBED ABOUT THE CHURCH
1st January 1977

Dear Fellow Catholics,
The ever increasing subversion at work within the Church today has reached such proportions, that very many Catholics feel that we have nothing left that we can do, but appeal to the Holy Father to intervene, if the Church of Ireland is to be saved from complete collapse. All of us, priests and laity, have a duty in conscience to defend our Catholic Faith, given to us, and handed down to us, with so much sacrifice and even martyrdom in ages past. Elements are at work within the structure of the Church, bent on emptying Faith of its meaning, undermining the Truths of Faith, reducing belief in the Supernatural to a 'hangover' from a superstitious past, and inculcating the belief that there is no other world but this miserable existence in which we live.

Appeals to the Bishop of the country, to take effective action against the pedlars of this evil neo-Modernism, remain unheard and unanswered. **Commissions** of priests and lay people seem to control every Bishop in the country.

We believe the time has come when every Catholic must turn to him, whose first predecessor was granted by Christ the task of governing the whole Church. Vatican II has repeated the basic doctrine of the Church, that the reigning Pope is the Superior Bishop in every diocese, and every local Bishop solemnly promised him obedience and loyalty on the day of his consecration – a promise that remains unfulfilled.

We suggest to all Catholics to send to Pope Paul VI, a personal letter of appeal; it should be simple, courteous and most respectful. He is not responsible for the chaos in the Church today, but we feel that a clear warning from him to the Bishops of the country, that if they are not prepared to defend the Church in their diocese from the ravages of Modernism, they should hand in their resignation. We also believe that while other countries in recent years have had appointed to the Hierarchy some staunch defenders of the Faith, no such Bishop has been appointed in this country, and we believe that spiritually and mentally strong Bishops are needed, noted for their unquestionable loyalty to the See of Peter.

Please remember the following, if your love for the preservation of the Church and its faith moves you to do something.

1. Write or type your letter clearly, and not excessively long.
2. Address it to, His Holiness, Pope Paul VI, Vatican City, Rome, Italia (Italy).
3. Address on the inside – Your Holiness, followed by the text of your letter which should have your name and address (clearly typed or written) at the end.
4. Most ordinary letters will weigh about 50 grams, and so the postage stamp will be 18p.
5. MOST IMPORTANT: If this appeal is to have real effect, it is important that the letters reach the Vatican during the same week. Hence, please, please, please, see that your letter is posted, so as to reach the Vatican during Holy Week 1977. That means not later than 4 April. Please make sure you do not forget.

Catholics who can reproduce this letter (by duplication or other process), are asked to do so, and send copies far and wide.

We give herewith some features of the Catholic Church in this country today, which disgust many, and to which you can refer in your letter, to some of them, not necessarily all.

Those who intend to write, should remember that they are not writing to tell the Pope the mistakes He is alleged to have made in the new Liturgy of the Mass. It is the interpretations of the Mass and the translations of its text that are at fault, but we suggest that your letter does not mention complaints against the liturgy as such.

FEATURES OF CATHOLICISM in this country today which should move you to action:-

1. When the present generation of Catholics has died out, the future generations will know nothing about Catholicism, as the schools are now giving a dose of Christian Sociology to replace it. Children of even Catholic schools, are entirely ignorant of the fundamentals of faith and are not taught any devotional prayers.
2. The degradation of the Mass and the Eucharist from homemade liturgy, lay people distributing the Eucharist without justification, and Communion in the hand, which was imposed by a desire to meet the requests of 'trendy priests' have robbed the Holy Eucharist of all love and respect once shown to it.
3. The scandal given by priests and nuns, who seem ashamed of their status in life, judging by their dress, contributes much to the death of Catholicism.
4. Bishops seem to have lost their Catholic faith, and close their eyes to the hideous and heretical doctrines and practices which are often welcomed into their dioceses, under the incredible title of 'renewal' of 'ecumenism'. Bishops take part in heretical services and attend revolting conferences which reject the very basic moral code of all Christians.
5. The Central 'Bishops Fund' which comes from an annual collection in every Catholic Church in the country, is used in a considerable proportion to advance the work of non-Catholic beliefs and Marxist-revolutionary activities. Catholics have to pay financially for the destruction of their Catholic faith.
6. Seminaries and college are factories for subversion and the production of false doctrines incompatible with Catholicism. It is questionable if newly ordained priests could even read a Latin Mass.
7. *Humanae Vitae* is still rejected – not openly but in private by priests in conferences, teachers in Catechetical schools and teachers training schools. The sanctity of marriage is ridiculed.
8. *Auricular* Confession is now being replaced by a General Absolution with no regard whatsoever to the conditions laid down by the Holy See as to when General Absolution is permitted. If things continue, we shall soon have no Mass, no Sacraments, no Churches, nothing but blank

humanism. The faithful ask for the bread of life and are given a stone. We urgently need orthodox Bishops, who have not only faith, but great courage in their hearts.

Rev. Father J.W. Flanagan.

AUTHORITY IN THE CHURCH – criticism of the 'AGREED STATEMENT' issued by the joint ANGLICAN-CATHOLIC COMMISSION

By Reverend Father J.W. Flanagan DCL STL.

The preface of this 'AGREED STATEMENT', which it states, will be known as the *Venice Agreement* – the others being *The Windsor Agreement* on the Eucharist, and the *Canterbury Statement* on the Ministry – has some extraordinary affirmation, that:-

'It was precisely in the problem of Papal Primacy that our historical diversions found their unhappy origin' and the eventual unity will 'enrich Roman Catholics by the presence of a tradition of spirituality and scholarship, the lack of which has deprived the Roman Catholic Church of a precious element in Christian heritage.'

Most objectively thinking historians ascribe the rupture of Anglicanism from the parent Church, to the unbridled desires of Henry VIII to rid himself of his legitimate wife, an event which occasioned the use of Papal power, when a declaration of nullity of his marriage was requested. As to the second point, it may be fairly said that Anglicanism, has no doubt, produced much scholarship, particularly in the realm of Biblical studies, yet the Catholic Church has not suffered any loss of its spirituality and/or scholarship by the 16th century break. The strong support given by well-known Anglicans to legitimise contraception and abortion, can hardly be considered as examples of outstanding sanctity of life, though it must be admitted that the views of Anglican Bishops do not always reflect the views of the Anglican Church. Yet, it is precisely on this point, that one becomes befuddled in speaking or writing on 'AGREEMENT, (or even disagreement) with the Anglican Church'. Who is it, who can speak or act on behalf of Anglicanism, which in itself, contains a thousand fragments? Will a document, signed by the Archbishop of Canterbury, who has no authority over his own Bishops, convey what is acceptable to the Anglican Church or just to some Anglicans?

The preface of the *Venice Statement* also tells us that 'for the reading of the document, and for the understanding of the method pursued, an awareness of the "ideal" (as willed by Christ) and the "actual", is important'. An enumeration or exemplification of the 'ideals' willed by Christ for his Church, as distinct from what He 'actually willed' would have clarified a paragraph of the document that must, as a consequence, remain gloriously obscure. Perhaps the Bishops McAdoo and Clarke, will inform us on how they know that one thing is an 'ideal', and something else is not?

On careful perusal of the document, one is struck by the absence of any reference, even by the 'Catholic' side, that Christ willed the transmissions of His doctrines, not through the Scriptures, but through a living 'Church'. The Apostles were commissioned to 'preach' and 'teach', while no mention is made by the Scriptures of any commission to 'write'. The failure of the Anglican-Catholic Commission to face this reality, means that the International Commission stopped short of excavating the foundations of the Christian Church, in their quest for the meaning of 'authority', and were content with leaving them undisturbed. Perhaps the explanation lies in what par.25 has to say on the 'method' followed:

'We have endeavoured to get behind the opposed and entrenched positions of past controversies . . . We have deliberately avoided the vocabulary of past polemics, not with any intention of evading the real difficulties that provoked them, but because the emotive associations of such language often obscured truth'.

We find this explanation entirely unpalatable. Truth must come first, however arduous the quest. It is easy to leave it buried and untouched, covered by phrases of alleged 'emotive association'. Truth and falsity be united by any bonds of false charity or excuse. Such a procedure only deepens and prolongs the agony, and the problems become more obscure.

Before embarking on a paragraph by paragraph analysis of the *Statement*, it is of fundamental importance to consider how we are to understand the word ***authority*** in the Church, as used by Catholics and by non-Catholics. Presumably a Catholic and particularly Catholic Bishops, as Bishop Butler and Clarke, realise that ***authority*** in this context, is the ***authority*** essential for a perfect society, as is the Church, and an ***authority*** which is of Divine origin. It is not then, an ***authority*** which can be bartered, humanly changed or modified. It is the ***authority*** which Christ has given to the ONE TRUE CHURCH, and any dialogue between the ONE TRUE CHURCH, and any other Christian denomination must conform to the rules laid down in this matter, notably *Reflections and Suggestions concerning Ecumenical Dialogue* issued 15 August 1970, by the Secretaries for the promotion of Christian Unity. Section IV, par.2 (a) of this document states that:-

'The participants . . . will not pass judgment on the willingness of one side or the other to be faithful to the Gospel. The Catholic participant, however, believing as he does, that the Lord has confirmed to the Catholic Church the fullness of the means of Salvation and all truth revealed by God, will be ready to give an accurate account of his faith.'

In these words, the author of the *Reflection and Suggestions* was not affirming a guideline different from what Vatican II itself taught. The constitution on *Ecumenism* par.3-4 and 11) is crystal clear on how representative of the Catholic Church must stand in dialogue with non-Catholics. It states:-

'It is through Christ's Catholic Church alone, which is the all embracing means of salvation, that the fullness of the means of salvation can be obtained. It was to the Apostolic college alone, of which Peter is the head, that we believe Our Lord entrusted all the blessings of the new covenant, in order to establish on earth the One Body of Christ, into which all those should be fully incorporated, who already belong in anyway to God's people (par.3) . . . It is of course, essential, that in dialogue, that doctrine be presented in its entirety. Nothing is so foreign to the spirit of ecumenism as a false conciliatory approach, which harms the purity of Catholic doctrine and obscures its assured genuine meaning' (par.11).

One wonders in how many dialogues with non-Catholics, apart altogether from the McAdoo/Butler/Clarke discussions, are the principles of Ecumenism stated above, affirmed by the Catholic representatives?

The Catholic Church has always claimed that it is a 'perfect society', i.e., one which possess within itself, all the means necessary to attain its end. Authority is essential to such a society and must arise from the same source from which the society itself (the Church) arises, on the principle *unde oritur societas, inde oritur auctoritas*. As Christ is the founder of the Church, He is the sole source of all authority within it. The Church, by Divine Law, is a juridical society, i.e., possessing power to impose on its members real obligations (legislative), to judge its subjects according to law (judical and penal) i.e., to impose penalties on transgressors. This authority was exercised from the Church's very beginning, and is not therefore any historical accretion.

The *Agreed Statement on Authority* is highly unsatisfactory, pars. 3-7 of the *Statement* revive the ideas of Rationalists (Harnack) and other Protestants of the last century, e.g. Sabatier, *Les Religions d'autorite et la Religion de L'Esprit,* who reject any Divine Constitution to a 'religious movement' founded by Christ. For those who drew up the *Statement*, it is the 'local Church' which is the Church. A merely spiritual bond existed between the diverse 'local Churches'; fostering a universal communion between the 'local Churches' merely consolidates the faith of the local community. Rome became the principle See of the early Christian world, merely through an accident of history.

The Bishop of Rome exercised his 'oversight' in order to guard and promote the faithfulness of the other Churches to Christ and to each other (par.12).

The universality of Christ's Divine power ('All power is given to me in Heaven and on earth' – John XX, 21); 'He that heareth you (the Apostles) heareth Me . . . Go ye into the whole world etc.,' are texts that cannot receive their full meaning if only addressed to local communities. The scriptures use the word 'Church' when speaking of the Church in a particular city or town, and the plural 'Churches' when referring to the Churches of a province. But, besides these 'Churches', there is a Universal Church, which is made up of members of individual communities and over which Peter and his successors preside with the same authority as Christ Himself ('the plenitude of power').

Professor Moran (Maynooth) in his excellent work, *The Government of the Church in the First Century*, clearly points out this basic Church structure. He writes:-

'We never hear of 'Churches' of Corinth or of Thessalonica or Philippi or Rome . . . but frequent mention of 'Churches' of a province, because each town in the province has its own Church. St Paul speaks of the "Churches" of Galatia, of Asia and Macedonia . . . Over and above this local community, there is a universal unity, a Church composed of all Churches, something like an empire composed of many principalities. This universal Church is not the sum total of all those who are just before God, as Luther considered the Church to be. For St Paul, the same faithful who form the local visible Churches, form also, when considered in their ensemble, the universal mission and authority from the Apostles' (pp.59-60).

In the *Venice Statement* (see pars 8-13, much loose thinking is indulged in, by the emphasis given to "local Churches", whose meetings give "authoritative decisions", when they express the faith and mind of the Church' (par.9) and Bishops of the prominent Sees acquire the oversight over other Bishops of their region . . . and it is within this historical context that the See of Rome, whose prominence was associated there, with the death of Peter and Paul' (par.12). It would be extremely difficult for the signatories of the *Statement* to reconcile the prominence of Peter as contained in "The

Acts of the Apostles" with his death which had not as yet come about.'

One of the most extraordinary statements in the *Venice Agreement* must be that contained in par.12, where we read:-

'The importance of the Bishop of Rome among his brother Bishops as explained by analogy with the position of Peter among the Apostles, was interpreted as Christ's Will for the Church.' Then it continues – 'On the basis of this analogy, the first Vatican Council affirmed, that this service was necessary to the unity of the whole Church. Far from overriding the authority of Bishops in their own dioceses, this service was explicitly intended to support them in their ministry of oversight.'

The *Statement* then goes on to affirm the inconceivable, that Vatican II, merely placed the episcopal function of the Bishop of Rome in the 'shared responsibility of all Bishops' . . . and communion with the Bishop of Rome does not imply submission to an authority that would stifle the distinctive features of the local Churches.'

Catholics who sign a document, which contains such an outrageous statement, force one to conclude that the signatories never read the Apostolic Constitution of Vatican I (Session IV), *Pastor Aeternus,* or that they have forgotten it, or, that they no longer accept it, even though there is no dispute as to its infallible nature (Denzinger-Schoenmetzer, No.3050 SS; Karl Rahner, *The Teaching of the Catholic Church,* No.370 SS). That Vatican, II could change the infallible nature of *Pastor Aeternus,* or that promulgated documents of the same Council are worded in such a way as to make possible such an interpretation as the signatories of the *Venice Agreement* arrived at, is entirely preposterous. Vatican II, in its Apostolic Constitution *Lumen Gentium* reaffirm in the clearest terms, the traditional teaching of the Church on the primacy of jurisdiction possessed by the Roman Pontiff, derived immediately from Christ, and which is not dependent on any other source or authority, for its exercise. This supreme authority of the Vicar of Christ, does not destroy the legitimate authority of the local Bishop, but rather affirms, strengthens, and vindicates it. (*Lumen Gentium* No.27).

Par.12 of the 'Venice Agreement' states that 'Rome became the principal centre in matters of the universal Church' because it was so prominently associated with the death of Peter an Paul there. How would the signatories of the 'Venice Agreement' explain the prominence of Peter BEFORE HE HAD COME TO ROME and WHILE HE WAS STILL ALIVE, as given to us in the 'Acts of the Apostles, chapter XV, where Peter, at the Council of Jerusalem claimed (with no dissenting voice) 'that God had made choice among them' (verse 7) and when he had given his decision 'silence fell upon the multitude' (verse 14). Peter's prominence in this case did not arise from the accidents of history which the 'Venice Agreement' assigns as an explanation of Rome's prominence. It was Peter who gave prominence to Rome, not Rome to Peter.

'The teaching of these Councils (Vatican I and II) show that Communion with the Bishop of Rome, does not imply submission to an authority which would stifle the distinctive features of the local Churches' (*Venice Agreement* par.12).

Papal authority has never been accepted, in the sense that it can be used to change the Divine Constitution of the Church, by the abolition of the Episcopacy. It is equally inconceivable that it would be used to abolish the whole Hierarchy of a country, or perhaps even a province. But other than excesses of this nature, Papal authority, as *Pastor Aeturnus* (Vatican I) shows, can be used to the betterment of the Church, and as judged by the reigning Pontiff. It is equally false, as the *Venice Agreement* states, that 'this service' (Papal authority) 'was placed by Vatican II, in the wider context of shared responsibility of all the Bishops'. These words are directly in conflict with 'Pastor Aeturnus' (Rahner, No.374) which infallibly declared, that it is not 'through the Church on Peter as her minister' that this supremacy is derived, but 'is bestowed immediately and directly upon Blessed Peter (and his successors) by Christ Himself.' Papal authority is unique to Peter and his successors, and cannot be shared with Bishops.

'Sometimes functions, assumed by the See of Rome, were not necessarily linked to the Primacy: sometimes the conduct of the occupant of this See, has been unworthy of his office: sometimes the image of this office has been obscured by interpretations placed upon it' (*Venice Agreement*, No.12).

It is not surprising that the signatories of the *Statement* should accept the above quotation. All through the document, it is clear that the Anglican signatories (presumably in good faith) consider the Church of Christ as a collective of local Churches, with no visible perfect Society of Christ existing on earth.

On the contrary, Vatican I has made it abundantly clear that the Church of Christ is a 'wholly self-contained unity . . . and is not distributed and divided among various societies that call themselves Christian' (Rahner par. 363).

Why reference should be made in the *Statement* to the conduct of the occupant of the See of Rome being occasionally unworthy of his office is difficult to see. If it comes to inserting unworthy conduct into what is supposed to be serious dialogue on structures of the Church of Christ, then it is clear that prejudice and animosity are not yet terminated. But it must be said that Catholics in general will appreciate the healthy opposition of the Anglican signatories to what they consider as unwarranted weakening of their own Anglican faith, as these same Catholics will deplore the many points of evidence, that the Roman Catholic signatories are only too willing to ignore truths of Catholic Faith to win some tactical position from which they can launch their 'ego' still further into the world of popularity.

At this stage of our reflection on the *Agreed Statement* it is worthy of note that, at the General Synod of the Church of England on Friday 18 February, numerous speakers showed 'often in criticism, that was at times fierce' (*Catholic Herald*, 25 February) how much in disagreement they were with the *Agreed Statement*.

Professor Lampe of Cambridge, regretted that the Commission had come to this topic before it had first done more prepatory work. He pointed out that 'Primacy of the Pope as here described' was 'quite incompatible with the Pope's universal immediate jurisdiction' . . . It means the dismantling of the *Curia* . . . no more encyclicals like *Humanae Vitae*. He did not like to look a gift horse in the mouth, but he felt that this one had too many rotten teeth to be able to last the course.' Professor Jones told the Synod that 'he thought the *Statement* on Authority and its two predecessors on the Eucharist, and the Ministry and Ordination, looked very Anglican documents. There is nothing in them that does not have its counterpart in honoured Anglican theology,' he declared. 'The Synod voted by an overwhelming majority to welcome the document.'

To Professor Jones' remark on the three *Agreed Statements* being very Anglican documents', we say 'AMEN!'

Even a superficial analysis of this *Statement* will bring to light its efforts to establish numerous ideas that are, to quote Professor Jones, 'very Anglican'. Only decisions of Ecumenical Councils of the first centuries (par.19) have binding force, so these alone formulate the central truths of faith. 'Bishops have a special responsibility for promoting truth and discerning error, and the interaction of Bishops and people in its exercise is a safeguard of all Christian life and fidelity' (par.18).

This passage implies the 'House of Laity' of 'Convocation' to be a divinely established source of authority.

A CRITIQUE AND OTHER CONCERNS 247

The *Venice Statement* in par.21, declares that 'Primacy fulfils its purpose by helping the Churches to listen to one another; it does not seek uniformity where diversity is legitimate.' Who, it may be asked is the final arbiter, of 'diversity being legitimate or not?' Who is to be the final arbiter, as to whether local Churches have or have not deviated from Christian life and fidelity?

Par.16 of the *Venice Agreement*, by attributing to local Councils held from the second century, and which determined the limits of the New Testament, some special assurance from the Lord Himself that He was present with His people, guiding them to know the Scriptures that were authentic, and those that were not, could place Protestants in an unenviable position. While they are expected to accept the 'Scriptures and Scriptures alone' as the 'Sole Rule of Faith', yet certain **local Councils** and not the Scriptures, told them how to distinguish the authentic Scriptures from the non-authentic. This would mean that the basic rule of faith in early Church were the assemblies of the faithful, with their Bishops, but later on, in the history of the Church, Luther's unalterable basic rule of faith became the 'Scriptures and Scriptures alone.'

The signatories of the *Venice Agreement* in this paragraph 16 even attribute to the 'people assembled' at the Council of Jerusalem the words which the Acts of the Apostles (XV.28) attribute to the mouth of Peter – 'It has seemed good to the Holy Spirit and to us.' Contrary to the teaching of Vatican I and Vatican II, the 'reception of conciliar definitions' by the faithful is essential for their validity. This 'response of the faithful' is indicative of the 'Holy Spirit's continuing guidance of the Church', we are told.

Par.17 of the *Venice Agreement* confuses the moral or pastoral leadership which came from the principal Sees, particularly the See of Rome, with authority which we are discussing. It is clear that the signatories of the 'Agreement' in paragraphs 17 to 19 continue to muddle the concept of pastoral or moral authority, with the authority which Christ entrusted to Peter and the Apostles.

Par.19 asserts that when the 'Church meets in Ecumenical Council, its decisions on fundamental matters of faith exclude what is erroneous'. The source of this protection from error is not Peter's unique position, as Catholics know, but the Holy Spirit. Even some Anglican Bishops (e.g. the Anglican Bishop of Norwich) were not slow to repudiate the claim contained in par.20, that a 'Bishop, after consulting his fellow Bishops, may speak in their name, and express their mind.' It is not necessary to specify the Bishops who would (and in fact have) promptly repudiated this statement.

In section VI of the *Venice Agreement* pars.24 and 25, we find material which should never have been endorsed by the signature of a Catholic Bishop.

In fact, the signature of any Bishop of the Catholic Church to these points, means he forfeits his duty to uphold the Catholic Faith. It should be borne in the mind of any student of this 'Agreement', that, while the Anglican members of the Commission who signed it honourably specified certain aspects and points of Catholic doctrine on which they could not agree and were not prepared to accept, the Roman Catholic Bishops showed no such faith or courage. They showed that they were prepared to accept numerous points of doctrine which are completely alien to Catholicism. We shall specify these items, in the course of this commentary. Not only did the Catholic Bishops evince acceptance of points of Protestant doctrine, and without any objection, but in view of their notoriously liberal Catholic mentality over a whole Catholic life and doctrine, one cannot but lament that it was such Prelates as Bishop Butler and Clarke who were appointed to this Commission. Only last year, Bishop Clarke in an ecumenical conference in Australia, declared that the Church of Christ had not yet reached 'Unity'. For him, the Church of Christ is composed of all divisions of the Christian people. This heretical doctrine is firmly repudiated in a pastoral letter, read in all Churches of the dioceses of Sandhurst, issued by, and ordered to be read by that indomitable Champion of Orthodoxy, Bishop Stewart.

No one in this country, acquainted with the liberal views of Bishop Butler, can have had doubts that this Auxiliary Bishop of Westminster is dangerously near breaking point in doctrinal unity, which is the essential criterion of whether one is a Catholic or not.

'Par.24 of the *Venice Agreement* tell us, 'Claims on behalf of the Roman See, as commonly presented in the past, have put a greater weight on the Petrine texts (Matthew XVI, 31-32; John XXI, 15,17) than they are generally thought to be able to bear. However, many Roman Catholic scholars do not feel it necessary to stand by former exegesis of those texts in every respect.'

COMMENT ON THIS SECTION: Bishop Clarke and Butler in signing this document accepted a doctrine in conflict with what the Fathers of Vatican II signed in the Constitution of the Church.

One does not have to go back to Vatican I to find official Church teaching on the value of those Biblical texts. Each one of the texts considered by Bishop Butler and Clarke, as overweighted by the Church in the past in favour of Papal Primacy, were considered by their brother

A CRITIQUE AND OTHER CONCERNS 249

Bishops of the world and by the Vicar of Christ, to retain their probative value, as traditionally understood, up to 21 November 1964, when the Apostolic Constitution on the Church was signed at the Vatican Council. Obviously then, Bishops Clarke and Butler only accept the portions of the Decrees of Vatican II, which are agreeable to their way of thinking. Who are these 'Roman Catholic scholars' who find it unnecessary to stand by former exegesis of those texts? Bishops Clarke and Butler thus give countenance to these views, or at least find them as acceptable interpretations as those given by the Church's *Magisterium*.

'The first Vatican Council of 1870 uses the language of 'Divine Right' of the successors of Peter. This language has no clear interpretation in modern Roman Catholic theology.'

COMMENT: 'If anyone shall say, that it is not by the Institution of Christ the Lord, or by divine right, that Blessed Peter should have a perpetual line of successors in the primacy over the Universal Church; or that the Roman Pontiff is not the successor of Blessed Peter in this primacy, let him be *anathema*'. (Pastor Aeturnus of Vatican I, *Denz.3058*). It is not necessary to tell Catholics that the above solemn teaching from Vatican I is such that those who deny it are cursed by the Church (*Anathema* sit) and are accordingly automatically excommunicated from the Church. Bishops Clarke and Butler are obliquely contesting Vatican I – it appears. Here again, as in the previous paragraph, these Prelates side with modern liberal Catholics holding that **Divine Right** in the Papacy, 'has no clear interpretation'. The time has come, when the Church in this country must recognise these Bishops for what they are. Their presence on any Church Commission is unfortunately no guarantee of immunity from doctrinal error.'Anglicans find grave difficulty in the affirmation that the Pope can be infallible in his teaching.'

COMMENT: It is understandable that Anglicans should find themselves in this state of uncertainty, not possessing as they do, the gift of Catholic Faith, which is the only key which unlocks all the problems in the Church. It is impracticable to view Revealed Religion without an absolute certainty as to what is revealed. The Anglicans seek the source of this certainty in the workings of the Holy Spirit, illuminating in the mind of the Christian as he studies the Scriptures.

This subjective criterion is both elusive and dangerous. The Catholic sees the foundation for absolute certainty in the design of the Church as fashioned by Christ, with His Divine Guarantee given to Peter and his successors.

'The conditions (for exercise of 'infallibility') preclude the idea that the Pope is an inspired oracle communicating fresh revelation or that the can speak independently of his fellow Bishops and the Church or on other matters not concerning faith and morals.'

COMMENT: It is inconceivable that Catholic Bishops and priests should sign a document as an 'agreement' which 'precludes the Pope from speaking independently of his fellow Bishops or of the Church', when such a dependence of the Pontiff on the Bishops or on the Church, has already been authentically and firmly rejected by Vatican II (Dogmatic Constitution on the Church, No.22) and the independence of the Roman Pontiff in the exercise of the primacy, is part of the solemn and infallible teaching of Vatican I *Aeturnus Pastor, Denz.* 3050 – 3054. It is for the educated Catholic to conclude how Catholic clergy now stand who sign a document as acceptable, which is in direct conflict with an infallible decision of the Church.

No doubt, Bishop Alan Clarke has been caught up in that liberal Catholic movement (which is in fact Protestant) and in the formation and development of which he played a big part, and to which he refers in his pamphlet, 'The Roman Catholic Church in England and the Ten Propositions of the Church Unity Commission'.

Here on Page 1, he states: 'In the Roman Catholic Church, there has begun a movement away from the model of a single centrally controlled worldwide Church, towards that of a Communion of Churches (dioceses) bound together by their union with the See of Rome.'

Surely, if the 'movement' is away from 'central control' the union with the See of Rome must be one of honour only?

This liberal mentality of Bishop Clarke has surfaced through the 'Agreement'. He has completely failed to conform to the ruling of Vatican II on ecumenism. He has made no effort to implement the Decree on ecumenism governing dialogue with non-Catholics V.12., that 'Catholic doctrine be presented in its entirety.

'Nothing is so foreign to the spirit of Ecumenism, as a false conciliatory approach, which harms the purity of Catholic Doctrine and obscures its assured genuine meaning.'

What, it may be asked, have Bishops Clarke and Butler stated in the three published *Agreements* on the Eucharist, the Ministry and Authority, that would lead the non-Catholic participant to conclude that the Catholic participants genuinely believed that the Roman Catholic Church alone contained all divinely revealed truth, and that it – and it alone – was the Church founded by Christ on earth? Yet that is what all authentic documents of Vatican II and those following the Council have insisted upon.

'For the Roman Catholic Church, the Popes' dogmatic definitions, which, fulfilling the criteria of infallibility, are preserved from error, do no more but no less than express the mind of the Church on issues concerning divine revelation.'

COMMENT: If ever there was a fuzzy-woolly definition of the exercise of Papal infallibility, the above quotation from the 'Agreement' must top the list. 'To express the mind of the Church is very different from an actual expression of the Church's teaching authority, as an exercise of Papal infallibility is. The Catholic signatories of the 'Agreement' should have refreshed their memories on the lines laid down by the Holy See for all who are involved in ecumenical dialogue.

It will be seen therein, that the decree of Vatican II on this point is both positive and negative. Positive – in that those taking part should establish their own belief – that the Catholic Church is the one true Church founded by Christ; and Negative – that they should avoid a false conciliatory irenicism.'

(Decree on the Liturgy, No.11) Both aspects of the Decree have been ignored by the Catholic signatories.

'Special difficulties are created by the recent Marian dogmas, because Anglicans doubt the appropriateness or even the possibility, of defining them as essential to the faith of believers.'

COMMENT: This is the second occasion when Anglican members of the Commission have the courage of their convictions, to express their opposition. We congratulate them on their courage, as we deplore the easy acquiescence with which Bishops Butler and Clarke permit numerous elements of Protestant theology to pass unchallenged. The paragraph quoted, shows not only opposition to Marian dogmas, but the reason for the opposition, that they are not contained in the Scriptures, reaffirms the Protestant stance unchanged. That is, the Scriptures alone, and not the '*Magisterium*', remain the ultimate source of Christian teaching.

'The Roman Catholic Church is today, seeking to replace the jurisdictional outlook of the nineteenth century, by a more pastoral understanding of authority in the Church.'

COMMENT: It is entirely untrue to allege that the Church can, replace its doctrines with Pastoral 'understandings' of the same. Vatican II was, as Pope John stated, when opening the Council, a 'Pastoral Council'. Yet, its two first documents were *The Dogmatic Constitution on the Church* and *The Dogmatic Constitution on Revelation,* which repeatedly reaffirm both *ex cathedra* and *magisteral* teaching of Vatican I.

The signatories of the *Agreement* will seek in vain in the *Dogmatic Constitution on the Church* for any relaxation of the authority given to the Church by its Divine Founder. Nor will they find therein any text which could even remotely be considered as a basis for their conclusions, given in the *Agreement.*

In fact, as the Council opened, its first promulgated Decree was on the liturgy (4 December 1963) which preceded both Dogmatic Constitutions, on the Church and on Revelation, (21 November 1963 and 18 November 1965, respectively) yet it is the Dogmatic Constitutions which occupy pride of place in all collections of Vatican II documents.

To dismiss then, Vatican II as a Pastoral Council is entirely erroneous. In fact no Council other than Trent, has so many reaffirmations of official Catholic dogmas as the Second Vatican Council. Pope John, in his inaugural address, spoke of a 'Council, predominantly pastoral in character', which must 'transmit doctrine pure and integral without any attenuation or distortion.' Vatican II's *Decree on Ecumenism* (par.11) warns those who would follow 'false conciliatory approaches which harm the purity of Catholic doctrine'. This warning does not seem to have been listened to by the signatories of the *Venice Agreement.*

In the final paragraph of the *Statement,* the Commission members claim that they: 'Have got behind opposed and entrenched positions of past controversies, and have come to the conclusions contained in the *Statement* which represent a significant convergence with far-reaching consequences' (par.25).

COMMENT: The writer of this article completely disagrees with the conclusions of the signatories. The *Venice Agreement* will only confuse members of both Roman Catholic and Anglican Churches.

The **convergence** is that created by compromise, and not that which can radiate from truth.

A CRITIQUE AND OTHER CONCERNS 253

Its publication can only be deplored by anyone objectively seeking the unification of Christianity as emphasised by Vatican II. Its frequent attempts to make Protestant theology appear palatable to the Catholic Church can only have disastrous consequences.

We have kept the most solid objection against the *Agreement* to the last. In paragraph 24, the signatories assert that the *Agreement* is a:-

'Consensus on authority in the Church, and in particular, on the basic principles of primacy, but it does not wholly resolve all the problems associated with Papal primacy.'

The places of Papal authority and primacy are so fundamental to the whole concept of authority in the Church, that it is contradictory to claim an agreement on the latter but not on the former.

Papal authority and primacy are the very bricks and mortar from which authority in the Church is built. It is preposterous to claim reconciliation of Catholic and Anglican views on authority in the Church if Papal authority and primacy are left unsettled and unaccepted. It is obvious, that the Catholic signatories of the *Agreement*, never fully appreciated the intrinsic link between one and the other. The convergence they claim to have reached, must have involved attempts to meet a false concept of Papal authority and primacy.

The work on the *Agreement* has involved time and money badly spent, and has ended in an illusory agreement.

It will take much true ecumenism to compensate for the damage done to both Churches.

P.S. As each year passes, the orthodoxy of Father Flanagan's many critical essays is further vindicated. His criticism of the *Agreed Statements* as contained in this biography, the deep reservations he expressed over Bishop Clarke's eagerness to sign them have just been corroborated by an Official Vatican response in the form of a letter written by Cardinal Ratzinger to Bishop Clarke.

In it, the Cardinal informs Bishop Clarke that:-

'It is not yet possible to say, that an agreement, which is 'substantial' has been reached on the totality of the questions studied by the Commission. There are several points, held as dogmas by the Catholic Church, which are not able to be accepted as such. Some formulation in the ARIC report can still give rise to divergent interpretations, while others do not seem able to be easily reconciled with Catholic Doctrine'.

Points taken from the full Vatican text of the letter to Bishop Clarke as published in *The Times*, 31 March 1982.

One is tempted to say to Bishop Alan Clarke – you were well told! Other articles (in pamphlet or booklet form) written by Father Flanagan in defence of the Church and its *Magisterium* can be obtained from:-

> The Keys of Peter Book Service
> 4, Boscombe Avenue
> London, E.10.

They are as follows:-

1. The Case against Communion in the Hand.
2. The Demolition of the Sacrament of Penance.
3. The War Against The Pope.
4. Teilhardism by Father Flanagan.
5. A Refutation of Moral Doctrine.

CATHOLIC HERALD

Article by Father Flanagan

1973 The *Catholic Herald*, 17 August 1973, in an editorial and in a column from **A Staff Reporter** contains an unconcealed and bitter attack on the Catholic Priests' Association and its efforts made to prevent the moral corruption of youth through the publication of the booklet *Choices in Sex*.

The time is long past when this paper can be called 'Catholic' and in the course of this letter I mean to expose the want of veracity – the want of justice and the want of charity on the part of a paper that in this very issue (August 17) deplores the absence of these on the part of the ICPA.

It is rather significant – at that very moment, the counterpart of the *Herald* in Ireland, the *Catholic Standard,* has been given an ultimatum by the Secretary of the ICPA to withdraw its libellous statement of a few weeks previous, that the editor of *Newsletter* was guilty of 'lifting' Bishop Daly's article *Christianity and Sex*.

Bishop Daly has now disassociated himself from the false charges also made in the same *Catholic Standard* involving himself and CPA.

The *Catholic Herald* of August 17 descends to the depths of mendacity by ascribing to the CPA what it is guilty of itself, when the editor of that paper tells its readers that we have been conducting a 'smear campaign for sometime, whereby the integrity of blameless individuals was being gradually undermined.'

We presume that it is Monsignor Barton's endlessly repeated accusations of 'forgery' to which the editor is referring. It was not the CPA who made the charge of 'forgery' – but the CENSOR, Monsignor Barton, who in six letters written between June 26 and August 8, in which he repeats no less than 14 times, that forgery has been committed, that our charges were based upon.

These letters were on the repeated request of the same Monsignor Barton made public to the national press in Ireland and to the Irish Hierarchy, but never at any time, as the *Catholic Herald* falsely states, has any communication been made to the 'NC' (Worldwide) News agency.

This is typical of the untruths published in the *Catholic Herald*. On the question of 'smear campaign', the *Catholic Herald* has a strict monopoly of this tactic, and we would not dare to intrude on its preserves.

The 'smear campaign' carried on, during the CPA defence of *Humanae Vitae* between 1968 – 1970, is not forgotten by the reading public.

We can well understand the editors desire, that the CPA should be considered 'totally discredited and never expect to be taken seriously again,' (editorial 17 August).

Any individual or organisation that is not afraid of popular opinion and defends orthodoxy of doctrine can be sure that, at some stage, the so called *Catholic Herald* will indulge in systematic 'besmirching' (to use Monsignor Barton's words against his 'forger') of the character or the integrity, when rational or theological arguments fail. We have seen this so often, that we expect nothing else from the paper concerned.

Monsignor Ralph Brown in the same issue of the *Herald*, gives us all a laugh when he bemoans 'the distress we (CPA) caused an elderly and distinguished priest, who served the Church so long and well.' The 'distinguished priest' is of course Monsignor Barton, whose very own letters were the ones which originally, and all through, levelled 'forgery' at someone (whose identity he has disclosed to me) working close to him in the Westminster Curial Offices.

Poor Monsignor Ralph! He does not seem to know whether he is coming or going.

Yet another laugh – not at the expense of Monsignor Barton but at the expense of Monsignor Brown when in the *Herald* he complains that the CPA 'should have checked any private correspondence with the Censor before making allegations public'. But it was the Censor's own six letters, with his photostat copy (3 in fact) his legal advisor, telling him to take action and not to spare the forger, that we had before us, when we made the allegation.

In fact, I did telephone the Monsignor twice, and he emphatically confirmed in conversation, what he had written so often, and expressed his appreciation that I would duplicate for him a letter to be sent to the Irish Bishops and Irish National Press, in which country his international reputation had, he believed, suffered most, by the unsuspecting reader, thinking that he had given the *Nihil Obstat* to this disgraceful book.

Poor Monsignor Brown! Your thinking powers seem to have gone astray in your efforts to pin the fault for the whole affair onto the poor CPA.

But, there is more to come, Monsignor Brown! You state, that the Censor now admits that he gave the *Nihil Obstat* in 'August of last year'. Monsignor Barton's letter to me, dated August 9 (one day only after his sixth letter, and his fourteenth statement to the contrary) admitted that he had given the signature 'at the end of last year'; there is still the period from August 24, when the book appeared, to the end of the year, to account for!

So Monsignor Barton acknowledged finally, after all the denials and consultations with others, in view of action, that he had signed, but it was too late to prevent the letters sent out at his request from reaching their destination.

Many will say that there is something fishy in this whole story, and they will recall that pressurisation takes place in more places than in an airliner.

Monsignor Barton, who was so anxious – and rightly so – that his international reputation should not be endangered by appearing to agree with the ideas contained in this book, now had admitted that he had agreed with them.

Monsignor Brown assures us, *Catholic Herald*, 17 August, that the 'Censor signs the *Nihil Obstat* only if he is satisfied the book makes no statements contrary to faith or morals.' O tempora! O mores!

But hold it, dear reader! The **Staff Reporter** of the *Catholic Herald* tells us that, 'The Cardinal, as a result of information and representations from other sources, decided some time ago, that the book was inappropriate for publication.'

Strange how these who made the representations found the book at fault and the Censor did not.

Equally strange to, that the Cardinal did not intervene until the forgery charge was made. But better late than never!

The *Catholic Herald* keeps the best wine to the end. It tells us that, before publication, the booklet was submitted to the scrutinising of 'leading Catholic Educationalists (named by other papers, e.g. Irish Independent, August 13) as Fathers Constant and Bullen and of course by the infallible

Enda McDonagh of Maynooth who wrote the postscript, recommending it to teenagers 'who take their religion seriously'.

The *Catholic Herald* did not tell us what other papers gave, quoting the authors of the book, who said of Fathers Constant and Bullen, who are called 'prominent religious educational experts' that you 'could scarcely be more careful about getting approval, short of going to the Pope himself' said Mr de la Bedoyere. (Author of book).

The Chairman of the 'Pastoral Development Group', Dr Oliver Pratt, quoted in the same *Catholic Herald*, assured the readers that *Choices in Sex* does not set out to give Catholic teaching on moral issues, but assumes that the reader is already aware of these. The booklet merely asks questions about sexual behaviour and attitudes, quoting a variety of views to help the reader to reach a fully thought out acceptance of the Catholic Church's views, which are, of course, those of the authors.'

Whatever Dr Pratt may know, he certainly does not know Catholic Theology when he presents the Church teaching through her *Magisterium* as a 'view', but there are other 'views' as well.

One only has to read, *Choices in Sex* even superficially to see that the booklet does 'not merely ask questions', it presents to teenagers, and to all readers a CHOICE between following the teaching of the Church, or a teaching that differs from the *Magisterium*. Catholics have NO CHOICE, but to accept the *Magisterium* of the Church, and accordingly the book must be condemned as a pernicious production, undermining the moral life of youth, and is the 'furtive and hole in the corner operation' which the *Herald* attributes to the CPA.

Yours sincerely
Rev FR John W. Flanagan DCL STL.

Continuing with this controversial subject, Father Flanagan decided to take this matter to a higher level, e.g. The Press Council.
I here give some extracts from his letter, as follows:-

The Press Council,	St George's Church,
New Murcury House,	Eastbourne Road,
81, Farringdon St.,	Polegate,
London, EC4A 4BL.	Sussex.
	13 December 1974

Dear Sir,
I wish to lodge before you the strongest possible complaint against

the unjust and flagrant violation, not once, but many times, of the very rudiments of justice and veracity, on the part of a weekly paper known as *The Catholic Herald* edited from 63, Charterhouse St., London EC1M 6LA.

The reasons for my complaint are as follows:-
1. The issue of *The Catholic Herald* for the 17 August 1973, accused me as Secretary of the 'International Catholic Priests' Association', of 'mendacious allegations of forgery'. This groundless charge was never retracted nor in any way corrected, though I have in my possession to this day the documentary evidence (no less than 14 in number) that the charge was correct.

It arose from the circulation of a book entitled *Choices in Sex* published with a *Nihil Obstat* and 'Imprimatur', which assure Catholic readers that there is nothing unsound or unsafe in the book concerned. The ecclesiastical authority of the Archdiocese of Westminster, who was reputed to have given the 'ALL CLEAR', has told me that his signature was a forgery.

He told me, not once, but many times. He even gave me a photostat copy of the forgery, and the legal advice of his Solicitor as to how he should proceed against the culprit.

With the full authorisation of this ecclesiastic and acting on his behalf, I disclosed this fact to the *Catholic Herald*. It later, published the libellous accusation, to which I refer above. If, as reported, the clergyman reversed his statement, and recalled giving the 'ALL CLEAR', that had nothing to do with me.

I am asking you to see that this scurrilous public statement by this paper is corrected. (End of extract).

2. The second charge against this paper is more recent.

I have been involved in the study of the 'Holy Shroud of Turin' from 1933 to the present date. It has been, for me, a life study and I have had a Sindonolical Centre here, where I live in Sussex, for many years.

In the issue of the *Catholic Herald* for 24 May and 19 July 1974, readers of this paper were astounded to read two half page advertisements, in which a gentleman named John Reban (also known as Kurt Berna) living in Stuttgart, Germany, claimed that he could prove from the 'Shroud of Turin' (which he accepts as authentic) that CHRIST DID NOT DIE ON THE CROSS. This doctrine is, as you are aware, contrary to the basic faith of all branches of the Catholic Church. I know from the *Catholic Herald* office that these two advertisements were sold for less than half price to the same John Reban – a reduction from £250 to £120 each. So a paper masquerading as 'Catholic' could sell its birthright. All efforts to have a letter refuting the false charges of this man printed in the *Catholic Herald* having failed, I had no option but to challenge Mr Reban to a public debate.

This was accepted, published in the *Catholic Herald*, and Mr Reban left to me details of time and place for the debate in question. The only hall I could acquire in time was one in Holland Park (London) which had a capacity of 100 people. I sent this fact to Mr Reban, who then decided he was taking some 200 press reporters to the debate.

As this number could not possibly be accommodated in the hall, I had no option but to postpone the debate – fixed for 21 November last (1974) – to a later date, perhaps nearer to Easter. Mr Reban was informed of this in my letter which reached him on November 6. He telephoned me twice after this and continued to insist that the debate was not postponed. He arrived in London 16 November and issued a statement to all new agencies that he did not know of the postponement until he reached London. This was absolutely false, and I have his own letter to prove it.

On Friday 29 November, the *Catholic Herald* published a letter from Mr Reban, falsely repeating this statement and the letter was followed by a note from the editor, that 'This correspondence is now closed.'

I protested to the editor, sent him a letter, to give the facts, but he has refused to publish it, so once more, as in August 1973, holding me up to readers of the paper as a LIAR and a COWARD.

Dear Sir, I expect prompt action from your Council to put the records right, and to see journalism, so debased by this paper, restored to credibility.

Sincerely Yours,
Rev FR John W. Flanagan

OUR QUARTERLY REVIEW OF CATHOLIC PUBLICATIONS

Newsletter Vol.V No.1 1975

CATHOLIC HERALD

It is difficult by any stretch of the imagination to consider this paper as entitled to the term 'CATHOLIC'. It is long overdue for the Hierarchy to tell its Board of Management that it has a better title to be called by any other name than by 'Catholic'. Looking back over the years since *Humanae Vitae,* I doubt whether any other paper in the Catholic world has given such open and unashamed approval to everything that is anti-Catholic than this paper.

The years 1968 to 1971 saw the Encyclical on birth control scoffed at, ridiculed, downgraded to a mere directive, by some of the country's most ardent supporters of Modernism.

Norman St John Stevas, in particular, over the months following *Humanae Vitae,* continued to hurl condemnations at the Encyclical, and when he was not attacking the Encyclical, he was discovering a new concept for the Papacy (like Bishop Butler in the *Sunday Times* Supplement, 24 October 1968).

The occasional 'sound' letter, or short article, seemed to have received publication, to offer occasion for the Modernists to go into the attack. One reader who did a survey of the number of orthodox articles in the *Catholic Herald* during six months, compared to the number of unorthodox, found the rates 1 to 12.

The *Catholic Herald* is certainly very selective in the letters and articles it publishes. One reader told me that she sent in a letter for publication, but it never saw print. Two months later, she sent in exactly the same letter but put 'Catholic Renewal Movement' after her name, and it was published the following week.

FINAL VERDICT OF THIS PAPER

If you appreciate your Catholic Faith do not purchase this paper, and tell priests to stop its sale at Church doors.

N.B. The good name of this priest was vilified after his death by at least two writers of this paper. It is a great pity they are not man enough to have tried this during his life. Father Flanagan could match them.

XX

THE LAST FIVE DAYS IN THE LIFE OF FATHER FLANAGAN
March 22-27 1977

BY THIS TIME, Father Flanagan's life was ebbing to a close. He had fought the good fight to the end. His task was immense, and how he defended the Church he so loved – but his Master would call him soon to his Heavenly home, where his eternal rest awaited him.

How little did I realise what the next five days had in store for us. How many times, prior to this week, did illness strike suddenly, both day and night. Always we were able to get him through each attack, and he would return in fighting spirit to carry on, once again, his priestly duties. Not this time!

On Tuesday 22 March, Father Flanagan retired to bed as usual at approximately 9.30 p.m. By 10.30 p.m., a moan from his bedroom signalled the onset of another cardiac attack. Soon, the doctor arrived – a cardiograph taken – drugs administered.

Father had endured a restless night, but by the morning, his condition had considerably improved.

This sustained improvement followed through the day and as the reader will recall from a previous chapter, it was at 3.30 p.m. of this day, that he finished the last sentence of his criticism on the *Venice Agreement*, when I report again his last words, on completion of that document – 'it will be now or never.'

On the night of the 23 March again another slight attack. His doctor (Dr Ashforth) arrived at approximately 11 p.m., and remained for the following two hours. Father Flanagan spent a more comfortable night, and by the morning, decided to celebrate Mass.

With anxiety we shared and watched, but all was well *Deo Gratias*. This Mass Father Flanagan had offered for my mother's soul – whose anniversary was the 22 March – as he had always done through the years.

On returning from the Church to the presbytery, and having had a small meal, Father Flanagan headed straight to his desk to tackle the correspondence of the past few days.

On completion, he decided to go to the village Post Office (quite near) to get his letters posted. No amount of persuasion could stop him from doing this.

He drove his car to the village, which would take about five minutes normally. Father Flanagan did not return for the next hour — then he drove into his garage, and very slowly, walked back to the house.

As I was later to learn (after his death) Father Flanagan drove to the home of a very dear parishioner, whom he had received into the Church on St Patrick's Day — one week previously. This new parishioner — Robert Mallon of Willingdon (Nr. Polegate) himself was a very sick man. Father Flanagan paid this last visit to Robert and his wife Breda telling them that his Mass of the following day would be their Mass. (Robert was to join him in their eternal home three months later.)

On the night of 24 March, again the feeling of illness overcame him and another sleepless night lay ahead. But to my surprise, at 5 a.m., Father Flanagan again stated his wish to get up and celebrate Mass. His own words to me — 'It is the Feast of Our Lady and people will expect it' and so, the pale-faced weary frame of Father Flanagan, robed in his white vestments, standing at the altar of our lovely Church of St George, celebrating the Holy and Unbloody Sacrifice of Calvary, will be an everlasting memory to all present — for the aura of sanctity and holiness at and around the altar was immense.

There were no Mass servers present, and so, I had that great privilege of answering the Mass from outside the Communion Rails. I was naturally very anxious, but felt very sure, that **OUR BLESSED LADY** whom he loved and venerated with all his heart, would stand by us in this hour of need — and she did just that.

(It was to be the Father's last Mass).

Mass was completed and Father Flanagan was in marvellous form. It was hardly believable. After his lunch, he headed straight for his desk where he worked right through the rest of the day. Finally at 8 p.m., desk work completed, he prepared to retire to bed. We talked over a cup of hot milk — myself wondering what this night would bring forth.

He seemed so well again — so happy, on this particular night, with not a single complaint of pain, that, looking back on those hard and difficult days of suffering, I feel sure, Father Flanagan even then, had a premonition of his nearing destiny, and his final resting place with his God.

On retiring, I found him reading as usual – but this last book was *The Holy Shroud*. All was well, and a good night's rest seemed possible. But at 10.30 p.m. the pain struck again, and this time it was severe and excruciating beyond words. No mistaking the coronary! With an agonising look in his eyes for the very first time ever – his words to me were 'Why have I to suffer so much?' 'It is the cross of Calvary,' I answered. 'Do you think so?' 'Yes Father'.

Such was the depth of this attack, and such was the resignation and fortitude shown that it was obvious to me the loss of our priest was near. No words can describe it. At 3 a.m., after the doctor had left the sick room, I sent for a parishioner friend, Nora Jones, herself a nurse, and between us, we got Father Flanagan safely through the night. Next morning at 11 a.m. Father Flanagan was again removed to Esperance Nursing Home. As he was carried on a stretcher to the waiting ambulance, one of his most faithful people, stood at the back door, looking and feeling distraught. This good person, who as a very young teenager in 1958, remained faithful to Father Flanagan all through the years – his name, Michael Smitherman. Father Flanagan looked towards Michael and said, 'Don't worry Michael I will be back.' That was not to be, for Father Flanagan his work for God and His Church, now completed. The Good Lord had given him the past nine years of 'borrowed time' to fight for orthodoxy, and teach others how to carry on. The responsibility must be theirs from now onwards. Priests and people, and the battle must go on unceasingly against the enemy of the Church of Christ – Modernism. Only in doing this, will they fulfil his great work for the defence of the Church, to which he gave his every hour, right up to the last day. Father Flanagan had received the Last Sacraments from Father Whatmore.

I accompanied Father to the Nursing Home. On my return to the Presbytery and with the great help of our parishioner, esteemed friend and sacristan, Mrs Molly Smart, we prepared and arranged with priests for the Masses of the following day – Sunday 27. Father Brady, our ever faithful helper, would be with us.

I returned to the Nursing Home at 3 p.m. Father Flanagan was sitting up in bed in a very jovial mood. He talked and joked with the Sisters and myself. Then Dr Ashforth arrived and told me that the Father was 'dying', the clot had moved to his leg and any movement could be dangerous. I returned to St George's, my feelings low.

At 8 p.m., I returned again to the Nursing Home, to keep the night vigil. One of the Sisters had asked me to come and be near. Still in good form, he informed me that Bishop Bowen was expected. I could hardly believe it! I was worried, knowing the treatment meted out to this priest in past years from the diocese – repeating again the Father's words 'they treat me like a hermit'. How would this final meeting take place. This time, they wouldn't be hounding for cash!! The Father was dying. This Bishop had made his first visit to St George's Church and Parish on the 10 March – his first visit in five years – in spite of the fact that we were under the constant strain of illness. Now this Bishop was making his final visit. It passed well – *Deo Gratias*.

At the Father's request Bishop Bowen had come to me and thanked me for my care of Father Flanagan and my help in building up both parishes. Then he left. On returning to the sick room, Father informed me that he had requested the Bishop to do this.

Time was ticking away and it was nearing midnight. Father Flanagan then spoke his last words to me. 'Sally, as long as you are all right – I don't care for any of them', and finally, 'Will you rub some Lourdes Water on my chest', that was the end – and he said it all. Father Flanagan had told me at different times that he had provided for my future.

From 1958, I had not taken a salary – for we were pioneering and paying large debts for the New Parish Development i.e. both St Joachim's and St George's Churches. This always worried him for I had parted with much of my own savings for the Church and had forfeited my Nursing post to do this. (This story will follow later).

At midnight I called the Sister to help me raise him up in the bed. This we did and administered oxygen – but in a flash – he became unconscious, never to regain it. For the next three hours, the Father sank deeper and deeper into unconsciousness. I prayed and prayed on my blue Rosary, which had touched the Holy Grotto of Lourdes, so often, and was now placed around the Father's neck with the Crucifix to his lips. At 3 a.m., I asked the Sister to send for Dr Ashforth. I knew he could do nothing, but I felt I needed him. He arrived promptly, stayed a few minutes and left – to return a short time with the Dean – Father John Sullivan. This priest remained until Father Flanagan died at 6.05 a.m.

As I left the room, and standing at the door, looking back at the still form of the Father's body on the bed, a heavy load descended, as if a cross weighed me to the ground. Little did I know – that cross was to become heavier and heavier as the months and years passed, with the scourging that was about to be inflicted on Father – in his grave – and on myself, to the point of a total nervous breakdown. (This story will come later).

Funeral arrangements were made, and the *Requiem* Mass fixed for April 1. Mourners packed the little Church, Church Hall and the grounds from all parts of the country, especially those who were part of his great work for the Church. A loudspeaker system set up by our faithful parishioners – Maurice Smith – M.C. in carrying out important duties during those sad days, carried the Mass to all.

Requiem Mass over, the funeral cortege proceeded to St Mary's Catholic Cemetery, Kensal Green, London, where Father Flanagan's faithful friend – Father Hugh Byron, carried out the committal ceremony. Many of the Father's friends who could not manage to be present at St George's awaited the arrival of his remains at the graveside.

Such was the love and esteem in which this priest was held.

An important incident to relate here:-
Two sisters, Mary and Gertrude – living in Stanley, Co. Durham were lay members of the ICPA, and close friends of Father Flanagan. When news reached them of his death, Mary became ill with shock and died (R.I.P.). The funerals were at the same hour 11 a.m. – 1 April 1977. They had both fought the good fight for Christ's Church, each in their own particular calling. They were now happy in the Divine Presence of God for all eternity.

XXI
TRIBUTES PAID TO FATHER FLANAGAN R.I.P.

Tribute No.1 From: *The Diocesan Newsletter* 1977
(ARUNDEL & BRIGHTON)

FATHER JOHN FLANAGAN, Parish Priest of Polegate, died in Esperance Nursing Home on 27 March 1977.

Born in Portarlington in 1912, he studied at the Dromantine Theological Seminary for Foreign Missions, Newry, N.Ireland; The Irish College, Rome; The Pontifical Institute of both laws (Rome); The Latetan University (Rome) and the Angelicum University (Rome). He gained a Doctorate in Cannon Law.

Ordained in 1936, he taught Moral Theology and Canon Law at the Foreign Mission Seminary, Newry 1937 – 1952.

He came to England and was stationed at Barnes 1953 to 1958. Between 1958 and 1965 he was Parish Priest of Hampden Park. From 1965 to his death, he was Parish Priest of Polegate.
MAY HE REST IN PEACE.

Readers – please note, the severe brevity of this tribute. Father Flanagan, was Parish Priest of St George's Polegate, from 1958 – 1977. This was the extent of the new parish he came to found, known as Hampden Park/Polegate.

Also, please note, that, following that brief tribute to a great Churchman – in this same *Newsletter* – followed a deeply extensive panegyric to another priest, recently deceased – also a parish priest. This priest (R.I.P.) was born in 1930. Father Flanagan was well on the way to Priesthood, as recorded here'. No further comment.

No. 2 TRIBUTE
Memorial Masses were offered in many parts of the country by members of the 'International Catholic Priests' Association.' The London Centre of

TRIBUTES PAID TO FATHER FLANAGAN R.I.P.   267

one such Mass was offered at St Osmund's Barnes, London, SW13, where in 1953 Father Flanagan had first started a life in the secular priesthood. Another such Mass was offered at Altrincham, Cheshire, arranged by Mr Raymond O'Brien, where the many tributes were read by Father Carney. I will include here, the cablegram which had arrived from Bishop Stewart of Sandhurst, Australia, in time for this Mass. It read as follows:-

'UNITE WITH ADMIRERS AND FRIENDS LATE FATHER FLANAGAN AT THE ALTAR OF SACRIFICE WHICH HE LOVED SO DEEPLY AND DEFENDED SO STOUTLY STOP OFFERING MASS SAME DAY FOR HIS NOBLE SOUL AND ASKING LIKE COURAGE FOR US ALL TO CONTINUE THE CRUSADE OF WHICH WAS SUCH A VALIANT LEADER STOP IT WAS MY PRIVILEGE TO KNOW HIS FRIENDSHIP AND ENCOURAGEMENT IN TODAYS DEEP CRISIS FOR HOLY MOTHER CHURCH.'

† *BISHOP STEWART*

No.3 Tribute From: FATHER GRANTLEY – FORMER SEMINARY PUPIL

This tribute arrived in the form of a letter to myself. It reads as follows:-

I feel I ought to convey to you the thanks of so many former students and admirers, for the care you gave to Father Flanagan for so many years. I was a pupil of his in Dromantine from 1942-1946. In addition to being an excellent teacher, he used to referee football games for us. So I have many happy memories of him and have offered Mass for him now.

Signed
Father Gantley S.M.A.

No.4 Tribute From: MONICA AND NOEL KING,
CO-EDITORS OF *DEFENDER*

It is very difficult, as well as painful, for those of us who were so closely involved with the work of Father Flanagan, to be able to assess, even remotely, the impact of his life on our times. This must be left to future Church historians.

There is no doubt, however, that the death of Father Flanagan has left a void which cannot be filled. Like the disciples who thought that the end had come, with the death and burial of Christ after the Crucifixion, so we too feel that all is lost, all is finished. In the words of the psalmist *'HOMO SICUT FOENUM DIES EJUS TAMQUAM FLOD AGRI SIC EFFLDREBIT'*. 'Mans days are as the grass, as the flower of the field. So shall he flourish' (ps.102). But when the wind shall pass over, it shall be no more.

He was taken from us at a time when, although he had suffered much from ill-health during his life, he appeared to have been given a new lease of life. He was writing pamphlets, dealing with correspondence and numerous other matters connected with the life of the Church, right up to the time of his death; and it was only a week or two prior to his death, that he had posted off his final *Newsletter* of the Catholic Priests' Association'. This latter publication was always very much looked forward to, by the priests and lay members of the Association. Why was this? Chiefly because Father Flanagan was not afraid to speak out on important issues as they arose in the day to day life of the Church. He was not only a mine of information, as to what was happening, but he was also a very effective exposer of error, whether it was to be found in high places or in low places.

His scholarly mind would get to the root of these errors and being the clear thinker and clear writer that he was, it was not difficult for him to expose false conclusions drawn from false arguments, and in such a way that all could understand.

Father Flanagan had a rare flair for being on the spot. For instance, when the vexed questions of Communion in the hand arose, and a pamphlet was produced by the National Liturgical Commission in support of the practice, he immediately brought out another pamphlet *The Case Against Communion in the Hand,* in which he corrected the errors and refuted the fallacious arguments of those who were trying to foist an unjustifiable option on unsuspecting Catholics, for he was not only a man of prayer, but a priest, ever guarding the Church's greatest treasure, the Blessed Sacrament. Had not Christ said 'WATCH as well as PRAY?' Perhaps the two things which he feared most would eventually destroy the Church if allowed to go unchecked, were the Commissions, which he felt were taking over the duties and responsibilities which pertained to Bishops, and the blind eye which the Hierarchy are turning towards ex-priests and ex-religious men who are allowed to roam the country speaking to groups here and there, poisoning the minds of other priests and religious people, as well as the laity, with their theories which are against Catholic truth, because they are against Catholic doctrine.

Father Flanagan maintained that the hour had come when we must present our petitions at the feet of the Holy Father himself, if the Church in this country is to be saved from the indifferentism to Catholic truth which has struck at its very roots.

Father Flanagan was attacked on all sides, but he never flinched. He longed for one thing and one thing above all, namely, the unity of the Church under the Supreme Pontiff. He loved the priests under his care with a great love. His love for his fellow priests was only second to his love of God, which was boundless. *ECCE SACERDOS MAGNUS QUI IN DIEBUS SUIS PLACUIT DEO* . . . Perhaps the greatest tribute we can pay him, is for each and every one of us to support that loyal band of orthodox priests, and pray for the Paraclete to come and strengthen us. May He send us one as full of zeal as Father Flanagan. Who will lead us into the way of TRUTH.

No.5 Tribute From: THE EDITOR OF *THE KEYS OF PETER* RONALD KING

'With the death of Father Flanagan the Church in England has lost a great Champion of Orthodoxy. His devotion to the Holy Father was all-embracing and was clearly demonstrated by his upholding of *Humanae Vitae* and lawful changes within the Church . . . Father Flanagan was plagued with poor health for many years.

A lesser man would have retired, but Father Flanagan persevered in his determination to uphold the authority of the Vicar of Christ . . . and the *Magisterium*.

No.6 Tribute From: CHRISTOPHER BELL, ST JOACHIM'S CHURCH, HAMPDEN PARK (EASTBOURNE)

'I will, for as long as I live, give thanks for the life of Father Flanagan. From the time, as a small boy, he received me into the Church, I have always felt he was someone very special.

I shall remember him in my prayers always, and most of all his wonderful love of Our Lady.'

No.7 Tribute From: **'STUBBORN UPHOLDERS'**
**CONTRIBUTED BY V.G. DAVIES, FROM THE *SOUTHERN CROSS*,
CAPE TOWN 22 MAY 1977.**

In the report headed 'CAMPAIGNING CONSERVATIVE PRIEST DIES', *Southern Cross,* 24 April 1977, there is reference to the ultra-conservative 'International Catholic Priests' Association.'

Readers may wonder what sort of people ultra-conservative Catholics are. Here is a description in a *Newsletter* issued by the Association 1974: 'A quarterly journal which boldly exposes many of the current fallacies now plaguing the Church, stubbornly upholds the *Magisterium* of the Church now so much under attack, and helps clergy and laity to face the problems confronting the Church in the world today with Christian confidence, fortitude and courage.'

'It strives in conformity with Papal teaching which is always sustained and supported to establish the primacy of Catholic Truth, the absolute purity and integrity of which can never be jeopardised; and without which, as Pope Paul has so often stated, no renewal is possible.' (See Allocution 4 July 1973).

When Catholics worthy of the name, would not wholeheartedly endorse the above?

What Catholic, then, worthy of the name, would not describe himself as 'ultra-conservative', if such designation now be necessary, in order to show that one is a true Catholic.

No.8 Tribute From: **THE TABLET, HOME NEWS, 2 APRIL 1977**

FATHER JOHN FLANAGAN R.I.P.

Father John Flanagan, Parish Priest of Polegate in Sussex, a cofounder of the self-styled Catholic Priests' Association (not to be confused with the officially sponsored National Conference of Priests) died on the 27 March, after an illness of many years, which almost to the end failed to quench his spirit and his resolution to fight for the truth as he saw it. His convictions were almost wholly opposed to anything that might be construed as stemming from Vatican II.

He was a last-ditch ultra-montane – a heresy hunter, never-hesitating to denounce – to the point of slander – or to delete Priests,

TRIBUTES PAID TO FATHER FLANAGAN R.I.P. 271

Bishops and even Catholic editors whom he suspected of departing from his special brand of orthodoxy.But he is to be admired for having the courage of his convictions, and will surely have found a peace passing all understanding.

From the Chairman of the 'Catholic Priests' Association' Reverend Father Whatmore. In answer to the above Tribute:- (from CPA *Newsletter*).

'Opening of the windows' as a signal to the demolition contractors and bulldozers to come in.

Father Flanagan had 'no special brand of orthodoxy'. Only seeking to follow the authentic teaching of the *Magisterium* and when, as occasionally in these confused and difficult times, individual Bishops seemed to differ – that of the Pope.

He fully subscribed to the adage of St Ambrose, *Ubi Petrus, ibi ecclesia,* where Peter is, there is the Church.

He looked to Rome, and not to Malines or Canterbury, for the first and last word. Only if one accepts an unacceptable and impossible dogmatic pluralism within the One and Only True Church founded by Jesus on earth, can one truly style Father Flanagan's views 'his special brand of orthodoxy'. It must be admitted that he thought *The Tablet* under its present editorship to be both anti-Catholic in general, and anti-Papal in particular.

No.9 Tribute From: **RAYMOND H. O'BRIEN –
ALTRINCHAM, CHESHIRE
UNIVERSE, 15 APRIL**

Sir – May I beg the courtesy of your columns to offer, in the great sorrow of his death, my personal tribute to that great and good priest, Father John W. Flanagan, of St George's, Polegate, and to plead for prayers of Catholics everywhere for the repose of his soul.

His brilliant mind was only equalled by his courageous heart, and his untiring efforts – in spite of serious surgery and heart attacks – in defence of Papal Authority authentic Doctrine.

THE HOLY SHROUD OF TURIN

Father Flanagan (now R.I.P.) previously stated, had given much time to the study of the Holy Shroud from 1933. This study continued right up to his death.

Many people will remember those lectures given by Father Flanagan in St George's Church hall and in many other centres, where he had been invited to lecture.

I have here, the Father's original notice of invitation to a lecture of April 16 1965, which will deal with the most awe inspiring object in Christendom, known as 'The Holy Shroud' and continues:-

WHAT THE POPES HAVE TO SAY OF THE SHROUD

'The Shroud is the most beautiful and precious object that one can imagine . . . It is 'mysterious and certainly not the work of human hands' Pope Pius XI, 8 August 1929.

'The Shroud is a glorious witness of the Passion of Our Divine Redeemer and is worthy of the Universal Veneration of all followers of Christ' Pope Pius XII, 19 September 1939.

The Holy Shroud is often referred to as the 5th Gospel for the 'Scientific Age'. The lecture will cover the findings of modern science, when concentrated on this Real Self Portrait of Christ.

Do not miss the opportunity of knowing something about this awe inspiring object – it will give you a new insight into the sufferings of Christ for all of us.

This lecture, recorded on cassette, has now gone to many parts of the world, with subsequent incorporation into the Wuenshal Collection – library at Esopus, U.S.A.

The story surrounding this, gives a clear picture of the Grace of God working. The story is as follows:-

While Father Flanagan suffered perpetual ill-health, he was never deterred from lecturing on the Holy Shroud when invited to do so. It was at one such request, feeling unwell before the appointed day, that he conceived the idea of pre-recording his lecture on cassette – to be played, should any difficulties arise. The subsequent recording which he made himself over a period of some days, was never used, and was not played until after his death.

I remember asking Father Flanagan to play it back, but he refused saying it was of 'poor quality' and he would do a better one later. That was not to be.

Providentially, after Father Flanagan's death it became my property, when I decided to carry on with joy, this aspect of Father Flanagan apostolate, by distributing copies of this recording, in cassette form, in order to spread further the knowledge of the sufferings of Christ for our sakes. So, this 'poor quality' cassette recording is today in many parts of the world, i.e. Madras (Salesians), Ceylon (Benedictine Monastery), W. Australia (Bishop Stewart), New Zealand (Schools), Ecuador (Irish Missionary) and New York. Used by H. Walsh (cassette-a-month) England, Scotland, Ireland – *Deo Gratias*.

Then to my great joy, I received a letter from the President, 'Holy Shroud Guild', Esopus, U.S.A., affiliated to the *Centro Internazionale di Sindonologia*, Turin, Italy, who wrote the following:-

'I have just listened to the tape, and I am amazed at the completeness of his treatment. Two things struck me.
1. His reference to Origins referring to the one leg being shorter, and to an image on the Shroud.
2. I was surprised when he mentioned the theory that the image was perhaps formed by scorch. However, later he mentioned Dr Willis. I was present in Turin in 1973 when Dr Willis mentioned the possibility of scorch.

It was the first mention of that theory that I know of. I shall incorporate the tape into the Wuenshal Collection – Library at Esopus'.

Sincerely
Adam J Otterbein CSSR.
(President)

Previous to this letter's arrival, 4 February 1981 I received the following words from an eminent Prince of the Church, His Lordship Bishop Stewart of Sandhurst, Australia (retd.) present address, Sacred Heart Cathedral, Bendigo, Vic.3550.

'I am most grateful for the tape 'Our Saviour's Holy Shroud.' It reveals a great deal of the character and holiness of the late lamented Father Flanagan. I do not think I have ever heard such a moving sermon on the Passion and death of Our Saviour, as revealed by the Shroud. Father Flanagan became known to me through his spiritual upholding and defending of the Church, particularly against the enemies within the Gates.

I heard of your great devotion to him and can understand something of your grief in is death. His photo is on the mantelpiece of my study among great men of our times – Cardinal Mindzenty, Bishop Quinlan of Korea, in addition to Cardinal Newman.'

Also on tape, *Tribute to Father Flanagan* compiled by his friends, and produced by C.V. PRODUCTIONS, 48 Cambridge Road, Gillingham, Kent. *Our Saviours Holy Shroud* from myself – LORETO, 6B Grange Road, Eastbourne, Sussex or from C.V. PRODUCTIONS (J. Edwards) above address.

XXII

THE 'GOOD SHEPHERD' OF SHEPHERD'S BUSH
The story of a priest who gave his life for his flock.
by the Editor of *Newsletter*   Father Flanagan

FOREWARD

THIS ARTICLE DEALS with the events that tragically terminated the life of Father Jeremiah Daly, Parish Priest of Shepherd's Bush. It is a documentary report. All letters used were the property of the deceased, who, in July 1974, and again only four hours before his sudden death on 13 December 1974, gave the author of this article, not only permission to use them, by every encouragement to do so.

When Father Jeremiah Daly was appointed Parish Priest of Shepherd's Bush in 1966, he had more than one problem to face.

The parish had been shaken to its foundations by the presence of a bogus priest, Monsignor Dowling, who, though never ordained to the priesthood, received the full faculties of the Archdiocese from Archbishop's House, and acted as a priest, hearing confessions, celebrating Mass, and doing all the pastoral work associated with the priestly ministry, with the exception of marriage. The story of his 'identical twin brother' served a useful purpose as an escape hatch when suspicions were aroused – it was always a case of 'my twin brother' when any pressure was on.

When finally he departed from Shepherd's Bush, he left the parochial cupboard bare, not to count the great number of anxious minds of people who had given him Mass Intentions, and who by now, knew that they would not be discharged. The Archepiscopal approval, so lightly given to this pseudo-priest, may perhaps be construed as an indication of the gullibility of those in charge, and may have tempted the small group, later to appear on the scene in order to oust Father Daly and who were motivated by the principle, that if one man can deceive the Archdiocesan Curia, a group could do the same.

Father Daly had also to deal, shortly after his arrival, with the unpleasant backwash that can be left in the wake of a youth club scandal. These two factors would weight heavily on the shoulders of any priest, however physically and mentally strong he may be, and which faced him in all his parish work. But Father Daly was made of strong stuff. 'A man of immense physique and a will of steel' is how a doctor was to describe him, at a later date. He was to need all his physique and willpower in the years to follow his appointment.

Father Daly was not an enrolled member of the 'Catholic Priests' Association', though he supported its aims and activities wholeheartedly. He told me once, why he would prefer not to be on the enrolled membership list. 'If I am asked by any of those, high up in the Diocese, I will have to tell the truth, and I know that the CPA is not looked upon favourably by them – it is too outspoken for their views'. So Father Daly remained an 'honorary member'.

In mid 1971, certain reports reached me, that there was a plot on foot to get rid of Father Daly. He was not prepared to tolerate false doctrine in the school or in the parish, and this situation invariably, in our present world, throws up elements who are prepared for anything to get their way. Character assassination, the imputation of 'failure to update', 'failure to relate and communicate with those of different views' (wording actually used in the decree of his dismissal later), 'failure to bring the parish into the post-Council Church', 'preaching an outdated Catholic doctrine', etc., etc., were some of the weapons of war employed by a small subversive group, entirely unrepresentative of the parishioners.

During the period of organising the opposition to Father Daly, these nominal Catholics worked in unison with some of their trendy clergy scattered throughout different parts of the Archdiocese. In turn, the link up was made, with other priests in an influential position, to bring pressure to bear on Cardinal Heenan for Father Daly's early removal. Meetings of small groups of these subversive elements took place both within and without the parish of Shepherd's Bush. Members of the group were not allowed to be inactive.

During this whole period of nearly three years, Father Daly was entirely unknown to me – I never had any communication with him, by letter or by telephone, nor had I even met him.

The victim of the plot was entirely unaware of the machinations that were around him. He did not realise that an impending storm was already visible on the horizon, and scarcely did he become aware, when the storm broke in all its fury.

Sifting through the dossier of correspondence to and from the Cardinal and his Vicar General, Monsignor Norris, it became abundantly clear to any neutral observer, that Father Daly was to be dispatched at all costs, and the reasons for this did not matter hence we find a continuous flow of contradictory reasons, and every effort being made to cover up the real reasons – the desire on the part of the Archdiocesan Authorities to placate at all costs, a group of revolutionaries.

A letter, from Cardinal Heenan, dated 15 January 1973, written to Father Daly, stated 'your priestly zeal is not in question, but there are good reasons for thinking, you would be better off, in a parish of your own.' In a letter from the Cardinal, written on 11 October, of the same year, he told Father Daly that 'I know that those who oppose you are a minority', though the Vicar General, in a letter to the victim of machinations could refer to 'voluminous complaints', to which Father Daly was later to reply (letter dated 5 February 1974). 'Midst the voluminous correspondence, I was never once give the opportunity of seeing a postage stamp, let alone a letter. While you hinted at a large number of complaints, the Cardinal in his letter to me (dated 11 October) referred to a 'minority group who were opposing me.' The intrigue becomes more clear even still, when we find the Cardinal (letter 14 March) writing to Father Daly that 'he was quite unimpressed by the evidence of certain of his parishioners'.

At this stage of trying to unravel the plot, it might be useful to quote *verbatim* the letter of the Secretary of the Parish Council, written to the author of this article (dated 5 March 1974). It reads:-

'Father Daly has, the last year or more, been the subject of complaints to the Diocesan Authorities by an apparently organised but unidentified group in the parish, in an effort to have him removed. We have heard of a petition to this effect having been taken around the parish for signatures, though no member of the Parish Council has been approached. As parishioners, we believe Father Daly to be an exemplary priest, in his devotion to his calling and in the holiness of his life, in his preaching of the Gospel without fear or favour in accordance with the doctrine of the Catholic Church . . . Father Daly would have preferred to resign, but realising that this would not solve the underlying problem, that the trouble makers would not thereupon cease their activities, we advised him to stay on.'

We sent a letter dated 17 April to the Vicar General, pointing out that we were the only body representative of the parish, and we should have been consulted before any adverse judgments were given, and natural justice required that the complaints be properly formulated and an opportunity given of answering them. Later, one of our members, a barrister, went to see the Vicar General, but failed to find out the cause of the complaint.

Later (23 May 1973) the Vicar General met all members of the Parish Council at Church House, Westminster, but we failed to find out the 'matters of complaint' beyond a vague criticism, without foundation in fact, that Father Daly was 'not active enough in obtaining an extension to the existing school in the parish.'

The final remark of this letter is interesting, as on two occasions, certain London newspapers carried criticism of the neglect of an extension for the overcrowded Catholic school.

These articles, with photographs, were made available to the Papers concerned, without any word, form or knowledge on the part of the parish priest.

In a letter dated 14 May 1974, Cardinal Heenan wrote to Father Daly – that the reasons for asking him to resign his parish were because of 'the divisions within the parish, which only another priest could heal.' The Cardinal asked for a reply, in writing, within two weeks, 'giving the reasons why you are not prepared to resign your parish', and regretting that this was the first time in his life, that he had to act 'in a legalistic way'.

Father Daly's reply (unfortunately not dated) deserves quotation. It is written to the Vicar General, Monsignor Norris, it reads:-

> 'I have decided to remain at my post and trust that it is a triumph of grace over nature. I am following my conscience and guidance from no less an authority than the Cardinal, who, in the matter of birth control, advocated this principle . . .
>
> 'Alleged reasons for my resignation are brought forward to ratify a decision which has already been made . . . they are not the real ones. It is one of the harsh facts of life that pressure groups exist. The pressure groups I have in mind, are the local Deanery, and the Senate of Priests. The lower down the scale one goes, the greater the number. Numerical superiority, which is well organised, is a dominant factor in any diocese. A Bishop, to survive must take cognizance of this fact. If the Cardinal complains that lay people now attack Bishops, what of those who are placed in charge of parishes, in which there is an Assistant who is determined to have autonomy without responsibility?

'The policy of containment will fall most heavily on the parish priest who tries to run a parish with the dice loaded against him. I believe that the Deanery I attend has such a pressure group. At a lay Deanery meeting a few months ago, the subject of clerical dress was put forward by a member of the Shepherd's Bush Parish Council, and it was agreed that it would be on the agenda for the next meeting, to be chaired by Bishop Guazelli, but this was withdrawn . . . At a subsequent meeting, my parish members were insulted by the intemperate language of one of the priests and the remarks of Father X, that the motion on clerical dress was an attack on him. In view of these considerations, your attempt to move me from my parish is a case of victimisation and my removal would impugn my good name.

'As to the clerical dress point, I intend to bring it to the notice of the Apostolic Delegate.'

The above extract from Father Daly's letter to the Vicar General, speaks volumes, as to the source and reasons for the plot to remove him from his parish.

But the scheming of the pressure group was not yet complete. It is now quite a common experience to find efforts being made to use KGB tactics on priests who are orthodox. It is briefly expressed in the words – 'If you're orthodox you're mental' and of course the psychiatrist should be called in.

A letter from the Cardinal dated 4 July 1973, stated:-

'I wrote, as agreed, to your doctor who kindly saw Monsignor Norris a few days ago. I wanted to find out as you know, whether it would be useful or desirable for you to see a neurologist or psychiatrist. Your doctor was quite agreeable.

I am writing today to ask Dr J.G. to give you an appointment. You may talk to him with the greatest confidence . . .'

COMMENT: It is an extraordinary procedure, when the Vicar General of a busy Archdiocese, instead of writing, or even telephoning to Father Daly's own doctor, has to call on him personally. It makes one suspicious! This suspicion is heightened by the reply of Father Daly to the Cardinal a few days later (in fact the very next day – 5 July 1973) when he wrote to the Cardinal as follows:-

'I went to see my doctor today, and he assured me that when he told Monsignor Norris during his visit the other day, that he had no objection to me seeing Dr J.G., it was also accompanied with the statement that it was "totally unnecessary".

My answer then is, an emphatic NO! I consider this as the greatest affront that I have ever received; an insult to my intelligence and to my priesthood . . . I intend taking this matter up with my lawyer, who is also a member of my parish Council, and well-acquainted with the events of the last few months. I intend to act on his advice and if the consequence is unpalatable publicity, then I presume you took it into account in the first place.'

COMMENT: The strong reactions of Father Daly to this effort to have him 'certified', would clearly indicate that by the 5 July 1973, Father Daly, whose reactions were always most mild, had become aware of the possible sinister reason lurking behind the move. May I add, that when this letter was written, the author of this article had no contact with the intended victim of the KGB tactics.

I had known of the plot against him long before this date, but the one to suffer from the plot was entirely unknown to me. I emphasise this, as otherwise some people may conclude that Father Daly's strong reaction to the suggestion of psychiatric investigation may have come from me. This would be entirely false.

A letter from Cardinal Heenan (14 March 1974) to Father Daly, states that the reason why he asked his Vicar General to have an appointment made with a Catholic psychiatrist to see Father Daly, was 'his convictions that you are a good and zealous priest, and that your attitude was probably due to some physical cause.' It is remarkably strange that the Cardinal would send one of his priests to a psychiatrist to discover a physical cause, and with no initiative or suggestion to do this coming from Father Daly's own general practitioner.

In the same letter from the Cardinal (14 March 1974), to Father Daly, three priests of the Archdiocese are mentioned to whom the Cardinal entrusts (to quote) the 'examination of the facts, interview the witnesses, and give their advice.'

The priests designated were Monsignor Dunderdale, Monsignor Kelleher and Canon Carr.

In mid-summer 1974, Father Daly was seen by the three Assessors designated above. The interview took place after the funeral of a priest of the Archdiocese. The three Assessors chatted with Father Daly over a cup of tea, and at the end, told him that 'he was right, justice was on his side.' There was no interrogation of witnesses, and no specific charges made against Father Daly, nor even a reference to 'dissension' in the parish.

That evening Father Daly telephone me, overjoyed that the Assessors had found justice on his side, and he naturally presumed that the case was over. But subversive elements never take a defeat, it only encourages them to exert greater pressure on the pressure points that are already weakening.

Did the Assessors give to the Cardinal a decision that they knew would please him, or did they give to the Cardinal the decision they had already give to Father Daly? We do not know. All we do know is, that the scope of their mandate from the Cardinal was – to quote a letter from Monsignor Dunderdale (1 April 1974):

> 'There is nothing in the way of a judicial enquiry and we must hope that, that will not be needed. My co-Assessors and myself have merely been asked by the Cardinal to advise him as to whether we think he is justified in what he proposes to do. It will be up to him to decide how he should act.'

Many questions could be asked at this point. Did the Assessors find their verdict set at nought by the Cardinal, or did the Assessors give one statement to Father Daly and the opposite to their Archbishop? In a statement to the press, after Father Daly's death, this 'friendly interview' with the Assessors, was referred to as an 'opportunity given him to present his case,' by a 'spokesman' of the Westminster Diocese (*West London Observer*, 6 December 1974).

Whoever the 'spokesman' was, it is obvious that he was entirely non-conversant with Father Daly's case, or he had received a false one. Father Daly was emphatic in his conversation to me within hours of the meeting the Assessors, that 'no charges were made' nor was he 'even asked to defend any allegations – the conversation was merely on the state of the Church in general'.

We now reach the crisis in the case with the issuing of the Decree of Dismissal from his parish, dated 25 November 1974. Here is the text:-

> 'Whereas the Reverend Jeremiah Daly, parish priest of the parish of The Holy Ghost and St. Stephen's at Shepherd's Bush, has shown himself to be possessed of an extreme rigidity of outlook coupled with an inability or refusal to communicate with members of his parish, who are not in agreement with his views, and even to disregard such disagreement as an attack upon his position.
>
> And whereas his failure to accommodate his views and attitudes

to meet the needs of a considerable number of his parishioners has produced to the detriment of good order and thus demonstrated his incompetence to an extent that made it necessary for the Cardinal to decide that he must remove him from his charge; Whereas Father Daly having refused to take another appointment, and having refused to resign, the Cardinal considered it necessary to take steps for his removal, according to the procedure laid down by the terms of *'Motu Proprio' Ecclesiae Sanctae* art. 20, and having taken such steps accordingly, and having now called upon Father Daly once more through his Vicar General to resign the above parish by Thursday 21 November, or in the event of failure to do so, be removed by decree. And whereas Father Daly has failed to resign as requested – 'I, acting as Vicar General for and on behalf of the Cardinal Archbishop, hereby decree that the Reverend Jeremiah Daly be removed from the office of parish priest of the above parish of the Holy Ghost and St. Stephen, Shepherd's Bush, and he is hereby removed accordingly, and that Reverend John Formby is hereby appointed to the office of parish priest in his place. This decree to take effect immediately.'

Signed
David Norris *Vicar General*
F.A. MILES *Chancellor*
Westminster
25 November 1974

Some Comments on the Above Decree

For the first time in all the correspondence between the Archdiocese and Father Daly, the specific charge 'of extreme rigidity of outlook, coupled with an inability or refusal to communicate with others . . . and his failure to accommodate his views and attitudes to meet the needs of . . .' is given. Those who knew Father Daly, knew quite well that he had 'no views' in the realm of the Catholic Church's *Magisterium*. There is no place for views within the official teaching of the Church; certainly from the *Magisterium*, which does not admit contrary views.

It is in this context that we can understand the words of Bishop Guazelli, Auxiliary Bishop of the same diocese, speaking at the funeral of Father Daly – 'He spoke strongly for authority in the Church. He had no time for anything that was not orthodox.' (*West London Observer,* 26 December 1974). The Vicar General refers to his refusal to take another appointment.'

This is not true, as he was never offered another appointment. A letter from Father Daly, addressed to Cardinal Heenan, and dated 27 October 1973 refers to a 'mention in the Cardinal's letter (15 January 1973) of a possible new appointment', but this was not mentioned when called to an interview with the Vicar General.'

'It is clear that I am not being offered another appointment, and I refuse to resign.'

The Decree of Dismissal makes a mention of a 'considerable number of parishioners' to whose views Father Daly was not prepared to accommodate his teaching. A survey carried out in the parish by 200 parishioners, asking their fellow parishioners if they were 'dissatisfied with Father Daly', failed to find a single one who did not both like and approve of the parish priest. How does Monsignor Norris reconcile his wording of this decree with the verdict of the only representative body in the parish – the **Parish Council.** They went as a body in 1973 to ask for an explanation from Monsignor Norris, as to the reason for the pressure on Father Daly to resign.

There is no one reading this Decree who will not get sick at heart to read such puerile efforts to cover up a grave injustice. At a time when we have the 'Commission for Justice and Peace', with its headquarters in the same Archdiocese, when all kinds of trendy priests and pseudo-Catholics are given not only the freedom, but at least the tacit approval of the Archdiocese authorities to spread their views (in conflict with the *Magisterium*) in Westminster, when books can be sold in the Cathedral which reject every truth of Catholicism, the treatment of Father Daly for his orthodoxy, will cry to Heaven for vengeance.

Let us continue that march of events in this tragedy of our days. Father Daly, having received this Decree (which incidentally was issued by Monsignor Norris after he was officially informed of the appeal of Father Daly's case to Rome) asked his successor already living in the presbytery, if he could stay until after Christmas, as he had no home to go to, received the prompt reply 'NO'. We do hear a lot of the virtue of charity these days, but its practice is another matter.

On the following Monday week (2 December) Father Daly left to take up residence with his sisters in South Wales.

He had hardly arrived there, before a former parishioner of Father Daly's, from a previous parish, hearing that he was dismissed, dropped dead.

This is the first tragedy of what ended in a double one. The son of the deceased lady motored down to South Wales to take Father Daly back for the funeral.

Father Daly phone me from London at 4.30 p.m., and he spoke his heart on the telephone – little did I realise that within hours, Father Daly would be dead.

In this last conversation with me, he repeated that his refusal to quit his parish was done in the common interest of the Church. He was at pains to emphasise that if the Church authorities surrendered to this small group of revolutionaries, the whole Church would be in danger, as the movement would proliferate.

Before long, the very ecclesiastical authority that issued one Decree of Dismissal, would itself be found guilty of 'refusing to communicate with those not in agreement with its views.' Cardinal Heenan, Monsignor Norris, and the lot, would find that the same weapon which crushed Father Daly, would crush them also.

While visiting the house of a friend in Brook Green (London) less than four hours after speaking to me at length on the telephone, Father Daly collapsed and died instantly.

God had prepared for him a better home in Heaven, where he would spend Christmas.

The shock waves that went through the parish, and even into parishes where Father Daly served in the past, could not be described. At one Church, the priest of the parish roundly condemned from the pulpit the gang that had brought about his monstrous injustice that had ended in tragedy. Within hours of his death, one of the subversives telephone the *West London Observer* to say that he had died from the causes on account of which he was removed from his parish. What a mendacious allegation, to cover up the perfidy of the few!

Even the Vicar General, Monsignor Norris issued a statement to the press – 'Father Daly had suffered from a heart condition for a number of years. We regret his death.'

Father Daly suffered from no heart condition. The postmortem verdict was 'coronary occlusion' which could happen to anyone, even in the best of health.

A 'heart condition' as stated by the Vicar General, meant a chronic condition, but any heart specialist will confirm that an 'occlusion of the coronary artery' is triggered off by emotional anxiety or deep upset.

If what the Monsignor seems to convey that his death fitted into the reasons for his dismissal, why were very different reasons given in the Decree of Dismissal?

Why did the Cardinal, in the first place, send him to a psychiatrist? Why was it, that the Cardinal appointed three Clerical Assessors to see him, and not three medical men?

As Father Daly's attorney and representative, I can write that Father Daly had anaemia some years before, and had an accident (knocked off his bicycle by a car) in October 1974. While he cycled his parish doing his pastoral work with one leg in plaster, he also attended hospital, where he was examined and found in perfect shape, but for the fractured ankle.

1. 'Sacked Priest dies of a Broken Heart' declared the *Evening News*, 18 December.
2. 'Sacked Priest died with Broken Heart' stated the *Shepherd's Bush Gazette'*, 19 December.
3. 'Sacked Priest predicted his own Death' read the *West London Observer*, 20 December.

In this last mentioned press report, we read the extract of the last letter of Father Daly. It reads:-

'Strange as it may seem, I have no doubt that the unpleasantness and pain of the past few years are part of God's mysterious plan . . . Who knows if my sojourn here (South Wales) is going to be a long one, or whether Divine Providence may intervene in some other strange way to terminate it.'

Yes, Divine Providence did intervene to see that this man of God, was not permitted to suffer any longer.

He was home for Christmas. Like the Divine Infant for whom there was no room in the habitations of man, an eternal home was ready for Jeremiah Daly. 'Consummatumn EST' – the cry of the Divine Victim from the cross is re-echoed from the cross of Father Daly's last years.

Perhaps at this stage of unfolding the tragedy that was Father Daly's it would be appropriate a little from his book *Random Thoughts*.

'In the last 2,000 years there were those who challenged the claims of Christ and denied His Divinity. However crude they may have been, they are preferable to those of our day, including 'theologians' and priests (and some nuns) who deny Christ's claim by implication. These are the 'learned ones' with special 'insights'. The curious thing is that the name Jesus Christ is more familiar to an irreligious world than ever before.

Christ's prophecy is being fulfilled. If those who should champion HIS cause fail to do so, then the very stones on the street will cry out.' (p.13).

The stones on the street cried out at Father Daly's funeral. Two *Requiem* Masses in the Church, that only two weeks previously had been his, saw an immense crowd of people, file past the coffin and assist at the Masses.

While an evening Mass was being offered in his old Church's at Shepherd's Bush, some miles across the city, in one of Father Daly's former parishes where he worked as an Assistant Priest, the parish priest of that parish was thundering in the pulpit against those who treated this dedicated priest so unjustly.

At the *Requiem* Mass at Shepherd's Bush, Catholics and non-Catholics alike were grief stricken and whispered one to the other – 'What wrong has this good man done to deserve this?' Women sobbed uncontrollably as his coffin was carried from the Church. A little girl kept repeating 'bye-bye'. 'Traffic came to a standstill as priests formed an arc around the hearse in Archbishop Grove' (*Shepherd's Bush Gazette,* 26 December 1974).

We have come to the end of this narration of the events that led up to, and followed the death of this true Priest of God. Amid the endless efforts of the guilty to find excuses and justification for their action, the ring of truth comes through – the numerous and conflicting explanations as to why Father Daly was dismissed – it was his failure to communicate, it was a heart condition which he had had for some years, he needed medical care for a psychological cause – none of the false explanations will cover the ignomy which someone must bear, the guilt which must haunt them to the grave, that in their own weakness, they were prepared like Pontius Pilate, to wash their hands of the injustice done, rather than offend the small gang of plotters, whose ultimate aim is to destroy the Church. We repeat, with the *West London Observer,* 20 December: 'When conspirators will not even be recalled, Shepherd's Bush Catholics will vividly recount the glorious deeds of this man of God.'

The Archdiocese of Westminster is in need of radical pruning. Who can forget the corruption in doctrine that went on at Corpus Christi College, for years, after all the facts were given to those whose task it is to defend the interest of the Church?

Who can forget the sordid book to which one can only apply the words of St. Paul *nec nominetur in vobis* and which received the *Nihil Obstat* and *Imprimatur* of the Westminster Archdiocese?

Who can forget the continuous denials of the Censor Deputatis of that diocese, that he ever gave the *Nihil Obstat,* and that it was forgery – and then suddenly (after 14 denials), he did give it. Was this statement made under pressure or freely?

Father Daly is, for all priests today, an example of absolute integrity in

'GOOD SHEPHERD' AND CORRESPONDENCE

his priestly life, abounding in charity, but never at the expense of the *Magisterium* of the Church, which was always placed first.

May he, in his enduring home, help all of us to stand up to 'the learned ones with special insights' – to quote his own work – until Peter's barque finds itself once more in calm and placid waters.

REQUIESCAT IN PACE

EXTRACTS FROM A LETTER
WRITTEN TO BISHOP BOWEN,
DIOCESE ARUNDEL AND BRIGHTON
From Father Flanagan

WHY ARE SO MANY CATHOLICS LEAVING THE CHURCH?

To:- February 1977
Right Reverend M. Bowen St. George's
Bishop of Arundel and Brighton Polegate
Sussex

Your Lordship,

I enclose herewith, a letter from a Mrs Diane Burrow sent to me on January 26, announcing her abandonment of her Catholic Faith, to join Jehovah's Witnesses. With her consent, I am sending it to you, together with other facts, in the hope that you may come to a realisation of the Church's state in your diocese at the present time. You, I understand did not have Catholic faith from the days when you suckled at your mother's breast, so may not fully appreciate the disgust and horror a born Catholic experiences, when matters so intimately linked with the priceless gift of faith, are held up for contempt, or reduced to the level of the merely profane.

Over the years since the end of Vatican II, an ever increasing number of men and women, young and old, of your diocese, have turned to me to help them preserve their faith. I have done so by giving them all the encouragement possible, and explaining to them, why it is, that the Mystical Body of Christ is now enduring the same scourging and torture that Christ's physical Body once endured. To the very many tortured souls of your own diocese, must be added, thousands more from all parts of the country, who constantly seek my aid, very many of whom travel long distances to receive even a glimmer of hope.

The stories of these bewildered, and often demented Catholics, have little variation, they are violently disturbed, because they are told by priests (and not seldom by nuns) that belief in such doctrines as Original Sin, Life after death, the Resurrection of Christ, the effects of Sin, the need of repentance, the place of Mary in the Catholic Church, the Rosary, etc., etc., have all been 'debunked' by the Church since Vatican II. Priests and nuns and teachers in Catholic schools, fill their minds with a hatred of everything the Church officially taught in the past. Papal infallibility and the Pope's appalling mistake in his teaching on contraceptives, are frequent targets for the most vitriolic attacks, by the newly enlightened 'experts' or our age, while, in the line of Christian 'mores' the unspeakable sexual deviations of the past, have now become the passport to advancement and enlightenment.

It has been my constant policy in dealing with these people, by letter or personal contact, to endeavour to encourage them to seek help and direction from their own local clergy or their own Bishop, but in recent times I have come to the conclusion that this is a waste of time, because it is their own local clergy, who are the source of the scandal, and their own local Bishop will remain silent.

I would like your Lordship to read carefully through the letter of Mrs Burrow, and you will have no difficulty in picking out the causes for her decision, a decision which I believe is also imminent in many other cases, where human beings can take no more. Unless a radical change takes place soon to defend the Church from the attacks of the ecclesiastical vandals which are in every diocese in the country, the late Cardinal Heenan's prediction (Times Supplement, December 24 1973) that there would be no Catholic Church in Britain by the year 2000, will be shown as far too optimistic.

Under the title Stern Warning for Church, a Dr C. McArdle of Derby writing in the *Catholic Herald,* 11 February 1977, shows a decline in Sunday Mass attendance from 2.06 million in 1968 to 1.75 million 1974, and allowing for an increase in the Catholic population, this means a severe drop in Mass attendance.

The number of children baptised in 1964 was 138,000; in 1974 it was 81,000.

At this stage of my letter, may I repeat that I am not, nor have I ever been, an admirer, and still less, a follower of the controversial character known as Archbishop Lefèbvre. I have condemned his stand against Vatican II, and his refusal to accept the revised liturgy of the Mass in particular. There are priests of Your Lordship's Diocese, who in their ignorance consider me an 'extremist', and who shun me as if I were a leper. They are welcome to their views, however groundless they are. My total allegiance and loyalty is, the CHURCH in its teaching and doctrine, as proclaimed by Pope Paul and the Council, and to its AUTHENTIC interpretations.

That the post-Vatican II days have numerous false interpretations and interpreters, can hardly be beyond doubt; they have been frequently referred to by Pope Paul in his letters to Archbishop Lefèbvre (e.g. 29 June 1975 in which he speaks of the many 'superficial interpretations . . . and which we suffer from'; letter 11 October 1976, has even a stronger condemnation of these same false interpretations of conciliar and post-conciliar documents).

It was in the days when this growth of 'false interpretations' first manifested themselves that Pope Paul issued his famous 'Apostolic Exhortation to the Bishops of the World', (8 December 1970, published in *L'Osservatore Romano,* 14 January 1971). This heart-rending appeal of the Supreme Pontiff to his fellow Bishops of the World 'Not to be reduced to silence for fear of criticism' produced no results.

As the years have gone by, Bishops all over the world have been paralysed by the fear of offending the creatures of their own making, – the 'COMMISSIONS' which have imposed a stranglehold on the Masters they were intended to serve. These 'COMMISSIONS' have done immense harm to the Church, as they are mostly composed of forward looking individuals with little faith and much arrogance. We have already seen, how much they have pushed in this country, since their inception.

They have pushed to the forefront, what few wanted – Communion in the hand, and no doubt, they will now pressurise the Hierarchy to introduce 'Optional Celibacy!' and a National Pastoral Council, which was the beginning of the end of the Church in Holland.

Returning to Mrs Burrows letter: Your Lordship will notice in the paragraphs (which I have numbered) how she refers to:-

'The sheer emptiness of spiritual deprivation' (par. 1).
'The Church is destroying itself' (par. 2), again repeated in paragraph 4.
'The people of God are being given blank humanism' (par. 3).
'Those opposing the Church's teaching are being permitted to remain actively within it' (par.5).
'No proper moral teaching in the schools, to say nothing of the seminaries' (par. 6).

May I comment briefly on her remarks which are alas all too true. Our Catholic schools no longer teach sound Catholic doctrine that will help youth all through life, but instead, the pupils are given a mixed grill of humanism and guru horizontalism. Sin is out and love is in. In a society that is oversexed, no moral control is inculcated. You must not mention the TEN COMMANDMENTS, 'they frustrate the growth in human dignity' as one Catholic teacher wrote to me some months back. Sex education is so advanced and of such a type, that one would think that all children are intended to become 'Specialists on Sex Perversions'. The seminaries are beyond hope, as they are run today, yet the faithful are expected to support financially institutions of half-baked Christianity. The dress and deportment of these seminaries are frequent topics of discussion among those who have to pay for them, and yet nothing is done to introduce even the rudiments of discipline.

Is it surprising (however regrettable) that so many broken-hearted Catholics are joining the Lefèbvre Movement?

Here at least, they see reverence, clerics dressed as clerics, the Mass with its liturgy carried out respectfully, no clowning in the sanctuaries, no hippies jumping around the altar. The Bishops, in their failure to stamp out the abuses that have grown up with the new liturgy, are the best recruitment agencies for the Lefèbvre Movement.

I will have more to say on the scandals of the sanctuaries later in this letter.

Can an explanation be given for the widespread use of so called 'experts' who are in constant conflict with the *Magisterium* of the Church, to give or conduct Clergy Conference, retreats, seminars of diverse kinds? Hans Kung, Bernard Haring and other theologians outstanding for their opposition to the teaching of the Church, seem always welcome as guest speakers, and have access to the mass media at a stroke of a pen, notwithstanding our **Mass Media Commission** with its Episcopal Presidents.

Why are such people as Dr Jack Dominian (notorious for his contempt of the Papal Encyclical *Humanae Vitae*, Dr Enda McDonagh, Father Eric Doyle – with the latters big doubts as to the Resurrection of Christ, the 'leading theologians' for conferences etc., even in your diocese?

These men have repeatedly and scandalously rejected or cast doubt on one or other of the teaching of the *Magisterium*.

Dr Dominian's recent publication *An Outline of Contemporary Christian Marriage*, a booklet revolting to the Catholic faith and conscience – was acclaimed by the Senate of priests of this diocese, as containing 'nothing whatsoever contrary to the teaching of the Church' *Ad Clerum*, 4 November 1976.

I doubt very much whether a single member of the Senate had ever seen the booklet, let alone studied its contents.

In a situation like this, one would expect the Bishop, at least to ask to see the evidence of one side or the other. A counter motion rejecting the criticism of Dr Dominian's book was carried unanimously. This sort of procedure only holds the Senate of Priests up to contempt, not contempt for the individuals who compose the Senate, but to the Senate, as an institution.

This letter cannot be terminated until I have drawn to your Lordship's notice, the following facts, as they are the source of much scandal to the faithful and the major factors in driving people out of the Church:-

The document *Immensae Caritatis* and its implementation.

The numerous references made by Pope Paul during 1976, on erroneous interpretations of conciliar and post-conciliar documents, as found in his correspondence with Archbishop Lefèbvre, and in his weekly allocutions, have, in so far as the Bishops are concerned, fallen on deaf ears.

The document *Immensae Caritatis*, 25 January 1973, (AAS, vol.65, p.264-271) which permitted the distribution of Holy Communion by lay people, in certain particular circumstances, has, in its implementation in this country, caused more Catholics to abandon their Church, than any other factor.

Why should the use of a Papally approved faculty cause such

disaster? For the obvious reasons, that only in the rarest cases, and on the rarest occasions, have the 'Conditions' for using the 'Permission' been fulfilled.

Hardly had the announcement of the Papal document been made known, before Bishop after Bishop of this country and of others, rushed to designate the men and women, boys and girls, who would be ready in any parish, to act as extraordinary Minister of this most Holy Sacrament.

Communion sent by letter, The Sacred Host carried in one's cigarette box, The Sacred Hose carried in a lady's powder bag, to be administered to a housebound person — these are but a few of the appalling cases which have happened (but not to my knowledge in this diocese — yet).

Communion distributed by an altar boy of 12 years, while two assistant priests chatted outside — this is one that did happen in this country, and will happen in your diocese unless steps are taken to anticipate the evil.

Nuns distributing Holy Communion on Sunday morning to a not full Church, a situation which the able bodied Parish priest was always capable of coping with alone, before *Immensae Caritatis* was known.

Nuns dressed in secular dress, distributing Holy communion while the priests of the parish took extra time in bed — this has happened, and to the best of my knowledge, is still happening in your diocese.

Divorced and remarried women who openly attack the Pope for his ruling on contraceptives and that women cannot be ordained, are among the 'Episcopally approved' Extraordinary Ministers of one English diocese.

There is hardly a parish Church which does not have its women ministers of the Blessed Sacrament, and in summer time, many of these females are anything but modestly dressed.

How does this widespread practice harmonise with the Conditions laid down by the Holy See? It just does not harmonise at all. How to reconcile it with Pope Paul's words uttered in his letter to the American Hierarchy (published in *La Documentation Catholique*, No.1703: 15 August 1976) that 'The Blessed Sacrament must be treated always with the greatest respect, and it is only in truly extraordinary circumstances, and which can only be existing in the most rare cases, that a lay person may be requested to distribute Holy Communion.'

How any open-minded person, studying the document itself, and Pope Paul's words in it, will conclude that the Bishops of this country have gone out of their way, to make what should be the 'rarest of occasions', the normal weekly practice.

COMMUNION STANDING ('The Blessed Bread' Queue, as it is called in some Churches).

The Instruction of the Congregation of divine worship called *Mysterium Eucharisticum*, 25 May 1967, must be one of the most violated Instructions of the Holy See in the post-conciliar days. Chapter 1 tells us that 'Mass on radio and television, should be celebrated with such dignity and discretion, as to be a model of celebration of the Sacred Mystery'.

The faithful see on T.V. in this country, televised Masses which must give great mirth in the pit of Hell. The profanation of the Eucharistic Mystery has been so shattering to onlookers (such as the televised mass from Cockfosters in January of this year) that it was compulsive switching off, for many. The same Instruction declared, that 'Communion may be received kneeling or standing according to the custom of the Church'. The Instruction does give authority to the National Episcopal Conference to decide which mode of receiving, taking into consideration the circumstances of the Church, and the number of the faithful. No decision of the National Conference of Bishops was ever promulgated in this country, and so the first method designated (kneeling) which is the one established by long custom in every Church in Britain and Western Europe should still be in use. The 16th century *Black Rubic* introduced by the Protestant Reformers, that Communion should be received STANDING as a sign of rejection of the Popish belief in the REAL PRESENCE, is a grave historical reason why STANDING should not be the normal manner of receiving THE BLESSED SACRAMENT.

Yet our National Liturgical Commission seems to have put into effect, almost overnight, what the persecutors of the 16th century failed to achieve. In not a few Churches priceless Altar Rails – often the gift of generous souls of the past, were thrown down, rooted up from their foundations, and cast on the scrap heap. This was to assist 'optional kneeling or standing' the liturgists will tell us. Is it surprising that less and less Catholics are donating objects to the Church? Donations are at the whim of the liturgical lunatics.

Is it surprising that so many Catholics have broken with the Church? If all the changing things associated with belief in the REAL PRESENCE are being carried out in the name of the Church, is it difficult to understand how so many faithful now conclude, that the Church has changed in its own beliefs?

The unprecedented vandalism or auto-destruction of the most sacred objects and practices of the Church has run riot in this country for years, and your diocese is no exception. These vandals are 'experts' in one or other of the Commissions that have fettered true Episcopal authority, and reduced it to silence. Is it not time that the place of 'Commissions' in Church affairs were reduced to a proper position, that of 'consultative voice' only, and not a 'deliberative voice' as we have seen so often?

The overriding by 'Commissions' of the Bishop and the Bishop alone being the final judge of the suitability of candidates to the priesthood has long been a scandal.

Remember the Richard Williamson case of some four years back, when after spending two hours with this candidate, you both affirmed verbally, and later confirmed in writing, that he was excellent and 'one of the finest you had come across', only to be later rejected by his interview with one priest, one man and one woman – The 'Commission'. Who has given lay men and women any say in judging the suitability of candidates to the priesthood?

GENERAL ABSOLUTION REPLACES INDIVIDUAL CONFESSION IN SPITE OF WARNING OF THE HOLY SEE

Whatever you may personally think of the place of General Absolution in the revised 'Rite of Penance', and whatever the Supreme Authority of the Holy See may assert, as to its exceptional use, and only in well defined conditions, all over the country, and in your own diocese, forces are at work to push 'auricular confession and personal absolution' out of existence. I have heard that you have refused certain parishes permission to use it. I congratulate you on this show of courage, but have no doubt, that the subversive elements in the Church and in your diocese will not take your refusal as final.

Parishioners of another parish have told me, that their priests will not hear of refusal for General Absolution and are already encouraging parishioners to demand it.

I give this report for what it is worth, but it is from reliable and conscientious people. Dioceses like Shrewsbury, Nottingham, Birmingham have already, unwarrantedly introduced this practice of General Absolution to entice people back to the Church and Communion.

This 'easy return' is not given among the circumstances which entitle General Absolution in the new 'Rite of Penance', yet in all those three dioceses, it was practised with great publicity (and received banner headlines from the Catholic papers), yet, when the Bishops of those dioceses were shown their mistake, authoritatively by the Holy See, we find no public statement to correct the error and to negate the scandal.

Cardinal James Knox, Prefect of the Congregation for Sacraments and Divine Worship, in a press report (10 February 1977) warned Bishop Dozier of Memphis, that the use of General Absolution was not justified on a day of 'Reconciliation' organised for his dioceses, 23 December 1976.

The Cardinal Prefect reiterated his warning, in a letter of December 8, sent to Archbishop Bernadin, President of the Episcopal Conference, and reaffirmed, that there should be simultaneously existing, three conditions for its use, (a) Few or no confessors, relative to the number who wish to confess; (b) Penitents would be deprived of the use of the Sacrament or of Holy Communion for a considerable time; (c) Access to personal confession and absolution could not take place for a considerable period, unless by General Absolution. The local Bishop is given the judgment as to whether the conditions are verified or not, but he is not authorised by the new 'Rite of Penance' to change the conditions or modify them.

Unless Your Lordship insists on the observance in every parish on the conditions laid down in the Vatican's *Ritus Poenitentiae,* auricular confession and personal absolution will have ceased to be practised in the diocese within a few years.

The National Conference of Priests, the Diocesan Pastoral Council, the Senate of Priests and other such bodies will see that the old distasteful practice will meet an early death.

No doubt, you will have in your diocese 'experts' who will hold that the observance of these conditions is not necessary.

Some laity have informed me already, that some of their own 'trendy' fellow parishioners, and their priests, are pushing for the introduction of the 'Reconciliation Room' (the rec-room, as it is called) on the alleged claim, that a few teenage girls may want to 'confess' on the knee of their long haired trendy clergy, but it would be uncharitable to surmise that the motive is not 'penance'. This rec-room concoction of the pseudo-liturgical experts, by results already achieved, could be more aptly called 'marriage advisory room for priests', as many of the priests who have advanced this gimmick already, are now living in the matrimonial state.

COMMUNION IN THE HAND – WHO WANTED IT?

It would be a great help to many priests and laity of your diocese, if some member of the Hierarchy could explain to the ordinary thinking Catholic, why it was that the vote of the Bishops of the world, sent to the Holy See in 1968, on the question of whether they favoured Communion in the hand or not, was so suddenly reversed.

With the Bishops voting approximately three to one against its introduction, followed by the detailed decision of the Congregation of divine Worship, confirmed and promulgated by the Pope, personally in his 'Memoriale Domini', with its wording – 'The Apostolic See, therefore, strongly urges the Bishops, priests and laity to observe most zealously this law (Communion to the mouth) . . . The Supreme Pontiff has judged the LONG RECEIVED MANNER OF DISTRIBUTING HOLY COMMUNION to the faithful should not be changed.' How is it that priests all over the country with the approval and connivance of Bishops, continued in defiance, the very opposite practice?

How can the ordinary priest or member of the laity be asked to believe, that the Bishops show obedience, both in word and in deed to the Pontiff?

No sooner was the 'Instruction', quoted above, promulgated, than the National Conference of Priests, demanded the immediate introduction of Communion in the hand. Did the Bishops order the removal of this proposal from the 'Agenda' of the N.P.C.? Of course not. In 1970 and 1971, the Pontiff declared that celibacy was not for discussion. In every year since *Memoriale Domini*, both **optional celibacy** and **Communion in the hand** were placed on the Agenda of the annual meeting of the N.P.C. Now really Your

Lordship, do you really think, that this repeated open defiance of Papal decrees, has enhanced your standing as Bishops in the Church, or your own example of obedience to your own Supreme Bishop? Of course not! It is here that priests abandon hope, and laity leave the Church in droves.

Not content with reversing the Bishops of the world's vote, the hardy Modernists decided that they would even change the nature of the indult, when it came, as they knew full well that the Bishops would eventually succumb to their pressure. How right they were! To make sure that The Blessed Sacrament would be desecrated as often as possible, the nature of the indult must be changed. An 'indult to distribute Holy Communion in the hand' would still leave conscientious priests refusing IT to the hand of the communicant.

So, the National Liturgical Commission, the tool of so many perversions in the past once more got to work, and notwithstanding the fact, that *Notitiae* (official organ of *Acta Congregationis pro Culto Divino*) reads *Indultum de Sacra Communione in Manu Fidelium Distribuenda*, the instant manipulators changed *Distribuenda* into *Recipienda*, thus leaving, as would appear, the final say on whether Communion could be received in the hand, to the judgment of the recipient.

Now, My Lord, I am too long dealing with Church legal matters, not to know, that an indult for distributing cannot be transferred to an indult for receiving.

Correspondence on this point with the revered Secretary of the 'National Liturgical Commission', only brought the reply that we 'used different languages'.

Priests and laity of the country have been 'had', and it is time that the Hierarchy awoke to the realisation.

Would it be asking you too much to awake your fellow Bishops to the fact I have mentioned, as it is possible that some of them at least, are unaware of the 'sacrilegious trick' worked out on the faithful of this country, by the National Liturgical Commission?

In case you might think that my distinction between an indult for 'distributing' and an indult for 'receiving', still leaves the final decision with the Communicant, I can assure you that it is not the case. The distinction is fundamental in Church jurisprudence, and is well known to even beginners studying the Church law.

Can you be any longer surprised that there is a mass exodus from the Church? One has only to see, or ask the parish priests where

Communion in the hand is distributed, to know the enormous scale of sacrileges and desecrations of the Eucharist committed in their Churches.

In mid-January, a parishioner of mine wrote to me that she had seen 'Communion under both kinds' (Sacred Host already dipped into the chalice) having been given into the hand of a little child. We know the consequences: the child wiped his Precious Blood dripping hand on his trousers. How many times does this happen in every diocese? I wrote to Bishop Casey of Brentwood, where it took place. He kindly acknowledged my letter some weeks later, told me that he had investigated the case and my complaint was true.

Another priest tells me, that after a children's Mass, at which he is weak enough to distribute Communion into little hands, he has to pick an average of four particles or parts thereof from the floor.

How can members of the Hierarchy sleep in their beds at night with the horror of such events on their conscience?

Locally, I have another problem. Within three miles of this presbytery there is a centre of Devil Worship.

If any Bishop thinks for one moment that I am under obligation to conform to the wishes of an occasional communicant and distribute Holy Communion into the outstretched hand, which can facilitate its transfer to the Devil Worship Centre where it can be sold for 50 pieces of silver (not just 30) and then in the orgies of hatred, subjected to the most unspeakable acts of desecration, including being urinated upon, then, that Bishop, whoever he may be, will have to think again!

I want to make it perfectly clear that there is NO COMMUNION IN THE HAND in my Church, nor will there ever be. My own parishioners whose love and devotion to the Eucharist is excellent, would hound me out of the parish. But apart from that aspect of the case. I will not make use of a permission fraudently acquired, and more so, fraudently interpreted by pseudo-experts of the Liturgical Commission of this country.

The 16th century saw the Hierarchy of this country surrender their birthright to an oversexed monarch. But, they had a lot to fear if they refused — they might have seen hanged, drawn, quartered, disembowelled.

What have you to be afraid of today in the defence of Pope Paul's teaching? Is it the scorn of the 'up-dating' lads that crowd the Commissions?

This letter is long and hard-hitting, but please make an effort to grasp the anguish of great numbers who have left the Church, and others on the way.

I respect your office, and would give my life in its defence . . .

Praying for your enlightenment, and growth in your Faith and courage.

Sincerely Yours in *Domino*
John W. Flanagan

Father Flanagan died one month later . . . March 1977, Communion in the Hand was distributed at Father Flanagan's *Requiem* Mass, and has continued ever since!

There is an exceedingly sad chapter to be written before the saga of this Priest's life can be said to be complete. This will now unfold in the following chapters.

PART TWO

XXIII

SUFFERING AND INJUSTICE

AT THIS STAGE we will deal in particular with suffering and it is designed to be a new enlightenment of events which followed the death of Father Flanagan and of which I will now relate. These events will include the unjust treatment meted out to myself in those sad days for me which followed the funeral.

Many people, particularly members of **The Catholic Priests' Association,** and its lay members, were shocked at the immediate stranglehold placed on the Association. It almost dwindled into oblivion overnight, save for a few issues sent to members by its Chairman, Father Whatmore. He refused co-operation with other founder members to continue, and handed over the complete affairs to the Diocese under the Dean, Father John Sullivan.

IT WAS A NON-DIOCESAN ASSOCIATION
This was to be the first stage of this Association's demise. It was also to be the end of a great priest's good name *(pro tem!)* for Father Flanagan's good and holy name was crushed stone dead by these very people, and calumny and detraction lashed upon it.

How did this all happen? The answer will follow, for as I am now their living victim – remembering that the soul of the virtuous is in the Hand of God – I will from here onwards, give the full truth of the suffering and crucifixion that was caused to myself, and as already stated, the calumny and detraction lashed upon Father Flanagan – in the grave and unable to defend himself.

Readers will also have learned of the part I played in the work of the Church towards the establishment of both parishes i.e., St Joachim's and St

George's Hampden Park and Polegate, from 1958 – 1977. Starting from the sum of 17 shillings, (I counted it!) in July 1958, to supplying entirely my own personal household equipment to start a new presbytery and relinquishing my professional post as Queen's District Nursing Sister and withdrawing my Superannuation contributions paid in since the beginning of my career when I was 20 years old. Now, I was 42 years old, and by this time had built up for a future retirement pension. I had nursed Father Flanagan through continuous illnesses, already described for this biography, and because of his poor state of health, forfeited all holidays for many years (13).

All this is reiterated in view of what is to follow:-
I had not taken a salary in all those 19 years of total commitment. Large debts to the bank for this new development were being paid. All debts were paid by 1974 which included both Churches i.e., St Joachim's and St George's, and all this done through the hard and laborious work of a Football Pool - against the continuous ill health of our priest. Dare we expect help from the Dioceses! Never. For under three successive Bishops, all Father Flanagan ever received was contempt. Those men, some now deceased were Bishops Cowderoy, Cashman and Bowen.

I will now continue with the treatment meted out to myself, and it is as follows:-
Father Flanagan made his Last Will and Testament in 1973 (September) and aware continuously of my position, had a duty in conscience to provide for my future in the event of his death. Because he had informed me of such, I had parted with much personal cash to Church requirements.

Provision for my future needs – as follows:-
Father Flanagan made this provision through investments placed in Dublin, because that country was paying a higher rate of interest, than England. It consisted of his own personal monies and gifts, especially a substantial amount from a close friend of mine from London – Mrs Edith Smart. She was my prized convert to Catholicism, whom I nursed for years. These investments, placed in his own name, would be transferred to my name after his death. **This never took place!**
After Father Flanagan's death and on the WILL being read, the shattering shock to me was, those investments for my future would not come to me 'they were not Father Flanagan's to give OR mine to receive.' Such were the words spoken! Through a small paragraph, poorly worded, a loophole was formed - and so through that loophole, chaos broke out, and grave

injustice was meted out to me, and those investments for my future stripped from me.

It was expected that the clergy involved, would rectify this, knowing my life's work for the Church. This could have been done, but indeed, far from doing justice to me, those clergy fell in with the loophole of the third paragraph of the WILL. This WILL was made by Father Flanagan, after suffering a severe coronary attack. This is how that loophole arose in the first place.

I will give an account of how Father Flanagan managed these investments and the cruel turn given. He made this known to me:- Father had had two accounts at a Bank namely PARISH (a) and Administration (b). Into the latter (Administration) was paid all incoming cash (other than parish) plus personal cash, which included substantial gifts from friends – plus International Catholic Priests' Association monies – and finally and most important, the six-monthly interest from those investments in Dublin. These Interest Warrants, together with a further sum added from time to time, were returned to the Capital Investment by cheque from the Administration A/c. In this way, through all the years, Father Flanagan was conscientiously providing for my future. 'You gave your life's work for the Church and me – but in the event of my death, you could be put on the street'. Words which shocked, but became true reality, and by the very men within the confines of the Church, later described. Moral justice was out, and the loophole was in.

Father Flanagan had written this Investment into his last WILL as a 'charity' (small c) emphasising emphatically, it wasn't a 'REGISTERED CHARITY'. I would need every penny to give me a home and enough to live on.

How I lived through those dreadful days, weeks and months I will never know. I had hoped for help from the clergy involved, but received the reverse.

On 20 September 1978, I had the first visit from a priest. Father John Sullivan came to see me at my home. Indeed, not to bring me the help I so needed – but to pose a threat. He told me that a Court of Law would take steps to remove Authority of the Will out of my hands, should I not agree to sign away my Rights as *Executrix*. If I signed, it would make progress easier, but if I did not do so, it really would not matter, as the above mentioned procedure would be enforced. He told me of the great scandal to Father Flanagan's name etc., etc!

I nearly expired. I felt desperate. I told him that I would have to think it over, and finally by the end of that memorable day – to avert such a dreadful act happening to the good name of our dear deceased Priest, I signed away my rights to executrixship, which then gave them the power to delete from the WILL, Paragraph three (III), which was done.

That form for my signature lay in my desk drawer for 18 months, unsigned. I would not give the power to delete. Now, with this thunderous shock levelled at me, on top of everything, I felt finished and had reached the point of a total mental breakdown – but for the Grace of God. I stressed the point to Father Sullivan that I was being deprived of my just rights. He did not appear to understand. I told him that Father Flanagan had requested five hundred (500) Masses to be said, after his death for any soul he might have forgotten, stressing the point that he could not remember having forgotten one. Nevertheless, this was his request to be carried out, when the Investment cash came to me.

Now, I was deprived, and had in conscience, to get those five hundred Masses celebrated from my own personal savings – as the Mass Stipend required (£500).

I have never been recompensed for this sum, nor have I received one penny from those investments intended for me by Father Flanagan towards my nineteen years of total commitment to the Church and its needs.

I was told by Father John Sullivan (Dean) that the whole case was being prepared for Rome. I asked him to make sure that my case re these investments was justly put across. He said he would, but he certainly did not do so, as I learned, on receiving a letter from a priest, enclosing the full text of Father Sullivan's Report to The Sacred Congregation of Clergy, The Vatican, Rome. Just one sentence describing me as a **housekeeper** who put up a claim for those investments, but that was safely in the past as I agreed to drop it. I never dropped it, and I was no **housekeeper** and well they knew it.

I will continue with the next phase re Rome and the *Acta* being and sent. It was never expected that I would do the same. I did, and I too contacted Rome and The Holy Father, which I may add, proved an almost impossibility to accomplish. A doctor of the Church, knowing all that had happened warned me of 'The big wheels there (Rome) turning with the big wheels here', and I had little chance of ever having justice done. I was determined to get the circumstances to The Holy Father, and I was successful, *Deo Gratias*.

Part II

The story will now unfold of an attack loaded with calumny and detraction made upon the good name of Father John Flanagan DCL STL., principally

SUFFERING AND INJUSTICE 307

from the pen of Father John Sullivan, Eastbourne, who as Dean, sent to the Sacred Congregation of Clergy, a Report, that would need to be read to be believed. This Report was endorsed by Bishop Cormac Murphy-O'Connor of this Diocese of Arundel and Brighton.

I have in my possession, this Report in full, as it was sent to Rome – its return to Bishop Murphy-O'Connor, with instructions and comments – and finally to Father John Sullivan with further instructions from the above Bishop.

The final blow was struck by the said Father John Sullivan on his deceased brother Priest – his own fellow countryman. He sent out to Priests of 'The International Catholic Priests' Association' a copy of the original Report, together with copies of letters from The Sacred Congregation to the Bishop. A personal covering letter was also sent.

As stated, I have this Report in full, plus the copies above mentioned, sent to me from another country by a Priest whom I had never met, nor indeed, had Father Flanagan ever met. But, from his note to me, written at top left-hand corner of Father Sullivan's personal letter to Priests, this is what he had to say:-

> 'Great harm has been done to the good name of Father Flanagan.
> Although I did not always agree with him, nevertheless, no Bishop or priest could walk in his footsteps.
> You are the only person in the world, who can bring justice.'

With this message to hand, I would leave no stone unturned to expose the cruelty meted out from the hierarchy and clergy. Father John Sullivan, who had only been appointed Dean a short time previous to the death by Bishop Michael Bowen (now Archbishop of Southwark), when in fact, Father L. Whatmore, Parish Priest of Hailsham, Sussex, and who was Chairman of 'The International Catholic Priests' Association', had actually been proposed unanimously by the Deanery, as its new Dean. In 1977 this act of Bishop Bowen upset Father Flanagan and he complained to the Bishop, sending a copy of this letter to Father John Sullivan. Father Flanagan's death followed a short time after, and Father Sullivan since then, in complete charge of affairs, which should have had only lasted for the period following the death, until the appointment of a new Parish Priest for St George's Parish (October 1977) as this was the total realm of his rights.

It did not work out that way. Father Sullivan, in the name of the Diocese – then governed by the Vicar Capitular, Monsignor Arthur Iggleden,

Parish Priest of St Mary of the Angles, Worthing, Sussex – took upon himself more than was his duty.

Father L. Whatmore, Chairman of the 'International Catholic Priest's Association' handed over to him full and total Authority of the Affairs of the Association, notwithstanding the fact, that co-Founder members were anxious to carry on, and rightly be involved in matters concerning this Association's business.

The Association was absolutely NON-DIOCESAN – stated continuously and emphatically by Father Flanagan, and its affairs should never have been handed over to this Priest by Father Whatmore.

Two of its co-Founder Members, Father Hugh Byron P.P. Wisbech, Cambs., and Father George Walker, then Parish Priest at Chesham Bois, Amersham, Bucks., (now retired) continuously pressed for possession of the Association's business – a 'legal' hold-up, was the excuse. These two Priests were well and truly kept at bay. the enemies had hoped to sing another *Requiem* – this time, over the 'International Catholic Priests' Association' – but the battle for justice was about to start. The work of this gallant Association of which Father Flanagan was co-Founder – guided and defended so valiantly against the snares of the enemy – especially from within the 'gates' – would rise again, in face of bitter opposition, and carry on, loyally upholding the Church and *Magisterium,* as their deceased leader would wish them to do. This is now in being. A new Executive Committee was formed on 30 September 1981. It is the Executive elect meantime, awaiting instruction from The Holy See before commencing. This Committee consists of a Chairman, Secretary, Treasurer and two others.

P.S.
To date, 12 July 1983, as I write, no instructions have as yet come from Rome!! This, in spite of efforts from the Executive Elect on many occasions since September 1981. Food for thought!

HAVE WE ALL BEEN WRONG UP TO NOW?

(Address by Most Reverend William J. Philbin, D.D., Bishop of Down and Connor to the Annual General Meeting of the Down and Connor Committee of the Catholic Truth Society of Ireland).

I.C.P.A.
For *Newsletter* October 1969

The purpose for which this Organisation exists, the exposition and defence of the Church's teaching, is assuming new importance in these days. We

SUFFERING AND INJUSTICE 309

are experiencing a great expansion of interest in religious and theological matters. In an age in which materialism and selfishness are so dominant, this in itself is a very welcome development. But unfortunately, much of what is being said and written is not the product of full or clear understanding of what Christianity is really about. A great deal of light-hearted thinking is current. The more novel and advanced one appears the more attention one attracts: this is the way to 'show character', to become fashionable. Repudiating the past is the great matter: the assumption is that what has been done up to now is almost necessarily wrong. The Holy Spirit, it would appear, began work in the Church again, after a lapse of some centuries, at the time of The Second Vatican Council; and the helpfully vague expression 'the spirit of the Council' is to be the universal guideline.

We need, it seems to go no further back.

Writing of this kind is selling very well. It has made quite undeserved reputations for learning and wisdom. Its general drift is at best unbalanced. At its worst it is quite dangerous and in some forms contrary to the first principles of our Faith. The numbers who are pushing these ideas are relatively very small, but they are very vocal. So few voices are raised to oppose them, that many people conscientiously trying to live Christian lives are worried and disturbed. They are asking themselves: have we all been wrong up to now? Do we need to change the whole pattern of our relationship with God?

Perhaps the most fundamental mistake underlying the new writing is its disregard, in any but the most superficial way, of the Scriptures. In the New Testament, we have accurately conveyed to us the deed of trust, the charter by which Christianity was established and our first obligation is to study all the features of that document and to be faithful to them.

So many people write about the Church today as if everything were in the melting-pot: in fact we should first study each proposed innovation not with the question of whether it is in fact in conformity with modern trends of opinion but with a view to finding whether it is in conformity with the blueprint of the Scriptures. St Paul said that even an angel from Heaven should not be allowed to altar the Gospel he preached. The Scripture test will eliminate much of what passes nowadays for progressive thinking.

Take for instance, the suggestion that concern with saving one's own soul has been greatly over emphasised in the past, and indeed may be dismissed as mere 'pietism'. We are now told we function and think primarily as a community and that philanthropic activities come before personal devotions. How anyone who attaches the slightest importance to the Gospel teaching could think along such lines, is difficult to understand. Have we forgotten that we must work out our salvation with fear and trembling?

Equally at variance with the New Testament is the theory that the Church must enter politics and become an active force in the field of secular government.

Have we forgotten how Our Lord resisted attempts to involve in the things that were Caesar's, how He evaded those who wanted to make Him a King? 'My Kingdom', he said, 'is not of this world'. To distort the Church's function in this way would be quite plainly to destroy the Church, and it is difficult to imagine how anyone could see it otherwise.

An alarming feature of the new writing is a trend to make less mention of Our Lord and or our dependence on Him. How long is it since we had the Church described as the Mystical Body of Christ, a conception so prominent in St Paul, and so great a source of inspiration in comparatively recent times? The whole essence of Christianity is that Our Lord gained for us the salvation we could not attain by ourselves and left us the means to apprehend that salvation. Without Him, we can do nothing. Much of what is written nowadays conveys the impression that we are working on our own, as a philanthropic society pursuing truth and charitable objectives by the aid of new enlightenment. Any presentation of our religion that fails to insist that our personal relationship with Our Lord, about which He preached so incessantly, is the all important matter, misses everything. It is not Christianity at all – Christianity is Christ.

In the field of worship we are in danger of thinking the external rites and ceremonies are more important than inner dispositions of faith and love. This would be to confuse ends with means. We may forget that we were told that true adorers, adore in the spirit and in truth: that prayer in secret was required.

Somebody has said that unless certain further changes are made in the liturgy of the Mass it will have no meaning for the people. Surely every Catholic ought to understand that no matter what ceremonies are used, the essential meaning of the Mass is found in the Consecration, where the act of Our Redemption is re-presented so that we can come near it and lay hold of it for ourselves. Can this come to mean little or nothing to Catholic people? What is essential in the Mass is laid down in a few sentences in St Paul – though this is not to say that the liturgy which the Church has assembled over the centuries we should now think lightly of and complete with one another in altering.

The same over concern with externals appears in what is being said about institutional changes. Unless these come and come quickly, some people say, large numbers will leave the Church. If people are thinking of leaving the Church because of impatience concerning institutional changes they should ask themselves what kind of allegiance they have towards the Church, what is the quality of their faith. The fact is that Our Lord established an institutional Church, with all the advantages and inconveniences involved, as a condition of salvation. We cannot have Him and not have His Church.

He allowed people to leave Him rather than abate His demands that His teaching be accepted: 'Will you also go away?' He asked His Apostles.

It is chiefly the authoritarian character of the Church that is at issue here. Again, the touchstone is the New Testament documents. For all His meekness and lack of human ambition Our Lord was the most absolute and authoritarian of all teachers, as he had most reason to. Latterly many interpreters of Christianity fail to realise that in accepting Christ, in making the act of faith He demanded, we forego a large part of our freedom to think and decide for ourselves. St Paul talks about Christ, 'bringing into captivity every intellect.' The special freedom of Christianity is not freedom to think and do as we like, as some are now suggesting, it is freedom through grace from enslavement to sinfulness.

The Gospels, the Acts of the Apostles and the Epistles all show as clearly as possible that Our Lord established an institutional Church to be the interpreter of His teaching and the administrator of the means of salvation. And the Church was not to be governed democratically, in the sense that its members, by voting or by exerting pressure, exercised decisive power. Government was to be the responsibility of the Apostles and their successors who were to receive the special help of the Holy Ghost to teach and put into practice what Our Lord had taught them. We can read in the New Testament that the pattern laid down was followed exactly in practice.

Currently efforts are being strenuously made to push us further and further away from what the Founder of Christianity prescribed in this matter. Authority, under Christ, must be seen in terms of service, not of self-assertion; but, as an exercise of the responsibility to instruct in what must be believed and done, it is an essential element in the religious system which Our Lord set up. Even the gentle use of authority, which Our Lord required and exemplified, will not satisfy some critics; ' paternalism' is as heavy a weapon of abuse as any other. Nothing will satisfy except the rejection of the whole principle of Church organisation established by Our

Lord. The ideal seems to be the position outlined on Television a few nights ago by an advanced thinker – not I believe a Catholic – who said that the clergy in future were merely to be expert students of the theological niceties, but lay people were to take over all effective power. For such people the New Testament might never have been written.

(With acknowledgements to the *Catholics Truth Quarterly*.)

XXIV

WRITERS OF LIKE MINDS

IN THE FIRST phase of Part II of 'The Great Defender' I have dealt with the suffering and injustice which followed the death of Father Flanagan.

I will now continue once again, by giving the reader a full account of the many eminent Churchmen associated with Father Flanagan in this fight for orthodoxy – a fight which was to take him to his death. I will again record verbatim, many of the very informative articles sent to Father Flanagan for inclusion in the 'International Catholic Priests' Association' *Newsletter*. I will also include a further number of articles written by Father Flanagan himself, in his continuing pressure to bring stability to the One, Holy, Catholic and Apostolic Church, now being dealt a crushing blow by its very own within the confines.

These articles have already been widely published between 1969-77, which was the Association's active life time. Now – in this EDITION as in the FIRST – these articles have been brought into book form.

I will record here at this point – that on sending that Report to The Sacred Congregation of Clergy, The Vatican, Rome, Father Sullivan did state that the 'International Catholic Priests' Association' was a 'myth' and 'Father Flanagan, a one man band.'

Let us hope, that while the story progresses, portraying the depth of defence by these faithful sons of God, no one will be under any misapprehension as to the above 'Association' being a 'myth' or, Father Flanagan – 'A ONE MAN BAND'.

IS ANATHEMA THE REMEDY?
by the Most Rev. William L. Adrian, D.D.
Former Bishop of Nashville, Tennessee

I.C.P.A. *Newsletter*
Autumn 1970

Most Catholics are convinced that today a grave crisis exists in the Church, and that it is becoming daily more acute. A few so called traditionalists like Dr Kellner, have even pronounced the present Church 'not the true Church of Christ'; that 'Pope Paul is an illegitimate Pope' and, therefore, 'The Sacred Vatican Council was illegitimate and its decrees heretical.' The 'progressives' go to the other extreme, asserting that the Church is out of date, that the whole structure of the present Church is man-made and needs reforming.

The great body of Catholics, however, are trying to remain faithful to the Church in the midst of the present turmoil and dissension within her walls. It is this latter phenomenon which has so confused and scandalised the faithful. Accustomed, nay even strengthened by attacks from without, Catholics were ill prepared for the anarchy which has raged inside the Church since the beginning of the Second Vatican II, these anarchists – many of them in responsible positions – have attacked or questioned almost every aspect of the Church: her doctrine, her discipline, her tradition, and her structure.

Is it any wonder
Do you wonder then, after all this has happened, that the Church is in disrepair? Could it be anything else? And what is the remedy? How to bring back that unity for which Christ so earnestly prayed back into His Church?

In the fourth century, St Justin wrote: 'To remain silent, knowing the truth, is to invite the wrath of God.' It stands to reason that, in the present crisis of disunion in the Church, to correct this evil, the cause of disunion must be removed. This evil is the toleration of error.

As the great French thinker Pascal wrote: 'It is written there is a time for peace and a time for war , and it is the law of truth that distinguishes the two. But at no time is there a time for truth and a time for error, it is written that God's truth shall abide forever. This is why Christ has said that He has come to bring peace, and at the same time that He has come to bring the sword, but He does not say that He has come to bring the truth AND the falsehood.'

THE HEART OF THE CRISIS

'This valuing of unity over the truth' insists Dr Dietrich von Hildenbrand *Triumph,* June, 'plays the central role in the crisis of the Church in our day; for the Church of Christ is based on the fundamental principle – The absolute primacy of Divine Truth which is the very primacy of God. It is the principle lying at the basis of the condemnation of all heresies in the course of the past 2000 years – the basis of all anathemas – the big reason for all her apostolic work. The Church has survived because she always condemned error. He goes on to say that in this crisis of faith, some Catholics, including some Bishops, argue that the most regrettable thing today is disunity among Catholics. This is not true. A far more important thing is, there be no priests, no lay people, no Bishops, who profess heresy; who profess theories incompatible with the deposit of Catholic Faith. The fact that many orthodox Catholics fight the heresies is not deplorable; on the contrary we should rejoice that there are still faithful Catholics, and that they raise their voices against heresies, for God expects that of them. St Paul says there always will be heresies and that God permits them to test the faithful. It is a crime to keep the peace when truth is violated. Thus, Christ said 'I have not come to bring peace to the Earth . . . but the sword. For I have come to set a man against his father, a daughter against her mother..' The truth of Christ must be preferred to even family unity and peace.

It is the opinion of many faithful Catholics today, that much of this turmoil in the Church will be stopped and true unity restored in no other way than by resorting to the time-honoured method of Anathema.

MEANS OF SURVIVAL

It is by imposing the anathema against heretics that the Church has survived, has kept her identity, down all the centuries. Although it has cost the Church many members – Bishops, priests, religious, laity – yet the Church authorities deemed it necessary to keep the integrity of the Church intact as Christ willed it to be. Thus in condemning the Arian heresy, almost one half of the Bishops, priests and laity defected. In the Protestant Reformation, the Church lost one third of Europe, including nearly all of England. Christ said of Himself, 'I am the Truth' and He cannot abide in the Church that does not maintain the truth and condemn error.

During his Pontificate, Pope St Pius X faced a situation in the Church much like we are experiencing today, because of the heresy of Modernism. While the Church suffered much in Pius' time, because many of the French Bishops defected by yielding to the law by the government of separation of the Church and State, we today have a like problem of secularism in the Church, resulting in defections for moral reasons. But the heresies that are afflicting the Church today are very similar to the errors of Modernism. As Pope Pius X said of Modernism, 'This attack is not a heresy, but the compendium and poison of all heresies,' so Pope Pius XII called the present errors afflicting the Church 'the cesspool of all errors.' They both aim to lay bare the very foundation of the Faith and to annihilate Christianity.

Neo-Modernists

The words Pope Pius X used in describing the Modernists can likewise be said of the dissidents today: 'The Modernists proclaim themselves as the champions of scientific truth, and their words and writing seems to many a true religious reaction against materialism. Excited and confused by the clamour and abuse, young priests – some of them being afraid of being branded as ignorant, others ambitious to rank among the learned, and both groups by curiosity and pride – not infrequently yield to temptation and give themselves up to the errors of Modernism. It is pride which causes them to seek to be reformers of others while they forget to reform themselves.'

When in 1907, Pope Pius X published his encyclical condemning Modernism and excommunicating those who in anyway taught these errors, he knew that the Church would lose many brilliant priests; but, he said, it must be done: 'We can no longer be silent lest we seem to be wanting in sacred strength, and the patience which we have hitherto shown in the hope of bringing them to their senses would be interpreted as neglect of duty . . . The security of the Catholic Church is at stake: to keep silence longer would be a crime.'

The Pope had waited 12 years hoping and praying. Then when he was convinced that nothing else would avail, and that he could not win over the obstinacy of the erring, he resorted to excommunication, adding: 'If we are forced to fight for truth, we must meet the enemy with love.' How like the Divine Saviour!

The historian comments: 'The hatred and mockery, which the ignorant adherents of Modernism and Freemasonry and Liberalism heaped on the Pope is unbelievable.'

The Sword of Truth

Whether Pope Paul VI will resort to excommunicating those who persist in preaching false doctrines of faith and morals – those who are leading the faithful into heresy and sin – we do not know. Judging from precedent there seems to be sufficient reason for doing so, and it may be the only way to bring these dissidents to their senses. It is true today, as it was true in the case of former heresies in the Church, that the Church may lose some Bishops and many priests and religious and lay persons who are too ignorant or proud or stubborn in their conceit to yield to the mandate of the Church, yet, aren't we now losing many, many Catholics and gaining fewer converts? Look at the statistics of last year; the loss to the Church of priests and religious and lay persons in 1969 over the previous year in the United States is appalling; besides, those who are in fact heretics and apostates, but still claim to be Catholics, are not listed, and must run into the millions.

Maybe that time has come to use the Sword of Truth as the means – the only means – to restore unity and peace to the Church. Christ, the God of Truth, wants unity in His Church, but not at the cost of tolerating error and corruption.

The Gates of Hell Shall Not Prevail

THE CHALLENGE TO FAITH
by the Most Rev. William L. Adrian, D.D.
Former Bishop of Nashville, Tennessee

I.C.P.A. *Newsletter*
January, 1971

If Satan were to draw up today a *Modus Agendi* (Manner of Acting) for the agents of his kingdom on Earth, he most likely would include as a top priority objective to corrupt the young and lure them away from religion by getting them interested in sex. He would also secure control of all the means of publicity; divine the people into hostile groups; destroy the people's faith in their natural leaders; foment civil disorders; and, by specious arguments, cause the breakdown of the old moral virtues – honesty, sobriety, continence – in order to encourage soft living.

Satan most certainly would promulgate special rules of action to promote the breakdown of the Church. For Christ and His Church are the most hated enemies of his kingdom. Satan well remembers how God had warned him after he had seduced Eve, that 'a woman shall crush thy head'; how Christ had humiliated him in the great temptation and later had accused him before the people of being 'a murderer and a liar – one who had no truth in him.'

When it became evident that Christ's mission on earth was to destroy his kingdom on earth, Satan schemed to have the Jews put Christ to death — and succeeded. But this, too, proved to be his own undoing, since Christ's Death and Resurrection became the very foundation of His Church — the very means to save souls from the Devil's deceitful snares. And ever since, Satan has made assault after assault on that Church, only to be frustrated and humiliated by the omnipotence of Christ, Who had declared: 'The Gates of Hell shall never prevail against it.' What a marvellous blessing this has been to Christ's followers in all these centuries!

SATAN VICTORIES

But Satan had also achieved some remarkable triumphs. From Christ's own words, and from the annals of history, we have reason to believe that many souls — perhaps the majority of mankind — have travelled, and are travelling, the 'broad way that leads to destruction.' But this is not for lack of power on the part of Christ. He became incarnate to save all men. To every man He says, as He did to St Paul: 'My grace is sufficient for thee.' There is no soul in Hell that is not damned because of its own free choice. Free will is a tremendous human faculty: even God, its Creator, so highly respects it, that He will never destroy it — no matter how evil it is in its choice of action.

What a blessing is free will to men, and what a curse it can be! Why an intelligent man should freely choose to follow the 'broad way that leads to damnation,' rather than the 'narrow way that leads to life everlasting' with God is hard to understand. The soul that chose the 'broad way' must forever reproach itself in Hell: 'What a stupid fool I was to choose Hell, when I could have attained Heaven with a little more effort by having been obedient to the Will of God.' 'And there will be weeping and gnashing of teeth,' Christ had warned.

NO EXCUSE

Nor can we plead even the excuse of Even and Satan to tempt man. NO! It is blasphemous. Christ warned us of the deceits of the Devil; He taught us to pray always that we be not lead into temptation. St Paul warned his people against the wiles of Satan 'For Satan disguises himself as an Angel of light' (2 Cor.11,13). St Peter warns: 'Be you vigilant, because the Devil like a roaring lion goes about seeking whom he may devour' (I Uet.5,8). The Holy Church, throughout her councils, Popes, doctors and saints, has warned us of the power and deceits of the Devil; but too often, men have ignored her voice or ridiculed it.

Is God cruel – unjust – that He permits Satan to tempt man? NO! It is blasphemous to entertain such a thought. God owes man nothing, man deserves eternal Hell fire because of his sins, and would inevitably end in Hell but for the infinite love and mercy of God in sending to men a Redeemer. Every man can save his soul if he does God's Will through the infallible voice of His Church – of the Pope and Bishops in communion with the Church. Man is free to choose. He can either obey God's Voice and be saved, or declare, like Satan did, 'I will not serve' – and, also like Satan, be forever damned.

For over 19 hundred years now, Satan has fought viciously against the Church – his number one enemy. He has used all the allurements of the world largely under his dominion; he has made use of man's unruly appetite; but for the most part, he has used men to be his agents – and especially men of little or no faith, and men sin, who are under his dominion. Seldom has he so blatantly revealed his plans for revolution as he is doing today. Not only have his agents literally carried out his programme for man's enslavement, but even more desperately, have similar tactics been directed against the Church.

The Devil within the Church

And what makes those attacks the more dangerous – the more seductive – is, that Satan is using those within the Church to carry out the nefarious schemes – some bishops, but primarily priests and religious and influential laymen, who by their vocation and office are bound to defend the Church.

To name only a few of these vicious attacks on the Church:

1. The unjust persecution of the Pope, accusing him of heresy, ignorance and injustice.
2, The numerous organisations – clerical and lay – that are advocating a 'New Church', a 'New Magisterium' a 'New Morality' to the destruction of the Church established by Christ and in defiance of moral laws made by God himself.
3, The almost complete domination of the Catholic means of communication – the Catholic newspapers and magazines, the public forums, the pulpits, the radio and television – by those Catholics who are highly critical of the Church, and often in open rebellion.
4. By those who poison the very wellsprings of Catholic doctrine in that they teach false doctrines in our seminaries, our colleges and our Catholic schools.
5. By those who openly advocate and practice birth control and oppose

by word and act, clerical and religious celibacy, after the Pope has definitely stated the position of the Church on these matters.

6. By those who are endeavouring to downgrade (often by ridicule) the dignity of some of the most sacred treasures of the Church: the Holy Sacrifice of the Mass and the Holy Eucharist, the Sacraments of Penance and Matrimony, the veneration of the Blessed Mother and the saints, and so on. And I repeat – these attacks coming from the very ones who by vow or position should be defenders of the Church and its teaching, makes their conduct all the more diabolical. One can almost see in physical form the Devil operating through these, his agents. Christ knows who they are, and his Church keeps warning the faithful; in the words of Christ: 'Those who are not with Me, are against Me.'

WHAT PRICE YOUR SOUL?
To be a faithful Catholic has never been easy, and it is harder now, but it is worth the effort. Christ puts the challenge to every faithful soul: 'What exchange can a man give for his soul? Even if he gain the whole world and suffer the loss of his soul, what will it profit him?'

Christ may well be using these attacks of the enemies of the Church to try the souls of men; it may be His way of sifting the chaff from the wheat. So we have need, as St Peter says 'to be humble under the mighty Hand of God, and cast all your anxiety on Him, because He cares for us' . . . 'Be prudent and watchful in prayer.' Resist the Devil and his agents by being 'strong in your faith'. (I Peter, Ch.4).

And the Divine Saviour on that last night before His terrible Passion, just after He had offered up that first Holy Sacrifice of the Mass, prayed thus: 'Heavenly Father, not for these only (His Apostles) do I pray, but for all those, who through their word are to believe in Me . . . Sanctify men in truth.' 'Fear not – only believe – I have conquered the world.'

COMMEMORATING THE FIRST VATICAN COUNCIL
by the Right Rev.Thomas Muldoon
Auxillary Bishop of Sydney, Australia

I.C.P.A. *Newsletter*
Autumn, 1978

Bishop Muldoon kindly sent the Catholic Priests' Association for publication in our *Newsletter*, the text of the address he gave in Sydney on the occasion of celebrating the First Vatican Council. We are grateful to the Bishop for his patronage and support.

What brings us together in this liturgical celebration this morning is gratitude: gratitude to Almighty God for a great gift to His Church – the gift of the First Vatican Council, the Centenary of which we are celebrating.

That 20th Ecumenical Council, summoned by Pope Pius IX, opened on the Feast of the Immaculate Conception, 8 December 1869. Due to the eruption of war, it met for the last time on 1 September 1870. On 20 October that year Pius IX now 'the prisoner in the Vatican' suspended the Council indefinitely. That Council gave the Church two great treasures for which we can never be sufficiently grateful. They were the two solemnly defined dogmatic constitutions *Dei Filius* and *Pastor Aeturnus* which decisively set the course of the Church for a hundred years, and will continue to do so until the end of time. I should like to say a few words about each hoping that you will read, or read again, these vitally important dogmatic statements of immutable Catholic Faith.

The Constitution *Dei Filius* was the Church's definitive answer to the numerous doctrinal errors of the times. We must remember that for more than a century, rationalism had been gathering into an immense force. The very foundations of religion were awash in the tide. Scorn and ridicule were heaped upon the idea of the existence of a supernatural order to which man is raised by God's grace. The concept of revelation was rejected as impossible; the idea of faith was spurned as unworthy of man; the notion of creation was cast off as a fantasy; the absolute autonomy of human reason was proudly and perversely exalted on all sides; the self-sufficiency of man and the evolving of man by an inevitable progress towards the possession of all truth and good were loudly proclaimed. Man did not need God and, if God did exist, He certainly had no contact with man, nor man with Him. Out of this morass came the systematic errors of crass materialism (nothing exists except matter); pantheism in its various forms; atheism; deism; and, at best, a great pall of agnosticism hung over the minds of men. As a result there was a widespread sickness throughout the whole of society, and the Church was affected by the disease.

Pope Pius IX was not exaggerating when he said, summoning the Council: 'It is now evident to all men what a terrible storm is tossing the Church about, and what vast evils are afflicting civil society. The Catholic Church, with its saving doctrine . . . and the Holy See's authority, are attacked and stamped upon by the bitterest enemies of God and man.'

The great Dogmatic Constitution *Del Filius* resolutely faced these fundamental aberrations and clearly defined the Catholic doctrine on all these points. Of supreme importance is its teaching on faith, reason and their interrelation. When one studies that superb conciliar document, one is struck again with this thought, which I leave with you: there is no rationalism so daringly rationalistic as Catholic rationalism. It is the Catholic Church that has always defended the transcendence of the human intellect. It is the Catholic Church that has always stated the paradox that man, though finite, is open to the Infinite; that his spiritual faculties of intellect and will, stretch out to the Infinite; and that nothing but the Infinite, concretely possessed, can still his craving aspirations and bring him beatitude. It is the Catholic Church that has ever taught man his true dignity, both in the natural and supernatural orders; and you will not find this teaching more authentically or clearly expressed than in the Dogmatic Constitution *Del Filius* of the first Vatican Council. For this we are profoundly grateful. If the Church had not thus solemnly intervened, where would we be today?

The second vital dogmatic teaching of the first Vatican Council is found in the Constitution *Pastor Aeternus*, promulgated on this day, 18 July 1870. In this document the Church irrevocably defined its teaching on the position of the Vicar of Christ, the Bishop of Rome in the universal Church. I urge you to read again this dogmatic Constitution, not only for the sake of the precious truth it contains in itself, but because the doctrine contained in it is absolutely essential for a right understanding of the second Vatican Council's most important document, namely the 'Dogmatic Constitution on the Church.'

We all know that in the First Vatican Council the authentic teaching authority in the Church, to whom alone belongs the authentic interpretation of Sacred Scripture, brought into full and everlasting light, the profound significance of the Petrine text read in today's Mass – (Mt.16, 13ff). We all know that the Council defined the Pope's supreme primacy of jurisdiction over the universal Church, and his infallibility when, in strictly prescribed circumstances, he teaches and binds the universal Church in matters of faith and morals as pertaining to the Revelation.

I should like to point out very clearly that the main issue at stake in the First Vatican Council was not the question of the Pope's infallibility in certain circumstances (for this is the most reasonable of all teachings, given the Revelation) but the question of the Primacy of Jurisdiction over the universal Church and individual churches and persons. I should like to point this out very clearly, because the question in raised again today, even by some supposedly learned theologians who, it would seem, have never studied the defined dogma of the First Vatican Council.

The First Vatican Council was at pains to point out that the primacy of the Pope embraces in itself the supreme power of teaching and binding in matters of faith and morals. I refer you to Chapter 4 of the Dogmatic Definition, (Denzinger 1832). Infallibility in matters of faith and morals, in the prescribed circumstances is included in the Primacy given by Christ to Peter and his successors. This, it seems, is not always understood. However, I wish to revert to the question of the Primacy of Jurisdiction which was the major issue and for some, inexplicably, still today. The defined doctrine of the First Vatican Council is lucid. The Pope, the successor of Peter and Vicar of Christ, holds the Primacy not only in matters of faith and morals but also in all matters of Church – discipline and government both as regards individual churches, be it the Church in Australia or Holland or New Guinea or anywhere else. I quote the defined doctrine of Vatican I: 'If anyone says that the Roman Pontiff has only an office of inspection and direction, and not full and supreme power of jurisdiction over the universal Church, not only in matters that pertain to faith and morals, but also in matters of discipline and government of the Universal Church; or if anyone says that He has only a chief part in these matters of discipline and government, but not the whole plenitude of supreme power; or if anyone says that this power of the Bishop of Rome is not inherent in his office and immediately effective in all the individual Churches in all countries and as regards all and every individual pastor of the Church, and all and every individual Catholic, let such a person be anathema.' (Ch.3 *Pastor Aeturnus*).

I want to stress this defined doctrine in the face of those who, today, say that the Pope's function is to preserve the Church's essential unity in faith and communion, but that it is not his function to intervene in matters of discipline and government in individual Churches. Such a position is not only false but plainly heretical.

The first Vatican Council dogmatically defined that the power of jurisdiction belonging to the Sovereign Pontiff, the Bishop of Rome, over the whole Church and each individual Church, and each and every individual person in the Church, be he Bishop, priest, religious or layman, is marked by four indisputable notes.

Firstly, it is inherent in his office as defined by Christ Our Lord, who gave him the keys of the whole Kingdom on earth and appointed him to pastor every member of the flock, without any exception whatsoever.

Secondly, it is immediate, that is, he is not bound to pass through anyone else, even the Bishop of a Diocese, in order to determine what is good for an individual Church or person.

Thirdly, it is full. This means that the Pope possesses the fullness of all the power entrusted by Christ to His Church. Such power of ruling is restricted only by the natural law and divine positive laws, to which the Pope is strictly subjected, as is every other human being.

Fourthly, it is truly episcopal, that is, the Pope's pastoral rule as a Bishop extends to each and every diocese in the world, and is in no way restricted to the Diocese of Rome.

From all this it is clear that it is not enough to be a subject to the Pope in doctrinal and moral matters, as some would have us believe. Submission must extend to all which he promulgates, both for the universal Church or for any particular Church; also to the precepts he may impose on individual persons. It is clear, then, that it is the Pope's function to co-ordinate and direct the whole of the Church's activity in all its aspects. This function is inherent in his office as the Supreme Head of the visible Church; and if you analyse it closely you will find that it is inherent in the theological concept of the Church as the Body of Christ.

It is for him alone to decide according to the Church's needs, which vary in the course of time, in what the Supreme power is to be exercised, both personally and collegially.

It is within the framework of that defined doctrine that the difficult task of working out the principle of collegiality must be undertaken. The First Vatican Council, going to the very heart of the matter, gave us the *Raison d'etre* of the Pope's universal primacy in these words: 'That the Episcopate may be one and undivided, and that, thanks to the close and reciprocal unity among pastors, the entire multitude of believers may be kept in the unity of faith and communion, Christ the Lord set Peter over the other Apostles and established in him the perpetual source and visible foundation of this double unity.' The Pope is there in order that the organic unity of the Church in faith, morals, worship and discipline may be preserved intact. But this presupposes a willingness on the part of all members of the Church to recognise and accept him in his Christ given role. In the final analysis this is a matter of faith in the strictest sense. One must examine one's Faith.

Some say, even today, that the Church, through the teaching of the First Vatican Council, placed an intolerable burden on one man. That is not the question; nor was the burden recognised by that Council for the first time, as though the doctrine were new. The only question is whether the doctrine is true or false; and to that question a Catholic can only give one answer if he wants to remain within the Church.

As we meditate the defined doctrine of the First Vatican Council (reaffirmed in its entirety by the Second Vatican Council, though that was not necessary) we are moved to a profound feeling of awe for the Christ given office of the Papacy. But, even more so, we are moved to deep compassion for the person upon whom a heavy burden falls. He is called to the complete service of God's People, yes; but his service is a service of strict authority in teaching, sanctifying and governing with utter fidelity to Christ, no matter what voices are raised against him, even from the most unlikely quarters.

Therefore, while we thank Almighty God for the treasures He gave His Church through the definitive teaching of the First Vatican Council, our minds and hearts go out to Pope Paul, the Vicar of Christ, with gratitude, love and complete loyalty and devotion. Ever so patiently and courageously does he carry the immense burden of his office in the midst of huge difficulties, often created by those whom he has the right to expect most support.

'May the Lord preserve him and give him length of days, and make him blessed on the face of the earth, and deliver him not into the hands of his enemies.'

Thomas Muldoon, Auxiliary Bishop of Sydney
18 July, 1970

A CAUSE WORTH FIGHTING FOR
by the Archbishop Robert Duryer, Oregan, U.S.A.   I.C.P.A. *Newsletter*
Autumn 1970

His Holiness Pope Paul VI, has given the endorsement vigorously and enthusiastically, to the New Order of the Mass. He has made it clear that he expects all Catholics of the Latin Rite to accept it, no matter how deep may be their attachment to the 'Tridentine Mass', the ritual published and promulgated in the 16th Century by Pope St Pius V and revised and re-edited under the authority of Pope St Pius X and Pope Benedict XV in the early decades of this century. Here is a typical act of the ordinary *Magisterium* of the Holy See. It does not invoke that note of infallibility which the Roman Pontiff exercises when necessary, under God, either as head of the college or Supreme Pastor, *motu proprio*. Nevertheless, in a matter so intimately associated with the very well springs of Grace and of Faith itself, it is inconceivable that the Common Father of Christendom could or would sanction a liturgical innovation which might in any way endanger the validity of that Sacrifice and Sacrament which Our Divine Lord left to us as our spiritual food and of a sign of our unity in Him.

Unquestionably, it was this consideration which caused His Eminence, Cardinal Ottaviani, to withdraw and repudiate his initial strictures upon it. No doubt he would prefer to see the Tridentine Mass preserved (as indeed it may yet be an alternative) but closer scrutiny and deeper reflection elicited from him an unfeigned declaration of acceptance. Once again, in his age and retirement, he has demonstrated the greatness and simplicity of his soul.

The sanction of the Holy Father was given, directly, to the official Latin text of the New Ordo. It may be remarked here parenthetically, that the promulgation of the recent liturgical changes in no way affected the status of the Latin, as the basic tongue of the Western Church. The mind of Vatican I1 expressed in the decree on the Liturgy is explicit, that Latin should and must remain the principle vehicle for Divine Worship; it was never intended that it should be supplanted by the vernacular.

Whatever virtues or advantages the vernacular may possess – and there are many – the Latin mass is still the norm, unless we are to consider the action of the Council to be a mistake and a dead letter. Thus, while for specific pastoral reasons, Bishops advocate and encourage the use of the vernacular for ordinary worship, it would be hard to justify, on the strength of the Council, a refusal to permit Mass in Latin when warranted, or for those special occasions when the solemnity of the Liturgy should be properly emphasised.

But what is to be thought or said of the translation of the New Ordo? Here, manifestly, the Holy Father is at the mercy (the word is used advisedly) of his consultants who are involved with the languages involved. Pope Paul VI may well be an accomplished linguist in his native Italian; he may command half a dozen languages (modern) to a greater or lesser degree, though it is unlikely that he would claim more than an amateur's appreciation of their literacy niceties. Certainly he would not be tempted to assert a mastery of English, that most baffling or tongues, which defies the average Southern European with much the same arrogance as Mandarin Chinese.

It is with mingled sorrow and indignation that we say, bluntly, that the English consultants of the Holy See, in this manner, whoever they may be in recommending for his approval the current translation of the New Ordo, together with those of the Scriptural readings, have rendered him a grave disservice and have done serious harm, if not irreparable harm, to the whole cause of the liturgical development in our time.

Their fault may not be as direct and personal as that of those agents who did the actual translating, but it is heavy enough to rob them of their rest. Translators and consultants both have demonstrated their incompetence, their insensitivity, and their indifference to the demands of absolute fidelity when dogmatic consideration make this obligatory. Hence it is, that to cite the Holy Father's approval given to the English text of the new Missal (or should we say – New Missal library?) is a very different thing than citing his official sanction of the Latin Text of the Order.

In the latter instance he is acting out of full, personal knowledge, placing the seal of his approval upon those liturgical modification deemed useful for the better presentation of the Mass. In the former he is simply assuming that those men whom he relies upon for advice, know what they are doing. Not to put too a point upon it, there is a very large doubt, shared by many who are concerned for the integrity of the liturgy and for the dignity and beauty of its prayer and worship, whether they acted wisely or well.

The point, to belabour it, is that the approval given by the Pope to any particular translation, be it English or Hottentot, does not imply that he has thereby exercised so much of his authority. It means no more than that he has taken another's word for it, that the text in question is an accurate and faithful rendering of the Latin which he has personally examined and promulgated.

So it follows that to counsel uncomplaining acceptance of the English version of the New Ordo, with all its inaccuracies, its crudities, its liturgical and literary blemishes, is by no means included under our 'reasonable service'. Nor is it being disloyal or disrespectful to the Sovereign Pontiff to keep on fighting for a revision in the hope that ultimately the English speaking Catholic world may possess the Mass in a vernacular rendering which will be true to the original, and meaningful and dignified in its language.

Let it be added, when it comes to the question of those parts of the Mass which are intended to be sung, that they be written so that a musical lines may be carried. As things are now, the horrendous response – 'And also with you', is one example, however glaring, of how men who have not the slightest ear for music can be turned loose, like so many bulls in the liturgical china shop, to wreak their havoc. It was John Ruskin, organ voice of Puritan England striving to recapture its Catholic past, who paid tribute in so many contexts, to the paramount influence of the King James version of the Sacred Scripture, both on his style and on his thought. Just as surely do echoes of the *Douai* version (so grossly underestimated and stupidly maligned) resound in our memory and seek imprint in fugitive maunderings.

But could any man living, imagine himself forming his style or moulding his cast of thought on the English of the liturgy as it is presently perpetrated?

No use sighing – How long, O Lord, how long? Here is the point of the attack; here is a cause worth fighting for – even if it means a broken head or two.

Robert J. Dwyer
Archbishop of Portland, Oregon

OTHER STATEMENTS FROM
THE SAME ARCHBISHOP ON THE VERNACULAR:-

'The I.C.E.L. has performed its task so poorly as to raise serious questions as to its competence. Never was there the slightest consultation with the Bishops of the English-speaking world. Here is a signal of bureaucracy inflicting its will by methods which can only be described as high-handed.'

(*Twin Circle,* 21 June 1970)

'We are in a veritable landslide of vulgarisation. What was intended by Vatican I1, as a means of making the liturgy more easily understood, has turned out like something of an orgy of stripping it of all sense of holiness and reverence, bringing it down to the level of commonness, where the people for whom the changes were made, now only yawn, out of sheer boredom . . . The New Ordo of the Mass, what crimes can be committed by men in committee? It might have been thought that in the interest of ecumencity, consideration could have been given to strengthening the old *Douai-Challoner* text with the great style of King James's version,. But no! In the minds of those commissioned by the Hierarchy to do the work, the great object on target, manifestly, was to denude the liturgy of its last claim to literary dignity . . . With polite, pious acquiescence, the Bishop received the results with no more than an occasional feeble, almost only grunted protest.

Thus do we lose a priceless cultural inheritance.'

(Published in **The Clarion,**
Archdiocesan Weekly,
26 July 1970)
(Editor, Father Flanagan)

THE SUPREME *MAGISTERIUM* OF THE POPE
UPHOLDS THE PURITY AND INTEGRITY OF THE FAITH

by Cardinal Ottaviani　　　　　　　　　　　　I.C.P.A. *Newsletter*
January 1971.

The above declaration is the substance of a statement by His Eminence Alfredo Cardinal Ottaviani, honourary prefect of the Sacred Congregation for the Doctrine of the Faith, which appeared in the *Cruzado Espagnol*, 15 May 1970, published in Barcelona. The following is a translation of that statement by our Paris correspondent, Paul Poitevin.

'One faith, one baptism, one Lord,' (Eph. IV, 5) – with this synthetical and eloquent formula Saint Paul has summed and explained the triple unity which rules and upholds the ecclesial family in doctrinal, liturgical and hierarchical field; this triple unity is rooted in the Papacy as it is personified in the Sovereign Pontiff, the Vicar of Christ on earth.

Una fides; we never will be able to thank God sufficiently for the gift which He made to His Church in giving it a leader, the successor of Peter, adorning him with special powers and charisma, especially the charisma of infallibility by which, as the First Vatican Council stated, the Roman Pontiff 'when he speaks *ex cathedra* – that is, as supreme pastor and teacher of all Christians – and when – acting with his supreme apostolic authority – he defines a doctrine concerning faith or morals which must be held by the Universal Church – by virtue of the Divine assistance promised to blessed Peter – (the Pope) possess this infallibility which Our Divine Redeemer wanted His Church endowed with to define faith and morals; and it is why these definitions by the Roman Pontiffs are irreformable by themselves and not by the agreement of the Church.'

Arius came, Luther arose and after them the Modernists, the seed of whom has not wholly disappeared. They attempted, and they still attempt, to break the unity of the faith of the Church, but always there was, and always there will be, a Pope to profess the *Credo,* as it was done by Paul VI at the end of the year of the faith, a profession which received the ecclesial agreement of an immense number of the faithful.

In the life of the Church there will be hard times; black clouds will darken the sky, storms will brew, but never will it be without a shining star – the light of the truth proclaimed by the *Magisterium* of the Pope.

Unum baptisma: the beauty of the Church is equally resplendent in the variety of the liturgical rite which enrich the divine cult – when they are legitimate and conform to the faith. Precisely the legitimacy of their origin protects and guards them against the infiltration of errors and excludes in these rites the arbitrary innovations which are the fruit of caprice and disorder, and which appear under the mask of false ecumenism.

The purity and unity of the faith is in this manner also upheld by the supreme *Magisterium* of the Pope through the liturgical laws. Thus is maintained — living and operative — the ancient principle: *Lex orandi, Lex credende*.

Unum Dominus; some deliberately refused to hear the Lord's prayer *ut unum sint*, and rejected the apostolic bond of unity through submission to Peter and to his successors; they parted from the true Church and dispersed themselves among various confessions, sects and churches — thus breaking all bonds of dogmatic, liturgical and hierarchical unity. They rejected all submission to Peter, and some of them fell into servitude — compelled as they were to serve a *caesaropapism*, of which in certain nations of today traces are still found.

Through the dogmatic Constitution *Lumen Gentium* the Vatican Council solemnly proclaimed the authenticity of the revealed Divine Word, as found in Holy Scripture — Tradition and the *Magisterium*. Those Christians who have broken with Tradition and refuse to submit themselves to the supreme *Magisterium* established by Christ in His Church, have renounced the riches of the divine wisdom from the pure spring of truth. It is by the supreme *Magisterium* of Christ's Vicar that we are guided on our way — in the light, out of darkness.

In my book *Baluardo,* I ended thus a chapter on the Pope: 'Whatever sorrow, whatever disgrace, obscurity, persecution, there may be, they all fade away when one comes to rely on a unique man, in whom shines always the light of eternal truth. The night of the world will perhaps become very dark, but it will never be without a star: the Pope.' (p.17).

THE WOOD HALL THEOLOGICAL DISCOVERIES
by Rev. Fr. John V. Flanagan　　　　　　I.C.P.A. *Newsletter*
April-June 1971

The **Pastoral and Ecumenical Centre** at Wood Hall, Linton, near Wetherby, Yorks., was the setting last June for the first National Conference of Priests of this country. It is a centre where numerous conferences take place during the year for various groups of people, priests, nuns, laity in general. In a previous issue of this *Newsletter*, Autumn 1970 pp. 35-36, we quoted a statement coming from the same centre and published in the *Leeds Diocesan Gazette,* 1969 p.17.

'We believe that religion is a vital factor in the lives of individuals and nations, but religion today must be relevant, Christian and non-denominational'. One wonders how this can be squared with Papal teaching, as it is typical of the 'Christian-humanism' that is fed to the faithful all over the country today, particularly from such places as Catechetical centres and Ecumenical welding factories. In the same issue of the *Newsletter* just referred to, we exposed certain unorthodox doctrines associated with this same centre. A reader has now sent us a copy of *De Ecclesia* – a neatly bound duplicated booklet of 41 quarto sized pages, taken, as we are told in the introduction – 'From the basis of a three day course on *De Ecclesia* held at Wood Hall, April 11 to 13, 1970.' The lectures were Monsignor Buckley, Mother Mary Bernard, and Harry Kenny. We are not told who gave the particular lectures which compose the booklet.

While many pages of the booklet are sound and seem unaffected by Neo-Modernism, certain parts of it must be challenged and one portion in particular which forms the final paragraphs of this article, is an utterly disgraceful attempt to bamboozle its readers into believing that certain historical discoveries made in recent years (around 1943) throw new light on the nature of the power of conferring Sacred Orders. It is deplorable that those attending this series of lectures may well have left the centre with entirely erroneous ideas on this whole matter. The booklet opens with a severe criticism levelled against Vatican II in its decree on modern means of communication which it describes as 'unworthy of serious reflection that went on during four years' while the decree on the Priesthood is viewed as 'no great credit to a conciliar body.' It, of course, places great emphasis on 'The Action of the Whole People of God' under the influence of the Spirit, and it reminds the clergy that 'it is not they alone who rule the Church . . . and it is not a gracious condescension when they accept suggestions from below.' 'Belonging to the Church has no longer a unique and restricted meaning; even the well disposed agnostic has some connection with the Church and is not a complete outsider.' (p.13) The great contribution of Vatican II may well be 'the emancipation of the laity'. 'The Bishops do not get their power and office from the Pope but from Christ as did the Apostles.' (p.19) These are but a few of the strange views put forward by the Wood Hall booklet.

It is when the authors of this production deal with the Episcopacy and its relationship to sacred ordination, that they indulge in a deliberate effort to twist and even present us with fiction for fact to help us swallow their ideas. On 'The Church and the Episcopacy' (p.14) we read:-

'Theologians seemed more intent on telling us the powers which the Apostolic College did not have, they were more preoccupied with defending Papal status and privilege than developing the theology of the episcopate.'

The authors then go on to state that owing to the fact that the 'Sacramental character' of ordination was 'atrociously handled by theologians', Episcopal consecration 'came more and more to be considered as a personal possession and privilege of the individual', when in fact it is 'a figurative expression of a man's irrevocable consecration and commission for a particular role in the Church' . . . 'It appeared as a ghostly property or quality of soul. The character was a playpen of theological fantasy. Some spoke of it in such a way that it seemed like a blot of ink spreading over blotting paper.'

So in the teaching of the authors of the 'Wood Hall' booklet, the Sacred Character of episcopal consecration with its indelible seal on the human soul, is an illusion of theologians of the past. Hence there is no difference between the consecrated Bishop and the validly ordained priest; the difference is not in the 'fullness of the priesthood', but in the extent of one's commitment to the Church. If there is no difference, then priests can validly ordain other priests – with due authorisation, of course, from the Holy See – but Episcopal Order is not required. This is the conclusion arrived at by the *periti* of 'Wood Hall', and to remove all doubt from the minds of those who might question their findings, readers are presented with some excellent examples of 'trumped up' evidence. Let us quote the booklet itself:-

'It was well known that the Pope could delegate any priest to confirm. So the power to ordain remained the unique and distinct power of the Bishop. The argument was simple: the episcopal consecration was a Sacrament because it gives the power. Trent was quoted as supporting this by saying that the power was *iure divino* reserved to the Bishop. Actually, recent research has shown that Trent left the divine institution an open question. It was a neat though unsatisfactory notion of the Episcopate. However, it was shattered when certain papal documents of late mediaeval times were unearthed seeming to show that a simple priest can be delegated by the Pope to ordain.'

The authors of *De Ecclesia* then designate the three discoveries of the age which showed that the Pope has in fact authorised simple priests to ordain to the priesthood – they are:

1. The Bull 'Sacrae Religionis' of Pope Boniface IX in 1400 AD.
2. The Bull 'Gerentes Vos' of Pope Martin IV Nov. 1427 and
3. The Bull 'Exposcit' of Pope Innocent VIII in 1489.

'The last document was the first to become known' write the authors of *De Ecclesia* (p.17) 'but it makes no mention of the priesthood. The other two have only just come to light. *Gerentes Vos* of Martin IV was found in the State Archives of Saxony. The corresponding entry was found in the Lateran Registers and published in 1943. There is no doubt whatever about the authenticity of these documents. With the appearance of the document of Pope Boniface, attempts were made to explain it away. This was rudely stopped by the 1943 publication. Men like Journet, Piolante, Michel Herve who had unhesitatingly taught that the Pope could not grant such a privilege, sought a different interpretation. The evidence of history has proved too strong and all no longer doubt the historical fact of this concession.'

We now come to the theological conclusions of the authors of the Wood Hall *De Ecclesia*, 'Within the last decade all reputable theologians have accepted the fact that an ordinary priest can be the extraordinary minister of Ordination' (p.18). That would mean that Bishops are now superfluous – 'One French theologian delivered a quaint verdict that Bishops had outlived their usefulness in a world moving towards unity it is necessary that the Pope should speak, speak often and direct all . . . The Bishops will lose their sovereignty leaving to Peter and his successors the general direction of the whole Catholic enterprise, of the whole apostolate.' (p.18). For the authors concerned there is no 'fullness of the priesthood' in the Episcopacy. The Bishop is just a simple priest 'committed' to the world of the Church: he has not personal episcopal character received through his consecration. All that he has (apart from ordination to the priesthood) comes to him from the Church. The authors state 'The Council re-directs our attention to the fact that the Sacrament is not a personal possession, the privilege of the individual, but is a Sacrament of the Church.'

What in fact are those three Bulls to which the authors refer and which were of 'ONLY RECENT DISCOVERY' (1943) and the 'unearthing' of which caused a 'FLUTTER' among theologians who held that a priest – a simple priest — could not be delegated to ordain to the priesthood? What monumental discovery was this at all? Why was it not blazed in the headlines of every paper in the world. Were all three of them 'unearthed' at the same time — 'RECENTLY' in 1943?

The Bull *Sacrae Religionis* of Boniface IX in 1400 gave to the Abbot of a monastery in Essex, then in the diocese of London, the authority *in perpetuum — Omnibus et singulis Canonicis praesentibus et futuris professis eiusdem monasterii omnes minores necnon subdiaconatus, diaconatus, et presbyteratus ordines statutis a iure temporibus conferre libere ac licite valeant*. For the sake of lay readers of this *Newsletter*, the words mean that the Pope conferred in perpetuity on the Abbot of this monastery and on his successors, the right of conferring minor order, as well as the *subdiaconate*, the *diaconate* and the priesthood on the professed monks of the same monastery.

This Bull, instead of it being 'unearthed' in 'recent' years — 1943 — is known to have been studied and commented upon by scholars from the time of its publication. It is listed in the Vatican Archives under 'Reg. Lat. 81, folium 264' and its revocation by the same Pontiff only three years later (February 6 1403) has also been the subject of study by scholars since the 17th century. The revocation is tabulated under No.108 folium 132. It is quite clear that the authors of *De Ecclesia* have not even read the text of the Bull and the circumstances under which it was granted. If they did they would have concluded that the Bull was giving to the Abbot of the Monastery the authority to grant Dimissorial Letters independently of the Bishop of London. This was a great concession at this stage of Church discipline and it was the beginning of the practice which later became general, of authorising Abbots of Monasteries to advance their own professed for Ordination — which later, where the priesthood was concerned, was always conferred by a consecrated Bishop. Canonists and theologians who flourished in the years following this Bull — all of whom knew of it and its contents (though we are asked to believe in *De Ecclesia* that it was unknown until around 1943!) never even raised the difficulty which would have been created if our Wood Hall writers' contention were true. With Father Cappello, S.J., in his *De Ordinatione* we conclude that the Bull. *Nihil aliud continet quam facultatem promovendi ad ordines sodales professos independenter a Episcopo diocesans*. (No.312)

The Bull *Exposcit* of Pope Innocent VIII (1498) conferred on the Abbot of the Cistercian Monastery of Citeaux and four other houses the faculty of conferring subdiaconate and diaconate on monks of the monasteries. It is understood by many Canonists and theologians as meaning that Pope Innocent authorised the Abbots concerned to grant Dimissorial Letters to their professed monks, which, as in the case of the Bull *Sacrae Religionis* of Boniface IX, was a great concession from the demands of the existing discipline. Vasquez (who testified to seeing the original Bull) and a host of other Canonists of past centuries – e.g. Reiffenstuel, Pirhing, Schmalzgruebar, Morinus, Giraldi and many others have discussed the text of this Bull – so obviously its 'UNEARTHING' in 1943 can only be compared to the tooth of the 'Piltdown Man' that Father Teilhard de Chardin 'unearthed' in his days.

We are living in a time of great scientific forgeries and so when the authors of *De Ecclesia* tell us that 'the evidence of history has proved too strong' (p.17) to preserve the traditional teaching of the Church on the necessity of a valid Episcopal consecration of the conferring of the Order of Priesthood, we can only sit back with a salt cellar near us and sprinkle the tail of this hairy monster! I wonder do the authors of *De Ecclesia* realise the consequences of the theory they put forward? At the very time that there is a cry to return to the Church of the past, they appeal to those three Bulls to show the accepted power of the Roman Pontiff to authorise simple priests to ordain to the priesthood. But this very same conclusion does not fit into the same authors' design to remove Pope Paul VI from the pinnacle of authority which in some unexplained way he holds over the Church. The Bulls referred to, if accepted in the sense in which the authors of *De Ecclesia* sustain, only conclusively prove the old axiom of *Ubi Petrus Ibi Ecclesia*.

It is difficult to understand why the Hierarchy of this country should continue to support – morally and financially – centre of 'New Theology' with experts who endeavour to prove that the Bishops have no real Episcopal Character given to them by virtue of their consecration, and that anything they have, comes from the Church – presumably from the Roman Pontiff. So, while on one hand the authors endeavour to upgrade the Bishops at the expense of the Roman Pontiff, they supply us with evidence that downgrades them in relation to the Pope. Episcopal approval for such a centre of 'New Theology' must be considered as the first step in a process of self-destruction – Episcopal *Hara-Kiri*.

When the authors of the booklet (p.16) tell us that a 'Number of theologians have been advocating . . . a rediscovery of the office and doctrine of the episcopate . . . and it would be wrong to think that it was only debates on the Council floor which brought about a new look' we could not agree with them more, but one could remind them that this is not the proper sphere of the theologians, who function it is faithfully to unfold and explain what has been decided on the Council floor – not to deviate from it. It is their desire to rush into untrodden, untested and unapproved realms that prompts them to consider the 'character' of episcopal consecration as only an 'external' element, 'a figurative expression of man's irrevocable commission to a certain role in the Church.' With theologians 'atrociously handling' the study of the 'episcopal character' in the past, it was reserved to the discoverers of the 'New Theology' to realise that the 'Sacrament of Order is not a personal possession or privilege of the individual.' *(De Ecclesia,* p.18.) The authors of course quote proof of their statement for this – it is 'The Council'. This indeed is a discovery of the greatest moment, as world shaking as the discovery of the tooth of the Piltdown jaw by Father Teilhard de Chardin. Unfortunately the authors do not supply us with the sources of the Council Documents where this new doctrine is found, and so we are forced to conclude that notwithstanding Pope John's emphatic statement that Vatican II had the task of transmitting the doctrines of the Church 'pure and integral without any attenuation or distortion'. And this doctrine includes no doubt the teaching of Trent, *Session VIII, Can 9,* that the character of the Sacrament of Order impresses a 'certain spiritual and indelible character on the soul' and that he who shall presume to state to the contrary is anathema. This solemn teaching of Trent if rejected or questioned by anyone, places that person outside the fold of the Church; no one can reject any infallible teaching and remain within the bosom of the Church. In the light of this fact can **Wood Hall** continue to be recognised as a Catholic centre, if those who propound false doctrine still continue to functions there? Can 'Wood Hall' continue to indoctrinate those who go there for lectures without action being taken by the Bishops to safeguard orthodoxy – the truth of God, the jewel of great price which prompts its possessor to lose everything in order to save it?

This criticism of the doctrines emanating from **Wood Hall** should not be complete without some reference to the views of the same authors on Collegiality. We read the following in *De Ecclesia* (p.19).

'By Episcopal consecration a Bishop admitted to the college shares the pastoral mission of the Apostles and receives the grace and power to do his job. He does not enter the college because the Pope appoints him to govern a See, but because by Sacramental consecration he has received the highest share in the priesthood of Christ. A Bishop is received into the college by three of its members. Nor do the Bishops get their office and power from the Pope, but from Christ, as did the apostles. The true nature of the

Church is not expressed in an external structure which stresses Papal primacy without episcopal collegiality . . . Vatican I on the office of papacy, tended towards uniformity which is damaging to the catholicity of the Church.'

These words do not convey the truth of the matter. Episcopal consecration does to number him among the successors of the Apostles, but gives him the fullness of the priesthood including the power of consecrating other Bishops. Neither does the fact that three Bishops take part in the consecration ceremony mean that he is *ipso facto* a successor of the Apostles. It is only in so far as these Bishops act in conformity with the mandate of the successor of Peter that incorporation into the College of Apostles takes place. Episcopal collegiality is meaningless except when understood as emanating from the head. As Father John A. Hardon, S.J., accurately puts it, 'the Catholic episcopacy has three powers inherent in it, firstly the power of consecrating, secondly the power of teaching authoritatively and sharing the Church's divine guidance of communicating revealed Truth, and the third is the right to direct the people of God according to norms of conduct binding their conscience. The first of these belongs to the Bishop by virtue of his episcopal consecration, but the others become operative only if a Bishop (or groups of Bishops) are in actual communion with Rome, and in obedience to the Holy See.' *L'Osservatore Romano*, 26 November, 1970).

The **Wood Hall** theologians confuse the power of order with that of jurisdiction. And to say that a Bishop or a group of Bishops receive today their 'office of power' not from the Pope but from Christ, is to make of the Church a many headed monster. No one today can be unaware of the constant efforts of Modernists and their friends to shackle the Primacy of St Peter's successor. 'It is damaging to the Catholicity of the Church' write the authors of *De Ecclesia* (p.19). This is dangerous nonsense unworthy of any priest who has studied the Divine Constitution of the Church. Collegiality has to be seen in relation to the primacy, without which it cannot be conceived. To give the impression – as so many Neo-Modernists and their friends do today – that Vatican II conceived collegiality as lessening the primacy of the successor of St Peter, is false. Those who worked on drafting the 'Constitution on the Church' recall that no question was more in their mind than how to express the place of the episcopal college without in anyway infringing the rights of Papal authority. For that reason, they went out of their way to make this crystal clear, emphasising no less than 33 times in the single chapter on the episcopate and 10 times in one paragraph where collegiality is described, the Supreme and utterly untouchable office of the Pope in relationship to the body of Bishops. This is a relationship between Pope and the Bishops which is not dependent on the whims of man, and is unalterable by any human power.

STAND UP AND BE COUNTED – IT IS NOW OR NEVER
I.C.P.A. *Newsletter*
Vols. III and IV, 1972
Edited by Father Flanagan

Pope Paul VI on June 29 of this year, declared in St Peter's in Rome that the 'turmoil in the Church since the Council is due to the work of Satan, the enemy of mankind, who has entered into the Church to scatter and destroy the fruits of the Vatican Council'.

This is a cry of alarm from the Vicar of Christ on earth, and an admission by him of what so many Catholics have believed during the last eight years. It has been often stated in the pages of this *Newsletter* that the evils in the Church are so great, so complex, so universal, and have arisen so suddenly, that they could not have an adequate cause except on a praeternatural level.

It was Our Divine Lord Himself who declared that the Evil One can only be driven out by 'prayer, fasting, and alms deeds'. We call upon all our members who are priests to consider arranging a weekly or monthly 'Holy Hour for Priests' in particular, as they are, to quote the Pope, the target of increased diabolical attacks. Many priests, aware of the dreadful situation, are now reciting the prayer to 'St Michael' (dropped some years ago) privately after Mass with their people.

It is time when more than ever before, we must show our Faith as stronger than ever. We must have confidence that the evil will be overcome, but we – all Catholics – must play our part. Stand up and be counted! Be fearless in defending your Catholic Faith – it is the jewel beyond price – to retain which our glorious martyrs gave their lives.

Every Catholic in the land can help to offset the Evil One. Take the initiative – recite the Rosary in your home or better still in your parish Church; invite your friends to join with you, so that 'Where there are two or more gathered together in My Name' there will Christ Himself be in the midst of them.

Our Catholic Priests' Association is engaged on every front in an almost global war with the enemies of the Church. Our overseas commitments are now vast, priests by the score and laity by the hundreds write to us for help and advice. Our once small and localised Association is now worldwide, and coping with its demands imposes great strains on all our resources. Help us to continue effectively — we need everything but above all spiritual and temporal help. Some convents have started a *Perpetual Novena* to help us spiritually. This is a wonderful assistance and much appreciated. Numerous Priests celebrate Holy Mass for our intentions each month — what a tremendous help!

Keeping our *Newsletter* going is a tremendous financial strain which would be much alleviated if all our registered members contributed a yearly subscription, but alas, this is not so. A small percentage of priests and laity make a tremendous sacrifice for our work — it is always the way, the people who can never do enough, the souls in whom the Gift of Faith does not lie inactive. You can help in a thousand ways — even tell your friends of our work, pass on our magazine — there are endless little ways.

The crisis in the Church demands courage more than any other virtue just now. Fear not those who will despise you and call you **divisive** for defending your sacred heritage. Good and Evil are by their nature **divisive**. Do not let the taunts of the tools of Satan upset your inner happiness and dedication to the Church. Has Christ not told us long ago what we must suffer for His cause!

The Secretary's Office will endeavour to answer all letters but on a priority of urgency basis.

God Bless you all,
Sincerely yours

Rev. Fr. John W. Flanagan, Secretary,
St. George's Presbytery,
Polegate, Sussex.

P.S.
Pray for Father Flanagan who after completing this magazine had a coronary thrombosis.

CHRISTIANITY AND SEX

by the Most Reverend Dr Cahal B. Daly, D.D.,   I.C.P.A. *Newsletter*
Bishop of Ardagh and Clonmacnoise, Ireland.   Vol. I and II, 1973

EDITOR'S FOREWORD: We welcome Most Reverend Dr Cahal B. Daly D.D., Bishop of Ardagh and Clonmacnoise, Ireland, as a contributor to *Newsletter*. Bishop Daly is a well-known writer in ecclesiastical matters.

There is perhaps no age in all human history when sex so preoccupied the attention of men as this age in which we live. It is 40 years since the great French and Jewish philosopher Bergson declared that 'our whole civilisation is aphrodisiac'. It is in this culture that we have to live our Christian lives. Is it any wonder that it is difficult in these days to be a Christian?

Of course there are some good aspects to the modern outlook about sex. The way in which sexual matters can be discussed frankly and honestly is, in general, a healthy thing. It is progress when people come to accept, as nearly everyone does nowadays, that sex education is a necessity for all young people and a duty for Christian parents and educators. It is both right and Christian that people should see sex, not as something shameful and indecent, but as something in itself beautiful and wonderful. It would be a tremendous benefit for the world and for the Christian if the new openness about sex helped us to see it as one of God's most splendid gifts to us, one of the noblest parts of his Creation; and led us to a greater admiration and respect and reverence for it.

But we can all see only too well that this is not always the case. It was often urged by advocates of permissiveness in the last generation that sexual freedom would take away all morbid curiosity about sex and put an end to obsessive interest in sex. Frankness and openness, it was argued, would bring about healthy freedom from sexual hang-ups. Now that we have had a decade of unprecedented permissiveness. I think few would be so optimistic. The preoccupation with sex seems more compulsive than ever. Much of modern culture and communication media seem to assume that men and women have no interest except sex, and no appreciation of entertainment other than sexual exhibition, no sense of humour other than sexual double meaning. This is often called being 'adult' about sex. But it is strictly the reverse. Psychologists tell us that voyeurism, which is what much of the modern entertainments industry is founded on is technically an 'adolescent stage' of development which the mature adult will have transcended. Many a film labelled 'For Adults Only' should properly be described as 'For Immature Personalities'. Some of them seem to be made for, if not by, the sick sort of people we know as 'Peeping Toms'.

Sexual freedom was also supposed to offer people, especially young people, a new and glorious happiness which the older so-called puritanism of Christian morality was held to deny them. Again the experience of our permissive age has been very different. The fruits of sexual permissiveness have often been disgust and despair instead of happiness; boredom instead of blissfulness; guilt-laden enslavement instead of joyful freedom. Overexposure to sexual titillation has driven many to perversions in search of new thrills; and this has only increased their loathing both of self and of sex. It is surely significant that contemporary literature is much more marked by sexual failure and despair than with sexual fulfilment and delight.

Sex and Creation

The Christian will not be surprised by this. He knows that sex is God's gift to man and that it can fulfil its purpose only if used with God's meaning and for God's intention. Sex like all God's gifts, but even more than others, is good and must, as St Paul's says, of all God's gifts be accepted from God with thankfulness. To accept sex from God with thankfulness means especially to offer sex back, to God again as our thanks offering, by using it as an expression of our answering love.

Even from the natural point of view, we can see that sex comes from the God of love and reveals to us glimpses of the infinite and eternal love which He is. Even the human language of love is full of allusions to God. Even popular love songs have words like 'divine', 'eternal', 'heavenly', 'for ever and ever'. There is always more to love between man and woman than either is capable of giving or explaining. Love always points beyond itself to God. Woman gives to man and man to woman more than just himself of herself – she gives him also some glimpse of God. One writer puts it; 'Woman promises to man what God alone can give.' Human love must always be one of the best starting points for our attempts to discover God and have some understanding of what He is like. For, as St John says:

'God is love and anyone who lives in love lives in God and God lives in him' (1 John 4:16).

This is something of what the Bible is telling us when it says that God made man and woman in His own image and likeness. It is important to note that it is as male and female that men are said to be made in God's image.

> And God created man to His own image;
> to the image of God He created him
> Male and female He created them

This is because it is as man and female beings that men and female come to learn the meaning of love, and it is love that makes them like God. For God is love. This is why God looked at sex, as He looked on all that He had made, and that it was very good.

Pornography and Eroticism

What a profanation of this likeness to God it is when the sacredness and God given loveliness of sex are made the subject of dirty jokes. What a degradation of sex it is when it is used to sell beer, cigarettes and detergents. What a sacrilege when God's image is turned into the lewd images of pornographic pulp literature and youth, who could be finding God through their own developing sexual beings, are instead exploited by cynical publicists with no God except the golden calf of their own bank accounts. We object to pornographic literature not because we think sex is dirty and should not be mentioned; but because we think it is sacred and should not be degraded. We want to protect youth from pornography not because we want to deny them freedom but because we want to keep them free – free to discover the image of God in sex and not be led by corrupted sex to wear the image of the Beast. It is a pity that the Women's Liberation Movement does not turn its attention also to this problem of cynical commercial exploitation of the female figure by modern salesman. It is one of the greatest signs today of discrimination against woman and woman's inequality to men. It is an insult to womankind. Bergson said the reform of an aphrodisiac culture would come only when women demanded equality with men.

One of the great sicknesses of modern society is pornography and eroticism in literature, theatre and film. It is really a form of moral cowardice and fear of not confirming to current conventions which prevent us from protesting more vigorously and persistently against these aberrations. Gone are the days when it could plausibly be called courageous to flaunt the conventions which sought to protect reverence for sex in writing, image or speech. A new conformism in our time takes the form of competition in sexual shamelessness. The true non-conformity and moral courage now consist in resisting the vociferous lobbies in favour of uninhibited sexual expression. Sufficient indication of this is already provided by the use of such emotive slogans as 'puritan backlash' to discredit criticisms of the new conventions; or by the unfavourable public images imposed by publicists upon opponents of contemporary eroticism. Even Christians, even we Bishops and priests have, alas, been tending to allow ourselves to be cowed or morally blackmailed into silence about these matters, from fear of losing a certain audience or of being dubbed 'reactionary'. We can easily enough surmise what the social elites of the Hellenistic world in, for example, a sophisticated city like Corinth, thought of St Paul's teaching on sex. But St Paul was not deterred or silenced. He was not 'ashamed of the Gospel'.

One of the immediate casualties of the new sexual exhibitionism is, paradoxically, literature and the dramatic and theatrical arts themselves. An acute analyst of modern society, Gustave Thibon, speaks of the purely 'epidermic tenderness' which many moderns take to be the whole of sexual love.

Somewhat similarly, though from an opposite standpoint, Andre Gide said that all human emotion is 'skin-deep'. Unfortunately, some contemporary literature, theatre and film are all too literally and merely skin-deep. The baring of skin becomes the facile and monotonous substitute for the revelation of personality and the probing of soul and spirit. Any mediocrity can strip the body. The true criterion of art is that it can reveal depths of the spirit. But it is only when sex is presented as an expression and sign of deep personal communication and self-revelation, only when it is treated as a language of the human spirit, that sex is true matter for art and literature.

It is more than a little of a paradox now to reflect that D.H. Lawrence, the writer around whose name the contemporary battle about 'four letter words' first raged, would be the most horrified of men, were he still alive, at the uses for which his example is now invoked. Lawrence had at least a deep respect and indeed a kind of quasi-religious reverence of sex. Lawrence abhorred pornography. He called it 'doing dirt on sex'. It is tragic that the words which used to be thought to mark the lout and the boor, became first the passport to notoriety of entertainers short of ideas and then a clichéd substitute for creativity by writers, before becoming the almost compulsive patter of many of today's youngsters. For these words 'do dirt on sex'. They are hateful on lips of cynical middle aged men or what used to be called dirty old men. But they are infinitely sad on the lips of the young of either sex. For the young are just those in whom and for whom sex should be loveliest and most full of admiration, wonder and delighted thankfulness. That young people should first hear sex spoken of or should themselves speak of it in terms of the gutter or of the underground, where sewers are, is a crime against the spirit as well as against sex, which is one of the noblest expressions of the human spirit. It qualifies for Shakespeare's description of 'the expense of the spirit in a waste of shame.'

Sex in man is never merely biological or physiological. It has only an external resemblance to sex in the animals. Human sex is marked by man's hunger for eternity, for immortal existence, for union with God. Sex in man reveals to him an emptiness and need for love which only God can finally fill, a capacity for love of which only God can be the source. The beauty and attractiveness of sex lies not in physiology but in wonderfulness of the spirit of man with which sex is pervaded. La Rochefoucauld was truer than perhaps he knew when he said 'were it not for poetry very few would ever fall in love.' Using the word at least in a broad sense, we might say that were it not for a religious respect for sex, no artist or writer could ever worthily treat of sex or significantly portray the glories and the sorrows of sexual love.

Censorship

One is by no means pleading here for a return to censorship as we once knew it in the past. This had in it much ignorance, narrow-mindedness and sheer illiteracy. But here, as in so many other spheres, the past can be left to bury its own skeletons. We have enough to do to weep for our own sins, and what is more important, to do something about them. Ignorance in the past is no excuse for irresponsibility in the present. Prudishness in the past is no justification for shamelessness in the present. It is true as no less a person than Cardinal Newman asserted, that there cannot be a sinless literature of sinful men. He said:

> 'Man's work will savour of man; in his elements and powers excellent and admirable, but prone to disorder and excess, to error and to sin. Such too will be his literature; it will have the beauty and the fierceness, the sweetness and the rankness, of the natural man of the noble, lawless savage of God's intellectual creation.' But it remains no less true that by far the truest and profoundest things ever said in literature and art, not just about man's goodness and greatness of spirit, but about his misery and sinfulness and also even about his sex, were said by writers and artists and in ages to whom and for which our contemporary sexual permissiveness would have been intolerable and unthinkable. Permissiveness encourages literary and artistic laziness and puts a premium on mediocrity. A reasonable reticence tends to add dimensions of depth.

Intimacy and Mystery

Reticence is anyhow a natural and spontaneous attitude before what we value most deeply and especially for something intimate we share with another and wish therefore to keep sacred and secret for that other. Sacred and secret – both words actually come from a similar root and belong with the holy and the wonderful. One of the great injustices we do to young people today is to rob them of the wonder and mystery of sex. So-called sex education which covers sex with cold, scientific detachment and clinical photographic realism, actually deals with everything about sex except its human meaning and value. In other words, it is omitting everything about sex which makes it human. Sex in the animal is not brutish; it is natural. Sex in man, when described or experienced only physiologically, is not natural but sub-human and therefore totally brutish. It is strange but significant that one way in which man is unlike the animals is this, that he can act the brute.

Sex without wonder and mystery, and therefore without love and reverence and thankfulness, is strictly sub-human. Modesty and purity, in dress and speech and behaviour, are simply safeguards of the mystery of sex. To strip all mystery from sex for the young is the same thing as to rob young people of their youth.

SEX EDUCATION

But mystery is by no means the same thing as ignorance. Wonder is something quite from the wonderland of prudish evasions or pious untruths about where babies come from. Mary, young virgin though she was, revealed no ignorance, no shock, at the announcement of coming motherhood. It was not ignorance which made her 'wonder at the words'. Her wonder was *Magnificat:* 'my soul proclaims the greatness of the Lord'. The true sense of mystery which authentic sex education must preserve or rather foster is that expressed in the words of Psalm 138:

> 'I thank You for the wonder of my being,
> for the wonders of all Your Creation.'

This very Psalm could well be called the Psalm of the scientific age, the Psalm of space travel. Just as today's great scientific conquest of space should enlarge one's horizon and extend one's vision beyond the bounds of space to the boundlessness of the Creator Spirit, so a more thorough knowledge of physiology and the most complete knowledge of modern progress in biology and bio-chemistry should lead us to cry out in wonder to the God of all the living:

> O where can I go from Your Spirit,
>   O where can I flee from Your Face?
> If I climb the Heavens,
>   You are there, If I lie in the grave, You are there
> For it was You who created my being,

Knit me together in my mother's womb.
See that I follow not the wrong path,
And lead me in the way of life eternal

Sex education must include 'the facts of life'. But the greatest and truest fact of life is that it comes from the Living God and reflects the goodness and the beauty of its Maker. Sex education can never be divorced from prayer and praise. It is an integral part of that Christian education which it is the first and gravest of all duties of Christian parents to give to their children. It is not short of scandal to Christ's little ones to let young people go out into today's world without question of whether the duty of imparting sex education lay on parents or on teachers. I confess that the question seems to me an academic one in the conditions of all pervasive erotic stimuli in our culture. The only important issue is that this education be given; that all concerned – priests, teachers, parents – recognise it must be given and ensure that it is; and that it be truly Christian.

It is vitally important that sex education be given in time. We must ensure that children and young people first learn of sex in an atmosphere of loving, unfrightened, thankful acceptance, respect and reverence; and that they first associate it with words and ideas that inspire and uplift. There are many in modern society competing with us – and also competing with one another to exploit sex. It is our Christian task to redeem it for Christ – or rather let Christ redeem it through us. We must help young people themselves to be instruments of Christ for the redemption of sex in the modern world. Young people themselves should be leading a crusade against the teenage pornography industry; for it is the young who are dishonoured by it.

COMMERCIAL EXPLOITATION OF SEX

It is, however, almost never the young who are the originators or the profiteers of it. In this, as in other spheres, many of the abuses for which we are prone to blame modern youth are not the sins of youth but the sins of the middle aged or older who seek to exploit the young for their own sick pleasure or greedy profit. One of the saddest signs of human sinfulness is that there are so few things men will not do, or say, or sell for the sake of money. One of the chief sources of problems and sorrows for young people today is, that this is the first generation of youth in Ireland perhaps ever to have had considerable spending power. It is youth's misfortune that many people are anxious to lay hands on their money and have little scruple what they supply in exchange. The mentality of the Roman Emperor

Vespasian still seems to persist. When scornfully criticised for putting a tax on sewer systems, Vespasian replied: 'But the coins don't smell'.

The fight to preserve reverence for sex is part of the struggle to preserve the human and the personal in the depersonalised world of production and consumption. People have coined the phrase **The Naked Society** – where the nakedness is not only carnal but also the prying camera, the eavesdropping publicist, the debunking biographer, for whom there is nothing sacred, no sphere of intimacy, of respect for persons for the need-stimulation of a bored consumer public. A French film of a few years ago had the title: *Boredom and its remedy: eroticism*.

In the consumer society there are no longer persons, only objects, units of consumption to balance quantums of production. People are in turn components of a labour pool, and then determinants of a graph of levels of marked saturation. In this process of dehumanisation of man by the productionist philosophy, capitalism and socialism are barely differentiated. Christians as a whole have still to grasp and to live the fundamental truth that the Gospel, stands for radical rejection both of capitalist and socialist ideology. The man whom Christ condemned, whose plan for increased production entailed pulling down his barns and building bigger ones, would in the modern world be a millionaire Oil Magnate or a Hero of Socialist Labour. Sex in such a society is merely another consumer product and indeed a perpetual occasion of the creation of new product needs. Never was it more necessary than in our day to restore and defend the sacredness of love.

SEX IN THE MYSTERY OF CHRIST

But our situation in the 1970's is not entirely new. Actually, in respect of sexual attitudes, it is not very different from the Greek world of the 70's when St Paul first brought the Gospel to it. Contemporary Europeans or Americans who advocate 'free love' and 'sex without guilt', would have felt completely at home in the *Graeco-Roman* culture of St Paul's time. The popular attitudes of the goddesses Venus and Aphrodite in whose names sex was worshipped, were quite comparable with the modern cult of the body beautiful which also has its own sex goddesses. The art devoted to these deities quickly degenerated into the equivalent of our pornography. Many of our terms for sexual excess come from these two pagan deities.

In this permissive pagan culture, one city stood out as notorious for sexual licentiousness. This was the city of Corinth. The word 'to Corinthise' had come to mean 'to live a life of debauchery'. 'A Corinthian Girl' meant a loose living girl. It was every bit as difficult for young boys and girls, for men and women, to be chaste in Corinth then as it has become for them in the world today. But it was to the boys and girls and men and women of Corinth that St Paul stated the firm demands, as well as depicting the beauty and the glory of chastity in the body for the Lord. His first Letter to the Corinthians deals with this problem in the form of what we would now call dialogue with the advocates of permissiveness who were to be found among the Christian community itself. The arguments they put up against St Paul are remarkably like those still used by spokesmen of today's **New Morality**. 'For me, there are no forbidden things,' they said. They appealed to a morality of love, not law; calling law mere legalism and opposed to the Spirit of the Gospel. They would live by the Spirit, not the letter. We are very familiar with it all.

The next of their slogans which St Paul quotes is: 'Food is only meant for the stomach and the stomach for food.' The point is, that sex is as natural as eating and should be as free. It is an argument often used by the prophets of sexual permissiveness. Bertrand Russell used this argument forty years ago in his famous book *Marriage and Morals*. 'Sex is a natural need, like food and drink,' Russell wrote.

St Paul quickly put things in their place. 'This would be true', he replied, 'if man was only like the animals, a body that dies and is then no more. But no; man's body is only part of being destined for eternal life.' Above all, man's body is redeemed, sanctified, consecrated by the Lord. 'The body', he declares, 'is not meant for fornication; it is for the Lord, and the Lord for the body.' This body, with the sexuality which so profoundly marks it, is to rise from the dead and be always with the Lord:

'God who raised the Lord from the dead,
will by His power raise us up too.'

The fundamental truth about man is that in Christ he has become a totally new being. Through baptism, his body now, mysteriously but really, is one with the Body of Christ. To sin with one's body, to sin sexually, is to desecrate the Body of Christ. St Paul says it:

'Do you think I can take parts of Christ's Body and join them to the body of a prostitute?'

To fornicate, he says is unlike other sins because it is 'to sin against you own body'. But we can never forget that our bodies are not our own.

Your body is the temple of the Holy Spirit. You are not your own property; you have been bought and paid for. That is why you should use your body for the glory of God.

There is the meaning of chastity as St Paul spelled it out for the Corinthians, as he would spell it out for us were he speaking here today. 'Give glory to the Lord Christ in your body.' That is what chastity does. It does not deny or downgrade sex. It uplifts sex to its true nobility and dignity. It gives sex its true beauty and glory. Chastity enables us through sex to give glory to Christ in our body. Chastity is a sharing by us in the mystery of Christ's Transfiguration. Chastity is already Christ's Risen Glory shining through our bodies in a real transfiguration of our sexuality. Chastity is in St Paul's words, 'Christ in us, our hope of glory'. Our last word on sex is again St Paul:

'When Christ is revealed – and He is your life – you too will be revealed in all your glory with Him.' (Colossians 3:4)

THE USE OF LATIN IN THE LITURGY
by Rev. E.J. Daly   I.C.P.A. *Newsletter*
Vol. I, 1970

During the past year, I have had repeated requests for a Latin Mass on Sunday. These requests have recently become more frequent, and it is interesting to note, that those who do ask, are not confined by any means to the older age group. Recently, I was asked by a small girl of only nine years old! There are also many youngsters, in the teenage range who have also made similar requests. I feel that, at last, their wishes should be met. Experience shows that those, of whatever age, who prefer Mass in Latin, are afraid to express their wishes or opinions, for fear of being ridiculed or shouted down on account of the things they stand for. But let them not be afraid. If more people came forward, and expressed their point of view with courage (a point of view, to which I may say, they are entitled) then we should not have reached our present pitch. If we are going to retain Latin in the Liturgy for the benefit of those who so desire, I think it only fair that we put the Church's point of view on this question. It is not a question of being **pro Latin** or **pro English;** it is a question of a fair and open-minded investigation of what the Vatican Council has said on the matter, and then, as a true Catholic, to accept it in a spirit of obedience and humility. If we are Catholics, and we claim to be certainly, then we should show in our own lives that obedience to the Holy See which is the hallmark of a true Catholic. We must be obedient to all points, and not merely pick and choose. There will soon be available the official Latin text of the Mass, so that those who wish can follow it.

Unfortunately, many of the provisions of the Holy See have been studiedly and sweetly ignored by sections of clergy and laity alike. But then, anyone can take the easy way. What has the Church to say on this question? What has the Holy See said? What have the Bishops in Council said? Let us take a look, shall we?

It is erroneous, but prevalent idea, that the **New Mass**, so-called, is the English or **Vernacular Mass** as opposed to the **Latin Mass**. Nothing, in fact could be further from the truth. The **New Mass** or more correctly, the *Missa Normativa* is a revised and simplified version of the older rite of Mass, in use for nigh on a 1000 years, from which it differs neither in substance, nor in language. This must be clearly understood, if we are to have things in perspective and proportion. The recently introduced liturgy is not, and I repeat, NOT a 'vernacular liturgy' from which all trace of the Church's ancient language has been expunged. It is, on the other hand, a LATIN liturgy, which, by the clear intentions of the Holy See and the Bishops of the world, ADMITS of the use of the VERNACULAR. But it is not, neither was it ever, the intention of the Holy See that Latin should be abolished. To adopt this latter attitude is, for a Catholic, be he priest or layman, an act of disobedience to the Church, to the Vicar of Christ on earth and hence to Christ Our Lord Himself. The mind of the Holy See is, in fact, crystal clear on the whole question, and we shall now see, from documentary evidence, just what Rome and our own Bishop have to say about it.

'Continue, therefore, according to the norms laid down in Vatican II, to use your native tongue in carrying out the sacred rites, together with the parallel use of Latin.' (Apostolic Letter to the Bishops of Czechoslovakia, 2 February 1969). The following paragraph is an excerpt from the Address of the Holy Father on 14 April 1969, to the ninth Congress of Church choirs:

> 'In fact, as may be seen from the sixth chapter of the Constitution on the Sacred Liturgy, the Council was concerned with fostering sacred songs in every way by founding and developing scholse contorum (n.114), by recognising Gregorian chant as the proper chant of the Roman Church, and giving it prime place (n.116).'
> The near complete elimination of such chant from the liturgy, and the virtually complete lack of pastoral response to the above directive of the Pope by liturgical commissions, and a vast percentage of clergy and laity alike seems incomprehensible. Yet the

Vatican Council clearly provided and laid down that 'Though existing special exemptions are to remain in force, the use of the Latin language is to be PRESERVED IN THE LATIN RITE'. Let us consider the following extract from the Constitution on the Sacred Liturgy which, promulgated by the Congregation of Rites in Rome, admirably indicates and, with unmistakable clarity, the mind of the Church:

'Priests shall take great care that the faithful, and particularly the members of religious organisations for the laity, also know how to SING or SAY together in LATIN, those parts of the Ordinary of the Mass, which are rightfully theirs.' (Const. art.54). There is not the least conceivable ambiguity about this, yet where do we see it?

A studied consideration of the Constitution on the Sacred Liturgy will, in addition, reveal the surprising fact that, although it is perfectly true that the vernacular may be used in the liturgy, provided that the decrees of the competent ecclesiastical authorities are approved by Rome, it is none the less true: 'Missals for liturgical use, however, must contain the Latin text, as well as the vernacular translation.' In 1966, the Hierarchy of England and Wales said that: 'definite steps must be taken to see to it, that knowledge of the Latin is not lost,' and on 6 May 1967, Monsignor Patrick Casey, then Auxiliary Bishop in the Westminster Archdiocese and now, of course, Bishop of Brentwood, addressing a a meeting of the Latin Mass Society, had the following observations to make: 'We none of us want to lose the priceless heritage which is the Latin Mass.' Our own Bishop of Arundel and Brighton in an Ad Clerum (letter to all priests of his Diocese for Advent 1966) had the following provision to make: 'The Latin Sung Mass should be preserved, in order that a Western Catholics of all nations and generations may continue to share a common heritage of liturgy and music.' I think that any open-minded person must agree that the words 'common heritage' have a special significance. The vital fact is, of course, that we are not a National Church, but a Universal one. The Bishop goes on in the *Ad clerum* in question to remind his clergy of their obligation to see that their people are able to sing at least the Ordinary in Latin, and refers them to article 54 of the Constitution.

In conclusion, Pope John XXIII wrote an Encyclical Letter on this very subject in 1962, entitled *Verterum Sapientia*. He speaks at some length in an earlier part of the document on the cultural value of the language. He emphasises the fact that, whereas spoken languages change owing to the impact of evolution, and indeed of slang (how many people have a facility with their own native English, let along any foreign tongue), Latin, on the other hand, remains unchanging. It is, like the Faith it represents, and through which it is expressed, immutable. No single modern language is superior to any other in authority. Thus it is, says the Pontiff: 'If the Truths of the Catholic Church are to be entrusted to any unspecified number of them, the meaning of these truths, varied as they are, would not be manifested to everybody with sufficient clarity and precision. There would, moreover, be no language that could serve as a common and constant norm, by which to gauge the exact meaning of other renderings. But Latin is to be affected by those alterations in the meaning of words which are the normal result of daily and popular use.' And yet there are still those progressive modern Catholics who will not accept this; who see no point in a Papal directive. Strange! The Pontiff continues: 'Finally, the Catholic Church has a dignity far surpassing that of any other human society, for it was founded by Christ the Lord. It is, therefore, altogether fitting that the language it uses should be noble, majestic and non vernacular'.

The Holy Father concludes his document with the following directive: 'Finally, in virtue of our Apostolic Authority, we will and command that all the decisions, directives, proclamations and recommendations of this our Constitution remain firmly established and ratified, notwithstanding anything to the contrary, however worthy of special note.'

Even as recently as the 22 August of last year, the Holy Father, in one of his regular addresses in Rome, revealed his intention to re-introduce the Latin and Gregorian Chants in the Mass. And rightly so. The Vicar of Christ sees in these Chants 'a means of bringing about a greater efficacy in prayer, and a renewed religious spirit.' *(The Times, 23 August 1973.)* With the continued emphasis on man in the new economy of Christianity, and the inevitable escalation in the blasphemous 'experimentations in the liturgy' which such diabolical humanism brings in its wake (especially in the sublime mystery of the Altar), the more prayer the better! The Holy Father says that the problem is not insoluble, owing to the demand from many parts of the world for the restoration of this ancient music. One might add that the problem would be greatly facilitated for the Pope, were a fair section of his Bishops to give him their unstinting, and above all, obedient and loyal co-operation in implementing his wishes, as expressed in the Decrees of Vatican II. Instead, the 'innovators' seem to be carrying the day, or at least so most of the evidence seems to indicate! He made it clear in his address, that the liturgical reforms should be applied: 'faithfully, diligently and intelligently'.

When you read this, dear reader, it should be apparent that it is not a question of 'plugging' Latin. It is not really a question of 'plugging' anything, if not obedience to the Authority of the Holy See, and those Bishops in the world who are in communion with her. There is a distinction to be made between what the Holy See and the Bishops have actually said on the one hand, and what so-called progressives, using as a cover the Council and the 'Holy Spirit' on the other, have tried to enforce in the name of Vatican II. But, a tree is known by its fruits! The gales that blow through the Church of God at the present time in the name of 'meaningful dialogue' etc., etc., do not by any means all represent the breath of the Holy Spirit at Pentecost.

WHERE HAVE ALL THE EXPERTS GONE?
by Simon Keegan   I.C.P.A. *Newsletter*
                              Vol. VI No. 1 & 2, 1976 (Double Issue)

When you come to think of it, the Church today at Diocesan level at least, both in Europe and America, should be flourishing, crowded Churches, substantial increases in baptisms, confirmations, receptions into the Church – but recent statistics published in the U.K., and in America, prove the opposite. One can rightfully ask what has happened to the endless number of 'experts', chosen by the Bishop of each diocese or by Episcopal conferences, to fill the important role of guiding the post-Vatican II Church to its intended objective?

While recuperating from recent illness, I reflected much on what has happened to those oracles of wisdom and right thinking, and I was more than amazed at what I found.

On this side of the Atlantic, Charles Davis' departure from the priesthood and his entrance into the bond of marriage, seems to have given an impetus and courage to a long list of the 'experts' to do the same. It would be extremely foolish of me to believe that I know the whole bunch, or that I know the chronological order of their abandoning the Church and taking to themselves a spouse. But this is something which developed out of my reflections.

Peter de Rosa, the darling of the late Cardinal Heenan, who after nearly 2000 years of Christian gullibility, debunked a score of dogmas, and liberated so many nuns from the yoke of dogmatism (incidentally, 'dogmatism' was defined as 'puppyism in development' in a book written in 1864) sending them back to the freedom of which they were robbed by the cruel religious vows.

Peter Hebblethwaite, one time Jesuit priest, and quasi-official spokesman on the *Mass Media* for the Church in Britain – as he still is. Fortified by the Sacrament of Matrimony, Peter is seldom out of the pages of one or other of the publications which have a 'Catholic dimension'. T.V. viewers and B.B.C. Radio listeners in Britain frequently hear his voice explaining 'The Runaway Church' – the title of his recent book.

Father Hubert Richards, whose theology since Vatican II was as much Catholic as Calvin's is the architect of the 'new thinking' which has characterised the Westminster Archdiocese for years. This great thinker was not content in foisting his brand of Catholic theology in Britain, but had to export it to Australia, New Zealand and America. His lecture tours of these continents dug up the old bones of every heretical *ism* that plagues the Church in the past, and Hubert gave them a new life, clothes them in the respectability of 'new insights' made possible by the re-awakening of the Holy Spirit who was dormant since the first Pentecost.

Time and space does not permit the list of departed 'experts' to be completed. The 55 'experts' whose infamous 'Letter to *The Times*,' all of them Catholic Priests, are reduced to 29, between 1968 and 1975. No doubt the remaining signatories of this letter against *Humanae Vitae* will have departed before very long.

Let us see how the 'experts' of America fared during the same period, particularly the ones whose writings and works became the *vade-mecum* of every updating Church 'person' in the U.K. and Ireland.

The false translations of the approved Latin text of the new liturgy, and which is still foisted upon us, owe much to the work of Fathers George Siegler and T. Sloane of the ICEL. Both these priests are now out of the ministry. Father Andrew Maloney, who denied the 'Resurrection' in an article published in 1974, true to the words of St Paul, said that if 'Christ be not risen from the dead then is your faith vain', and so he left the ministry. Father Maloney married a woman for whom he had been doing 'marriage counselling' and later, to the shock of the faithful Catholics, it was discovered that a certain Mr Andrew Maloney, Professor of Theology at the University of St Thomas, at Houston, Texas, was none other than the former 'Father' Andrew.

Father Anthony Padovano, the darling of nuns' conferences, and an 'expert' on education, left the priesthood and was, followed shortly afterwards, by Father Quentin Quesnell, S.J., who during the few years which preceded his departure, exploded numerous 'scriptural myths'. He was, after all, a 'Biblical Scholar of the Marquette University' and his deep insights into the Scriptures, enabled him to show the gullibility of a 1000 scholars from St Jerome's days.

Father Walter Imbiorski, Director of the 'Cana Conference' in Chicago for over 15 years, and one of America's famous 'Sex Educators', left the priesthood but not before thousands of good Catholic parents were forced to withdraw their children from Catholic schools, because of the outrageous sex indoctrination they were receiving. He was the author of *Becoming a Person* which chilled the very spines of Catholic parents when they realised what their offspring were receiving in Catholic schools. He married his secretary, Frances Marzec, with a civil ceremony only.

Father Peter Riga, of St Mary's College, California, considered one of the (Modern) Church's greatest authority on marriage and sexuality, and who held thousands of nuns spellbound as he addressed them in many areas of the United States, also left the priesthood and entered nuptials.

Father John McCall, S.J., who dissented from *Humanae Vitae* and denounced (as did many priests and others in the U.K.) the Encyclical on T.V., but whose voice can still be heard on tapes distributed by the National Catholic Reporter, left the Jesuits and the priesthood.

Father John L. McLaughlin, ex-President Nixon's highly publicised speech writer, married Anne Larentein Dore before a civil judge, Ann being a divorcee.

Father Anthony Wilheilm, C.S.P., author of the work *Christ Among Us*, a book which oozes with Teihardian errors, and who also publicly rejected *Humanae Vitae*, left the priesthood and married a divorced woman. This book *Christ Among Us* is considered, by Modernism infected teachers, as the last word in adult religious education, and is found in several convent and college libraries in Britain.

Father James Carroll, column writer for the *National Catholic Reporter*, left the priesthood, with the intention of 'acquiring new social justice in the world.' He alleged he was not marrying, but that celibacy was 'out', nonetheless, in so far as he was concerned.

Father Robert Griffin, S.J., Chaplain at Harvard University, abandoned the Jesuits and the priesthood in February 1975. Before leaving he uttered this opinion about the Jesuits: 'A convincing model of what Religious Orders should be — they have given up the rigid dogmatism of the past.'

Before ending our 'few examples' taken from the long litany of priests who have left the ministry, let us refer once more to some on this side of the Atlantic.

Father Nicholas Lash, described by an American publication as a 'leading theologian and a Marxist' 'Serviam, No.67, 1975), left the priesthood and still continues to pour out the Modernistic muck which made him the darling of the Northampton Diocese.

In Ireland Father James P. Mackay abandoned the priesthood and married.

Father Donal Flanagan, one time Professor at Maynooth, and founder of the 'Association of Irish Priests', and who was looked upon by the Irish Hierarchy as the oracle of true theology, also turned his back on the priesthood.

Let us terminate the list here, as otherwise it would go on to include thousands of other 'leading' theologians.

No Catholic can take gratification in surveying the long list of successors of Judas Iscariot (did not Pope Paul describe defecting priests in these terms one Holy Thursday a few years ago during a public allocution in St Peter's, Rome?) which characterises our present era. The shipwreck of men who once stood at the Altar of God, and preached His Word from the pulpits, and who were the instruments for the reconciliation of sinners with Christ, can only sicken of us at heart, and in all humility all of us can repeat the words 'There go I, but for the Grace of God.' But there is another aspect to the whole tragedy which we must face, the downward plunge to destruction which these 'experts' have taken, still continues, and in fact there are many indications that the momentum will gather force as time goes by.

Throughout this country (Britain) and throughout the English speaking world, the seeds of Modernism have been sown by these men, and as the tare grows and develops, more and more are being deceived that the tare is true wheat, just embellished and purified, and which they should consume in ever increasing amounts. How many more priests, nuns, and laity must be lost to the Church, before the satanical Modernism, so subtle, so dangerous, so much in conflict with Christianity, will be contained and finally destroyed? How many more young people are to be brainwashed, their faith and morals made a mockery of by 'leading theologians', before some Bishop will awaken to discover the situation in the Church today? No aspect of Catholic Faith and morals is safe today from the re-formulators of Catholic dogmas; no precept of the moral code that will not be emptied of its binding force under the pretext of liberation or rediscovery. The sphinx of the Egyptian deserts look over great areas of waste and desolation. Our Hierarchies' vision will soon be the same, as congregations slump, and liturgical and doctrinal scandals from which the faithful are unprotected, drive them to the feet of the Oriental Guru or into atheistic humanism.

Perhaps the following extract taken from the Paris Newsletter of St Joseph's, Upminster (Westminster Archdiocese) will drive home our conclusion. It reads:-

'**Swami** Bharyananda will speak on *Meditation and Prayer* on Thursday, 18 March (1976) at 8 p.m. in the fifth form Common Room of the Sacred Heart of Mary Convent, St Mary's Lane, Upminster. The **Swami** is from the Rma Vedanta Centre.'

CONCLUSION

From this brief sample of articles sent to Father Flanagan for inclusion in the International Catholic Priests' Association *Newsletter,* which I now bring together to present this *Sequel to The Great Defender,* readers will have no doubt as to the courage, stamina and above all else, the love for his God, his Church and *Magisterium,* which perpetually emanated from this holy and revered priest, and which spread to all parts of the world.

Other very informative articles from eminent Churchmen and laymen from many countries i.e. India, Poland, America, Australia, New Zealand, etc., poured on to Father Flanagan's desk daily – too numerous for my inclusion in this 'Part Two', but sufficient to say, here was 'The Man of God' at work, in defence, in this dark and dangerous period of turmoil which followed Vatican II.

As already stated, all this was completed against the ever persistent cross of illness which he daily endured with such fortitude. His fight over, God called his good soul to Himself, and so to rest in the everlasting joy and light of the Beatific Vision.

Requiescat in Pace

S.F. MORRISON

INDEX

abortion, 70, 130, 227-228
abrogation, 202
Adolf, Father, 31
Adrian, Most Rev. William, 314-320
aggiornamento, 101, 166
Alfrink, Cardinal, 37, 88
anathema, 314-317
Anglican/Roman Catholic Commission
  Statement on Authority in the Church, 240-254
  Statement on the Eucharist, 152-159
    CPA reply, 156-159
    critique, 153
Anglican/Roman Catholic International Commission, question of mutual recognition of Holy Orders, 181-182
Arundel and Brighton Diocesan Newsletter, tribute to JF, 266
Ashforth, Dr, 13, 161, 162, 261, 263, 264
Atkins, Anselm, 32
authority
  within Church of England, 240
  within Roman Catholic Church, 241

Baptism, conferred in other Christian Churches, Hierarchy's document on, 125
Barton, Monsignor
  and *Choices in Sex*, 178, 230, 231
  forgery of signature, 255-256, 258
  use of *Nihil Obstat*, 122
Beck, Archbishop, 129
Beech, Mr and Mrs, 22
Beeze, Mrs, 10
Bell, Christopher, 269
Bell, Eileen, 10
Bengsch, Cardinal, 55
Berna, Kurt, 258-259
bishops, 76-82, 235, 237, 296
  duties and responsibilities, 167, 169, 213, 290
  as target of JF's ire, 235-237, 239
Black Rubric, 154-155, 293
Bouyer, Father, 28, 29, 35
Bowen, Bishop, 263-264, 287, 304, 307, 351
Bradley, Father, 14-15
brainwashing, 115
Brey, Father, 48
Britain, question of Church treasures for sale, 111-112

Brown, Father Raymond, 108
Brown, Monsignor Ralph, 255-256
Brussels Congress, 106-109
Buckley, Monsignor, 190, 331
Bugnini, Archbishop, 195
Bullen, Father, 256-257
Burrow, Diane, 287, 289-290
Butler, Bishop, 73, 113
and Anglican Roman Catholic Commissions, 248-249, 250, 251
as target of JF's ire, 77, 79, 236
Byron, Father, xvi-xvii, 265, 308

Calderone, Dr Mary, 41, 118-119
Campbell, Hubert, 85
Campion, Father, 91
Carey, Father, praised, 211
Casey, Bishop, 61, 122, 351
Cashman, Bishop, 14, 21, 304
catechetical centres, 121-122, 131-132
catechetics, International Catechetical Congress, 139-140
Catholic Church
compared with Church of England, 249-250
interrelationship of parts, 100

Catholic Herald, 218-219, 254-259, 260
threatened libel action against, 178
Catholic Priests' Association (CPA), 82, 178, 338-339
after JF's death, 303, 307
Catholic Herald attack on, 254
early days, 17-18, 19-20
and tributes to JF, 266-267
Catholic Radio and TV Centre, 167

Catholic Teachers' Federation, 86
Catholic Truth Society of Ireland, 308-312
Catholicism, importance of doctrinal unity, 236
Catholics, true nature defined, 193
celibacy, clerical, 31-32, 42, 144
and National Conference of Priests, 136-137, 209
see also clergy, married
censorship, 344
Cephas *see* Catholic Priests' Association, early days
Challoner, John, 180
chastity, meaning of, 349
Choices in Sex, 225-229, 254, 257-258
Christian Order, 189-193, 203
Christianity, 95-103
and sex, 339-349
Church of England
and authority, 240, 246
compared with Catholic Church, 249-250
see also Anglican/Roman Catholic Commission
Clarke, Bishop Alan, 20, 235-236, 253
and Anglican/Roman Catholic Commission
Statement on Authority in the Church, 248-249, 250-251
Statement on the Eucharist, 156, 168-169
and Anglican/Roman Catholic International Commission, 182
clergy, 75, 102, 132
clergy, married, 37-38, 57, 180
see also celibacy, clerical

INDEX

361

Clergy Review, 121
Coderre, Monsignor, 187
collegiality, 69-70
Collins, Sister Mary, 29
Commissions, xii, 235, 237, 289, 294
   Commission for the Laity, 167
   Justice and Peace Commission, 142
   Mass Media Commission, 217
   see also Anglican/Roman Catholic Commission; International Commission for English in the Liturgy; Theological Commission; *Venice Statement*
Communion, 124, 292-293
Communion, first, 139
Communion in the hand, xi-xii, 232-234, 268, 296-299
   at JF's *Requiem* Mass, 299
   potential for abuse, 298
   as target of JF's ire, 120, 124, 175-176, 239
communism, 171-172
Confession, Auricular, 239-240, 294-296
Confession, first, 139
Congar, Father, 109
Congregation of the Doctrine of the Faith, 66-67
conscience, 71-74, 140-141
Consecration, 46-47
contraception, 41, 53, 67-83, 222-223, 226
Corcoran, Father, 15
Corpus Christi college, 131-132, 133, 176
Corsilla Movement, 115
Cowderoy, Archbishop, 9, 174, 176, 304

Cowper, Dom Fabian, 215-216
Crane, Father Paul, 189, 190-193, 198, 200
creation, and sex, 341
Cross, Tony, 182

Daly, Bishop Cahal, 254, 339-349
Daly, Father Jeremiah, 234, 275-287
Daly, Reverend E.J., 349-353
Davies, Michael
   arguments refuted, 200, 201
   and question of force of new liturgy, 198
Davis, V.G., tribute to JF, 270
Davis, Charles, 28, 77, 353
de Chardin, Father, 27, 28, 145-151, 335, 336
de la Bedoyere, Quentin and Irene, 225-226, 257
de Nantes, Abbe, 195-197, 198
de Rosa, Father, 79, 113-114, 131-133, 353
Delarue, Bishop, 31
derogation, 202
Digby Stuart Teachers' Training College (Roehampton), 176
Dominian, Dr Jack, 114, 220-224, 291
Dowling, Monsignor, 275-276
du Plessis, David, 183
Dulac, Pere
   arguments refuted, 190-191, 192, 199, 200-201
   quoted by Father Wathen, 195, 196-197
Duryea, Father, 123-124
Dutch Catechism
   see Holland
Dwyer, Archbishop, 325-328

ecumenism, 183
Emmerick, Venerable Catherine, 143
English Hierarchy, on *Humanae Vitae,* 74
Ernest, Bishop, 37
eroticism, 342-344
Eucharist, 28
   see also Theological Commission
Eucharist Presence, discussions with Anglicans, 142
European Charismatic Leaders' Conference, 183
excommunication, 164, 316-317
Existentialism, 27-28

Fabian, Father, 169-170
Family Planning Association, 224-225
Felici, Cardinal, 72
Fisher, St John, 79, 81, 82
Flanagan, Father John, DCL STL (Polegate), *xiii,* 1-9, 12-13, 82-83, 160-162, 304-306
   and death, 234-235, 261-265
   pictures, *viii, ix, xx*
   tributes to, 266-274
fornication, 70, 348
Fox, Cora, 10
Frazer, Hamish, 139, 186-187
Friesen, Father, 84

Gaden, Gertrude, 15-17
*Gaudium et spes,*70, 71, 72
Gauzzelli, Bishop, 225, 228, 282
General Absolution, 239-240, 294-296
Gerstner, Dr Elizabeth, 111
Giese, Father, 54
Gilkey, Professor Langdon, 107

Grantley, Father, 267
Greek Orthodox Church, 168

Hampden Park, 9-12, 14-15
Haring, Father, 56, 91, 92, 134
Harris, Father, 114
Hastings, Father, 180-181
Haughton, Rosemary, 108
Hebblethwaite, Father Peter, 134, 216-217, 353-354
Heenan, Cardinal, 88-90, 121-122, 131, 353
   and removal of Father Daly from parish, 276, 277, 278, 279, 280, 283
Henry VIII, 40, 41
heretics, 36, 54, 315
Hoefnagels, Father, 32
Holland, 78, 86, 88, 135-136
   Catholics in, 31-32, 36-38, 56-58
Holland, Bishop, 217
Holy Hour, 212, 338
Holy Martyrs of England and Wales, 104-105
Holy Orders, question of mutual recognition, 158, 181-182
Holy Shroud of Turin, 258-259, 271-273
homosexuality, 38, 214-215, 216, 236
Horizontalism, 33
Hovda, Father, 86, 87
Howell, Father, 86, 87
Humanae Vitae, 67-83, 142, 180, 239, 354
   and Cardinal Heenan, 89-90
   and *Catholic Herald,* 260
   and Dr Jack Dominian, 222, 223
humanists, 235

INDEX

Hurst, Mrs D. P., 62-63

IDO-C, 133, 134-136
Iggleden, Monsignor, 307-308
Immensae Caritatis, 291-292
infallibility, 69, 322
infanticide, 70
Instruction of the Congregation for Divine Worship, 110
International Catechetical Congress, 139-140
International Catholic Priests' Association *see* Catholic Priests' Association
International Commission for English in the Liturgy (ICEL), 34, 38, 44, 45-46, 328, 354
and translation of *Missa Normativa,* 49, 53-54, 93
International Consultation Committee on English Texts, relationship with ICEL, 54
Irish Standard, The, threatened libel action against, 179

Jaegar, Cardinal, 66
Janiwreck, Peggy, 122, 230
John XXIII, 24, 351-352
Jones, Nora, 263
Journet, Cardinal, 149
Justice and Peace Commission, 142
Justin the Martyr, description of the Mass, 50-51
Keane, Father, 60
Kearney, Father, 210, 211, 212
Keegan, Simon, 353-357
Keys of Peter, The, 128-129, 269
King, Monica and Noel, 267-269
King, Ronald, 269
Kirkendell, Dr, 41

Konstant, Father, 140, 256-257
Kung, Hans, 27, 56, 77, 107, 108, 129-131

Lafond, Dom, 52
laity, priesthood of, 26
Lance, Derek, 114
Lane, Bill and Bert, 10
Lash, Father, 114, 152, 156, 355
Laurentin, Abbe, 134
Lawrence, D.H., view of pornography, 343
Lawson, Father, 166
Lefebvre, Archishop, 289, 290
liturgy, 25, 44-45, 170-172, 183-185
liturgy, Latin, 59-60, 349-353
liturgy, new, 43-44, 50, 110-111, 189-190, 193-208
locutions, mystic, 143-144
Logos, 168
Lorenz, Cardinal, 66
Lucey, Bishop, 228
Luther, Martin, 40

McCabe, Father Hubert, 212
McDonagh, Father Enda, 186, 228, 230, 257
McDonnell, Father Killan, 183
McKey, Father James, 180
McQuaid, Archbishop, 84
Madiran, Monsignor, 198
Magisterium, 69, 329-330
Mainberger, Father, 30-31
Mallon, Robert and Breda, 262
marriage, mixed, 58-59, 66
Martin, Mrs, 10
Marty, Martin, 62
Maschio, Father, 212
Mass, 49, 50-52, 120-121, 124, 190

363

Mass Media Commission, 217
Mass, Old, article in *Christian Order,* 189-193
masturbation, 214, 225, 226-227
Maximos V, Patriarch, 168
media, and Vatican Declaration on Sexual Ethics, 219-220
Missa Normativa, 43, 45, 93-94, 192, 235, 350
translation and interpretation, 48-56, 190
Missale Romanum, 196, 203
mixed marriage, 58-59, 66
Modernism, 17-18, 135, 150, 179-180, 184, 214 and Corpus Christi college, 132, 133
errors of, 56-57, 315-316
insidious growth, 52, 105, 153, 175, 193, 209
progressives at October Synod, 91-93
threat to Church, 190, 237, 356
see also Renewalism
Molloy, Father, 1-5
Moore, Father, 30
Moralists, 71-72
Moran, Professor, 243-244
More, St Thomas, 226
Morris, Frank, 89-90, 92
Morrison, Sarah, 6-12, 264, 304-306
Mortier, Jeanne, 147
Muldoon, Bishop, 320-325
Murphy, Father Francis Xavier, 91, 93, 134
Murphy-O'Connor, Bishop, 307

National Catholic Fund, 142-143
National Conference of Priests, 136-138, 208-212, 237, 296
Neo-Modernism see Modernism
Neville, Patrick, 10
New Franciscan, The, 28
Newman, Cardinal, 169, 344
Nihil Obstat, and *Choices in Sex,* 228-229
Nolan, Father, 91, 92
Norris, Monsignor, 277-279, 281-283, 284
Novus Ordo Missae, 196, 325-328
effect of, 191, 192, 193
Nugent, Father, 165

O'Brien, Raymond, 267, 271
O'Connor, Father Patrick, 90
O'Doherty, Winifred, 11
O'Neill, Nora, 10
Ottaviani, Cardinal, 52, 326, 329-330
Otterbein, Adam, 273

Paisley, Reverend Ian, 114
Papacy, 49, 104-105, 245
Paul VI, 84, 86, 148, 235, 238-240, 296
and celibacy, 133, 136-138, 144
and liturgy, 191, 196, 204-208
periti, 27, 36, 38, 95
Perry, Father, 131-132
Philbin, Bishop, 308-312
Pius X, 163
Pius XII, 24-25
pornography, 342-344
Pratt, Mrs, 62-63
Pratt, Dr Oliver, 61, 62-63, 257
Press Council, 257-259
priesthood, 75, 102, 132
Private Revelations, 183
Pro Fide Movement, 127-129, 139

INDEX

Protestants, and ICEL, 54

Rahner, Father, 27
Ratzinger, Cardinal, 253
Reban, John, 258-259
reform, 101
Reformation, 40
religious objects, sale of, 63-64
Remnant, 200-202
Renewalism, 57, 60, 78, 121
  threat, 97, 102-103, 124
  see also Modernism
Richards, Father, 113, 114, 121, 354
Robinson, Bishop John (Anglican), 31, 236
Ryan, Archbishop, 84

sacred orders, and first National Conference of Priests, 331-338
St Augustine, 27
St John Stevas, Norman, 88, 114, 130-131, 214-215, 260
St Thomas Aquinas, 70
Salleron, Louis, 198, 199-200
Sartre, Jean Paul, 27-28
Satan, question of agenda, 317-320
Schillebeeckx, Father, 66-67, 194
  as target of JF's ire, 27, 29, 31, 56, 77
schoolchildren, 171-175, 239
Schoonenburg, Father, 27
Scott, Father, 14
sensitivity training, 115-117, 119
Sensus Fidelium, as target of JF's ire, 211
Seper, Cardinal, on bishops' duties, 169, 176
sex, 185-186, 187
  Bishop Cahal Daly on, 339-349

sex education, 41, 118-120, 224-228
  Bishop Cahal Daly on, 344-346
  and *Choices in Sex,* 178, 186
  sensitivity training, 115-117, 119
Sexual Ethics, Vatican Declaration on, 214-221
Sigler, Father, 26, 34, 35-36, 53
simony, perils of, 39
sin, modernists' attitude towards, 109
Smart, Edith, 304
Smart, Molly, 13-14, 263
Smith, Maurice, 265
Smitherman, Ella and Colin, 10
Smitherman, Michael, 263
Society of African Missions, 1-2
Sower, The, 167
Spencer, Anthony, 85
Stansky, Father, 91
Stewart, Bishop, xv, 267
Strand, Father, 175, 176
Suenens, Cardinal, 42, 88, 106-109
Sullivan, Father John, 18-19, 264, 303, 305-306, 307-308, 313
Sunday Independent (Ireland), 229-231
Surtees, Dr, 162

Tablet, The, 270-271
teacher training colleges, 121-122, 176
teachers, lectures for, 112-114
Theological Commission, 152-159
Thorpe, Janet and Stewart, 10
Thurian, Max, 50
Thuring, Father, 37
Tomlinson, Monsignor, 60, 212
transubstantiation, 157
Trent, Council of, 47

Tridentine Liturgy, 190-193, 235
Turin, Holy Shroud of, 258-259, 271-273

Universe, 179

Vatican Council, first, 320-325
Vatican Declaration on Sexual Ethics, 214-221
Vatican II, 24, 39, 131, 140, 190-191
  aberrations in name of, 110
  consequences, 24, 98, 235
Venice Statement, 240-254
  see also Anglican/Roman Catholic Commission, Statement on Authority in the Church)
Vergote, Father, 109
Vertical dimension, 33
visions, of Our Lady, 143
von Balthasar, Father, 36
von Hildebrand, Dr Dietrich, 73, 74, 315

Walker, Father George, xviii-xix, 308
Wall, Patrick, M.P., 128
Walsh, John J., encouraged by CPA, 177-178
Wathen, Father James, 193-194, 195-198
Watson, Father, 180
Westminster Religious Education Centre, 171-172
Whatmore, Father, 21-22, 161, 263, 271, 307, 308
White, John C, 212
Wilson, Dr Bryan, 184-185
Winkley, Austin, 112

Wood Hall Pastoral and Ecumenical Centre, 330, 336
Woodard, Father, 120-121
Worlock, Bishop, 61, 62, 125-127, 211-212, 215
Worship, 34-35
Wright, Molly, 10

Young, Father Godric, 28
youth, corruption of, 224-228

Zwartkruis, Bishop, 36, 58